Reconciling Trade and the Environment

Reconciling Trade and the Environment

Lessons from Case Studies in Developing Countries

Veena Jha

UNCTAD, Geneva, Switzerland

Anil Markandya

University of Bath, UK

René Vossenaar

Chief, Trade, Environment and Development Section, UNCTAD, Geneva, Switzerland

UNITED NATIONS CONFERENCE ON TRADE AND DEVELOPMENT
GENEVA, SWITZERLAND

Edward Elgar

Cheltenham, UK • Northampton, MA, USA

Published by
Edward Elgar Publishing Limited
Glensanda House
Montpellier Parade
Cheltenham
Glos GL50 1UA
UK

Edward Elgar Publishing, Inc.
136 West Street
Suite 202
Northampton
Massachusetts 01060
USA

A catalogue record for this book is available from the British Library

Library of Congress Cataloguing in Publication Data
Jha, Veena, 1959–
    Reconciling trade and the environment : lessons from case studies
in developing countries / Veena Jha, Anil Markandya, and René
Vossenaar.
    1. International trade—Environmental aspects—Case studies.
2. Developing countries—Commercial policy—Environmental aspects–
–Case studies. 3. Developing countries—Commerce—Environmental
aspects. I. Markandya, Anil, 1945–   . II. Vossenaar, René.
III. United Nations Conference on Trade and Development. IV. Title.
HF1379.J48   1999
382'.09172'4—dc21   99–12802
                                                                      CIP

Publisher ISBN 1 84064 072 3 (cased)
United Nations Sales no: E.98.II.D.9
United Nations ISBN: 92–1–112432–8

Printed and bound in Great Britain by Biddles Ltd, Guildford and King's Lynn

Contents

v

Tables and boxes

TABLES

BOXES

Acronyms

ABNT	Brazilian Technical Standards Association
ACOPLASTICOS	Plastic Industry Association of Colombia
AFTA	Asian Free Trade Area
ANALDEX	Associacion Nacional de Exportadores (Colombia)
AOX	Absorbable Organic Halogens
APEC	Asia-Pacific Economic Cooperation
ASCOFLORES	Colombian Association of Flower Growers
ASCOLTEX	Colombian Association of Textile Producers
ASEAN	Association of South East Asian Nations
BMR	Bangkok Metropolitan Region
BNDES	National Bank for Social and Economic Development (Brazil)
BOD	Biochemical Oxygen Demand
BOI	Board of Investment (Thailand)
BPM	Best Practicable Means
CEPT	Common Effective Preferential Tariff
CERFLOR	Forest Raw Material Origin Certificate
CET	Common Effluent Treatment
CFC	Chlorofluorocarbons
CIAT	International Tropical Tuna Commission
CINSET	Corporation for Socio-economic and Technological Research of Colombia
CITES	Convention on International Trade in Endangered Species in Wild Fauna and Flora
CMEA	Council for Mutual Economic Assistance (Poland)
COD	Chemical Oxygen Demand
COMESA	Common Market for Eastern and Southern Africa
CPO	Crude Palm Oil
CRM	Coastal Resource Management
CSD	Commission on Sustainable Development
CTC	Type of tea
CTE	WTO Committee on Trade and Environment
DDT	Dichlorodiphenyltrichlorethane
DIW	Thai Department of Industrial Works

DNP	Colombian Department of National Planning
DNRC	Direct Natural Resource Coefficient
DOE	Malaysian Department of Environment
DRC	Domestic Resource Cost
ECF	Elemental Chlorine Free
EFTA	European Free Trade Association
EIA	Environmental Impact Assessment
ELP	Environmental Labelling Programme (Zimbabwe)
EMS	Environmental Management Systems
ENRAP	Environmental and National Resource Accounting Project (Philippines)
EPSS	Export Promotion Support Scheme (Zimbabwe)
EQA	Environmental Quality Act (Malaysia)
ESCAP	Economic and Social Commission for Asia and the Pacific
EST	Environmentally Sound Technologies
EU	European Union
FAD	Fish-Aggregating Device
FDI	Foreign Direct Investment
FEDECAFE	National Federation of Coffee Growers (Colombia)
FEDESARRALLO	Name of a Colombian research institute
FELDA	Federal Land Development Authority (Malaysia)
FFBs	Fresh Fruit Bunches
FSP	Fisheries Sector Programme (Philippines)
FTZ	Free Trade Zones
FUNCEX	Foundation Centre for Studies on International Trade (Brazil)
GATT	General Agreement on Tariffs and Trade
GDP	Gross Domestic Product
GEF	Global Environment Facility
GNP	Gross National Product
HBFC	Hydrobromofluorocarbons
HCFC	Hydrochlorofluorocarbons
IBAMA	Environmental Protection Agency (Brazil)
IMP	Industrial Master Plan (Malaysia)
INBio	National Institute for Biodiversity (Costa Rica)
INDIRENA	Colombian Institute of Renewable Natural Resources and Environmental Resources
INPA	National Fishing Agency (Colombia)
ISDEMIR	The Iskenderun Iron and Steel Factory (Turkey)
ISIS	Institute of Strategic and International Studies
ITC	International Trade Centre
ITTO	International Tropical Timber Organization

LGC	Local Government Code (Philippines)
LINHUM	Lineal Indicator of Sharp Toxicity against Human Health and the Ecosystem
LMWF	Licensed Manufacturing Warehouse Facilities
MEA	Multilateral Environmental Agreement
MERCOSUR	Mercado Comun del Sur – Argentina, Brazil, Paraguay, Uruguay
MIDA	Malaysian Industrial Development Authority
MINAE	Costa Rican Ministry of Environment and Energy
MITI	Japanese Ministry of International Trade and Industry
MMPA	Marine Mammal Protection Act (USA)
MOSTE	Ministry of Science and Technology
MP	Montreal Protocol
MPEDA	Marine Products Export Development Authority
MTC	Methyl Chloroform
NDP	National Development Policy (Malaysia)
NEB	National Environmental Board (Thailand)
NEQA	Enhancement and Conservation of National Environment Quality Act (Thailand)
NGO	Non-Governmental Organization
NIC	Newly Industrializing Country
NIE	Newly Industrializing Economy
NTB	Non-Tariff Barrier
ODP	Ozone-Depleting Potential
ODS	Ozone-Depleting Substance
OECD	Organization for Economic Cooperation and Development
OER	Official Exchange Rate
OPP2	Second Outline Perspective Plan (Malaysia)
PCD	Pollution Control Device
PCP	Pentachlorophenol
PIDS	Philippine Institute for Development Studies
POME	Palm Oil Mill Effluents
PORIM	Palm Oil Research Institute of Malaysia
PPMs	Processes and Production Methods
PROTUGRES	Colombian Association of Small Producers
SACIM	Southern African Centre for Ivory Marketing
SELA	Latin American Economic System
SIRIM	Standards and Industrial Research Institute of Malaysia
SITC	Standard Industrial Trade Classification
SME	Small and Medium Sized Enterprise
SMI	Small and Medium Sized Industry
SMK	Stichting Milieukeur (Dutch Foundation for Eco-labelling)

SPS	Sanitary and Phytosanitary
TBT	Technical Barrier to Trade
TCF	Totally Chlorine Free
TED	Turtle Excluding Device
TEI	Thailand Environmental Institute
TNC	Transnational Company
TSE	Turkish Standards Institute
UNCTAD	United Nations Conference on Trade and Development
UNDP	United Nations Development Programme
UNEP	United Nations Environment Programme
UNIDO	United Nations Industrial Development Organization
USIJI	United States Initiative for Joint Implementation
VOC	Volatile Organic Compounds
WTO	World Trade Organization

Foreword

UNCTAD and UNDP have been cooperating on trade and environment issues since 1992. Under the joint UNCTAD/UNDP project on 'Reconciliation of Environmental and Trade Policies' a series of country case studies has been carried out (1993–1996) by local research institutes in developing countries. These studies, the first attempts to analyse trade and environment linkages in developing countries, are summarized in this book. In fact, these studies themselves were an important exercise in capacity building as they necessitated several rounds of consultations with major stakeholders in the areas of trade and environment policy-making.

The studies concentrate on the effects of environmental policies on trade as well as the environmental effects of trade liberalization. The effects of environmental requirements on market access and international competitiveness are issues of great concern to developing countries. The studies show that certain environmental requirements can act as barriers to developing countries' exports. One important lesson, however, is that in many cases competitiveness concerns can be addressed by the adoption of appropriate policies and measures at both national and international levels. Such measures include the timely provision of information, capacity-building and support for access to and transfer of technology.

Government policies to support private sector research and development also facilitate the ability of firms to respond to trade and environment challenges and, in the process, contribute to sustainable development. Improvements in the environmental infrastructure play an important role in reducing the costs of compliance, particularly for small firms. Similarly, the establishment or upgrading of certification bodies can be of key importance.

The studies also examine the environmental effects of changes in production patterns associated with trade liberalization and globalization. It is shown that such effects are unlikely to be either universally positive or universally negative; such effects vary according to country, sector and commodity. Where environmental pressures may increase, the studies make it clear that it is important to introduce appropriate environmental and macroeconomic policies to mitigate the negative pressures resulting from freer trade.

Analyses generated by these studies have had a catalytic effect. The secretariats of the Association of South East Asian Nations (ASEAN) and the United

Nations Economic and Social Commission for Asia and the Pacific (ESCAP) have sponsored further country case studies on trade and environment linkages. Some of this work has also generated further studies within the framework of the programme of work between UNCTAD and the UN Environment Programme (UNEP).

All these efforts have helped to promote dialogue between trade, environment and development communities and a better understanding of opportunities for improved policy coordination at the national level. Many of the recommendations are being followed up by UNCTAD/UNDP country projects aimed at strengthening government trade and environment policy coordination at the national level, involving civil society as well.

One important benefit of these studies is that fears of major conflicts between trade and environment policies have been alleviated. This has made it easier to move to build an agenda on trade and environment that reflects developing countries' needs and concerns. UNCTAD and UNDP will continue to cooperate on this agenda.

These studies have also helped to create greater understanding in developed countries of the implications of their environmental policies for developing countries as well as of ways to avoid unnecessary adverse effects on developing countries' exports. This is of key importance for bilateral and multilateral aid agencies.

The studies have been undertaken under a UNDP funded project. In addition to the core team, represented by the authors of this volume, thanks are also due to the research teams in developing countries for their untiring efforts to carry out these studies as well as to the many government officials and UNDP offices in developing countries who have given their support.

We are grateful to Luis Gomez-Echeverri and Karen Jorgensen at UNDP for their guidance in the development of the project, as well as to Leena Alanen, Shipra Das, Roland Mollerus and Rafael Sanchez at UNCTAD for their assistance in its implementation. Last, but not least, we thank Nick Dale and Tim Taylor (University of Bath) and Valerie Normand of UNCTAD for their contributions to the preparation of the manuscript.

Gus Speth

UNDP

Rubens Ricupero

UNCTAD

1. Overview and lessons learnt

Anil Markandya

1.1 INTRODUCTION

Under the joint UNCTAD/UNDP project on 'Reconciliation of Environmental and Trade Policies', which is itself part of a larger effort of policy-oriented research being undertaken by UNCTAD in this area, a number of country studies have been carried out in developing countries and transition economies by local institutes, in order to understand better the linkages between trade and the environment. The following countries have been participating in the programme:

Africa:	Zimbabwe
Asia:	China, India, Malaysia, Philippines, and Thailand
Latin America and Caribbean:	Brazil, Colombia, and Costa Rica
Other Regions:	Poland and Turkey

The studies address a wide range of issues and use a number of different methods of investigation. Although there has not been a coherence of methodology in analysing the data, in almost all cases some primary data have been collected. This has been done principally through interviews with enterprises that are likely to be affected, either by the changes in the trade regimes, or by the changing framework of environmental regulation, both in the exporting country and in the international markets to which it exports.

This chapter synthesizes the main findings from the studies and sets these in the wider context of the research that is ongoing on environment–trade linkages.[1] The central questions that need to be addressed are presented in Section 1.2, with Sections 1.3 and 1.4 dealing with the specific trade–environment questions. Section 1.5 provides some overall conclusions and reflections on how these studies have deepened our understanding of the key questions in the environment–trade debate. Further details of the case studies referred to here are to be found in Chapter 4 of this book.

1.2   ENVIRONMENT AND TRADE: WHAT ARE THE KEY QUESTIONS?

There has been a considerable increase in interest on the linkages between trade and the environment, both in seeing how changing trade regimes affect the environment and in the question of how stricter environmental regulations (as well as a general increase in environmental awareness and concern) affect trade. This has led to several papers and books which have helped improve our understanding of the subject. Frequently, however, one finds that the analysis is limited because there is an information gap. *In theory* many environmental impacts could result from, for example, the liberalization of trade. But how likely and how quantitatively important are these impacts in practice? In many cases this is simply not known. There is general agreement therefore that more *empirical* research is required. The UNCTAD/UNDP programme has attempted to help fill that gap.

We can divide the issues into two broad groups. One deals with the impacts of changes in trading rules and regimes on the environment, and the second with the effects of changes in environmental regulations (and other measures deriving from a concern with the environment) on the international trade prospects of developing countries and transition economies. The first group of issues has particularly come to the forefront as more and more developing countries and transition economies are moving towards liberal trade regimes. The shift derives partly from an increased conviction that a country's economic growth and the standard of living of its citizens are enhanced as a result of such policies; and partly from the pressure that such countries have come under from the international financial institutions (IMF, World Bank) as well as the GATT, to liberalize their trade regimes. The measures involved consist of some or all of the following: removal of non-tariff barriers to trade, reductions in tariff rates, reductions in subsidies to exporters, and competitive devaluations.

Have these policies affected the environment negatively, as in principle they might? For example, removal of an export tax on forest products, and/or a fall in the real exchange rate of a country that produces such products *could* result in increased logging and, indeed, there are some studies that show this. On the other hand, there are also studies that show that the more open an economy is, the less environmentally damaging are its economic activities (see below for examples of both cases). The question of interest here is whether these particular countries have observed a link between trade liberalization and environmental degradation and/or improvement. This is examined in Section 1.3.

The second set of issues relates to changes in environmental requirements through growing public concern for a better environment. How do they affect the trade of a developing country or economy in transition? There are a number of questions that need to be addressed here:

(a) Are the stricter environmental regulations in the trading partners of a particular country leading to higher costs for the exporters, as well as a reduced volume of trade?

(b) What impacts are the stricter environmental regulations in the developing countries and economies in transition having on their exports and imports?

(c) Following on from (a) and (b) above, there is the question of what impacts, if any, result from differences in environmental standards between richer and poorer countries. In particular is there any tendency for the more polluting and dirtier industries to relocate in poorer countries, thereby avoiding the higher costs of operating under stricter environmental regulations?

(d) Are programmes instituted on a voluntary basis in developed countries (such as the eco-labelling programme) having a detrimental impact on the exports of the countries being studied, or are they offering new market opportunities to those countries?

(e) There are several international treaties that have been acceded to in recent years that have significant trade implications. In the countries concerned, what impacts have they had on the trade flows? These treaties include the Convention on Trade in Endangered Species (CITES), the Convention on the Transboundary Movement of Hazardous Wastes (the Basel Convention), the Protocol on the Phase Out of Ozone Depleting Substances (the Montreal Protocol), and many others.

This set of questions is dealt with in Section 1.4. For each question some background on the current state of thinking on the issue is provided. This is followed by a review of the findings in the eleven country studies cited above. The countries are generally reviewed alphabetically.

1.3 HAVE THE CHANGES IN THE TRADE REGIMES HAD AN IMPACT ON THE ENVIRONMENT?

In assessing the impacts of changes in the terms under which trade is carried out it is important to recognize that observed increased levels of pollution are not themselves evidence that the policy is undesirable. If the liberalization policy is successful there will be an increase in economic activity which may well result in some increase in environmental damage.[2] The important policy point is to ensure that the cost of such damage is kept to a minimum, for any given increase in economic activity.

The above is important and should be kept in mind. Nevertheless it is instructive to know whether trade liberalization has resulted in increased environmental damage, and what the extent of that damage is. Previous studies provide conflicting evidence on this question. One study in the Philippines (Boyd *et al.*, 1993) seems to indicate that the removal of tariffs as existing in 1988 would result in substantial increases in deforestation. Similar results are derived from another study of the Philippines (Cruz and Repetto, 1993). At the same time a study by Birdsall and Wheeler of 25 Latin American countries over the period 1960–1988, showed that 'openness' of the economy was a significant factor in explaining pollution intensity (pollution levels per unit of GDP). Increased openness was found to imply *reduced* intensity (Birdsall and Wheeler, 1992).

The case studies carried out in the UNCTAD programme also shed some light on this question.

In the case of Brazil (Chapter 4) the picture is of an economy which had made some little move towards trade liberalization but had seen a trend for more environmentally harmful exports. Trade and investment policies since the 1970s were based on reducing the impacts of external factors on the economy, and included import restrictions, export promotion, and openness to FDI. Exports increased rapidly (and erratically after 1985), particularly in the livestock, forestry and mining sectors, putting heavy pressure on the exploitation of natural and energy resources. Exports of manufactured products also expanded rapidly over this period although they are concentrated in products with relatively low levels of technology, with pollution intensive industries accounting for a particularly high share of total exports of manufactured products compared to other developing countries. Furthermore, unlike OECD and developing countries, this share increased from 21.6 per cent in 1975 to 44.4 per cent in 1990. In general, exports are concentrated in sectors with declining participation in world trade, suggesting that Brazil's international competitiveness may be fragile. Hence, although the paper does not say much about trade liberalization it does provide the message that, in the case of Brazil, a development policy based on import substitution and controlled trade did not protect the environment; in fact the level of resource exploitation increased and, as one suspects, so did the degradation of the environment.

The China study (Chapter 5) gives a mixed message. Since the move to market reforms and increased openness, it declares that growth and trade may have been associated with a partial improvement in the environment. New technologies are less harmful and polluting than the ones they have been replacing. At the same time the sheer scale of expansion, especially in the small-scale industries (township factories), has been creating serious ecological problems in certain areas *through loss of biodiversity and depletion of natural resources*. The structure of trade is also believed to have improved as far as natural resources are concerned, with the share of primary products declining from 54 per cent in 1978 to 23 per cent in 1992. The latter, however, may not reflect less primary product use in total, but simply more domestic processing of primary products which are then exported in other categories.

The Colombia case study (Chapter 6) identifies the following products as ones where trade liberalization could potentially affect the environment: cotton products, leather tanning, printing, woven and final textile products, wood products and refining of petroleum. The study reports two indicators of industrial contamination from 1974 to 1992. Both of these *fell* during the first period of liberalization (1979–81) and *rose* during the second period (1990–1992). 'This suggests that industrial pollution exhibits a behaviour independent from foreign trade policy' (Gaviria *et al.*, 1994). The growth of contaminating industries during the whole of this period has more to do with conditions of domestic development than trade factors. On the import side similar conclusions are drawn. There does not appear to be any strong correlation between liberalization of the economy and increases in contaminating industry imports. In other words, the domestic contaminating industries did not face a significant increase in competition as a result of the liberalization moves.

Two exceptions to the above conclusions are cited. One is the impact on the basic iron and steel metallurgy industry which was traditionally overprotected and heavily polluting. As liberalization took place, imports increased substantially and domestic production declined. This should have resulted in less environmental damage domestically. The second is the impact of liberalization on the domestic recycling of paper and packaging material. Colombia has started to import large quantities of paper waste from the US, especially New York. It is of better quality and very competitively priced (partly as a result of subsidies from firms in New York transporting it for free and paying a fee to the receiving agent). Consequently it has reduced the demand for domestic recycling and increased the amount of paper that goes into domestic landfills. In other words, liberalization has helped solve 'other countries trash problems, to the detriment of Colombian environment and society' (Gaviria *et al.*, 1994).

The Costa Rica study (Chapter 7) identified the period 1985 to 1990 as one of export promotion with a slow opening of the economy, and the period since 1991 as one of a more rapid opening of the economy. There was found to be a recent trend towards the development of environmentally harmful industries. However, this is not considered to be related to economic and export promotion policies. Although overall industrial pollution has not increased more than real production, further research is recommended for sectors showing a higher growth in their pollution indicators, such as foods, beverages, and tobacco; paper, printing and publishing; and chemical industries. Case studies were undertaken on three environmentally sensitive major export sectors: bananas, coffee and forestry. Although details are given of the environmental effects of increased production in these sectors, there is no indication of the extent to which these effects are attributable to changes in the trade regime.

The Indian case study (Chapter 8) cites the increase in exports following a more export-oriented policy, as raising some environmental problems in selected industries, particularly tanning and shellfish. At the same time it acknowledges that solutions exist through the adoption of appropriate technologies and the use of the Polluter Pays Principle. The imposition of trade restrictions to resolve these problems would be inefficient, and perhaps also ineffective.

The Malaysia case study (Chapter 9) points out that the country's open and export-oriented economy has resulted in exports increasing from 50 per cent of GDP in 1970 to 81 per cent in 1990. There have also been fundamental changes in the composition of exports over this period, with rubber and tin significantly declining in importance, and crude petroleum, palm oil and timber becoming the most important export commodities. Exports of manufactured products have dramatically increased in importance, accounting for only 17 per cent of total export value in 1975 and 70 per cent in 1993. Environmental problems have been associated with trade liberalization and the study gives two major examples of how these have been alleviated through domestic environmental policies.

In the case of palm oil, which was the country's worst source of water pollution in 1975, the introduction of environmental quality regulations allowed high rates of export growth to be achieved at the same time as significant environmental improvements. In the case of the electronics industry, which has rapidly expanded to account for 30 per cent of total export value in 1993, potentially serious environmental problems have been successfully controlled through environmental quality regulation, with high rates of compliance attributed to multinational companies installing emission control equipment. Toxic wastes remain the most significant problem and lack of treatment facilities have resulted in accumulations at industrial sites and the export of such waste. However, a central waste treatment facility is soon to be operational. Thus, the study points to a situation where a strategy of liberalization combined with proper environmental controls can achieve export and economic growth as well as a protected environment.

The Philippines study (Chapter 10) is not as forward looking as the studies by Boyd *et al.* (1993) and Cruz and Repetto (1993). It evaluates the impact of past trade-restrictive policies on the environment. The ban on the export of logs from the Philippines, which has been in place in one form or another since 1976, is shown to have resulted in wasteful investment in wood processing, with high wastage rates for wood. This, combined with restrictions on imports of logs for the domestic furniture industry, has resulted in increased deforestation. Thus a trade-restrictive measure is shown to have been harmful to the environment.

In the case of fisheries, the reductions in import tariffs (cut from 78 per cent to 40 per cent in 1980) certainly resulted in a sharp increase in imports, which helped reduce pressure on the domestic resource base. The role of increased imports in this regard is considered particularly important as domestic fish stocks are dwindling and there is pressure on these resources through increased population and poverty.

On the export side, total volume and value have increased consistently since 1985. The main category for which this has been the case is crustaceans. These accounted for 91 per cent of exports in 1990, compared with 43 per cent in 1980. The increased production of crustaceans has had negative impacts on wetlands where aquaculture is practised, giving an example where liberalization has resulted in some environmental damage.

Thus, while the two examples point to some environmental problems resulting from trade liberalization, they also point to some advantages (for example, the increased availability of fish imports). In overall terms the Philippines study concludes that exports have shifted from natural resource intensive sectors, including agriculture, fisheries, and mineral-based products, to human resource intensive sectors with lower pollution intensity during the last decade. This coincided with the period of trade liberalization and reform.

The Polish case study (Chapter 11) focuses on the market reforms that have been central to the economic changes in that country during this period of transition. In assessing the trade and environmental impacts, it does not try to distinguish between these reforms and trade liberalization, something which would be very difficult to do. As these reforms take place, the economy is shifting from energy-intensive, heavy engineering activities to a mix of output that is more like that of developed Western countries. Given that it is starting from an industrial structure that is particularly energy and pollution intensive, this shift will take some time. Over the last few years, as prices were liberalized internally and as trade regimes have shifted from a centralized, partially barter system, to one of decentralized commercial trade, Poland has seen a drop in the exports of electrical and engineering goods and an increase in the exports of 'light goods' (clothing, knitting and leather), wood and paper, and metallurgical goods. At the same time imports of almost all items have increased, particularly chemicals, wood and paper, food items and agricultural products.

The environmental impacts of the trade shifts are difficult to analyse. A preliminary assessment shows that the items whose exports have fallen most (electrical and engineering goods) were not particularly energy or pollution intensive. Among the items where exports have risen, the metallurgical industry is energy and pollution intensive, and the wood paper industry destructive of forest resources which are being used unsustainably. The light industry sector is, by and large, low in terms of domestic pollution and energy use (most of the raw materials are imported). Thus the picture is mixed, with the increase in metallurgical exports being particularly damaging to the environment.

Thailand (Chapter 12) has been a high-growth export-oriented economy since the mid-1980s. However, the case study found 'few systematic effects' of export production on the Thai environment, pollution was mainly a domestic issue caused by rapid growth. The study did identify some environmental effects of export production. Diversification of exports has mainly reduced deforestation and soil erosion due to agriculture, but led to new environmental problems such as water pollution caused by textile production, deforestation due to timber production, use of ozone-depleting substances, and creation of hazardous wastes by the electronics industry. The study concludes, however, that it is difficult to isolate the impact of production for export from production for the domestic market, and that the impact of export growth may well be positive if it has provided resources for environmental measures. Since the early 1990s Thailand has changed its trade policy from export promotion to trade liberalization. The report states that the effects of this have still to be evaluated.

The Turkey case study (Chapter 13) looks at the iron and steel industry which has been among the most important industrial exports since the switch to an export-oriented trade strategy. The products and processing facilities located in the Iskenderun Bay area have transformed that area from one of considerable natural beauty to a heavily polluted industrial environment. Similar developments are noted in Izmit Bay, Istanbul and Izmir regions. The study also describes some of the serious environmental problems in the trade-oriented agricultural sectors, especially those associated with cotton production and its use of pesticides.

In the Zimbabwe case study (Chapter 14) little is said about trade liberalization and its impacts on the environment. It is noted that the 'removal of tariff and conventional quantitative restrictions ... as a means of liberalising trade is occurring simultaneously with imposition of restrictions based on environmental concerns' (Nkomo *et al.*, 1994). Much of the case study is concerned with the impacts of these environmental regulations on Zimbabwe's trade.

In conclusion one can say that these studies do not provide emphatic evidence that trade liberalization has systematically hurt the environment. There are specific situations in which environmental pressures have been reduced and others in which they have been increased. Where they have been increased, some of the case studies have identified policies that, if effected, could mitigate the damage without losing the benefits of the trade liberalization. In fact one could argue that in all cases where negative impacts have been identified, some policies of environmental protection that were acceptable from a trade point of view could have been introduced to reduce that impact.

1.4 WHAT ARE THE TRADE IMPACTS OF CHANGING ENVIRONMENTAL REGULATIONS AND PRACTICES?

As countries become more concerned about environmental degradation they are taking a number of measures to reduce, or at least keep under control the damage caused to the environment by the production and consumption activities of society. The instruments used to achieve these objectives include: (a) internalization of environmental costs and (b) increased awareness and information programmes that assist individuals in making ecologically sound decisions. In both cases, there is the concern that the measures undertaken will have a detrimental impact on trade, especially on the exports of developing countries and economies in transition. Should that prove to be the case, the prospects for economic growth in these countries could be seriously damaged, thereby making sustainable development in the North dependent on economic stagnation (or at least reduced growth) in the South. Related to this is a suspicion, especially among countries of the South, that some of the measures being proposed under the guise of sustainable development are in fact *designed* to restrict access to the markets of the North for the developing countries and economies in transition.

At the same time, developing and transition economies themselves need to take similar measures to make their development paths more sustainable. There is tension within these countries between those who wish to enact stricter environmental regulations and those who argue that economic growth is a priority. In so far as there is a conflict between these objectives, one way in which it may arise is through reduced competitiveness of these countries in world markets. Hence it is important to review the evidence on the effects of environmental regulations on competitiveness, employment and growth in the countries being studied.

This section examines the five questions identified in Section 1.2 that relate to different dimensions of the link between changes in environmental regulations and changes in trade.

Are stricter environmental regulations in developed countries leading to higher costs and lower volumes for exporters in case study countries?
The regulations governing trade place certain restrictions on the ways in which one country can impose its standards, environmental or otherwise, on its trading partners. In principle each country can set its own environmental standards but it cannot impose them on its trading partners. Global environmental problems should be addressed through international environmental agreements. Although this is clear enough in principle, many issues arise in practice. In order to

ensure that goods classified under a particular commodity classification are in fact the same commodity, product standards have been set up, both at the international as well as at the national level. The GATT made a clear distinction between standards that define products and those that refer to processes. A country may define its own product standards but it must apply them without discrimination and should wherever possible seek consultation before introducing changes.[3] However, it cannot apply process standards on its trading partners (Article III). An example of a product standard would be specifications about a particular kind of steel. A process standard would state how that steel was produced. A similar distinction is being elaborated by the successor to the GATT – the WTO.

The distinction between product and process standards, however, is not easy to maintain. By specifying certain products in a very narrow way, a country can more or less determine *how* certain goods are produced. Moreover, in some cases it is impossible for an importing country to ensure that product standards have been met without inspecting the production facilities. Food processing is a case in point and the European Union, for example, inspects meat and drug production facilities in countries such as India and Zimbabwe (see below) before approving exports to its region. This gives rise to a direct involvement in the process of production.

In the existing literature it is generally acknowledged that developing countries have had to adjust their production processes in response to changing environmental requirements in developed countries. Measures such as changing pesticide residue levels permitted in foodstuffs, changing emissions standards for machines, and changing packaging requirements for all commodities, have placed a burden on the exporters who are subject to these requirements. What is less clear, however, is whether these measures have had any significant impact on trade.

The Brazil case study suggests that the country is vulnerable to external environmental requirements for three reasons. First, the high natural resource and energy intensity of exports; second, the large share of exports of homogeneous products, with little product differentiation potential, competing on the basis of price; and third, the high share of exports to markets where environmental requirements are stringent, for example, exports of food products, timber and timber products, paper, textiles and footwear are principally destined for OECD countries. An estimated 25–30 per cent of exports to OECD countries are in sectors where environmental requirements are already emerging.

A case study of the pulp and paper industry concludes that it is particularly concerned with recycling requirements and the use of voluntary instruments. However, the large companies surveyed had generally been able to comply with such requirements 'without significant adverse effects on their competitiveness' (Veiga *et al.*, 1995, Chapter 4 of this book). The iron and steel industry is said to be less affected by external requirements, and the EU, where requirements tend to be most stringent, is only a relatively small export market for Brazil.

The study concludes that since sectors tend to be heterogeneous in terms of firm size and level of technology, the competitiveness effects of environmental regulations tend to be differentiated evenly within sectors. Small and medium enterprises (SMEs) tend to have greater difficulties with compliance than large firms.

The China case study takes the view that foreign laws and regulations have led to some loss of exports but does not cite specific cases. At the same time it does give several examples of the adoption of environmentally sound technologies (EST) (partly in response to foreign requirements of product quality) that have resulted in reduced wastes *and* increased profits for the enterprises operating them. These include a cement plant in Quju, a valve plant in Tanjing and many others. The study definitely takes the view that the adoption of EST is inevitable for companies involved in the export sector and that those that lag behind will be uncompetitive in the international economy.

In the Colombian case study, a survey of exporting firms was conducted. It showed that most industries had not perceived or experienced major effects of international environmental standards: 63 per cent said they had not perceived pressures from international regulations and only 16 per cent said they had. Part of this is due to Colombia's trade patterns. The European market is not the most important one for Colombia; Germany, for example, which has the most stringent standards, accounts for 2.4 and 7.6 per cent of non-traditional and traditional exports, respectively.[4]

The most significant problem exporting firms face with regard to environmental regulations in developed countries is the lack of sufficient up-to-date information. Colombian exporters of tropical fruit to Europe faced this problem with regard to the German Packaging Ordinance. Confusion also exists about the Green Dot Program and changes in packaging requirement legislation.

One case where foreign, environmentally driven regulations had a significant impact on Colombia was the US Tuna Fish Embargo. That market accounted for 32 per cent of Colombia's exports of tuna and the ban resulted in a loss of between $20 million and $32 million. It is also argued that the 'dolphin safe' method reduces the volume of captured tuna.

Less cases of actual export restrictions were found in the Costa Rica case study than in other national studies. In the survey of 39 firms there was little evidence of external environmental regulations affecting trade, with compliance costs in the majority of cases under 2 per cent of total operating costs. Some small enterprises had difficulties adapting to new norms, but only one firm, in the fishing sector, had experienced a decrease in competitive advantage due to the cost of technological changes necessitated by external environmental measures. Nevertheless, external environmental regulations are perceived as a potential threat due to Costa Rica's heavy dependence on export products based on natural resources. It is estimated that 40 per cent of the total value of exports are potentially susceptible to environmental regulations in their market destinations, and concern remains over the country's lack of institutional capacity to respond to such restrictions.

The study gives several examples of the vulnerability of Costa Rican exports to environmental protection measures in developed countries, although these have not had significant impacts on total export values. The examples include, first, the 1995 US requirement to use 'Turtle Exclusion Devices' in the shrimp industry which was expected to cause a loss of about \$2 million per year in foreign currency for the country. Second, the secondary effects on tuna canning companies of a US Tuna Embargo placed on Mexico aimed at dolphin protection. The effects have not been quantified but are believed to be significant.

The Indian case study looked at exports from two important sectors (leather and shellfish) and concluded that the increasingly stringent export standards have certainly raised the costs of production, especially for the leather sector, where costs of environmentally preferable methods are nearly three times as high when compared to non-environmentally preferable products. However, nothing is said about whether the producers can recover the higher costs with higher prices, thus leaving profitability unchanged.

Particular concern has been expressed about the German Packaging Ordinance, which requires the use of packaging materials not readily available in India. Other industries that have been affected by foreign regulations are motor vehicles and pharmaceuticals. A factor that affects exports in a big way is obtaining information about changes in regulations and the fact that they vary from country to country.

The higher costs resulting from these regulations will impact most seriously on small producers, who will need assistance to install the equipment required to meet the production requirements. However, there is only anecdotal evidence that overall exports are suffering as a result of these requirements. On the other hand there are indications that industry is flexible and able to adjust to the requirements without too much difficulty. Another Indian study (Achanta *et al.*, 1994), looked at the technologies required to meet changing environmental standards in the importing countries. They found that exporters had managed to acquire the necessary technology, often with assistance from the importers. Joint ventures were one way in which more sophisticated products were produced using the relevant technology.

The Malaysia study states that the country's export sectors that are vulnerable to external environmental requirements include timber, textiles, air conditioners and electronics. The study focuses on timber exports which fell from 20.4 million m^3 in 1990 to 9.3 million m^3 in 1993. Bans or restrictions on the use of tropical timber have been implemented by a number of developed countries.

Although sawlogs have remained largely unaffected, sawn timber exports have been affected by external restrictions, notably those of the Netherlands. Although export earnings from timber have fallen drastically the study does not isolate the effect of external regulation because the reduction is partially due to domestic policies.

The Philippines study concludes that foreign regulations have not *per se* posed a serious constraint on Philippine exports. This is based on a limited number of interviews with company managers. They believe that stricter foreign regulations will have the greatest impact on the prices of raw materials and research and development costs. Investment in pollution control devices for domestic reasons will be required in all sectors in the future, but especially in the livestock production and manufacturing sectors, such as printing, non-ferrous metals, food processing and pottery. The additional costs of meeting these and the requirements of foreign importers are not deemed to be large, and should be affordable for most producers (see the following section).

The sector where future regulation could seriously impact on exports is 'sustainable forestry management' (Intal *et al.*, 1994, Chapter 10 of this book). This is likely to impact on the country's furniture exports, as sources of local sustainable timber plantations are very limited.

The Polish case study focuses mainly on the stricter standards that have to be met if it is to become a member of the EU. The costs of meeting EU standards are considerable; according to one estimate they amount to $30 billion. Given that the country has set a target of achieving membership within 10–12 years, it is likely that many local producers will not be able to meet the standards and therefore will be unable to export (or even produce for the home market). At the same time, the decision to join the EU and the time period over which to phase in the stricter standards were those of the Polish government and cannot be said to have been imposed from outside. In this sense, the impacts of stricter standards here are different from those of other countries examined in this report. It is also worth noting that the cost of meeting the standards is not fixed but is a function of the policies implemented to bring about the higher standards. The use of market-based instruments could help to substantially reduce these costs.

The Thailand case study states that, although some exports are concentrated on specific markets making them vulnerable to external regulations – for example 70 per cent of fruit exports go to the EU – in general Thai exports have been flexible enough to adapt to such measures, often behaving proactively. An estimated 42.2 per cent of total exports were in products identified as sensitive to external regulations. Two product groups – fish, tuna and shrimp, and textiles and footwear – account for 80 per cent of all sensitive products.

In the case of fish, tuna and shrimp exports, these have been the subject of a number of potentially damaging external regulations. However, in two in-depth interviews cited in the study, producers have been able to adapt so that they have hardly been affected by these regulations. First, the Japanese Anti-additive Import Regulation of 1991 threatened Thai exports of shrimp and shellfish. By adapting production methods exports have, however, continued to grow. Second, tuna exports, which amounted to US$5 billion in 1994 making Thailand the world's largest exporter of canned tuna, have been affected by US restrictions. Again, Thai producers have changed their sources to comply with these restrictions. A French ban on fishery product imports for health and safety reasons in 1994 has not enabled such adjustment, although an indication of the effect on export values is not given.

In 1995 the textiles industry, which after electronics is the biggest Thai exporter, was faced with a German ban of Azo dyestuffs. Dyeing firms had to switch to substitutes at a cost increase of 5–20 per cent. Smaller firms were found to have had difficulties absorbing the higher costs.

In the Turkish case study a survey of major exporters in Turkey was conducted. It was found that environmental requirements in the markets to which they exported were virtually never a problem. The exporters accepted the standards as inevitable and often worked closely with their trading partners, who would sometimes specify the processes to be adopted. The necessary technology was mostly available in Turkey and the volume of exports was unaffected by the imposition of stricter regulations in the European Union, including the new packaging directives. One issue raised in the survey was that of different environmental standards. As with India, exporters found some loss of economies of scale in meeting the requirements of different markets.

The Zimbabwe study cites a number of examples where foreign standards are hampering its export requirements. One is ostrich production. It feels that the restrictions on exports of the live birds or the meat to the EU and Australia (including costly blood tests and quarantine regulations) are unnecessarily strict, having been designed in part to make Zimbabwe's exports less competitive. A second is phytosanitary standards for the export of beef to the EU, where European importers have to inspect all produce before it leaves the country of origin. This imposes higher costs on Zimbabwean exporters and may dissuade some producers of beef from looking for export markets. A third is the German Packaging Ordinance, where there is some concern about the cost and availability of recyclable materials, as well as difficulties in submitting packaging for evaluation and certification. To assist exporters, producers associations are running courses on packaging technology. A fourth is the restrictions on the textile industry where certain drying and sizing processes are not being allowed. As a result it is necessary to change and improve the processing technology, which is costly. A fifth is footwear, where leather tanned using PCB is banned in the international markets. This has necessitated a shift to different chemicals and processing techniques.

For all these examples, however (with the exception of ostrich production), it is not clear whether the international requirements have had a significant impact on levels of exports.

To conclude, the evidence from these case studies on how foreign environmental regulations impact on a developing country or transition economy is mixed. Many of the larger exporting countries claim that the effects have been small, and in most cases manageable for the exporters. In several cases the adoption of the stricter standards not only decreases environmental damage, it also increases efficiency and profits for firms.

The exceptions to this favourable picture are:

(a) smaller producers are more affected by the increasing number and variety of regulations. This, in turn, has implications for future economic growth, and for competition inside the country itself;

(b) several studies point to the difficulty firms have in simply keeping themselves informed of the changes in regulations. Lack of information is resulting in reductions in exports; and

(c) some countries believe that the regulations are cumbersome, complex and at least partly designed to make exports uncompetitive. They find that the costs of meeting them have affected exports. This is particularly true for Zimbabwe.

What impacts are stricter environmental regulations in the case study countries themselves having on trade?

Relatively little information is available on the economic impacts of domestically generated environmental regulations in developing countries. Industrialists frequently claim that the imposition of stricter standards will result in loss of competitiveness, employment and growth but such claims are largely unsubstantiated.[5] Furthermore one should not ignore the costs of environmental degradation on the business community, in terms of work days lost, congestion, and so on.

There are several studies that look at the same issues, but for developed countries, principally the US (see Dean, 1992 for a survey). In general their findings are:

(a) the costs of pollution abatement measures in the US have been only a small proportion of industry's costs (around 1.5 per cent);

(b) the percentage decrease in output attributable to environmental control costs in the US has averaged less than 1 per cent (the exceptions are industries such as petroleum);

(c) when allowance is made for general equilibrium effects, the cost impacts are lower and more evenly spread throughout the economy;

(d) if abatement costs were to raise prices by 1 per cent in the US, one study estimated the impact to be a reduction in exports of 2.7 per cent, with sectoral impacts varying from virtually zero (special industry machinery) to 7 per cent (copper) (Robison, 1988). Another study, however, using a different methodology, concludes that the impact on exports is negligible.

These results can be useful in evaluating similar measures in developing countries but some caution is warranted. First, the costs of environmental regulations as identified in the above studies (which are incremental costs) may be underestimated. They do not include workplace, health and safety protection costs (Chapman, 1991). Also, developing countries are starting from a lower base in terms of pollution abatement capital. Second, the effective response of industry requires it to be able to finance the capital expenditures and to respond flexibly to changes in relative prices. These factors are more acute in developing countries and so hinder the evaluation of the impact of stricter regulations on trade in developing countries.

In contrast to the negative impacts of environmental regulation there are also some positive effects to consider. There will be some growth of a domestic pollution abatement industry. Even if much of the technology is imported, various studies have shown that adaptation to local conditions is almost always necessary. This will generate some economic activity. Then there is the view that stricter regulations will benefit the more innovative and enterprising firms (Porter, 1991). This may be because they are able to find ways of meeting the standards at lower cost, or because they can respond more quickly and more effectively.

In the case studies there is little to suggest that, apart from in the case of Poland, stricter locally imposed standards have had a major impact on trade.

In the case of Brazil environmental policy was first established in 1981 but little evidence is presented in the case study about the overall effect on trade. A principal example given is that of legislation introduced in the early 1990s in the State of Minas Gerais prescribing that by 1998 all charcoal consumed must originate from non-natural or sustainably managed forests. Charcoal consumption accounts for up to 70 per cent of the production costs of pig iron which is a major Brazilian export, and therefore, this legislation initially had significant trade effects. However, with the help of fiscal incentives and programmes to support the financing of forest plantations these standards have been successfully introduced and trade effects have been negligible. Interestingly, the regulation that is of most concern to the iron and steel industry is that related to the imports of scrap. It is argued that this restriction could result in a decline in the competitiveness effects of domestic production, as supply prices for inputs will rise.

In the China study it is noted that the country only started introducing environmental measures in the 1970s and there is still a wide gap in pollution control between itself and developed countries (perhaps as much as 20–30 years). Where enterprises have made changes to production processes they have generally benefited both in terms of the environment and in terms of foreign exchange earned. Examples quoted include the Zhuzhou hard metal alloy factory which was a large, extremely dirty factory with extensive environmental damage. After a major attempt to improve its environmental performance, the situation improved substantially in that regard, as well as in terms of exports, which exceed $800 million. The paper gives a few other examples of a similar nature, and one can assume that they are intended to show what is believed to be a general picture.

In the Colombia study a survey of about 300 exporting firms is reported where the question of how domestic environmental standards has affected competitiveness was posed. Here, 29 per cent responded that complying with national environmental standards had affected their competitiveness *positively*, and only 4 per cent thought that it had had a negative effect. When asked whether the recent creation of the Ministry of the Environment and the consolidation of a national environmental policy would hinder or benefit them, 52 per cent said they thought it would affect them positively, 8 per cent thought it would affect them negatively and 38 per cent did not know. Similar percentages emerge for the question of whether these trends will affect their international competitiveness.

The Costa Rica study explains that considerable effort has been made in recent years to update the institutional framework regarding the environment. Most actions have been in the form of domestic governmental regulations, particularly in the cases of banana, coffee and some industrial products. In the case of bananas, the real cost of adapting to domestic environmental measures is hard to determine. Some rough estimates suggest, however, that these are no more than 4 per cent of total costs. In the coffee sector a three-stage plan has been developed to address the problem of water pollution, with the estimated costs of investments needed for compliance by coffee processing plants given as around 5.5 per cent of total cost of the plant. There is no indication of the effects these costs have had on trade, although the two products given as examples are the major traditional exports which continue to have a strong export performance.

The Indian case study focuses almost entirely on foreign environmental requirements. However, there are some examples of how the costs of domestic compliance differ from those of international compliance. For the leather sector, price increases in leather and leather products resulting from domestic pollution abatement rules were estimated at 1.5 per cent. Even this small average amount would, however, have an impact on small producers, as there is a substantial fixed cost component to it. But compared to the costs of meeting international standards it is tiny; the cost increase for international products is 300 per cent, presumably most of which is recovered from a higher sale price. For shellfish the costs of an effluent treatment plant for the fish processing industry, introduced for domestic reasons, would have a very small cost (0.2 per cent of turnover).

The Malaysia study details the substantial developments in domestic environmental policy since the 1970s. However, there is no overall view on how these have affected trade. The timber case study states that domestic regulations on sustainable forest management under the National Conservation Strategy has caused a reduction in logging areas and timber production, but the impact of this on trade is difficult to isolate from external and other domestic policies. As stated earlier, the palm oil and electronic industries are examples where high rates of export growth have been achieved at the same time as the implementation of domestic environmental quality regulations.

The Philippines study is the one that looks at this question most systematically. It computes first the share of abatement cost to meet domestic standards as a percentage of total sector cost for all the major sectors. The only ones where this cost exceeds 2 per cent are: public administration and defence, poultry and poultry products, forestry, agricultural crops, and livestock and livestock production. It is less than 1 per cent for 51 of the 61 sectors. It then calculates the competitiveness of different sectors with different levels of environmental costs being imposed on them. If the costs that are imposed are as given above (generally less than 1 per cent and almost always less than 2 per cent) the ratio of domestic private costs to earnings (which is a measure of private profitability, with values less than one indicating that exporting is profitable) remains less than one for all sectors on average, except inland fishing. However, it is possible, and likely, that marginal firms (those with costs above the average) will be affected in selected sectors. These include aquaculture and fish processing. Unfortunately no calculations are presented for agro-processing, forestry products, livestock and poultry. Apart from these sectors, it appears that local environmental standards would not have a significant impact on overall sectoral competitiveness.

The Poland study makes the strongest case for export losses resulting from changes in domestic environment and environment-related regulations. Many of Poland's exports are characterized by a high level of raw materials and energy. As part of the market reforms prices of both raw materials and energy have risen sharply in Poland. These reforms have also impacted positively on the environment, but they have contributed to a loss of international competitiveness. One special case of this is the export of electricity, which Poland exports to the Czech Republic and Germany. Its price advantage is derived partly from the fact that it does not have to capture the sulphur emissions. As flue gas desulphurization is introduced, export of electricity will probably become uncompetitive (costs of generation will rise by as much as 40 per cent). Similar factors apply to coal mining, where stricter ecological conditions on saline water discharges are making production uncompetitive (costs will rise by 10–15 per cent). In the case of coal it is estimated that, if all current environmental standards are met, exports in year 2000 will fall from around 25 million tons to 7–10 million tons. The increase in electricity prices is also conjectured to affect the export of the following energy-intensive goods: fertilizers, plastics, organic chemicals, metal products and building materials. At the same time, however, some of the environmentally sound technologies will increase efficiency. For example, with steel it is estimated that the market restructuring will reduce capacity by a large amount and reduce environmental damages by 70–80 per cent. Those plants that are left will be more efficient, with production costs down by $20–25/ton. Finally, another positive aspect of the stricter environmental regulations is the development of a pollution control industry that Poland, being a leader in environmental abatement among the economies in transition, hopes to be able to export to other transition economies.

The Thailand study does not give details of the effects on trade of domestic environmental regulations. However, in the context of thirty years of rapid industrialization, environmental legislation, such as the National Environmental Quality Act (1992) which applies the polluter-pays-principle and the Factories Act (1992) which can levy fines for non-compliance with environmental standards, has only been introduced relatively recently. Even this has been relatively ineffectual. No details are given about the effects of these regulations on exporters' costs and the value of exports.

The Turkey case study focuses almost exclusively on the demands of foreign markets. In the domestic market enterprises interviewed made the interesting point that stricter national standards would actually *benefit* them because: (a) they were currently facing different standards in the home and export markets and this was adding to their costs; and (b) producers in other developing countries were selling, in the Turkish market, goods that met the lower standards, thus making it difficult for local producers to compete with their higher standard goods.

The Zimbabwe study has little to say about local standards and competitiveness, but makes the point that environmental regulations in the country are poorly enforced. Thus large enterprises effectively avoid any impact on competitiveness by simply evading the regulation or obtaining exemption permits which are easily granted for exporters.

Is the migration of 'dirty' industries to less strictly regulated countries a problem?

The decision of where to locate a production facility involves a number of factors, including the cost of labour, access to markets, social and political conditions in the country concerned, the infrastructure facilities in the country concerned and the regulatory framework. The last includes environmental regulations but they are only part of the set of regulations. A lot of evidence exists to the effect that investors look not only at *current* regulations but also at the stability of the regulatory framework (how frequently governments change the rules).

To evaluate whether firms locate in countries to take advantage of lax environmental regulations it is necessary to look carefully at the quantitative importance of the different factors that determine location decisions. Studies of multinational corporations have shown that these decisions are most influenced by such factors as labour costs, access to markets and the existence of a developed industrial base (Wheeler and Mody, 1992). Factors such as environmental regulations and corporate tax rates emerge as less important. At the same time, however, study of majority-owned affiliates of OECD-based companies in developing countries shows that those involved in pollution-intensive industries did increase their investment slightly faster than did all manufacturing industries (Jaffe *et al.*, 1993). This statistical evidence offers only weak support of the pollution-migration hypothesis as it does not point to any significant change in investment patterns. What is observed could be explained by other factors such as the changing structural pattern of demand in the developing countries themselves.

More recent studies have supported these findings. Dean (1992) in a comprehensive survey of studies published up to 1990 concludes that there is little evidence of industrial relocation because of different environmental regulations. Grossman and Krueger (1992) analyse the *maquiladora* programme (which permitted US firms to locate on the Mexican side of the US–Mexico border on advantageous terms) and find that pollution abatement costs were not a significant determinant of the trade generated by the programme.

Even when pollution-intensive industries do locate in developing countries, they do not adopt a minimalist approach in terms of meeting environmental regulations. Often corporate policy dictates the use of the same technology and pollution controls in all foreign countries where plants are located as in the home country (subject to, of course, meeting the local standards where the latter are more strict). This is partly in response to the public image of which they are very conscious, and partly in recognition of the fact that regulations are almost certain to become more strict in the developing countries, and pre-emptive action may well be cost-effective (Jaffe *et al.*, 1993).

The case studies undertaken here say little or nothing about this issue. Only the ones from China, Colombia and Thailand address the question. The China study states that some overseas enterprises did locate in China due to stricter regulation regarding the environment in developed countries, particularly in the leather goods, paper, smelted products, chemicals and pharmaceutical industries. However, there is no specific evidence provided to support this assertion.

The Colombia study supports the conclusions of the main studies in this area. First, Colombia has relatively strict local pollution and environmental standards.

Second, it is not particularly well situated for multinational companies to select it for location; Central America or South East Asia would be preferable locations from which to take advantage of lax standards. Of the 20 multinational companies surveyed none appeared to have established themselves in Colombia for environmental reasons and most of them were already meeting OECD standards.

The Thailand study states that there are some indications that foreign companies are using the country as a 'pollution haven' and shifting ODS consuming production there to take advantage of its Annex A status. The significant increases in ODS imports between 1986 and 1991, and the fact that 97 per cent of Thai production using solvents is undertaken by Japanese, European and US firms or is part of a joint venture with Thai firms, is taken as evidence for this trend. In recognition of this situation the Thai Department of Industrial Works has entered into agreements with the US Environmental Protection Agency and the Japanese Ministry of International Trade and Industry, which encourage Transnational Corporations (TNCs) to halt the use of solvents in their Thai operations on the same timetable as their domestic operations.

To conclude, it appears that industrial location for reasons of different environmental standards is either not perceived as a relevant issue, and therefore not investigated, or is not found to be significant when actually investigated. The one exception is the case of Thailand where, as a result of special privileges for Thailand under the Montreal Protocol, some TNCs have located their operations inside the country. But the government has acted to control this situation and the impacts should be temporary.

What impacts are non-official pressures for more ecologically friendly goods having on the exports of the developing countries and economies in transition?

Many of the recent actions taken in developed countries do not have an official status, or may only have government support but are not backed by laws. Examples of such measures are the demands by individual importers for specific processes in the exporting factories, even to the extent of demanding changes in social conditions. There are no government-to-government rules about such demands but they are nevertheless real and it is hard to see how they could be effectively legislated against. If an importer only wants to trade with an exporting company that meets its standards of acceptability in production, and the exporter is willing to meet those terms, there is little that governments or trade bodies can do to prevent it. Nevertheless it is important to find out how significant such pressures are on producers in developing and transition economies, and what their impact on costs and exports has been.

A related set of pressures arises from the various programmes to label goods as environmentally friendly – the so-called environmental labelling programmes.

This is a major topic that is currently being studied in some depth. There are a number of different labelling schemes that come under this general title. The schemes included range from single criteria labels (recyclability, degradability, and so on), to others based on a life cycle assessment of the product's environmental assessment. A number of developed countries, as well as some developing countries, have such schemes. In all cases so far they are voluntary schemes, with the extent of government involvement varying from active participation to some administrative support and encouragement. As sources of information to consumers about the products, and as encouragement to be more ecologically aware they are a positive development. However, there is the danger that they could become barriers to trade. Rege (1993) argues that labels will be regarded as causing non-tariff barriers to trade if:

(a) the criteria on which they are awarded are not based on objective or scientific considerations, or fail to take into account adequately the production processes in other countries;
(b) procedures for verification are unnecessarily strict, making it almost impossible for an outsider to obtain the label; and
(c) the system is adopted for a product that is almost entirely imported and the right to grant a label rests with the importing country.

Reviews of eco-labelling systems in a number of countries (Jha *et al.*, 1993; Iba, 1993; Pearson, 1993) conclude that:

(a) although foreign products have access to the schemes, they find it more difficult to participate in them owing to lack of information and a proportionately higher cost of obtaining the label;
(b) within the countries in which they are awarded, the labels have not always had an identifiable impact in terms of sales of products under the relevant categories. In the Blue Angel scheme in Germany, for some commodities such as low-pollutant coatings the share of labelled products is significant. However, that may have been the case even without the label. Certainly 'eco-friendly' products are known to be attractive to some consumers, who are willing in some cases to pay higher prices for them;
(c) the trade impacts on developing countries are also difficult to measure. Many of the products covered by the labels are not exported by developing countries. If labels are developed which cover products that these countries do export, the impacts could be significant and they could be seen as technical barriers to trade. One such case was the attempted Austrian legislation that products made from tropical timber should be marked as such in the market. This was objected to by the ASEAN countries on the

grounds that it discriminated against imported products (the 'like product rule' under the GATT);

(d) developing countries are introducing similar schemes in part to promote the exports of their products, and in part to promote environmentally friendly products at home. The success of the schemes to date has been very limited.

There is also some evidence that developing countries may actually turn the system to their advantage by marketing their own 'eco-friendly' products more aggressively. The development of 'green food' labels in China, 'green cotton' in India and the possible use of natural fibres such as jute in packaging are cases in point (see below). To be successful this will require cooperation with the importing countries, to define the appropriate labels and even to modify the importers' own labelling schemes (see also Scholz and Wiemann, 1993).

Almost all the country studies reviewed here have something to say on this set of issues. The Brazil case study states that Brazilian industry may be more vulnerable to voluntary requirements, related to inputs and PPMs, than to mandatory product regulations. The study highlights the potential effects of eco-labels on exports and states that several of the product categories for which criteria are being set in the EU eco-labelling programme are of export interest to Brazil. In the case of pulp and paper, the emphasis of the EU programme on recycling could have significant trade effects since competitiveness is largely based on quick-growing eucalyptus while recycling has not been well developed. In the case of textiles, producers consider that it would be difficult to comply with EU criteria limiting use of pesticides and chemicals in cotton growing. In the case of footwear, the study found that although compliance costs would be high, producers would in general be in a position to comply with most eco-labelling requirements, and market shares would not be affected.

At the time of writing there were two proposals for Brazilian eco-labelling programmes. The Brazilian Technical Standards Association has proposed a 'Green Seal Programme', and the Brazilian Forest Development Society has proposed the Forest Raw Material Origin Certificate. Both these were facing difficulties over the response from domestic producers and exporters.

In the China case study it is stated that the country has instituted its own 'green sign' system which is in effect an eco-labelling system. It has also launched a 'green food' programme in which the label is awarded to products on the basis of low pollution in production and transportation, high nutrition value, and recyclability of the packaging. A life cycle method of evaluation is used for these labels, of which 384 have been awarded. The current volume of trade in these products is not given although plans for future production are high, as is the current demand for these products.

The study makes no comment on whether foreign private/voluntary schemes of environmental control have had any impact on China's exports. One can only reiterate the previous conclusion that, in general, China sees the need to meet foreign standards as beneficial to itself, as well as being feasible in terms of the technology requirements. It states, 'In a word the influence of correct environmental protection laws and regulations on Chinese foreign trade growth is positive . . . Its negative influence is temporary' (Lu *et al.*, 1993; Chapter 5 in this book).

In the Colombia case study exporters were asked whether they felt that they faced increased competition in foreign markets from producers who had eco-labels. A total of 85 per cent of them said they did not face such competition and only 13 per cent, or eight firms, said that they had dealt with competing firms with such seals. When asked, 66 per cent said they did not think that the implementation of eco-labels in international markets posed a threat to the competitiveness of their products. So far only 10 per cent of firms have applied for, or already possess, an international eco-label. However, 84 per cent of the firms responding said they would be applying and 81 per cent said they would be willing to take part in an educational programme for domestic producers.

Overall, the results do not suggest that eco-labelling is a serious issue in Colombia. This may be because the majority of Colombian exports go to the US, Central and South American markets where eco-label schemes are non-existent or weak.

In the Costa Rica study no specific details of the effects of external non-official pressures for ecologically friendly products are given. The survey of producers indicates that there is general awareness that environmental requirements will play a key role in future market access. Some sectors have been proactive in this regard; for example, in 1992 the PRO-O.K. seal started to be used in the country. It offers certification to banana producers interested in environmentally sound production. One firm estimates that production costs of certified bananas are about 2 per cent higher than non-certified, however none of the participating firms have as yet reported that they received a price premium. In the case of forestry only the largest projects are certified by the Green Cross seal, and the study found that producers feel that forest certification is costly and not profitable for smaller firms.

In India, the government has launched an eco-labelling scheme for products that, when properly used and disposed of, reduce the damage to the environment. It is essentially a promotional device and is not very popular with industry at present. The study also reports interviews which show that Indian exporters are not interested in subscribing to international eco-labelling schemes. They are 'not confident of the promotional aspects of [such] schemes for their products. For example in garments most exporters were of the opinion that fashion was of primary concern among the buyers and environmental considerations were of secondary importance even in Germany at present' (Parikh *et al.*, 1993; Chapter 8 in this book). At the same time it is acknowledged that in future the situation may change, and some exporters have complained that marketing certain products to Germany is becoming more difficult because of the 'green dot' label relating to packaging of the products.

India has recognized the profitability of some environmentally preferable products and is promoting them in a number of ways. One of the most important is organically grown cotton (or 'green cotton'). The federal government has identified 1000 ha of land in two states for producing organic cotton on a pilot scale. Of course this is only a start (India has 8 million ha under cotton) but it is a promising move. The benefits are not only to the producers, who can receive a 20 per cent price premium over cotton grown using chemicals, but also to the country where more than half the pesticide consumption is accounted for by cotton production. India is also beginning to grow some naturally coloured cotton, thus avoiding the use of dyes. This fetches a very high premium in foreign markets. Hybrid seeds for this, however, are still being locally developed, as India was unsuccessful in obtaining them from the US where such cotton is now being grown (*Financial Times*, 16.6.94).

A similar promotion is taking place for jute and its products, which lost much of their market due to competition from synthetic products but are now seen as eco-friendly. If terms can be agreed for their use in packaging to the European markets, they may have a big increase in demand. Other products where exporters recognize the benefits of environmentally friendly production are food products and leather.

The Malaysia case study states that mandatory and voluntary labelling requirements have had an adverse effect on exports but does not give an estimate of the size of this impact. The country has officially opposed the use of unilateral trade measures for environmental purposes including eco-labelling. However it also sees some benefits; for example, in the use of timber certification as a marketing tool for access to green markets. In the case of the timber trade, the study states that as a result of responses such as market substitution, development of higher value-added products, changes to production methods and the use of certification itself, unilateral measures (including non-official pressures) in export markets have not significantly affected exports.

The Philippines study makes no comment on whether eco-labelling schemes have had a detrimental impact on its exports. At the same time it identifies certain products that are being developed specifically for environmentally conscious consumers. These include hand-made paper charcoal briquettes and fertilizer/pesticide-free agro-products.

Although it has no specific comments about eco-labelling schemes as such, the Poland study is less optimistic about the possibility of taking advantage of 'green consumerism' in the West but at the same time acknowledges that

Poland will have to respond to such changes. It states 'The market for ecological products and so called "health foods" in EFTA and EU countries expands quickly but . . . it is subject to a very strong competition and exceptionally strict and fully observed regulations. We emphasise this fact because all the programs of ecological agriculture development in Poland are to a significant extent linked to the expansion of "green product exports"' (Fiedor *et al.*, 1994; Chapter 11 in this book). At the same time it notes that Poland does have favourable conditions for eco-agriculture because of its big rural population, low pesticide use and low labour costs. In this regard it notes that the current trend of manufacturers of some pesticides that are banned in developed countries to aggressively market their products in Poland is proving an obstacle to the development of eco-agriculture.

In the case of the Thailand study the impact of eco-labelling schemes is said to have been negligible so far in the key markets of North America, East Asia and Europe. The majority of eco-label criteria developed do not currently apply to the main export products. The study notes, however, that in the case of one eco-label developed in Germany to apply to textiles, Thai producers are not keen to comply as the market niche is not large enough to justify changes in product standards. If pressed to comply, some technologically less advanced textile producers said that they would prefer to switch to alternative markets. The attitude of footwear producers to eco-labelling is said to be more positive because newer and more advanced technology is used. For example, producers stopped using PCPs because this was requested by export markets. Various 'Green Labels' have been introduced in Thailand but these are still at an early stage of development and the report suggests that a national scheme based on life cycle analysis is needed to help producers to comply with developments in external eco-labelling.

Another area of difficulty for Thai producers has been packaging requirements. For example, the fisheries and frozen products processing sector has been affected by the German 'Green Dot' scheme, although the compliance costs have not been prohibitive.

In Turkey a group of institutions together award the 'friend of water and the environment' label to approved companies and products. Most companies regard this eco-label as a marketing device. They have not applied for or been granted any foreign eco-labels. Certainly foreign companies have actively been influencing production processes in Turkey, but local manufacturers are not opposed to this.

The Zimbabwe study does not say much about non-official schemes that promote environmentally friendly products in the West. It simply notes that eco-labelling schemes will mean that local companies will have to invest in new capital and technology. With these changes they can compete anywhere but the problem is the difficulty in obtaining the necessary capital and servicing the high interest costs.

In conclusion, these studies are not strongly negative about voluntary schemes that encourage more ecologically friendly products. Many producers do not feel that they have (as yet) affected their exports significantly. A number of others see such schemes as *opportunities* to develop new products. Only a few cases are cited where they have had a detrimental impact. One should caution, however, that these studies are based on past experience, covering a period when eco-labelling schemes were only just getting started. It may be that views about them will change as they become more widespread.

What impact have international treaties had on the trade of developing countries and economies in transition?

Whereas environmental standards can properly be set at the national level for impacts that are confined to national boundaries, the same does not apply when the domain of the impact is international, or even global. In the case of such issues as greenhouse gases, ozone-depleting substances (ODSs) or the conservation of threatened species international agreements are essential. These mandate specific actions to address the environmental problems that arise, *and* specify how the responsibility for the actions is to be divided up between countries.

Frequently, the required actions include some form of restriction on trade. For ODSs the original agreement in 1985 included trade sanctions against non-members that violated the Montreal Protocol condition banning trade in ODSs between members and non-members. The latter was intended as an incentive to join the Protocol and in fact proved to be an important factor in encouraging some countries to become parties. It is important to note, however, that the sanctions have never been imposed and, according to some commentators, it would be against the GATT to impose them (Sorsa, 1992). The same applies to any restrictions on trade in products not containing ODSs but made using them.

Restrictions in trade are central to other international agreements, such as the Basel Convention on Trade in Hazardous Substances, and CITES, the Convention on Trade in Endangered Species. Although such treaties can override GATT rules in so far as the contracting parties waive their GATT rights voluntarily, the same does not apply to non-members to the treaties. Also, members who were to face sanctions for not complying could take issue with the use of these instruments. There is no experience with any such cases before the GATT, which could approve the use of sanctions in connection with global environmental treaties as long as it was treated as last resort measure with all other options having been exhausted (Sorsa, 1992). The situation with respect to WTO, the successor to GATT, is still unclear as regards such treaties.

The studies under review indicate that these countries have suffered some loss of trade as a result of such treaties. Under the Montreal Protocol, as ODSs are being phased out, developing countries that had a large export of products using such chemicals (such as refrigerators) are finding that the markets are being squeezed as buyers want to shift to versions based on substitutes.

In the case of Brazil, the study states that the value of exports to OECD countries of products that are potentially affected by ODS phase-out policies represented US$726 million in 1989 but declined by 45 per cent between 1989 and 1992. The decline of exports of manufactured goods as a whole to the OECD over the same period was 7 per cent. Exports of products which may contain CFCs to developing countries increased quickly in the early 1990s. However, this was commensurate with export growth in manufacturing products as a whole. No data are given on the overall changes in value of ODS-related trade since 1989. The study also gives the example of the effect of the Basel Convention on trade in scrap metal. The iron and steel industries import scrap to make up for fluctuations in domestic supply. Although imports currently only account for a small proportion of the total supply of scrap, trade restrictions could adversely affect competitiveness in the event of shortages of scrap.

The China case study quotes a decline in the volume of exports of refrigerators of 58 per cent between 1988 and 1991. Similar declines were noted for other products using ODSs. It is as a consequence of this decline that China has stepped up its phase-out programme and hopes to phase out ODSs faster than would be required for developing countries under the Protocol.[6]

The Colombian study states that the impact of the Montreal Protocol on international competitiveness is not clear. While some firms will not be able to afford the new technology, there are funds available from the parties to the Protocol to assist in the transition. If the climate change convention results in a carbon tax, or if fossil fuel consumption is restricted in international markets in other ways, Colombia will lose out as a net exporter of oil and coal. An increase in the price of fossil fuels based on their carbon content would impact on exports of stone, glass and ceramics.

The Costa Rica study concludes that in general the application of Multilateral Environmental Agreements (MEAs) has been perceived as a generator of new opportunities. Thus the Convention on Climate Change has been declared a priority for the national development strategy. In the case of the Montreal Protocol the study states that it is difficult to quantify the effect this has had on the trade of CFCs, although the overall cost of reconversion resulting from the Protocol required by the country is expected to be no more than $5 million. The use of CFCs and halogens in aerosols has already been prohibited, but this is thought to have had little effect on trade due to the availability of substitutes. Products requiring refrigeration, such as bananas, fruit and meat, represent an important part of the country's exports and could potentially be affected by the phase-out of ODSs.

Although there are no precise estimates of the amount of trade in Costa Rica in products covered by CITES, it is known to be an insignificant percentage of total exports and therefore the commercial effect of its application is thought to be limited. The study gives the example of orchid dealers who have complained that the 5 per cent tax on all imports and exports of wildlife species reduces their competitiveness although this is not quantified.

No data exist on the commercial effects of the Basel Convention in Costa Rica; however, those consulted by the study suggested that these would be low.

The Indian study simply notes in passing that international agreements such as the Montreal Protocol will result in many export sectors being severely affected as a result of the need to adapt to the new standards.

The Malaysia study concludes that ODS phase-out as a result of the Montreal Protocol has had relatively little effect on Malaysia's trade and competitiveness. This is due to close co-operation between government and industry in the national phase-out strategy. Malaysia's production of refrigerators and air conditioners has not been greatly affected by cost increases. In spite of an accelerated CFC phase-out in developed countries, Malaysian exports of air conditioners have increased sharply as it has invested in the capacity to produce equipment that runs without CFCs.

Malaysia acceded to the Basel Convention in 1993 but no view is given on the actual or predicted effects of this treaty on exports. The country acceded to CITES in 1977. It is concerned that some countries are using conservation measures in this treaty as disguised trade barriers.

The Philippines study notes that most of the successful global agreements such as the Montreal Protocol, CITES, etc., affect commodities that are not significant Philippine exports. One potential treaty it is concerned with is that on trade in tropical timber. Such an agreement would impact significantly on the country's exports of furniture as local sources of sustainable plantations are very few and unable to expand quickly due to the long gestation period for hardwood plantations. As far as regulating open-sea resources is concerned, the 1989 Wellington Convention for the Prohibition of Fishing with Long Driftnets and the UN Moratorium on Driftnet Fishing are poorly monitored and enforced. In fact better enforcement would benefit the Philippines as driftnet fishing is not a major method in Philippine fishing.

The Poland study states that it is premature to estimate the influence of most international treaties on Polish trade as of this time (its participation in most treaties dates from 1990). Nevertheless it notes that both the Montreal Protocol and the Climate Change Convention can be expected to have an impact on Poland's foreign trade; the first through the increased cost of the technology that replaces ODSs and the second because of the loss of export markets for fossil fuels, particularly coal.

The Basel Convention that controls the transboundary movement of hazardous wastes has major implications for Poland. On the one hand it has resulted in a major reduction in the importation of wastes into Poland, where some of them (for example, scrap paper) are often useful inputs into production processes. On the other hand there are other products such as scrap metal where restrictions might benefit Poland, which lost a lot of this much needed material through exports. Finally Poland is losing out from this treaty through the loss of transport business (Poland is a corridor for the shipment of materials from Russia and Ukraine).

Another case where an international treaty has had negative impacts is fisheries. With the establishment of 200 mile exclusive economic zones, Poland was forced out of traditional North Sea fishing areas. Since then some new areas have been made available but overall the country is in danger of losing its fishery export industry.

There are also a number of regional treaties that will influence Poland's structure of industrial and agricultural production and hence its foreign trade. The Convention for the Protection of the Marine Environment in the Baltic Sea will result in increased fees for water intake and sewerage discharge, thus affecting the exports of water-intensive goods such as artificial fibres, cellulose and paper, coke, sulphuric acid, and so on. At the same time it will have to import a large number of water recycling systems. With regard to the transboundary movement of air pollution, Poland, Germany and the then Czechoslovakia concluded the so-called Black Triangle agreement that relates to the improvement of the environment in the three countries. This has resulted in reduced sulphur emissions from power stations, the costs of which are reflected in higher prices and less export of electricity from Poland. Finally, Poland has concluded or is concluding agreements on nature protection with the Ukraine, Slovakia, Belarus and Russia. These combine restrictions on the use of nature reserves with the development of alternative economic activities that could promote trade between Poland and the neighbouring countries.

In the Thailand case study, producers are said to have been only marginally affected so far by MEAs. As the country qualifies as an Article 5 country of the Montreal Protocol (which permits phase-out by 2008 instead of a much earlier period for most developed countries) ODS phase-out has been slow, with consumption of the most utilized ODSs increasing three-fold between 1986 and 1991. Therefore no negative effects on trade have yet been observed. The study warns, however, that if phase-out is undertaken at the last minute, additional compliance cost and the rising costs of CFCs could adversely affect producers.

Thailand became a signatory to the Basel Convention in 1992 and is in the process of applying regulations to the trade in hazardous wastes. Toxic waste imports have increased considerably in recent years but are predicted to reduce drastically as regulations come into force. Detailed global figures for waste trade are difficult to obtain due to widespread illegal trafficking.

Thailand's commitment to CITES has affected the major trade of orchid plants, with one whole family of orchids now prohibited from exportation. Artificially propagated species have partly replaced wild orchids in many export markets. Trade in crocodile and crocodile products has also been affected by CITES but the exact impact of such restrictions is generally hard to determine partly due to the level of illegal trade.

The Turkey study does not comment on the links between international treaties and the country's foreign trade.

The Zimbabwe study identifies trade benefits arising from the Bamako Convention which restricts the import of wastes into Africa and controls the transboundary movement of wastes within Africa. Although clearly restrictive of trade this is seen as beneficial as far as Zimbabwe is concerned, because it safeguards against serious environmental hazards. On the other hand the study sees the convention on trade in endangered species (CITES) as damaging to the country's interests. This is primarily because of the ban on trade in ivory, which hurts Zimbabwe, where elephants are not endangered and where it could gain significantly from trade in ivory were it permitted. In fact the revenues from such trade could provide much needed resources for managing elephant habitats. Zimbabwe's position on this issue is of course well known and a major source of disagreement within CITES.

The tentative conclusion therefore appears to be that these international conventions certainly will restrict or limit trade in some form or another. In some cases the restrictions can be significant and countries may wish to seek some compensation or exemption for the losses suffered on that basis. These treaties are voluntarily entered into and it may be possible for groups of countries with similar abilities to negotiate suitable terms. To some extent this is what was done in the Montreal Protocol, and the same could be done in other treaties, such as the Basel Convention. In any event, it will be important to know what these trade impacts *are*, prior to carrying out such negotiations.

1.5   CONCLUSIONS

In spite of the fact that data have been limited and the conclusions often negative, these eleven studies have provided a lot of useful information on trade and environment links. In this synthesis chapter these have been divided into those that arise as a result of trade measures and those that arise as a result of environmental measures.

On the trade–environment link the focus has been on the impacts of the various recent attempts at trade liberalization. Past studies have shown that such measures could both harm the environment as well as protect it. The studies reviewed here did not provide any emphatic evidence that trade liberalization has systematically hurt the environment. There are specific situations in which environmental pressure has been reduced and others in which it has been increased. Where it has been increased, some of the case studies have identified policies that could mitigate the damage without losing the benefits of the trade liberalization. In fact one could argue that in all cases where negative impacts have been identified, some policies of environmental protection that were acceptable from a trade point of view could have been introduced to reduce that impact.

On the environment–trade link five questions were posed. The first was whether environmental regulations in developed countries were hurting the exports of the countries under study. There is much talk of such effects but little hard evidence. These case studies looked for such evidence and found some situations where such pressures were significant. This was particularly true for the smaller countries. The larger exporting countries claimed that the effects generally have been small, and in most cases manageable for the exporters. In several cases the adoption of the stricter standards not only decreases environmental damage, it increases efficiency and profits for firms. The situations where problems have been identified are: (a) where exporters are small producers, in which case they are affected by the increasing number and variety of regulations; (b) situations where there have been a large number of changes in the regulations, where a lack of information is a serious problem; and (c) where there is a perception that the rules are unreasonably cumbersome and complex and at least partly designed to make exports uncompetitive.

The second question was whether domestic environmental regulations were hurting exports or encouraging imports. Apart from Poland, there was little evidence to suggest that they were hurting exports. Most country studies concluded that the costs of environmental protection could be met without seriously affecting competitiveness. In some cases there was even a gain in competitiveness as a result of imposing such regulations. The Poland case is rather special, as it entailed a very large number of changes in energy prices which were beneficial to the environment but undoubtedly damaging for exports which previously had had access to very low cost raw materials and energy.

The third question was whether there was any evidence that polluting industries were migrating to countries with less strict environmental standards. Only three studies offered any comments on this but they support the general finding that such migration is not a common problem. There are special cases where it does occur, however, and where action is needed to control it.

The fourth question was whether consumer-led movements in developed countries, such as eco-labelling, were having major impact on the exports of the countries being studied. In general the studies were not particularly negative about voluntary schemes that encourage more ecologically friendly products. Many producers did not feel that these had (as yet) affected their exports significantly. A number of others saw such schemes as *opportunities* to develop new products. Only a few cases were cited where they have had a detrimental impact. One should caution, however, that these studies are based on past experience, covering a period when eco-labelling schemes were only just getting started. It may be that views about them will change as they become more widespread.

The final question was about the effects of international treaties on trade. Such treaties were found to have had significant trade impacts in some cases. In other cases, countries managed to meet the conditions of the treaty and still have their exports in related fields grow. In yet other cases, there is concern that the treaties are having serious detrimental effects on trade and, indirectly, on national development. This is an area where changes may be necessary to reconcile such national interests with those of the international community. One way in which this reconciliation can be made is to compensate those who are seriously adversely affected by the measures.

NOTES

1. For a recent survey and evaluation of this literature see Markandya (1994).

2. The relationship between the level of development and the quality of the environment is now formalized in the so-called 'Environmental Kuznets Curve'. This postulates that the environment deteriorates in the early stages of development but then starts to improve once a certain level of living standard has been attained (Selden and Song, 1994).

3. Under the prospective Uruguay Round Agreement, greater emphasis is being placed on internationally determined product standards.

4. Traditional exports, representing 44 per cent of total exports are oil, coffee, coal and ferronickel. Non-traditional exports are fruits, flowers, fish, textiles, leather, chemicals and plastic, and resin.

5. One study which has looked at the effects on a developing country's exports of higher environmental costs is Low and Yeats (1992). This examined the effects of a pollution abatement and control expenditure tax (PACE) on Mexico, raising its costs to the level of the US. The results obtained show that such a measure would have very modest trade effects, amounting to at most 2 per cent of Mexico's export revenues.

6. The reduction in exports of refrigerators could also be due to the very rapidly growing domestic market. Nevertheless, it does appear that the loss of export opportunities had some impact.

REFERENCES

Achanta, A., P. Dadhich, P. Ghosh and L. Noronha (1994), 'Requirements of environmentally sound technologies (EST) to India for compliance with environmental standards and regulations in OECD countries', Tata Energy Research Institute, Delhi, prepared for UNCTAD-TERI, New Delhi.

Aruoba, C. *et al*., (1993), 'Impact of environmental regulations and standards in European and North American markets on Turkish Exports', Report 1: Environment–Trade Link, Second Draft; Report 2: Trade–Environment Link, First Draft, Geneva: UNCTAD.

Birdsall, N. and D. Wheeler (1992), 'Trade Policy and Industrial Pollution in Latin America: Where are the Pollution Havens?', in P. Low (ed.), *International Trade and the Environment*, World Bank Discussion Papers No. 159, Washington, DC.

Boyd, R., W. Hyde and K. Krutilla (1993), 'Trade policy and environmental accounting: a case study of structural adjustment and deforestation in the Philippines', mimeo, Athens, OH: Ohio University.

Chapman, D. (1991), 'Environmental standards and international trade in automobiles and copper: the case for a social tariff', *Natural Resources Journal*, **31** (3), 449–61.

Cruz, W. and R. Repetto (1993), *The Environmental Effects of Stabilization and Structural Adjustment Programs: The Philippines Case*, Washington, DC: World Resources Institute.

de Motta Veiga, P., M. Reis Castilho and Galeno Ferraz Filho (1995), 'Relationships between Trade and the Environment: the Brazilian Case', study carried out under the joint UNCTAD/UNDP project on Reconciliation of Environmental and Trade Policies (INT/92/207), July.

Dean, J. (1992), 'Trade and the Environment: A Survey of the Literature', in P. Low (ed.), *International Trade and the Environment*, World Bank Discussion Papers No. 159, Washington, DC.

Fiedor, B., S. Czaja, A. Graczyk and J. Rymarczyk (1994), *Linkages Between Environment and Trade: A Case Study of Poland*, Geneva: UNCTAD.

Gaviria, D., R. Gomez, L. Ho and A. Soto (1994), *Reconciliation of Trade and Environment Policies: The Case Study of Colombia*, Geneva: UNCTAD.

Grossman, G. and A. Krueger (1992), 'Environmental Impacts of a North American Free Trade Agreement', in P. Garber (ed.), *The US–Mexico Free Trade Agreement*, Cambridge, MA: MIT Press.

Iba, M. (1993), 'Japanese environmental policies and trade policies: trade opportunities for developing countries', mimeo, Geneva: UNCTAD.

Intal, P., E. Medalla, M. de Los Angeles, D. Israel, V. Pineda, P. Quintos and E. Tan (1994), *Trade and Environment Linkages: The Case of the Philippines*, Geneva: UNCTAD.

Jaffe, A., S. Peterson, P. Portney and R. Stavins (1993), 'Environmental regulations and the competitiveness of US industry', report prepared for the US Department of Commerce, The Economic Resources Group, Cambridge, MA.

Jha, V., R. Vossenaar and S. Zarrilli (1993), *Eco-labelling and International Trade: Preliminary Information from 7 Systems*, Geneva: UNCTAD.

Low, P. and A. Yeats (1992), 'Do "Dirty" Industries Migrate?', in P. Low (ed.), *International Trade and the Environment*, World Bank Discussion Papers No. 159, Washington, DC.

Lu, R., Y. Xia, J. Li, J. Zhang and Y. Lu (1993), 'A study on environmental and foreign trade development in China', draft, Geneva: UNCTAD.

Markandya, A. (1994), 'Is free trade compatible with sustainable development', *UNCTAD Review*, 9–22.

Nkomo, J., B. Zwizwai and D. Gumbo (1994), 'Trade and the environment: Zimbabwe case study', draft, Geneva: UNCTAD.

Parikh, J., V. Sharma, U. Ghosh and M. Panda (1993), *Trade and Environment Linkages: A Case Study of India*, Geneva: UNCTAD.

Pearson, C. (1993), *Trade and Environment: The United States Experience*, Geneva: UNCTAD.

Porter, M. (1991), 'America's green strategy', *Scientific American*, April, 168.

Rege, V. (1993), 'GATT law and environment related issues affecting trade of developing countries', mimeo, Geneva: UNCTAD.

Robison, H. (1988), 'Industrial pollution abatement: the impact on the balance of trade', *Canadian Journal of Economics*, **21**, 187–99.

Scholz, I. and J. Wiemann (1993), *Ecological Requirements to be Satisfied by Consumer Goods – a New Challenge for Developing Countries' Exports to Germany*, Berlin: German Development Institute.

Selden, T.M. and D. Song (1994), 'Environmental quality and development: is there a Kuznets curve for air pollution?', *Journal of Environmental Economics and Management*, **27**, 147–62.

Sorsa, P. (1992), 'GATT and Environment: Basic Issues and Some Developing Country Concerns', in P. Low (ed.), *International Trade and the Environment*, World Bank Discussion Papers No. 159, Washington, DC.

UNCTAD (1993), *Reconciliation of Environmental and Trade Policies: Description of the Programme of Work*, Geneva.

Wheeler, D. and A. Mody (1992), 'International investment location decisions: the case of US firms', *Journal of International Economics*, **33**, 57–76.

2. Environmental policy, market access and competitiveness: the experience of developing countries

René Vossenaar and Veena Jha

2.1 THE ISSUES

One important question examined in the country case studies is how environmental policies, standards and regulations affect international competitiveness and market access for developing countries. Enhanced understanding of this question is important for several reasons. First, developing countries need to know what policies and measures the government and the business community could adopt, at the national level, to mitigate possible adverse trade and competitiveness effects of environmental policies, standards and regulations as well as to allow businesses to take advantage of new trading opportunities. Second, developed countries need to be aware of the implications of their environmental policies on developing countries and to identify ways and means of avoiding unnecessary adverse effects on developing countries' exports. Third, there is a need to examine how bilateral and multilateral aid agencies can assist developing countries in maintaining and, where possible, expanding market shares in the light of environmental factors. Finally, there has been interest in examining the extent to which the rules and principles of the multilateral trading system facilitate legitimate environmental policies, standards and regulations as well as ensuring adequate transparency and sufficient safeguards against possible protectionist abuse. The purpose of the case studies was to improve understanding of the issues raised, based on empirical studies at the country level.

2.1.1 The Competitiveness Issue

This chapter highlights two issues: (a) the 'competitiveness issue' and (b) the impact of environmental policies on developing countries' access to developed country markets. With regard to (a), the relationship between environmental policy and competitiveness has been an issue of intensive debate in both developed and developing countries. This debate has evolved over time. When this project was initiated in 1992, the debate in both developed and developing countries was largely characterized by concern that environmental policies would have predominantly negative effects on competitiveness. In several respects the debate had a strong North–South dimension, as there were potential sources of friction between developed and developing countries.

In developed countries, the major worry was that the introduction of more stringent environmental regulations in the domestic market would result in loss of competitiveness *vis-à-vis* industries in countries where standards are less stringent or where enforcement is difficult, or that industries facing relatively high pollution abatement costs would relocate to such countries. This was sometimes seen as 'unfair' competition, resulting in calls for measures to 'level the competitive playing field'. Developing countries, on the other hand, were concerned that increasingly stringent environmental regulations in the developed countries could adversely affect market access for their export products and that this could erode part of the improvements in market access negotiated in the Uruguay Round of Multilateral Trade Negotiations. Thus, there was concern over 'green protectionism' and over the need to adjust products and production processes to the environmental regulations of the developed countries, which were not necessarily the priorities of the developing countries. Many in developing countries considered that it was 'unfair' that they had to make such adjustments to address problems which were caused by the developed countries in the first place. Examples of this perception can be found, for example, in the India study.

The country studies have contributed to advancing the international debate and to eliminating sources of potential friction. For example, it has not been possible to find evidence to substantiate fears that trade liberalization negotiated under the Uruguay Round would lead to competitive deregulation and a race-to-the-bottom in environmental standards. On the contrary, the case studies provide examples of the potential of international trade in diffusing environmental standards across markets. Furthermore, by and large the studies have not found any significant relocation of polluting industries to countries with less environmentally stringent policies. This issue has been examined, for example, in the Colombia study.[1]

In addition, several country studies reject the view that differences in environmental standards across countries would result in 'unfair' competitiveness advantages for firms in developing countries. They also reject 'eco-dumping' as an important issue. Indeed, the point is made that 'strategic policies' aimed at obtaining trade benefits from deliberately setting standards at an artificially low level (or from not enforcing them) are unlikely to be practised on a rational basis.[2]

Another reason why the competitiveness issue has become less controversial is that recent analyses and debate have also focused on positive linkages between environmental stringency and competitiveness and on the potential for 'win–win' situations. According to the 'Porter hypothesis',[3] for example, well designed environmental policies can improve competitiveness by inducing innovation or creating incentives to increase efficiency.[4] The country case studies provide some examples of win–win situations. Generally, win–win situations could arise in cases where increased resource productivity can be achieved or where price premiums are available. One reason why developing country firms may be at a certain disadvantage in taking advantage of win–win situations is the weak demand for 'environment-friendly' products in the domestic market.

2.1.2   Market Access

Whilst the studies do not reveal that developed countries' environmental policies, standards and regulations have generalized trade and competitiveness effects on developing countries, they can result in limited access for specific sectors and specific firms, particularly small and medium sized enterprises (SMEs) and producers from the informal sector. It should also be taken into account that compliance costs of environmental policies may become more significant in the future. For example, increased efforts to avert the problem of climate change may have strong trade and competitiveness effects on certain sectors.

   The rest of this chapter analyses a series of factors which has a bearing on the effects of environmental policies, standards and regulations on market access and export competitiveness for developing countries. It also discusses policies and measures at the national and international levels aimed at alleviating adverse trade and development effects as well as strengthening any positive effects.

2.2   EMPIRICAL ANALYSIS

2.2.1   Trade and Competitiveness Effects

As mentioned above, a concern in many developing countries is that there could be an erosion of gains arising from recent trade liberalization if compliance with environmental regulations were to lead to cost increases or discrimination against their exports. Concern has also been expressed that environmental measures may be adopted for protectionist reasons. Are these concerns justified?

   A priori, there are grounds for such concern in the case of many developing countries, in particular for the following reasons: (a) environmental regulations in the developed countries are emerging in many sectors where developing countries have become particularly competitive, such as fishery and forestry products, leather and footwear, textiles and clothing, and certain consumer products; (b) small and medium-sized enterprises (SMEs), which, particularly in the case of developing countries, may find it relatively difficult to respond to environmental regulations, often play an important role in these sectors (see below); and (c) other characteristics of developing country exports. Each of these is considered below.

With regard to (a), it should be noted that environmental regulations and consumer concerns in the developed countries are to a large extent sector-specific, affecting such sectors as fishery and forestry products, leather and footwear, textiles and clothing, and certain consumer products. A number of product regulations such as bans on the use of specific chemicals and eco-labelling apply to these sectors. Most country case studies presented in this book show that a significant share of developing country exports is in product categories which already have to comply with environmental regulations of developed country markets. An analysis carried out by UNCTAD indicates that, on average, about one-third of the value of total exports and about half of the value of manufactured exports of developing countries originate in such sectors. This is particularly relevant for Asian developing countries, since over 60 per cent of their manufacturing exports, in value terms, originate in such sectors. It is to be noted, however, that the ability to respond to environmental regulations also varies across regions. This may explain why a recent UNIDO survey found that the perception that foreign environmental regulations already hinder market access was slightly lower in South and East Asia (53 per cent) than in Sub-Saharan Africa (59 per cent) and Latin America and the Caribbean (67 per cent).[5]

Concerning (b), a recurrent theme in the country studies is that adapting to environmental regulations may be more difficult for small and medium-sized enterprises (SMEs) than for large firms. It is also to be noted that in many developing countries SMEs have a large participation in total exports. In India, for example, SMEs accounted for 32 per cent of the value of total exports in 1994–1995. Their participation was as high as 90 per cent in sectors such as textiles and leather and leather products; that is, in sectors where environmental regulations are now emerging. Furthermore, developing countries' export strategies are often based on SME's large potential for export expansion. Taking again the example of India, this potential can be illustrated by the fact that while SMEs account for 90 per cent of the exports of textiles, these exports still represent only a small part of total sales. Indeed, much of the recent export growth has come from SMEs, and the same is true for leather products. This may explain why concern over external environmental policies in India, which exports a relatively small portion of its Gross Domestic Product (GDP), would appear to be more accentuated than in many Asian developing countries with a much higher exports/GDP ratio.

With regard to (c), several studies have identified certain characteristics which may render developing country exports relatively vulnerable to the new environmental standards and regulations. For example, in many cases the competitive advantage of exporters from developing countries is largely based on their ability to sell standardized mass-produced products at low prices. The Brazil study points out that product differentiation is more difficult in the case of such homogeneous products, and producers generally find it difficult to recover through price premiums increased costs owing to environmental improvements. In addition, since the home demand for environment-friendly products may be insignificant, it is difficult for developing country firms to recover incremental costs in the domestic market.

2.2.2   Environmental Measures with a Potential Trade Impact

The country case studies show that environmental requirements can take the form of standards and regulations, product-content requirements (such as regulations limiting the amount of hazardous substances contained in a product), recycled content requirements, labelling and packaging requirements as well as a range of voluntary measures, such as eco-labelling. Apart from voluntary standards and mandatory regulations implemented by governments, private firms or importers may impose certain requirements on their foreign suppliers. Finally, non-governmental organization (NGO) campaigns may influence market access conditions.

The studies also show that environmental requirements may be different from other technical standards and regulations in several respects. For example, a relatively large number of environmental 'regulations' tend to be voluntary in nature; environmental regulations may be based upon non-product related process and production methods (PPMs); and channels of information dissemination may be less clearly established in the case of environmental requirements.

Standards and regulations
Environmental standards and regulations applicable to traded products have emerged in various sectors. Food standards and strict limitations on the use of certain substances are likely to have the most significant effects on market access. Among the problems reported by exporters, for example in the India and Zimbabwe studies, are the costs and difficulties of testing and verification procedures; perceived lack of scientific data for specific thresholds or limit values; and the uncertainty arising from rapidly changing requirements in overseas markets. Several studies report cases which are perceived as protectionist.

Regulations can imply bans for products not meeting specific requirements or containing certain substances. The studies indicate that bans on environmental grounds are becoming increasingly frequent due to the widespread public concern over hazardous substances and because it may sometimes be easier to legislate bans rather than importing technical standards which involve complex risk assessment.

Bans on substances which are hazardous to the environment or public health will affect trade in products containing such substances. Such bans are also emerging in sectors of export interest to developing countries, such as textiles, leather and footwear. For example, in Germany products containing pentachlorophenol (PCP) have been banned for several years, and the use of hazardous substances, such as dioxin and formaldehyde, has been restricted, affecting leather exports from developing countries. Sales of clothes and bed linen manufactured using azo dyes as well as materials containing these chemicals have also been banned.

Packaging requirements
The country case studies show that packaging requirements in the developed countries have at times created uncertainty among developing country exporters, in particular with regard to the type of packaging materials that will be acceptable to importers. The problem of a lack of precise and timely information is aggravated by the existence of differences in requirements among countries. Unintended effects of certain packaging requirements on developing countries are illustrated in the Colombia study. The study reports that as a result of the German Packaging Ordinance coffee exporters felt obliged to use plastic (inherently less environment-friendly packaging material) rather than jute (a traditional, environment-friendly material) because they perceived that importers would prefer materials which would be more easily recyclable.

This particular case has generated some debate. The Federal Ministry for the Environment in Germany acknowledged that many of the difficulties concerning imports from developing countries which have come to its attention related to jute packaging (the main products imported in jute packaging are coffee, cocoa, wool, cotton, tobacco, herbs and dried fruit).[6] However, the Ministry pointed out that there was no reason to generally substitute jute packaging, as it is both reusable and recyclable. Several companies in Germany, and in other countries, offer recycling services for used jute packaging. The recycling capacity in Germany for jute is about the same capacity as in the field of plastics packaging (50 per cent). Thus there is no reason to substitute jute with plastics because of a lack of recovery capacities. As for the markets for recycled jute these materials have been used for some time in the car, building and furniture industries.

Another question is whether certain requirements have to be met by jute packaging for it to be reused or recycled. Certainly there are such requirements stemming from technical details of the recovery processes. Problems have arisen in the use of certain batching oils, metal clips, cotton stickers and toxic substances in the packaging used. But none of these problems are problems which generally prevent the reuse or recycling of used jute packaging. They can be solved by adaptations in the packaging design or by more advanced recovery processes. According to the German Ministry of the Environment, such adaptations are not a problem specific to jute packaging but affect all packaging materials.

The country cases studies seem to suggest that, in general, initial problems with packaging requirements tend to be resolved after some time on the basis of adjustments in the importing countries as well as knowledge and experience acquired by exporters.

Recycled content requirements

The principal purpose of recycled content requirements (which prescribe that a product should contain a minimum percentage of recycled materials) is to create a market for recycled materials, in particular where market forces alone do not create sufficient demand for such materials.

The Brazil study observes that recycled content criteria in the context of an EU eco-label on tissue products could reduce the demand for pulp and threaten the competitiveness of Brazilian paper mills. The Brazilian forestry industry derives part of its comparative advantage from plantation forests, and Brazilian producers have made significant investments in the sustainable management of their forest base.[7]

Eco-labelling

Eco-labelling can have different types of trade effects.[8] At times, eco-labelling may result in *de facto* discrimination against imported products and in technical barriers to trade. For example, the Brazil study found that European Union eco-labels for tissue products discriminate against Brazilian exports. Eco-labelling may also have an impact on cost competitiveness and on the attractiveness of a product (whether labelled or unlabelled) in the market. The significance of any such effects depends to a large extent on the importance of eco-labelling in the market place. In many cases, trade impacts may be relatively small because eco-labelling targets only certain segments of the market, or because markets fail to react to eco-labelling. Effects may become more important, however, to the extent that market responses become more significant. In the pulp and paper sector, eco-labels may already have more significant effects than in other sectors as issues such as recycling and deforestation are important factors within consumer preferences and buying policies of importers in the developed countries.

Unilateral measures

A recurrent theme in the country case studies is the concern over unilateral measures with extraterritorial application. As a result of unilateral measures by the United States, the Colombian tuna industry would have lost 20 per cent of its revenues, or US$20 million. Even when Colombian vessels complied with the required fishing techniques, the Unites States continued to apply the embargo for a considerable time. Unilateral actions facing trade in shrimp harvested without using turtle excluding devices have also been examined. Whilst compliance cost would be low, concern is nevertheless expressed over the unilateral and extraterritorial nature of such measures. Both cases have been brought to WTO panels.

NGO actions

Several country studies have expressed concern over the effects of campaigns by certain non-governmental organizations (NGOs), affecting a range of products such as coal and flowers in the case of Colombia. Such campaigns raise the issue of accountability, as imprecise and incorrect campaigns could prejudice the foreign trade of another country.[9]

Campaigns by environmental NGOs and consumer organizations frequently target tropical timber. The Malaysia study strongly condemns unilateral action, but does not believe that effects on Malaysia's timber exports have so far been significant. It attributes this in part to successful policies and measures to counter such actions, such as export diversification, the adoption of sustainable production methods and Malaysia's own campaigns. The study underlines that timber certification can be used as a marketing tool that can help to gain access to 'green' markets, but lists conditions for non-discriminatory labelling.

2.2.3 Awareness and Strategies of the Business Community

Many of the country case studies have examined the state of awareness of the business sector in developing countries, their sources of information, their perception regarding some key issues as well as their marketing strategies in the light of differences in domestic and external environmental regulations.

Awareness

The extent to which the business sector in developing countries is aware of domestic and external environmental regulations was found to vary from case to case, depending on factors such as destination of exports. In Colombia, two-thirds of the respondents to a survey conducted among industries and industry associations were not aware of environmental regulations emerging from export markets. However, a survey among over 60 exporting companies in Turkey in 1993 revealed that all interviewed companies were well aware of newly emerging environmental regulations in the European Union and the United States. This was attributed to the publicity given in Turkey to the German Packaging Ordinance and to continuously changing quality standards in the European and North American markets, part of which were linked to environmental concerns. In addition, public interest in environmental matters in Turkey itself was increasing rapidly.

Sources of information
The country studies also show that access to information is of key importance. Lack of timely and precise information can be an obstacle to trade. Whilst large firms obtain timely and accurate information directly from importers in developed country markets and various other sources, SMEs tend to depend on secondary sources, basically government sources, often implying considerable time delays. For most companies interviewed in Turkey the principal sources of information on environmental regulations in Europe and the United States were importers in these countries. Other studies, however, indicate difficulties in obtaining information and stress the importance of improving information flows.

Perceived influence of external environmental regulations
Several country studies examine the perceived influence of external environmental regulations on production and sales practices and the reactions of the business sector to such regulations. The India study notes that environment-related product requirements in developed country markets can have significant impacts on the choice of production processes in developing countries. Another concern, which is expressed, for example, in the studies on India and Zimbabwe, is that environmental standards and regulations increasingly require developing country producers to source materials and technologies from the importing countries imposing such standards.

In Turkey, more than half of the interviewed companies asserted that recently emerging regulations and other requirements emerging in export markets, in particular packaging requirements, had some impact on their manufacturing or exporting practices. Almost all these companies stated that environmental regulations in various degrees influenced the use of raw materials and intermediate goods.

The issue of external influence on domestic process and production methods (PPMs) also comes up in some of the country studies. A general interpretation of WTO rules is that an importing country should not make access to its market conditional on the use of specific PPMs in the exporting country. This would be interpreted as an extraterritorial application of domestic environmental laws. In practice, however, market forces already have an impact on PPMs used in different countries. For example, more than 40 per cent of the interviewed Turkish companies, in particular in the food, textile and garment sectors, stated that importing companies had influenced their process and production methods, either by requesting detailed information or through plant visits. Turkish manufacturers appeared to accept certain interference with their process technologies as a 'normal' condition of doing business, and did not question the legitimacy of customers in external markets having certain influence on domestic PPMs. Other studies, however, indicate that the business sector perceives specific PPM-related requirements as unjustified and protectionist.

Sales strategies in the light of differences in domestic and external regulations
In Turkey, almost all companies which produce both for the domestic and for external markets mentioned that one aspect of increasingly stringent external environmental regulations was the need to manufacture products of different quality for different markets. For example, firms were using different quality raw materials and intermediate goods according to the destination of the final product. This could adversely affect competitiveness.

Where external environmental requirements are different from domestic requirements, transaction costs may arise if firms have to manufacture different products for the domestic and external markets. If exports are significant, governments may introduce domestic regulations which are similar to external regulations. Win–win situations may exist where environmental policies can induce both improved environmental management *and* increased export competitiveness. A study on India recommends that governments should take proactive stands, in particular where domestic environmental concerns coincide with those in major export markets. The Indian government has already intervened in the case of benzidine content in dyes, and pesticide usage in tea and other agricultural products.[10]

A different situation arises if compliance with external environmental requirements, while entailing significant cost, is of limited environmental benefit to the country of production. Here, incurring such cost may be a good investment from a commercial point of view, for instance to maintain export markets, but may yield inferior results from an environmental point of view compared to other investments. The India study points out that at times there may be trade-offs between addressing domestic environmental concerns and investments in specific environmental improvements in response to requirements emerging from external markets.

2.2.4 Factors Having a Bearing on the Trade and Competitiveness Effects of Environmental Policies

This chapter does not intend to draw generalized conclusions on the trade and competitiveness impacts of environmental policies on developing countries. It was found that such impacts depend on many factors. Rather, it tries to determine these factors, based on the analysis contained in the country case studies presented in this book.

Among the many firm- or sector-specific factors influencing the competitiveness effects of environmental policies are the following: destination of exports; cost structures; basis for export competitiveness; firm size; the availability of raw materials, specialized inputs, technology and information; corporate structures; and the relationship with foreign firms.

Destination of exports
Environmental regulations vary largely across different markets. Thus, in the case of Colombia, given the product composition and geographical distribution of exports, only a relatively small share of exported goods faces significant environmental regulations.

Cost structures
The competitiveness effects of increased environmental compliance costs largely depend on the share of corresponding cost categories in total production costs. Thus low-value-added products may be relatively vulnerable. For example, packaging requirements may have more significant effects on certain fruit and vegetables than on high-value-added products.

Another example is textiles in which a number of environmental regulations have been applied referring to the use of dyes and chemicals. The India study estimates that on average raw materials, of which dyes are a significant proportion, represent around 60 per cent of the cost of production. Thus, switching to more expensive environment-friendly dyes may have a significant bearing on production costs. In this context, the India study notes that while benzidine dyes cost only US$3 per kilo, non-benzidine dyes are priced at US$8 to 10 per kilo.

Basis for export competitiveness
Increased production costs may make a product less competitive in segments of the international markets where competition is based largely on the ability to sell at low prices, particularly if the prices of competing products have not increased similarly.

Firm size
Perhaps the most important conclusion from several studies is that in general it is more difficult for small firms to comply with environmental regulations and standards, both domestic and external, than it is for large firms. This topic is analysed in more detail in the next section.

Availability of raw materials, specialized inputs, technology and information
The availability of raw materials, inputs, and so on, is of key importance for the production of environment-friendly products. For example, complying with environmental regulations in the textiles and footwear sectors poses special

conditions on dyes and leather. Environment-friendly materials may often be several times more expensive than conventional materials.

Corporate structures

The Brazil study suggests that the relationship between producers of finished goods and sectors producing input materials, such as chemicals and leather, is also an important factor. In the case of textiles, compliance with requirements related to the use of chemical input materials depends to a large extent on the market power and negotiating capabilities of textile companies. The more a company is vertically integrated, the greater its ability to control environmental factors throughout the product's life cycle.

Relationship with foreign firms

Companies that have links with foreign firms often find it easier to comply with environmental regulations. Several studies note that subsidiaries of TNCs often have relatively stringent environmental management standards as well as easy access to environmentally sound technologies.

2.2.5 The Case of Small and Medium-Sized Enterprises (SMEs)

Several studies highlight the point that efforts to reconcile trade and environment policies may have to pay special attention to the situation of small and medium-sized enterprises (SMEs). The studies on China and Colombia point out that SMEs make a relatively large contribution to industrial pollution. At the same time, the Thailand study stresses that there is great potential for improving environmental management in SMEs provided that the proper supporting infrastructure is set up. Many practices which are cleaner than present methods of production are feasible for SMEs, but one important obstacle is lack of information on available options.

Many of the difficulties that SMEs may encounter in responding to either domestic or external environmental requirements are no different from other difficulties arising from the characteristics of their operation. Environment-related requirements, however, may create some additional difficulties. For example, certain installations (such as waste treatment facilities) require certain economies of scale. Several studies show that operating costs (even for common effluent treatment plants) may be relatively high for SMEs. In addition, environment-friendly input materials, which may represent a considerable portion of total variable costs, may be expensive. For example, in the leather tanning sector in India, the costs of chemicals required to meet international standards were approximately three times higher than the costs of conventional chemicals. While large firms may use their bargaining power to obtain inputs at competitive prices, this may not be possible for SMEs. Similar results were found in the study on Brazil.[11]

SMEs may find it difficult to obtain the required input materials (for example dyes or chemicals) or to verify their suppliers. Once a new regulation emerges from an external market, it is often a long time before substitutes become available on the domestic market. While large firms may engage themselves in import activities or can influence their domestic suppliers to switch to environment-friendly materials, such opportunities may not be readily available for SMEs.

The India study expresses concern that rather than incurring cost increases in response to environmental regulations, SMEs often prefer to divert sales to the domestic market or to those external markets where environmental regulations are less stringent. It thus follows that environmental regulations could have an important bearing on export strategies. As an example, take the case of azo dyes which were recently prohibited in Germany, an important market for small-scale textiles exporters from India. Around 70 per cent of dyes used in India are azo dyes and 25 per cent of them are now banned in Germany.

2.2.6   Trading Opportunities for Environment-friendly Products

Consumer preferences for environment-friendly products in developed countries can create trading opportunities for firms in developing countries. There are several examples of these, including 'green cotton' from Uganda, India and some other countries, and the certification of jute packaging for OECD markets.

Although such markets have some promise, there are also a number of problems with moving trade in this direction. Thus, a range of obstacles needs to be removed. First, the market for environment-friendly consumer products is generally still small.[12] Projects aimed at promoting trade in environment-friendly products have been successful on a small scale and when benefiting from considerable donor and other support. But would they be successful in the long run on a more commercial basis? This depends on several questions such as the size of the market for the product, the availability of supplies of specialist inputs, the extent to which costs will fall as production expands and the viability of production without the implicit and explicit subsidies currently provided. Unfortunately there is currently not much information on these important questions.

Second, it is also not clear to what extent significant premiums from environmental investments can be generated. Developing countries, will need to analyse the conditions necessary for such market premiums to accrue and for the additional costs of organic production to be fully recovered. Also, while the market for ecological products and organically grown products in developed countries may expand quickly, it is subject to very strong competition and strict regulations.

Third is the question of certification. This may be expensive, particularly when domestic certification facilities are poor or when certificates issued in developing countries are not accepted in the importing countries. Also, there is a potential conflict between mandatory national labelling of organic products, and labels or schemes established by NGOs and exporter or importer groups. This raises difficulties for exporters who find themselves having to meet multiple labelling requirements.

Fourth is the problem of information. Buyers are faced with a bewildering choice of products with claims from producers and marketing agencies of the green nature of whatever it is they are promoting. At the same time sellers have only a vague idea as to which environmental aspects of their product have the greatest appeal and how price sensitive the demand for the products is relative to less green products.

Fifth, as shown in the Colombia study, there may be some trade-off between the 'environmental' quality of a product and other factors determining product quality such as the presentation of a product. Examples cited refer to bananas and packaging materials.

Some have noted that 'green trade' remains a very small part of overall trade, and the evidence on market trends for green products in the OECD countries is mixed. It may be misleading to encourage developing countries to switch on a large scale to green products, when market opportunities remain limited, or are growing relatively slowly. However, this is certainly an area deserving the full attention of the business community, policy-makers and the international donor community. The challenge is to increase the number of developing countries and enterprises that can turn this potential into financial, social and environmental gains.

2.2.7   Import Competition and Environmental Performance

Industrial restructuring for improving production efficiency may also result in environmental improvements, provided that costs are reduced in the process. However, the process of industrial restructuring could also be accompanied by rising costs and decreasing competitiveness. In this case firms will be less inclined to invest in environmental improvements. Increased openness will generally make it easier to access raw materials and technologies, thus reducing the competitiveness effects of environmental policies.

A study on Argentina indicates that increased import competition and changes in relative prices as a result of trade liberalization have induced firms to reduce costs by increasing process efficiency.[13] This has also resulted in environmental benefits. The study notes, however, that obtaining economic benefits from improved environmental management is likely only in a limited number of situations and under specific conditions, which to a large extent are sector-specific.

To illustrate this point, the study distinguishes three approaches that firms can follow to introduce or improve their environmental management:

type 1   The use of environment-friendly technologies, that is the adoption of (new) production processes with reduced environmental impact, or the development of green products;
type 2   Process optimization (the improvement of process efficiency, cost savings from reduced use of inputs and/or from reuse of by-products and waste);
type 3   End-of-pipe treatment.

With regard to the economic effects of environmental management, type 1 and type 2 approaches can provide returns in terms of reduced operational costs, and market signals can induce firms to introduce them. Type 3 approaches, however, normally add to a firm's costs, without any economic return. In practice, type 3 approaches will be adopted only in response to regulations.

A closer examination of three sectors (pulp and paper, leather and steel) suggests that while in the case of Argentina type 1 approaches are rare, environment-friendly technologies are often embodied in new equipment available in international markets. Investments which incorporate cleaner technologies or processes eventually induce some in-house technological efforts to develop or adapt processes. The study quotes examples in the steel and pulp and paper sectors, but not in the leather sector.

More examples were found, however, of type 2 approaches, and these had, to a large extent, been triggered by Argentina's import liberalization and industrial restructuring processes, which had forced firms to reduce costs in order to maintain market shares. Many efforts to reduce costs had resulted in environmental improvements as well. The clearest relationship between increased process efficiency and environmental improvement was found in the steel industry. In the leather sector, while tanneries had increasingly adopted chrome reuse processes resulting in cost savings (reduced costs on inputs and effluent treatment) possibilities for cost savings were found to be more limited than in the steel and pulp and paper sectors.

With regard to type 3 approaches, investments in effluent treatment or in end-of-pipe technologies generally add to production costs. Consequently, environmental investments which have no, or only a relatively low, economic return (for example efforts aimed at reducing the content of pollutants in effluent or waste treatment) are less frequent, as firms are often reluctant to make such investments. Thus, in the leather sector, tanneries rarely invest in sulphur and secondary effluent treatment facilities. Similarly, in the steel industry few efforts are made to improve end-of-pipe treatment of solid waste with low recovery value.

2.3 POLICY IMPLICATIONS

The previous sections have indicated that there is no empirical evidence to suggest that existing environmental policies have widespread effects on market access. However, effects could be more significant for some sectors and for small and medium-sized enterprises. Environmental policies may have differential competitiveness effects on developed and developing countries. In most cases, however, competitiveness effects of environmental policies can be addressed by appropriate policies at the national, regional and international levels.

2.3.1 Addressing Competitiveness Concerns at the National Level

What policies and measures could the business community and the government in developing countries adopt, at the national level, to mitigate possible adverse trade and competitiveness effects of environmental policies, standards and regulations as well as to allow businesses to take advantage of new trading opportunities? A related question is how programmes such as UNDP's Capacity 21 could assist in implementing such policies and measures.

An important conclusion of a number of the country case studies is that increasing the ability of firms to respond to environmental challenges in the first place requires sustained economic growth and sound macroeconomic and environmental policies. The strong commitment of many developing countries to sustained economic growth and openness through the promotion of trade and investment, together with improved environmental management, are key elements of their sustainable development strategies. The Malaysia study underlines the role of government policies in supporting private sector led growth, for example through support for research and development.

In addition, a number of areas of policy reform that will help address the competitiveness concerns include the following:

Infrastructure development
Several studies stress the important contribution of improvements in environmental infrastructure in reducing the costs of compliance with environmental regulations, for example with effluent standards. The Colombia and India studies highlight the role of common effluent treatment (CET) plants. The Malaysia study stresses the need to establish a facility for the treatment of hazardous waste. The Philippines study observes that a dollar spent in

infrastructural development can make a greater contribution to environmental improvements than a dollar spent in pollution abatement.

Testing and certification
As noted above, the certification of environment-friendly products may be costly and confusing; in particular when producers in developing countries depend on testing and certification bodies in the developed countries. The creation of standardization bodies or the expansion of existing bodies in developing countries and steps contributing to their international recognition are of key importance.

Capacity for innovation
Innovative and cost-saving responses to environmental regulations determine whether compliance costs can be offset or even competitiveness improvements gained. To promote innovation, governments can either provide broad enabling conditions for innovation, or take a more active part in fostering innovation. The study on Malaysia stresses that the central role of technology within Malaysia's development strategy is vital for environmentally sustainable economic growth.

Cooperation between government and industry
Cooperation of industry with the authorities in the standard-setting process can ensure the design of feasible standards and facilitate their implementation. For example, the Malaysia study points out that cooperation between government and the private sector has helped to identify cost-effective approaches for the phase-out of ozone depleting substances based on the incorporation of sector-specific elements into a national strategy.

Special measures for SMEs: dissemination of information
As has been indicated above, SMEs tend to have more difficulties than large firms in obtaining information and in adjusting to environmental regulations. The study on India proposes the following steps for improving the channelling of information and availability of environment-friendly input materials to SMEs:

- improve the registration of SMEs so that the government and other agents know where to direct information on environmental regulations;
- improve the provision of timely and accurate information to SMEs;
- provide relevant information to suppliers of input materials, such as dyes and chemicals;
- improve the availability of environment-friendly input materials for SMEs, by providing information, facilitating imports if substitutes are not

supplied locally, supporting research and development or the acquisition of appropriate technology for the domestic production of substitutes;
- develop domestic regulatory measures or other policy instruments to support the development of environment-friendly substitutes;
- support the establishment of adequate testing and certification facilities.

Experience indicates that larger firms tend to cooperate with each other, for example in the exchange of information on existing and emerging environmental regulations in external markets. Capacity-building efforts may help promote a process whereby the know-how and experience acquired by larger firms is transmitted to smaller firms.

2.3.2   International Cooperation

International cooperation is of key importance in preventing environmental policies having unnecessary adverse effects on trading partners, particularly developing countries. This implies that developed countries should make certain provisions when designing and implementing such policies. For example, the WTO Agreement on Technical Barriers to Trade provides for notification of new standards and regulations and for the possibility to provide comments. The country studies have identified and/or recommended further forms of international cooperation, both on a bilateral basis as well as through the work of multilateral aid agencies. In this context, the OECD's Development Assistance Committee has paid considerable attention to trade and environment issues. Private sector initiatives are also important.

Company-to-company cooperation
Experience shows that cooperation between importers and exporters and company-to-company cooperation greatly assist developing country exporters in adapting to external environmental regulations, for example in terms of the provision of timely and accurate information on standards and regulations, sources for environment-friendly materials, availability of testing regulations and facilities, as well as market trends and strategies. In many cases, importers and retailers implementing green purchasing policies discuss corresponding guidelines with foreign suppliers, and provide other forms of assistance. Apart from cooperation between companies in developed countries and their overseas suppliers, there are also many examples of cooperation between subsidiaries of transnational corporations (TNCs) and their local suppliers in developing countries. Cooperation between importers and retailers in developed countries and producers and exporters in developing countries is also of key importance in the promotion of exports of environment-friendly products.

Although such cooperation is undertaken within the private sector, governments in importing and exporting countries as well as bilateral and multilateral aid agencies can create an appropriate environment for such cooperation as well as sponsor activities which may encourage private sector cooperation.

Bilateral cooperation

Developed country governments increasingly assist their major developing country trading partners in adapting to environmental standards and regulations, for example through consultations prior to the introduction of new standards, the organization of workshops aimed at disseminating information and technological cooperation. For example, CBI, the Netherlands Bureau for the Promotion of Imports from Developing Countries, has been active in organizing 'azo' workshops in a range of developing countries. The India study refers to the successful cooperation between India and Germany in terms of the use of pentachlorophenol.

Lessons for multilateral aid agencies

Aid agencies can also provide technical assistance aimed at assisting national standardization bodies in establishing or improving domestic testing and certification facilities and, where appropriate, in undertaking pilot studies on national eco-labelling programmes.

It should be noted, however, that representatives from developing countries sometimes express the view that donors offering technical assistance in the trade and environment area are partly motivated by their own environmental and economic objectives and not necessarily those of the recipient country. This means that the donor support has to be seen to be designed with the priorities of the recipients in mind, and with donor advisers taking a 'back seat' in policy advice.

Capacity-building efforts could focus on the identification of sources of information on product standards and regulations in external markets, as well as the establishment of information systems for exporters. In addition, dissemination of information, technical assistance and technical cooperation are important, particularly when there may be a negative trade impact of such measures.

2.3.3 Implications for the Multilateral Trading System

As mentioned at the beginning of this chapter, there has been interest in examining the extent to which the rules and principles of the multilateral trading system facilitate legitimate environmental policies, standards and regulations as well as ensure adequate transparency and sufficient safeguards against possible protectionist abuse.

In the recent debate on trade and environment, competitiveness has been set aside as an important issue in the context of the multilateral trading system. It is widely recognized that the case for trade-restrictive measures to 'level the competitive playing field' is very weak indeed. Thus, governments have taken a strong stand against the use of trade-restrictive measures, for example so-called 'green countervailing duties' which were sometimes proposed to compensate for negative competitiveness effects, whether real or perceived, of environmental policies.

A second issue examined in this chapter is market access. Existing environmental policies and measures in developed countries would not appear to have generalized effects on market access and export competitiveness for developing countries. However, environmental measures and regulations may affect competitiveness and market access opportunities for firms in some sectors and, in particular, SMEs. Therefore, it is recognized that certain provisions should be made when environmental policies and measures with potential trade effects are designed and implemented. This has been discussed in the previous section.

So far, the WTO Committee on Trade and Environment (CTE) has concluded that no modifications to WTO rules are required to ensure adequate transparency for existing trade-related environmental measures.[14] However, it was agreed that the CTE should keep under review the adequacy of existing transparency provisions. The CTE also noted that different WTO members are dealing with some notifications differently. However, the relationship between some types of environmental instruments, such as the ISO 14000 series on environmental management standards and the TBT Agreement, is not clear. This chapter has also highlighted the concern over NGO campaigns and the issue of accountability.

The future debate on market access in the CTE is likely to focus also on the environmental benefits that may arise from improved market access and the removal of trade restrictions and distortions, such as high tariffs, tariff escalation, non-tariff barriers to trade and export subsidies. More analysis is needed in sectors such as agriculture, tropical and natural resource based products, fisheries, forestry products, non-ferrous metals and textiles and clothing.[15] Possible guidelines for further analysis are included in the final chapter of this book.

NOTES

1. Some possible exceptions are referred to in the China study (Chapter 5).

2. UNCTAD (no date) *Trends in the Field of Trade and Environment in the Framework of International Cooperation.*

3. Porter, M. (1990), *The Competitive Advantage of Nations*, New York: Free Press.

4. Porter, M. and C. van der Linde (1995), 'Green and competitive', *Harvard Business Review*, September-October, 120–34.

5. UNIDO (1997), 'Survey of the trade implications of international standards for quality and environmental management systems, (ISO 9000 and ISO 14000 series), draft.

6. Delbrück, K. (1997), 'The German Eco-label "Blue Angel" and International Trade', in S. Zarilli, V. Jha and R. Vossenaar (eds), *Eco-Labelling and International Trade*, London: Macmillan Press, pp. 189–94.

7. de Motta Veiga, P., M. Reis Castilho and Galeno Ferraz Filho (1995), 'Relationships between trade and the environment: the Brazilian case', study carried out under the joint UNCTAD/UNDP project on Reconciliation of Environmental and Trade Policies (INT/92/207), July.

8. Eco-labelling and international trade has been covered extensively in UNCTAD secretariat reports, particularly 'Eco-labelling and market opportunities for environmentally friendly products' (TD/B/WG.6/2, October 1994) and 'Trade, environment and competitiveness aspects of establishing and operating eco-labelling programmes' (TD/B/WG.6/5, August 1995). An UNCTAD secretariat seminar on 'Eco-labelling and international trade' was conducted in 1994. The results have been published in Zarrilli, Jha and Vossenaar (1997), see note 6 above.

9. Becerra, M.R., 'Some annotations on sustainable development: trade and the environment. The impact of trade-related policies on export competitiveness and market access', presentation at UNCTAD's Trade and Development Board at the first part of its forty-first session (unpublished).

10. Bharucha, V. (1994), 'Impact of environmental standards and regulations on India's exports', study prepared for UNCTAD.

11. A study on Brazil illustrates that compliance with the criteria related to the use of chemical input materials depends to a large extent on the market power and negotiating capabilities of companies. Large textile firms, for example, often exert pressure on chemical industries to supply – either through local production or imports – the input materials required in European countries; they are unwilling to pay higher prices for these input materials, as this would affect the competitiveness of their prices on foreign markets. SMEs do not have this power. In this context, Brazil's pulp and paper industry, which has achieved a high level of vertical integration, is in a better position to control the environmental attributes of input materials.

12. The OECD report quotes some estimates that, for example, organic cotton forms 0.1–0.3 per cent of total cotton exports, and for organic food the market share is around 1 per cent. The study on Colombia points out that while there is interest in exploring trading opportunities for environment-friendly products, world demand for such products is still small. In most cases, shifting to environment-friendly production processes in order to gain access to small markets for environment-friendly products would not appear, under the current circumstances, justified from a commercial point of view. The study observes that consumers in developed countries are not willing to pay a sufficiently high price to allow cost internalization in the developing countries. In addition, access to environmentally sound technologies required to supply markets for environment-friendly products has generally not been forthcoming.

13. Chudnovsky, D. (coordinator), 'International trade and the environment: the Argentine case', carried out by the Centro Internacional para la Transformacion (CENIT, International Centre for Transformation, Buenos Aires, Argentina) under the joint UNCTAD/UNEP project on Capacity-building on Trade and Environment. The study has also been supported by the Ministry of Foreign Affairs of Argentina (unpublished).

14. WTO, Report of the Committee on Trade and Environment, Press/TE 014, 18 November 1996.

15. See also, WTO, CTE, op. cit. paragraphs 198 and 199.

3. Policy instruments in Multilateral Environmental Agreements: experience of developing countries

Multilateral Environmental Agreements (MEAs) address environmental threats which are transboundary or global and where it is generally recognized that solutions should be multilateral.[1] The Rio Declaration, through Principle 7, recognizes the responsibilities of all countries, developing or developed, in addressing global environmental problems: 'In the view of the different contributions to global environmental degradation, States have common but differentiated responsibilities. The developed countries acknowledge the responsibility that they bear in the international pursuit of sustainable development in view of the pressures that their societies place on the global environment and of the technologies and financial resources they command.'

MEAs are an important means to improve environmental management and to achieve sustainable development. However, the means for evaluating environmental resources/factors remain unclear and underdeveloped, which makes it difficult to assess the benefits and costs of MEAs (including possible trade and income losses). Moreover, mechanisms for enforcing the provisions of MEAs remain unsatisfactory for a number of reasons. Trade measures have been used by a few MEAs to enforce compliance, but it is an open question as to whether they are necessary, effective or sufficient. It is also not clear whether non-fulfilment of the obligations undertaken by a party to an MEA can be referred to in any form of binding arbitration. The inducement to join an MEA may take the form of positive measures such as financial, technological, capacity building or other forms of assistance. However, some parties, particularly developing countries, are reassessing whether, on balance, the costs of joining an MEA outweigh the benefits.

The actual structure of MEAs varies considerably.[2] Many agreements have operated without any clear and explicit sanctions and have relied on informal and non-binding mechanisms, such as negotiations and consultation, supplemented by conciliation, arbitration and judicial settlements. Trade measures have also been written into some MEAs, but only to be used as a last resort in the event of non-compliance. Of the 180 MEAs negotiated, only 18 provide for the use of trade measures, including the Montreal Protocol on Substances that Deplete the Ozone Layer, the Basel Convention on the Control of Transboundary Movements of Hazardous Wastes and their Disposal, and the Convention on International Trade in Endangered Species (CITES).[3] Technical and financial assistance has been incorporated into a few MEAs, such as the Basel Convention, but is not a common feature of MEAs.

Available evidence on the effects of MEAs on trade and competitiveness is limited to only a few agreements such as the Montreal Protocol, the Basel Convention and CITES. Thus most of the empirical evidence used in this chapter relates to these MEAs, but is particularly concerned with the Montreal Protocol. The Conference of Parties, for example, under the Montreal Protocol, has recognized that trade and competitiveness effects may be relatively more significant for developing countries, and has proposed facilitating mechanisms which are discussed below.[4] This chapter is organized as follows. First, there is a discussion of the role of trade-restricting measures, which are potentially important in any discussion of trade effects of such measures. Second, it looks at the direct trade impacts of the MEAs, drawing on country case studies wherever possible. Third, it discusses the adequacy of the facilitating mechanisms, and finally it offers some conclusions on the role of MEAs in the trade and environment debate.

3.1   THE USE OF TRADE MEASURES

The use of trade measures in MEAs has several purposes. First, the fulfilment of environmental objectives may be based on trade measures, particularly those among parties, for example the Basel Convention and CITES. Secondly, trade measures against non-parties are aimed at preventing free-riding, that is, non-parties continuing to reap the benefits of the MEA without bearing the costs. Thirdly, trade measures may aim at persuading countries to accede to an agreement by making the cost of not joining higher than that of joining.[5] All these factors have guided the use of trade measures in the Montreal Protocol. One important issue is whether the use of trade measures could lead to a situation where Principle 7 of the Rio Declaration was not upheld. This is because, while Principle 7 squarely puts greater responsibility on developed country parties for current global environmental problems, trade measures are a blunt instrument which apply equally to both developed and developing country parties. In fact they may be more easily enforced on developing country parties than on developed country parties, as is borne out by the experience with the Basel Convention.

3.1.1   The Montreal Protocol[6]

The trade provisions and the trade effects of the Montreal Protocol are complex. One provision is the restriction on trade with non-parties: since trade with non-parties is banned, their supplies of ozone-depleting substances (ODSs) and most of their export markets for products containing controlled substances are virtually cut off. However, with regard to the original Montreal Protocol, the distinction between parties and non-parties has become virtually irrelevant as the Protocol has achieved quasi-universal membership. In addition, while parties to the Protocol may trade controlled substances among themselves, such trade is constrained by the phase-out of production and consumption. Since the latter is defined to include trade, parties that have reached their consumption limit may not import any more controlled substances unless they export an equal amount. Thus, in practice, trade between parties, as well as between non-parties, is constrained.

While a number of commentators, particularly from the OECD countries, have noted that trade measures may have been important in inducing countries to accede to the Montreal Protocol, case studies conducted by UNEP and UNCTAD do not lend universal support to this view. For example, the study on India shows that the role of trade measures in the decision to phase out CFCs was quite unimportant in most sectors, but may have been far more important in the case of halons used in fire-extinguishers.[7] Two other factors appear to suggest that for a number of developing countries the threat of trade restrictions may not have had a significant effect on their decision to join the Protocol. The trade threat would have been important if countries which were going to be cut off from ODS supplies were either major importers of CFCs or major exporters of CFCs. Most developing countries do not fall into the latter category. As far as importers of CFCs are concerned, in most developing countries the major users are TNCs, who, with or without trade restrictions, would have had fewer problems in accessing substitutes than comparable local firms. Thus the problem of trade restrictions would only be biting for such countries where CFC producers and users were primarily dominated by local and domestically owned firms and by the extent to which such firms were dependent on the international markets for supplies of CFCs or their substitutes. This narrows the choice set to very few developing countries and indeed case studies on India, the Republic of Korea and Thailand show that the trade threat, while important for Korea and India, may have been less important for the others on account of the high local participation in firms producing, using and exporting CFCs in the former.

3.1.2 The Basel Convention

The Basel Convention came into force in 1992. Under its original terms, hazardous wastes could generally not be traded between a party and a non-party (except via Article 11), whereas transboundary movements are permitted between parties, under certain conditions.[8]

Normally, the conditions would require the pre-notification to, and consent of, the recipient country prior to export. These restrictions were introduced primarily because transboundary movements of hazardous waste could create a disincentive for properly managing and reducing hazardous wastes at the source, and because the hazardous waste trade resulted in the transfer of damaging pollution often to countries ill-equipped to cope with it.

Any transboundary hazardous waste transaction taking place in contravention of the provisions of the Basel Convention is considered 'illegal traffic'. According to Article 9 (illegal traffic), the state responsible for movement of hazardous wastes has the obligation to ensure its environmentally sound management, if necessary by reimportation into the state of origin. In conformity with Article 8, if disposal is not carried out in accordance with the terms of the contract, the state of export has a duty to reimport. In addition, if a transaction takes place in accordance with relevant provisions, but disposal cannot be carried out as foreseen, the state exporting has an obligation to ensure reimportation of the wastes if alternative arrangements cannot be made for their environmentally sound disposal.

The second meeting of the Conference of the Parties (March 1994) decided to ban exports of hazardous wastes from OECD member states to non-OECD member states. The ban was to take immediate effect for exports for final disposal and for recycling as of 31 December 1997. However, a decision to amend the Convention to this effect was taken by the Conference of the Parties in 1995 and will only come into force once ratified by three-quarters of the parties. This ban is in response to the fact that hazardous wastes had been exported from developed to developing countries for the stated purpose of recycling, but without the importing country having the technical capacity to manage such waste in an environmentally sound manner. The Basel ban is an export ban as well as an import ban, and thus for enforcement the onus does not fully fall on the importing non-OECD country, which is least likely to accomplish this, but on the OECD exporter with the greater resources and infrastructure for enforcement and implementation.

Perhaps the principal stimulus to transboundary movements of wastes between developed and developing countries is the substantial disparity in costs of disposal, including costs of compliance with technical standards.[9] Given the great difference in costs of disposal in various countries, if trade is prohibited it may be anticipated that an incentive for illicit trade will grow.[10] Nevertheless, it is anticipated that the ban will reduce the total amount of waste traded.[11]

Thus, while a ban on the export of hazardous wastes which cannot be disposed of in developing countries is a legitimate precautionary measure,[12] one important issue is whether these countries have the infrastructure to effectively control (and detect) illegal trade in hazardous wastes. While the obligations for reimportation of illegally exported wastes apply to parties, non-parties are not under any such obligation. Arrangements concerning liability could perhaps better meet the objectives of the Convention.[13] It should be noted that such a Protocol on Liability and Compensation has been proposed within the framework of the Basel Convention, to provide incentives to minimize trade in hazardous wastes.

It is not entirely clear whether trade measures have served the role of inducing parties to join the Agreement. According to a UNEP study about 50 per cent or more of the wastes generated at the global level originate in the United States, which continues to remain outside the Agreement.[14] It is also not clear whether illegal exports of wastes have increased over the past few years or whether trade between parties and non-parties has decreased. It is equally unclear whether restrictions on trade in wastes are actually leading to better waste management practices and therefore whether the ultimate environmental goal is being addressed.

3.1.3 CITES

The Convention on International Trade in Endangered Species (CITES) regulates commercial trade in endangered and other species. When a species reaches a certain level of vulnerability, the parties to the Convention list it in one of three appendices. This placement determines the extent to which trade is permitted in the species. Appendix I species are those 'threatened with extinction and are or may be affected by trade'. Trade in Appendix I species is prohibited for 'primarily commercial purposes'. Appendix II contains species that 'although not necessarily now threatened with extinction, may become so unless trade in specimens of such species is subject to strict regulation in order to avoid utilization incompatible with their survival'. Trade in Appendix II species is prohibited if authorities in the country of export determine that the export will be detrimental to the survival of the species. Appendix III lists species that a country has identified as 'subject to regulation within its jurisdiction for the purpose of preventing or restricting exploitation, and as needing the cooperation of other parties in the control of trade'. Unlike species in Appendices I and II, the listing of species in Appendix III does not require a vote of the Conference of Parties. Trade in these species requires the presentation of appropriate export documents at the time of importation.

It is to be noted that CITES is likely to have totally different impacts depending on the particular species being regulated. For example, while there is a global ban on trade in tiger skins, tiger populations continue to be decimated. However, the ban on trade in ivory has had a beneficial effect on populations of African elephants. Less is known about the effects on populations of Asian elephants.

Trade provisions of a global nature may in some cases be contentious from a local perspective. For example, while elephants may be globally endangered, in a particular country, such as Zimbabwe for example, they may exceed the sustainable number of herds and endanger other species. At the June 1997 meeting of the CITES Conference of the Parties, it was decided to downlist Botswanan, Namibian and Zimbabwean elephant populations to Annex II. The permission to trade, however, concerns only stock-piled and registered ivory and is limited to trade with Japan.

3.2   TRADE AND COMPETITIVENESS EFFECTS OF MEAs

MEAs may have trade and competitiveness effects irrespective of whether they have trade provisions. However, for each MEA such effects may be quite different, depending on the mechanism used and the environmental problem addressed. Effects may be more significant for developing countries than for developed countries for a number of reasons. First, whereas the unit costs of adjustment may be the same between developed and developing countries (or may even be higher for developed countries, on account of higher development costs of technologies), the overall difference in income levels would make the relative costs of adjustment higher in developing countries. This would be so particularly if capital costs of adjustment were high and the technologies required to meet the obligations of the MEA were harder to obtain or more expensive. Secondly, growth and export patterns of countries tend to be such that during the early stages of industrialization they may be more reliant on the export of products which are banned or restricted by MEAs. This hurdle may in turn affect their growth prospects. For example, a convention on forestry could have significant effects on tropical timber exporting developing countries. Similarly, at comparable levels of per capita income, the trade and competitiveness effects of the Montreal Protocol are likely to be more significant in tropical developing countries than in temperate zones, given the increased dependence on refrigeration and air-conditioning. Short-run and long-run effects of MEAs on developing countries may differ considerably because of technological and other developments.

In the case of Poland, there are also a number of regional treaties that will influence its structure of industrial and agricultural production and hence its foreign trade. The Convention for the Protection of the Marine Environment in the Baltic Sea will result in increased fees for water intake and sewerage discharge, thus affecting the exports of goods such as artificial fibres, pulp and paper, coke, sulphuric acid and so on. At the same time, Poland will have to import a large number of water recycling plants. With regard to transboundary air pollution, the so-called Black Triangle Agreement (between Poland, the former Czechoslovakia and Germany) has resulted in reduced sulphur emissions from power stations, the costs of which are reflected in higher prices and lower exports of electricity from Poland.

3.2.1 The Montreal Protocol

Trade and competitiveness effects of the Montreal Protocol on the developing countries' industries may be significant for several reasons: (a) the phase-out of controlled substances in developed countries and the subsequent closing of production facilities may affect the competitiveness of developing countries to the extent that controlled substances or their substitutes are expensive or not available;[15] (b) exports of products containing controlled substances may themselves become less competitive; (c) sectors relying on refrigeration, such as fruits and dairy products, may encounter cost increases; and (d) production lines and technologies may themselves have to be changed in order to use substitutes, and existing technologies may become difficult to service.[16] Developing countries' concerns are further heightened since most developed countries are now on the fast-track towards phase-out rather than a 50 per cent reduction, as was originally scheduled in the Montreal Protocol. The Multilateral Fund is meant to address the issue of additional financing required by developing countries seeking to comply with the Protocol.

With regard to (a), studies indicate that trade and competitiveness effects would differ according to whether or not the countries themselves produced controlled substances. A study on Poland, which did not produce controlled substances, found that the costs of polyurethane used in upholstering furniture rose substantially.[17] The case study in India shows that the use of CFCs is higher in life-supporting sectors such as drugs and pharmaceuticals, as compared to air-conditioners. Thus, given the social importance of the sectors involved, the room for adjusting or cutting down on the use of CFCs is relatively limited. Recent studies show that the price of methyl dose inhalers would triple if CFCs had to be substituted in India. Frequently substituting for CFCs may also lead to a decrease in the efficiency of the product as may be the case in the electronics sector.

The competitiveness effects of the Montreal Protocol on the refrigeration and air conditioning industry have been examined in a study on India.[18] Since food preservation and drug and pharmaceutical manufacture all use refrigeration, the use of CFCs assumes a critical role. While it is difficult to judge whether the costs increased faster than those in other developed countries, recent estimates from a number of countries show that the Multilateral Fund has covered to date only about 20% of the cost of phase-out in developing countries. The rest of the costs have been met by the countries themselves. Thus competitiveness concerns become linked with equity aspects.[19]

Other countries, such as India and the Republic of Korea, which were just becoming self-sufficient in the production of chlorofluorocarbons (CFCs), reported additional costs of closing down their production facilities.[20] In fact firms were unable to pay back the investment in these plants.[21] More importantly, at the time of signing the Protocol many of the plants used for manufacturing CFCs were relatively new and had not completed their payback periods.

With regard to (b), as ODSs are being phased out, developing countries that export products using such chemicals (such as refrigerators) are finding that their markets are being squeezed as buyers want to shift to versions based on substitutes, which may require additional investment and new technology to produce. Some developing countries, because of their high rate of growth, relied on the use of CFCs (or their substitutes) in the manufacture of such products as electronics, refrigerators and so on, both for export and domestic markets. Developing country exports to OECD countries of some products, such as refrigerators and freezing equipment, which could contain controlled substances, have been growing more rapidly than the exports of all manufactured products, and certainly much more rapidly than intra-OECD trade in such products.[22]

However, the stipulations of the Protocol helped one Chinese company to increase its exports of freon-free air-conditioners, while exports of refrigerators declined by 58 per cent between 1988 and 1991. Other adversely affected export items from China include air-conditioners with refrigerants, cleaning articles with blowing agents, chemical products and some miscellaneous organic and other products.[23] It is as a consequence of this decline that China has stepped up its phase-out programme to a pace faster than would be required for developing countries under the Protocol.[24]

Poland's commitment to cease the use of freon in refrigerators, freezers and freezing counters could, in the short run, reduce exports of these products. Poland did not have the technology to eliminate ozone-depleting gases and the importation of such technology would increase costs for the refrigeration industry. Similarly, studies on refrigeration and air-conditioning industries in India have revealed that these sectors recognized that new investments in non-CFC technology were required, but information on such technologies was not forthcoming and as yet there are very few CFC-free refrigerators in the local markets.

However, a study on Malaysia's exports of air-conditioners to the developed country markets shows that they have continued to increase strongly in recent years.[25] This could be attributed to the dominance of TNCs in this sector. Similarly, in Thailand while the phase-out of CFCs in the electronics sector has been very rapid on account of the presence of TNCs, that in refrigeration and air-conditioning has been very slow on account of lack of substitute technologies.

With regard to (c), a case study on Colombia indicated that the industries potentially affected are those which rely on CFCs for refrigeration, in particular producers of flowers, bananas and processed meat. Similarly, in Poland exporters of products reliant on refrigeration, such as dairy products, fruit and vegetables, may meet increased costs of refrigeration. However, no cost estimates were provided by the country studies. In a case study on Zimbabwe, where methyl bromide is used in horticulture and in bulk grain storage, concern was expressed that the detection of methyl bromide in exported products could imply difficulties in accessing the markets of countries, if these countries were to implement product content requirements.[26]

In Colombia, the direct effects are likely to be small, but the indirect effects of the Protocol may be felt more strongly. For example, the industries which may be affected are not those which produce ozone-depleting substances but those which rely on CFCs for refrigeration, including flowers, bananas and meat processing. Theoretically, these industries have until the year 2006 to adjust, but imports of ODSs had declined by 1995, because of the shutdown of American and European plants. Thus, concerns about the price of ODSs is likely to increase and so will the costs of refrigeration, perhaps leading to an increase in the price of fruit.[27] Of greater significance are the limits on the use methyl chloroform for fumigation of food exports.

With regard to (d), the cases where technological changes may increase costs can be divided into two groups. The first group includes large firms which are consumers of ODSs, but with access to the Multilateral Fund. In Colombia, for example, for the largest consumers of ODSs the estimated incremental costs of technology switching would be in the range of US$55 million. In 1994, projects for a total of about US$8 million were approved by the United Nations Development Programme (UNDP) in the framework of Colombia's country programme. The second group comprises small firms which in practice cannot access these funds easily. However, it should be noted that special provisions are being designed for small users of CFCs through providing funds to foundations which can then channel investments to SMEs. According to the Multilateral Fund, funding SMEs is a problem on account of the cost-effectiveness and counterpart funding criteria used in approving projects. However, given that phase-out would be difficult without involving SMEs, the Conference of Parties will discuss whether exemption can be obtained for SMEs from these two criteria.[28]

Research and development costs will also increase, as well as the cost of products using refrigeration. An early phase-out strategy by 1999 would be less costly for India as the costs would be mostly borne by the producers of ODSs and not by the users, either directly (for example refrigerators) or indirectly (for example food). In the late phase-out by 2010, most of the cost would be borne by the users rather than producers. On balance, a late phase-out may be more expensive.

At the sectoral level, a study on India has estimated that the adjustment cost of adopting new technology is about 30–35 per cent of total costs for refrigerators and about 5–10 per cent for air-conditioners. One of the problems that producers face in adapting to the Montreal Protocol is that of the difficulty of obtaining information on new CFC-free technology available in OECD countries. The problem of obtaining the appropriate technology is further compounded by the fact that these technologies are rarely tested in tropical conditions, and thus although an early phase-out would be more desirable from an economic point of view, whether such a strategy will prove feasible is more doubtful. This depends on the research and development capacity in India itself, and on the feasibility of developing indigenous substitutes for CFCs.[29] The information available appears to suggest that obtaining the technologies for producing CFC substitutes has proven to be difficult, if not impossible, in the Republic of Korea, China and India.[30]

The study on Thailand shows that research and development is concentrated in large firms, while there appears to be a tendency for the small firms to obtain interim chemicals rather than to change processes. An additional concern is how the Thai economy will eventually adjust to the requirements of the Protocol. Key sectors such as the electronics industry must consider the overall feasibility of such shifts, including the composition of foreign versus domestic investment or small-scale versus large-scale firms. Foreign and large firms tend to be better placed to benefit from the funds under the Protocol.

Detailed studies conducted by the United Nations Environment Programme (UNEP) have shown that the prospects for ODS phase-out are affected by different combinations of factors in different countries. Economic and political systems and structures, technological development, and the level of international economic activity vary widely among developing countries. In the context of the existing Montreal Protocol, the consequence of these differences means that the feasibility of a global phase-out scenario is determined by the countries that eliminate ODSs last, rather than by those that phase out sooner. This further emphasizes the role of enabling mechanisms in helping countries to eliminate ODSs.[31]

The overall costs of meeting the obligations of the Montreal Protocol have been estimated by some countries. For example, the Republic of Korea[32] has estimated that the incremental costs of meeting the obligations would amount to US$1.9 billions; for India and China figures in the order of the same magnitude have been estimated.[33] These estimates, however, do not take account of the fact that cheaper substitutes and technologies may become available in future. According to recent studies however, the cost of technology acquisition for the manufacture of CFC substitutes was found to be prohibitively high and probably higher than estimated costs on account of the proprietary nature of the technology.[34]

3.2.2 The Basel Convention

The competitiveness effects of the Basel Convention on developing countries and countries in transition can be positive or negative, at both the firm and national level. Few empirical studies, however, have investigated these effects.

At the national level, bans on transboundary movements may decrease the cost of cleaning and prevent soil and water contamination.[35] However, if there are scale economies there may be an actual increase in costs. To the extent that hazardous wastes exported to developing countries result in the contamination of soil and adjacent waters, the future productivity and economic uses of these natural resources may be reduced, besides endangering human, animal and plant life.

With regard to the effects of the Basel Convention on competitiveness at the firm level, an important question is to what extent the Basel Convention prohibits the recycling of waste materials. This depends largely on whether or not waste materials, particularly waste metals, fall under the definition of 'hazardous waste'.[36] In determining whether or not metal wastes are to be considered hazardous, the waste management practices of the importing country are of material importance. For example, even if only a small quantity of lead content is present, a metal may nevertheless be considered hazardous if there is a risk that lead might enter into the environment of the importing country, and particularly if lead contaminants are already close to the permissible level.

Although there are a number of problems with regard to the classification of different waste streams, whether bulk trade and recycling of secondary metals may be affected is an open question, giving rise to uncertainty among users of metal wastes. Some industries which obtain part of their inputs from recyclable wastes may be affected by the Basel Convention. For example, the iron and steel industry in Brazil has expressed some concern about the sourcing of their inputs.[37]

The country study on Poland reported that a branch potentially affected by restrictions in waste trade is the metallurgical industry: import limitations on scrap iron are likely to result in price increases of these secondary materials in the domestic market and, ultimately, to increased production costs.[38] On the one hand, it has resulted in a major reduction of imports of wastes, where some of them (for example scrap paper) are often used as inputs in production processes. On the other hand, the domestic industry using scrap metal may have benefited from export restrictions. Finally, Poland is losing out in economic terms from this treaty through the loss of transport business (Poland is a corridor for the shipment of materials from the Russian Federation and Ukraine).

The Basel Convention has not yet elaborated limit values on concentrations; however, the Convention does recognize all national definitions of the countries involved and therefore makes use of existing limit values. The 'grey' areas with respect to contaminants found in scrap metals are currently being elaborated at an accelerated pace in the Technical Working Group. Work is aimed at ensuring that trade in metals containing only relatively small and harmless amounts of hazardous contaminants is not affected by the trade ban. This concern may be particularly relevant for metal wastes as metals never occur in nature free of alloyed 'contaminant' metals.

3.2.3   CITES and Other Conventions

CITES could sometimes result in unintended trade and competitiveness effects on some parties. For example, if a country using national measures is able to manage specific controlled species sustainably, then trade measures could result in unnecessary economic losses with little environmental gains. Put another way, the lack of rewards in CITES for managing species sustainably gives parties little incentive to do so. Zimbabwe, for example, as a party to CITES, reports significant trade losses with regard to crocodile farming and the ivory trade. Elephants and crocodiles are not endangered in Zimbabwe, but under the Convention trade in these products is banned. Three years after the introduction of the ivory trade ban in 1989, Zimbabwe had accumulated from culling operations an estimated stock pile of US$12 million worth of ivory that it could not sell legally.[39] Thus, in Zimbabwe's view, the ban on the ivory trade is counter-productive in that it prohibits legal and controlled trade in animal products whose management is sustainable.

The effects on exports also depend on the products which are being exported. For example, in the Philippines MEAs have had no significant effect on exports. However, an agreement on trade in tropical timber would impact significantly on the country's exports of furniture as local sources of sustainable timber are very few. On the other hand, some MEAs would actually benefit the Philippines' exports. MEAs regulating driftnet fishing, such as the 1989 Wellington Convention for the Prohibition of Fishing with Long Driftnets and the UN Moratorium on Driftnet Fishing, are good examples as driftnet fishing is not widely practised in the Philippines.[40]

In the case of Poland, it is premature to estimate the influence of international treaties on trade as its participation in most treaties dates only from 1990. Nevertheless, it is possible that both the Montreal Protocol and the Climate Change Convention may have an impact on Poland's foreign trade, either through the increased cost of the technology that replaces ODSs or because of the loss of export markets for fossil fuels, particularly coal.[41]

Zimbabwe derived some environmental benefits arising from the Bamako Convention, which restricts the import of wastes into Africa and controls the transboundary movement of wastes within Africa. On the other hand, CITES appears to have been of doubtful environmental value to Zimbabwe. This is primarily because of the ban on trade in ivory, which hurts Zimbabwe, where elephants are not endangered and which could gain significantly from exporting ivory. In fact the revenues from such trade could provide much needed resources for managing elephant habitats. For Zimbabwe, this issue has been a major source of disagreement within CITES.[42]

The Basel Convention may also have effects on competitiveness. For example, restrictions on trade in scrap have potential effects on the steel industry. For steel mills using scrap as a secondary raw material, restrictions on trade may increase costs. On the other hand, in countries which currently export scrap, using scrap instead of iron ore would require an across-the-board replacement of technologies.[43]

3.3   ADEQUACY OF FACILITATING MECHANISMS IN MEAs

There has been either an implicit or explicit recognition that the formation of MEAs may have more than proportionate trade and competitiveness effects on developing countries. These effects may need to be addressed if the MEAs' environmental objectives are to be met in accordance with Principle 7 of the Rio Declaration.

3.3.1   The Montreal Protocol

Perhaps the clearest recognition of Principle 7 of the Rio Declaration can be found in the instruments used for the implementation of the Montreal Protocol. Two instruments are of relevance in this context: (a) differential phase-out schedules for developing and developed countries; and (b) financial assistance for Article 5(1) countries party to the Protocol.[44] It should be recognized that these two positive measures are almost the first of their kind; no other MEA has such provisions.

Differential phase-out schedules and other enabling mechanisms
The implementation of differential phase-out schedules between developing and developed countries may have both positive and negative effects. Developing countries were given a grace period so as to spread their adjustment over a longer period of time, given the paucity of resources and technologies. However, as developed countries are now on a fast track towards phase-out, supplies of CFCs and other chemicals may decrease, and substitutes may be expensive or simply not available. In this scenario, the grace period granted to developing countries

may have become less relevant, except for countries which are producers of CFCs.[45]

As far as availability of CFCs is concerned, according to the Ozone Secretariat, supplies currently are largely sufficient to meet the demand of the developing countries. However, according to the Technical Committee Report of the Montreal Protocol, it appears that while there may be over-supply in the case of some CFCs, there may actually be shortages in others.

Consumption of CFCs in a sample of 16 developing countries had increased by 45 per cent in the period 1986 to 1992.[46] The Montreal Protocol allows for an increase in the consumption of CFCs in developing countries. Such increases may be indicative of the increased dependency of developing countries on the imports of controlled substances and their high growth rates. Increased dependency on CFCs, however, may imply higher costs of eventual phase-out, particularly in terms of trade displacements and input price increases.

In addition, there may in theory be a possibility that differential schedules imply that industries using controlled chemicals may relocate to developing countries. There is some support for this proposition in the case of Thailand.[47] The Thai example shows that differential phase-out schedules and the corresponding trade restrictions imply that firms located in countries already bound by a phase-out schedule may be motivated to relocate to an Article 5 country, such as Thailand, which has virtually no restrictions on ODSs consumption until 1999.[48] This is evidenced by the fact that new importers, particularly small subsidiaries of multinationals, have entered the market in recent years and demand for CFCs has surged.[49]

It has been reported that the Thai Government has entered into an understanding with the United States Environmental Protection Agency (EPA) and the Japanese Ministry of International Trade and Industry (MITI) that encourages multinational companies to apply the same schedule for their phase-out as their domestic operations. It is to be noted that according to this study solvents constitute 40 per cent of Thailand's CFC usage, and that up to 97 per cent of these are used by Japanese or United States companies, and joint ventures.

The Conference of Parties to successive amendments of the Montreal Protocol recognizes the potential problems of developing countries in obtaining ODSs. For example, developed countries are permitted a national production slightly higher than the national consumption level for exports to developing countries, in order to enable them to meet their 'basic domestic needs'.[50] Concern over the supplies of ODSs and ODS alternatives during the grace period and thereafter could be relieved if broadly based recovery, recycling and banking operations were established. The role of economic incentives and other policy instruments in recycling and reclaiming CFCs, and the repair and retrofitting of CFC-using equipment would strongly influence the amount of CFCs available to service existing equipment. So as to facilitate such policies, the parties have agreed that the recovery and reclamation of controlled substances will not be counted as production.

The Montreal Protocol also recognized the importance of specific substances used by developing countries in connection with key exports for which substitutes are not available. For example, while the Copenhagen Amendment to the Protocol provides for a freeze on the production and consumption of methyl bromide at 1991 levels from 1 January 1995, the use of the chemical for quarantine applications (which includes pre-shipment quarantine fumigation) is to be excluded from the calculation of a party's consumption and production levels. This amendment would specially benefit agriculture-based developing countries.[51]

The preceding mechanisms for mitigating the competitiveness effects on developing countries while alleviating the short-term problems may in some cases prolong or even increase long-term dependency on controlled chemicals, unless specific provisions can induce developed countries to either provide substitutes or technologies to developing countries. Given that an accelerated phase-out has been negotiated in successive amendments, developing countries' needs for new technologies and substitutes have become even more pressing. Moreover, a number of country programmes indicate that an early phase-out has become less expensive than a late one. This implies that the differential schedule would be more beneficial to developing countries if additional funds, technologies and substitutes were provided to them at an early stage of their phase-out.

Evidence from country case studies conducted by UNCTAD and UNEP suggests that at least three countries have encountered problems in accessing technologies for the production of CFC substitutes. The Ozone Secretariat has also acknowledged these problems.[52] Moreover, guidelines for determining the incremental costs of producing CFC substitutes in developing countries have not as yet been established.

Finance and technology transfer

The Multilateral Fund of the Montreal Protocol provides a financial mechanism to assist developing countries in meeting their obligations and in purchasing new technologies. For example, according to a UNEP study, some developing countries such as Brazil, China, India and Mexico, which already produced CFCs, wanted to be able to produce any new substitutes and expressed concern that no special provision had been made for the transfer of technology on preferential terms.[53] The Montreal Protocol, in Article 10A, contains some provisions to encourage the transfer of substitutes and related technologies to developing countries under fair and most favourable terms.[54]

Since the creation of the Multilateral Fund, agreed contributions have amounted to around US$695 million. A budget of US$540 million was adopted for the period 1997–1999, of which US$74 million would be provided by funds unallocated during 1994–1996, requiring a replenishment of the Multilateral Fund of US$466 million. This total corresponds to 15 to 20 per cent of the estimated cost of meeting the current target of phasing out ODSs in Article 5 countries by 2010. Most of the funds have gone to Asian countries, followed by Latin American and African countries. Enterprises which have benefited most are those which are large and able technically to implement projects. Smaller firms often find it difficult to access the Multilateral Fund. This is of particular concern to India and China. Also, it has been noted that dissemination of information on technology choices has paid relatively little attention to SMEs in developing countries.[55]

Some commentators, however, have observed that although the Fund itself may appear adequate, several problems have arisen in disbursing finances to the developing countries. This could be partly due to the fact that the countries themselves have had major difficulties in putting together projects which can serve their needs and gain the approval of the Multilateral Fund. In several cases, the infrastructure required to absorb the funds coming from the Multilateral Fund under the Montreal Protocol may not be in place in the countries themselves. For example, a study on Colombia has indicated that small companies manufacturing ODS-containing products (30 per cent of Colombian ODS consumers are SMEs) had no access, in practice, to the Multilateral Fund. The study suggested that the competitiveness of these small firms would probably be substantially affected by the need to switch to CFC-free technologies.[56]

Although it is difficult to determine the magnitude of technological transfer to developing countries, the majority of firms which have actually received new technology were either foreign joint venture partners or subsidiaries of transnational corporations (TNCs). In the Philippines, for instance, the main users of CFC113 and other solvents in the Philippine electronics industry were foreign owned companies and had recently phased out most of their use of ODSs, with the assistance of the Multilateral Fund. Similarly, in Kenya, total ODS consumption decreased by two-thirds during the period 1989 to 1993 through voluntary actions encouraged by parent companies in non-Article 5 countries, which were able successfully to access technologies with the assistance of the Multilateral Fund. The Philippines and Kenya are examples of what has happened in many other Article 5 countries. A total breakdown of projects according to TNC ownership is, however, not available from the Multilateral Fund.

With regard to FDI, for example, according to a recent UNEP report, many Japanese, North American and European automobile, chemical, consumer product, electronics, and petroleum companies pledged to help the Government of Vietnam to protect the ozone layer by investing only in modern, environmentally friendly technology in their Vietnam projects.[57]

Concern has been expressed about the administrative costs of disbursing the funds. These were estimated to be as high as 35 per cent of expenditures, on average.[58] Problems have also arisen in that there are substantial arrears to the Fund[59] on account of which a number of useful projects have not been funded. This in spite of the fact that Article 10 makes it clear that the agreed incremental costs of developing countries whose consumption is below the limits specified in Article 5 will be met.

3.3.2 The Basel Convention

The Basel Convention requires parties to take 'all practicable steps to ensure that the hazardous wastes or other wastes are managed in a manner which will protect human health and the environment against the adverse effects which may result from such wastes' (Article 2, para. 8 of the Basel Convention on the Control of Transboundary Movements of Hazardous Wastes and their Disposal, Final Act). In this regard, although the Convention does lend its support to technology transfer for handling waste in an environmentally sound way, it does so by providing 'clearing-house' functions. The Basel Convention proposes the establishment of regional and sub-regional centres for training and technology transfer regarding the management of hazardous and other wastes and for minimizing the generation of such wastes.

The Basel Convention provides for the conclusion of separate agreements between its parties, and also between parties and non-parties, under certain conditions, via Article 11, provided that such an agreement does not circumvent the purposes of the Basel Convention. Article 11 requires that such agreements be 'compatible with the environmentally sound management of hazardous and other wastes as required by this Convention'.

One question which arises is whether governments have the legal provisions to induce the private entrepreneur to reimport wastes which may have been illegally exported to developing countries. Under the Basel Convention, governments have the obligation through their national legislation to impose appropriate measures on their private entrepreneurs involved in the transboundary movements of hazardous wastes. In addition, the exporter/generator of wastes may need insurance coverage, bank guarantees, bonds, and so on in order to enter a transboundary transaction. However, there is no provision in the Basel Convention for making the exporter liable for the costs of cleaning land and waters in the period that the waste is in the importing country prior to its reimport into the exporting country.

3.3.3 CITES

In the case of CITES, the problems posed to certain countries by the worldwide trade ban on ivory or other products have been mentioned earlier. To make the agreement function better for such countries in the event that the ban cannot be relaxed, consideration could be given to allowing countries to establish clearing-houses for products from culling activities. One proposal was to establish a Central Ivory Market. It could provide a labelling scheme for exporters who could be permitted to sell legally products obtained under sustainable conditions, such as ivory obtained from culling operations.

3.4   CONCLUSIONS AND RECOMMENDATIONS

Trade flows have been affected by some MEAs, either directly or indirectly. The extent of trade and competitiveness effects pursuant to the signing of an MEA calls into question whether existing positive measures, such as funding and technology transfer, are sufficient to ensure that the development process of poor countries is not impaired. More research is required to analyse and evaluate the trade and competitiveness effects of MEAs, particularly with regard to their effects on small firms. In addition, there may be a need to make interim evaluations of MEAs. There is a need to further examine such effects, particularly in negotiating future MEAs.

Trade provisions in MEAs may have broad economic effects which tend to differ across countries, inter alia in accordance with their level of development. Principle 7 of the Rio Declaration recognizes that developing countries need facilitating mechanisms to assist them in incurring the incremental costs required for meeting the multilaterally-agreed environmental targets of a particular MEA. It is generally recognized that positive measures which are feasible and equally or more efficient and effective should be preferred over trade restrictions. Negotiators of an MEA should consider the feasibility, necessity and environmental effectiveness of the package of measures available to them. MEAs have a variety of tools, including non-trade measures. Therefore, the menu of remedies in MEAs should consider alternative non-trade measures so as to minimize the risk of trade restriction. As such, a mechanism to make an overall judgement concerning the best method from both an environmental and trade perspective needs to be developed.

Any measures chosen should be considered against a carefully designed set of criteria or guidelines. These criteria or principles could make an important contribution to advancing the aim of making international trade and environment policies mutually supportive and to promoting an informed dialogue between trade, development and environment communities as called for in Agenda 21. Guidelines could be aimed at assisting environmental policy-makers in their consideration of the possible future use of trade measures in MEAs and these would make it more likely that new trade measures in MEAs would operate in a WTO-consistent manner, and would help to promote compatibility between trade and environmental policies.

NOTES

1. An unresolved problem in the trade and environment debate centres around what constitutes a multilateral environmental agreement. It is often difficult to distinguish between trade effects and trade measures or provisions which may be included in an MEA.

2. For a fuller discussion of these see Sands, P. (ed.) (1993), *Greening International Law*, London: Earthscan; and Beyerlin, Ulrich and T. Marauhn (1997), 'Law-making and Law-enforcement in International Environmental Law after the 1992 Rio Conference', *Research Reports of the Max Planck Institute for Comparative Public Law and International Law*, No.4, Heidelberg.

3. 'Trade measures for environmental purposes taken pursuant to Multilateral Environmental Agreements: recent developments', note by the Secretariat, Preparatory Committee for the World Trade Organization (Sub-committee on Trade and Environment), PC/SCTE/W/3, 13 October 1994:1. For the description of the MEAs containing trade provisions up until 1991, see Appendix I of GATT's *International Trade*, Volume 1, 1990–1991, pp. 45–7.

4. See Brack, D. (1996), 'International trade and environment', mimeo, Royal Institute of International Affairs, London.

5. See Housman, Robert F., Donald M. Goldberg, Brannan Van Dyke and Durwood J. Zaelke (eds) (1995), 'The Use of Trade Measures in Selected Multilateral Environmental Agreements', *Environment and Trade*, Volume 10, UNEP.

6. The Montreal Protocol of Substances that Deplete the Ozone Layer, hereafter referred to as the Montreal Protocol, was adopted in Montreal in 1987 and entered into force on 1 January 1989 with 29 parties. Initially parties agreed to freeze their consumption of chlorofluorocarbons (CFCs) at 1986 levels, followed by a 50 per cent reduction in accordance with an agreed timetable. Taking into account the results of periodic scientific and economic assessments, in subsequent negotiations 'amendments' were made to add new chemicals and 'adjustments' were introduced to make limitations more stringent and to reduce the timetable for reductions. Following the London and Copenhagen amendments, rather than a 50 per cent reduction, most developed countries committed themselves to completely phase out the consumption and production of Ozone Depleting Substances (ODSs) as follows: halons, by 1 January 1994; CFCs, carbon tetrachloride and methyl chloroform, by 1 January 1996; hydrobromofluorocarbons (HBFCs), by 1 January 1996; and hydrochlorofluorocarbons (HCFCs), by 1 January 2030.

7. See Das, Shipra (1997), 'The impact of trade measures and other measures in the Montreal Protocol on selected industries', mimeo prepared for the UNCTAD/UNEP project.

8. Under Article 11 of the Convention, imports and exports of covered wastes between parties and non-parties are allowed where the transboundary movements are subject to another appropriate bilateral, multilateral or regional agreement. Basel Convention, supra preface, note 4, at art.11.

9. According to a study made by UNEP, the average disposal costs for one ton of hazardous wastes in Africa was between US$2.50 and US$50, while the equivalent costs in industrializing countries ranged between US$100 and US$2000. See Kummer, K. (1994), 'Transboundary Movements of Hazardous Wastes at the Interface of Environment and Trade', *Environment and Trade*, Volume 7, UNEP.

10. See Greenpeace (1990), *The International Trade in Wastes: A Greenpeace Inventory*, 5th edn.

11. *Ibid.*

12. See Greenpeace (1994), 'Lead, astray: the poisonous lead and battery waste trade', Waste Trade Case Study No.5, Series: Recycling.

13. Under the Basel Convention, a Protocol on Liability and Compensation will be discussed. A three tier approach comprises: (a) making the exporting firm liable for the costs of reimport or clean-ups, (b) a Compensation Fund in cases where the exporter cannot be identified, and (c) making the State liable. There are different degrees of acceptability of the three tiers among the parties to the agreement.

14. See K. Kummer, op.cit.

15. Controlled substances and their substitutes may sometimes be less expensive in developing countries than in developed countries.

16. It should be noted that these arguments have also been made by firms in developed countries in the process of negotiating CFC phase-out schemes in these countries.

17. Fiedor, B., S. Czaja, A. Graczyk and J. Rymarczyk (1994) 'Linkages between environment and trade: a case study of Poland', study carried out under the joint UNCTAD/UNDP project on Reconciliation of Environmental and Trade Policies. A synthesis of this study is contained in TD/B/WG.6/Misc. 10/6 November 1995.

18. See Bharucha, V. (1994) 'Impact of Environmental Standards and Regulations on India's Exports', in Jha, V. *et al.* (eds) (1997), *Trade, Environment and Sustainable Development – A South Asian Perspective*, London and New York: Macmillan and St Martin's Press.

19. See for example Thailand Environment Institute (1997), 'Thailand and the Montreal Protocol', study conducted for the UNCTAD/UNEP project.

20. UNEP (1994), 'Report of the Economic Options Committee (EOC) on the Montreal Protocol on Substances that Deplete the Ozone Layer'.

21. The indicative list of categories of incremental costs covered by the Multilateral Fund, approved by the fourth meeting of the parties 1992, includes costs of closing down production facilities under certain circumstances.

22. Trade statistics do not distinguish between CFC-containing and CFC-free refrigerators and freezing equipment.

23. Lu, R., Y. Xia, J. Li., J. Zhang and Y. Lu (1993), 'A study on environmental and foreign trade development in China', draft study carried out under the joint UNCTAD/UNDP project on Reconciliation of Trade and Environment Policies.

24. A number of developing countries listed under Article 5 of the Montreal Protocol qualify for technical and financial assistance.

25. Institute of Strategic and International Studies (1995), 'A Malaysian case study', prepared for the UNCTAD/UNDP project on Reconciliation of Environmental and Trade Policies.

26. Whether it is possible to detect traces of methyl bromide in products is not resolved.

27. Gaviria, D. *et al.* (1994), 'Reconciliation of trade and environment policies: the case study of Colombia', study prepared under the joint UNCTAD/UNDP programme.

28. Hetherington, T. (1997), 'The multilateral fund and its activities', paper presented at UNCTAD's Expert Group meeting on Positive Measures and MEAs, 3-5 November.

29. See Bharucha, op.cit.

30. Studies on India and the Republic of Korea done for UNCTAD indicate these factors. The Ozone Secretariat reported similar complaints from China.

31. 'Report on the Review under Paragraph 8 of Article 5 of the Montreal Protocol', UNEP/OzL.Pro/WG.1/11/4.

32. See UNCTAD/UNEP (1997), '*Case study on the Montreal Protocol in the Republic of Korea*', mimeo.

33. UNEP (1994), 'Report of the Economic Options Committee of the Montreal Protocol on Substances that Deplete the Ozone Layer'.

34. See Watal, J. (1997), 'Technology transfer and the Montreal Protocol- a case study on India', mimeo prepared for UNCTAD/UNEP project.

35. See Kummer, op.cit. and 'Export gevaarlijk afval gaat in alle stilte gewoon door' in *Internationale Samenwerking*, 7 August 1995, (in Dutch).

36. Since metals hardly ever occur naturally in their pure form, metal wastes usually consist of a main component and several minor components. The minor components are often substances that may come within the scope of the Basel Convention. The definition of hazardous wastes includes any category contained in Annex I to the Convention, unless it does not have any of the hazardous characteristics listed in Annex III thereto.

37. See de Motta Veiga, P., M. Reis Castilho and Galena Ferraz Filho (1994), 'The country case study of Brazil', prepared for UNCTAD. A synthesis of this country case study can be found in TD/B/WG.6/Misc. 9, 3 November 1995.

38. It should be noted, however, that the Basel Convention does not regulate iron, steel, aluminium, copper and zinc and indeed does not intend to regulate such scrap unless it is contaminated with hazardous substances.

39. See Nkomo, J., B. Zwizwai and D. Gumbo (1995), 'A case study of Zimbabwe', University of Zimbabwe, and Development Activities, prepared for UNCTAD.

40. Intal, P., E. Medalla, M. de Los Angeles, D. Israel, V. Pineda, P. Quintos and E. Tan (1994), 'Trade and environment linkages – the case of the Philippines', study carried out under the joint UNCTAD/UNEP project on Reconciliation of Trade and Environment Policies.

41. Fiedor, B., S. Czaja, A. Graczyk and J. Rymarczyk (1994), 'Linkages between environment and trade: a case study of Poland', study carried out under the joint UNCTAD/UNDP project on Reconciliation of Environment and Trade Policies.

42. Nkomo, J., B. Zwizwai and D. Gumbo (1994), 'Trade and the environment: Zimbabwe case study', draft study carried out under the joint UNCTAD/UNDP project on Reconciliation of Environmental and Trade Policies.

43. de Motta Veiga, *et al.*, op. cit.

44. Article 5(1) countries are broadly classified as 'developing', but more accurately they are those with annual per capita consumption of ODSs of less than 0.3 kg at the date of entry into force or at any time thereafter until 1 January 1999.

45. See Twum-Barima, Rosalind and Laura B. Campbell (1994), 'Protecting the Ozone Layer through Trade Measures: Reconciling the Trade Provisions of the Montreal Protocol and the Rules of the GATT', *Environment and Trade*, Volume 6, UNEP.

46. According to the Ozone Secretariat, based on data available as of 9 May 1994. *Ibid.*

47. See UNEP, EOC, op.cit.

48. Developing countries are eligible for assistance under the Financial Mechanism and are referred to as 'Parties operating under paragraph 1 of Article 5'.

49. See note 47.

50. Bharucha, V. (1994), 'Impact of environmental standards and regulations on India's exports', report prepared for the Project RAS/92/034 on Institutional Capacities for Multilateral Trade.

51. UNEP, EOC, op.cit.

52. Statement by Mr K.M Sarma, head of the Ozone Cell at UNCTAD's Expert Meeting on Positive Measures and MEAs, 3–5 November, 1997.

53. UNEP, op.cit.

54. See Article 10A of the Montreal Protocol.

55. UNEP, EOC, op.cit.

56. Gaviria, op.cit.

57. UNEP, Technology and Economic Assessment Panel. Report to the Parties. November 1995, p. II-23.

58. UNEP, EOC, op.cit.

59. According to the opening statement of the Executive Director to the Open-ended Conference of Parties to the Montreal Protocol in September 1995.

4. Brazil

4.1 INTRODUCTION

A study on trade and environment linkages in Brazil was carried out by the Foundation Centre for Studies on International Trade (Fundaçao Centro de Estudos do Comercio Exterior, FUNCEX). FUNCEX also prepared a study on the potential effects of eco-labelling in the European Union on Brazilian exports. This chapter provides a synthesis, prepared by the UNCTAD secretariat, of the following studies:

(a) Pedro de Motta Veiga (coordinator), Marta Reis Castilho and Galeno Ferraz Filho, 'Relationships between trade and the environment: the Brazilian case', July 1995.[1]

(b) Pedro de Motta Veiga, Mário C. de Carvalho Jr, Maria Lúcia Vilmar and Heraldiva Façanha, 'Eco-labelling schemes in the European Union and their impact on Brazilian exports', paper prepared for the UNCTAD workshop on Eco-labelling and International Trade, 28–29 June 1994.

The first study contains a comprehensive analysis of the vulnerability of Brazil's exports to environmental requirements, based *inter alia* on their product composition and destination as well as on environment-related factors, such as natural resource and pollution intensity of production. It also includes detailed surveys of the iron and steel, pig iron, and pulp and paper sectors, including their business strategies in response to domestic and external environmental policies, standards and regulations. In the second study, the possible effects on Brazilian exports of eco-labelling programmes in the European Union are analysed on the basis of case studies covering pulp and paper, textiles and footwear. Both studies contain recommendations.

The sector-specific analyses in both studies include an examination of a series of factors that determine the potential competitiveness impacts of environmental requirements at the firm level, such as firm size, share of exports in total production, destination of exports, patterns of competition in export markets, and corporate structure, particularly in terms of vertical integration. The studies stress that since sectors tend to be quite heterogeneous in terms of firm size and level of technology, the competitiveness effects of environmental regulations tend to be differentiated even within sectors. Small and medium-sized enterprises (SMEs) tend to have more difficulties in complying with environmental requirements than large firms. However, even large firms may have difficulties in complying with certain stringent environmental requirements emerging from external markets.

Both studies point out that Brazil's exports may be vulnerable to environmental factors, for two reasons in particular. Firstly, in the case of Brazil, international competitiveness is derived to a large extent from the intensive use of natural resources and energy. Secondly, a significant share of exports consist of homogeneous, low-value-added products, which compete in international markets on the basis of price.[2] Therefore, possibilities for product differentiation are limited and producers generally find it difficult to recover increased costs arising from the need to comply with environmental requirements through price premiums. The point is made, however, that while pollution-intensive sectors account for a relatively large share of total exports of manufactured products, the more dynamic export sectors have also achieved relatively high levels of pollution abatement, which seems to suggest that participation in international markets would encourage improved environmental management.

The studies further argue that, in the case of Brazil, external environmental requirements related to inputs and to Processes and Production Methods (PPMs), for example in the context of eco-labelling, may pose a greater potential threat to market access and export competitiveness than product regulations, even though compliance with the former is not mandatory.

External environmental requirements, however, are not always the most important factors contributing to improved environmental management. Growing concerns over the environment can be observed at the levels of the business sector, in particular larger firms, and the government. Furthermore, public sector financial institutions are implementing programmes to support investment in pollution abatement, and their financial support for investment projects in general is conditional on a company's compliance with all relevant environmental legislation.

4.2   RELATIONSHIPS BETWEEN TRADE AND ENVIRONMENT: MACRO ISSUES

4.2.1   The Economic Development Model

In the 1970s, the Brazilian economy was growing at an annual rate of approximately 10 per cent. Following the oil shock, Brazil resorted to foreign debt and an intensification of import substitution policies to reduce the impact of external factors on the economy. Trade and investment policies were based, *inter alia*, on import restrictions, export promotion and openness to foreign direct investment.

Large investments were made in agricultural and industrial activities as well as in infrastructure, increasing the average scale of production units. In the agricultural sector, for example, large-scale production of soybeans and oranges (for exports) and sugar (for the production of alcohol to reduce Brazil's dependence on oil imports) were promoted. Similarly, export-oriented projects were implemented in the Amazon region for the development of livestock, forestry and mining. Large-scale investments were also made in the energy sector (including the construction of several huge hydroelectric plants) and in infrastructure.

Furthermore, investment programmes were implemented to expand the production of intermediate goods, such as cement, pulp and paper, fertilizers, chemicals, steel and aluminium. As will be pointed out in various parts of this report, the ability of manufacturers of final products to comply with specific environmental requirements may depend to a large extent on the environmental policies of suppliers of raw materials and intermediate goods.

This growth strategy put a heavy pressure on the exploitation of the country's natural and energy resources. Until recently, the attention of local and foreign environmental groups as well as international agencies focused on deforestation caused by projects in the Amazon region. Currently, attention is focusing not only on the environmental impact of primary exports, but also on the environmental impact of industrial production[3] and on the linkages between the natural resource and pollution intensity of industrial production, and international competitiveness. This synthesis report focuses on the latter set of issues.

4.2.2 Domestic Environmental Policy-making

Environmental policy in Brazil in essence started in 1981 with the enactment of Law 6938, which established the 'National Environment Policy' and created the National Environmental System[4], to implement this policy.[5]

In Brazil, State Governments may legislate on environmental issues provided that this does not conflict with federal legislation. State Governments thus have a relatively high level of autonomy in environmental management.

The study by FUNCEX holds that Brazil's National Environment Policy has achieved some success in recent years. IBAMA, Brazil's Environmental Protection Agency, has become more effective in controlling forest clearing and logging, while the Ministry of the Environment, Water Resources and the Amazon Region has managed to strengthen the consideration of environmental factors in government agencies, in addition to promoting initiatives designed to attract foreign investments in environment-related projects. Some CONAMA (an advisory and executive council on the environment) regulations have been instrumental in promoting the use of environmental impact studies (which are mandatory in the case of large-scale projects).

Furthermore, Law 6938 made the financial support that public-sector financial institutions may provide to companies for investment projects conditional on the company's compliance with all relevant environmental legislation. The incorporation of environmental considerations in the management of public-sector support for investment projects was reinforced in subsequent legislation.[6] This has strengthened the consideration of environmental issues both within financing agencies as well as by their beneficiaries. An example could be found in the context of the BNDES (National Bank for Social and Economic Development) system, the government's principal long-term credit agency with a budget of over US$3 billion per year. In addition to requiring compliance with environmental legislation, the BNDES has encouraged companies which benefit from BNDES support for programmes aimed at increasing productivity and improving the quality of products and production processes to include the control of environmental impacts in these programmes (including through a more efficient use of inputs).

BNDES offers loans for pollution abatement programmes developed by government agencies[7] and in the context of industrial projects. In the period 1990 to 1993, environmental disbursement (representing US$276 million in 1993) typically accounted for 6 to 7 per cent of BNDES' total disbursement.[8] The BNDES Planning Superintendency believes that over the next ten years this share will increase to up to 20 per cent.[9] Table 4.1 indicates that three sectors (iron and steel, pulp and paper, and chemicals and petrochemicals) absorbed 71 per cent of total environmental investments made under the BNDES System in 1993.

Other institutions such as FINEP (an agency which provides financial support for projects and studies) also have programmes to support environmental protection. In Brazil, FINEP is the implementing agency of the Multilateral Fund of the Montreal Protocol. At the time of drafting, various projects were being analysed for funding, principally in the refrigeration sector, which would need financing of some US$15 million. FINEP has also earmarked funds for scientific and technological research in the environmental area. Approximately US$20 million has been budgeted for this purpose, drawing from the National Scientific and Technological Fund, which depends on transfers from Brazil's National Treasury.[10]

FUNCEX points out that, apart from the government, the business sector is also becoming more concerned about environmental management. A survey conducted in 1993 among 23 major industrial groups with considerable export activities (half of them derived more than 50 per cent of their revenues from exports), operating in 34 sectors, indicates that environmental issues are important factors in their management strategies.[11] Almost all groups had already been engaged in environmental auditing or were planning to do so in the near future, even though auditing was not mandatory under Brazilian legislation. In some cases auditing had been prompted by importers in overseas markets. Among the principal benefits expected from audits the following were mentioned: improved corporate image; better relationship with environmental supervising agencies; differentiation from competitors; and increased exports.

Table 4.1   Brazil, National Bank for Economic and Social Development (BNDES): support to environmental investments in 1993 (US$ millions)

Sector	Total investment (1)	Environment investment (2)	Share (3) = (1)/(2)	BNDES contribution to environmental investment		
				Value (4)	% Share (5) = (4)/(2) × 100	Distr. by sector (6) (%)
Total	–	432.2	–	276.2	63.9	100.0
Cattle raising and agro industries	35.2	0.7	1.9	0.4	53.7	0.8
Alcohol and sugar mills and plants	3.0	3.0	100.0	2.2	75.0	0.8
Automobile parts	23.4	9.1	39.0	2.3	25.2	–
Food	3.2	0.2	4.7	0.1	50.0	–
Beverages	14.2	0.2	1.0	0.1	50.0	0.2
Energy	198.2	0.8	0.4	0.6	67.8	15.4
Pulp and paper	370.0	130.0	35.0	42.6	32.8	2.9
Oil products	24.1	24.1	100.0	8.1	33.4	11.1
Chemicals and petro-chemicals	62.6	44.8	71.0	30.7	68.7	44.6
Iron and steel	727.7	184.2	25.0	123.3	67.0	0.2
Textiles	18.6	0.8	4.3	0.6	80.0	0.6
Transportation	671.5	15.8	2.3	1.7	10.9	23.0
Others	28.6	18.7	–	63.5	–	

Notes
1. Sum of own and third-party resources invested in the project by the entrepreneurs.
2. Portion of the total investment assigned to environmental preservation and control.
3. Environmental investment financed by the BNDES system (BNDES/FINAME).
4. Participation of the sector in total environmental investments financed by the BNDES system.
5. Includes support for pollution abatement programmes developed by government agencies.

Source: BNDES.

4.2.3   The Structure of International Trade

The value of Brazil's exports increased rapidly during the 1970s and early 1980s, exceeding the rate of growth of world trade as well as that of many other dynamic developing countries. Exports showed an erratic development between

1985 and the early 1990s, strongly influenced by changes in the domestic macroeconomic situation. The value of exports amounted to US$38.7 billion in 1993 (see Table 4.2). The growth in the volume of exports exceeded that in value terms, thus more than compensating for a decline in export prices, in particular for semi-manufactured and manufactured products.[12] It is to be noted that in the case of these products, Brazil's exports are concentrated in products with a relatively low level of technology and for which international markets

Table 4.2   Brazil: total exports and imports by main commodity groups, 1975–1993 (millions of US dollars).

Commodity groups	1975	1980	1985	1990	1991	1992	1993
Imports							
(in value)							
Total	13578.3	24948.8	14329.2	22457.7	22976.3	22338.0	27288.3
Food and agr. prod.	1039.7	2728.9	1529.9	2689.4	3181.7	2743.0	3835.5
Fuels	3550.9	10749.1	6766.7	6009.4	5398.6	5155.6	4558.9
Ores and metals	567.2	1281.1	586.1	1032.9	995.2	895.7	881.7
Manufactured goods	8417.5	10180.1	5430.9	12734.0	13395.2	13541.9	18010.3
(share in percentages)							
Total	100.0	100.0	100.0	100.0	100.0	100.0	100.0
Food and agr.prod.	7.7	10.9	10.7	12.0	10.2	12.8	10.1
Fuels	26.2	43.1	47.2	26.8	6.1	5.5	3.8
Ores and metals	4.2	5.1	4.1	4.6	3.9	3.7	2.7
Manufactured goods	62.0	40.8	37.9	56.7	76.6	74.3	76.1
Exports							
(in value)							
Total	8669.5	20132.1	25638.7	31397.3	31610.4	35995.5	38679.4
Food and agr. prod.	5026.2	10110.2	10097.6	9777.8	8954.1	10320.0	10960.8
Fuels	200.7	357.5	1629.7	678.1	430.7	568.5	639.2
Ores and metals	1071.8	1894.4	2408.3	4257.0	4535.6	4275.5	4094.4
Manufactured goods	2192.4	7491.9	11215.5	16300.1	17342.7	20489.7	22768.1
of which:							
Chemicals	185.6	722.4	1674.0	1979.5	1968.8	2176.4	2381.0
Paper	27.6	154.2	262.7	693.1	733.7	804.3	894.5
Steel	171.6	881.5	2174.3	3587.2	4132.1	4150.4	4195.8
Textiles	373.0	792.2	835.6	1015.1	1128.8	1358.0	1338.2
Footwear	165.1	387.9	907.6	1106.7	1176.7	1409.1	1859.6
Machinery	896.2	3392.3	3900.0	5807.5	5830.8	7443.1	8063.6
Others	373.3	1161.4	1461.3	14189.0	14970.8	17341.3	18732.7
(share in percentages)							
Total	100.0	100.0	100.0	100.0	100.0	100.0	100.0
Food and agr. prod.	58.0	50.2	39.4	31.1	28.3	28.7	28.3
Fuels	2.3	1.8	6.4	2.2	1.4	1.6	1.7
Ores and metals	12.4	9.4	9.4	13.6	14.3	11.9	10.6
Manufactured goods	25.3	37.2	43.7	51.9	54.9	57.0	58.9

Note: Food and agricultural products consist of SITC 0+1+2+4 less (27+28); Fuels consist of SITC 3; Ores and metals consist of SITC 27+28+68; Manufactured products consist of SITC 5+6+7+8 less 68.

Source: UNCTAD, based on COMTRADE, various years.

are relatively less dynamic in terms of growth. Indeed, a 1993 study by Brazil's National Bank for Economic and Social Development (BNDES) shows that Brazil's exports, in general, tend to be concentrated in sectors with declining participation in world trade. This suggests that international competitiveness may be fragile and vulnerable to any requirement leading to an increase in production and marketing costs. These characteristics, in combination with the geographical distribution of exports, to a large extent determine the vulnerability of Brazilian exports to external environmental requirements.

4.2.4 Export Shares of Products from Pollution-intensive Industries

An examination of world trade patterns corresponding to industries with high pollution abatement and control expenditures shows that these industries account for a relatively high share of Brazil's exports.[13] In the case of Brazil, pollution-intensive industries account for a particularly high share of total exports of manufactured products (47 per cent in 1990), compared to other countries (see Table 4.3).[14] Furthermore, while in OECD countries and Asian developing countries this share has decreased significantly, in the case of Brazil it increased from 21.6 per cent in 1975 to 44.4 per cent in 1990. These figures indicate that a high share of Brazilian exports may *a priori* be vulnerable to environment-related pressures.

Table 4.3   Brazil: share of pollution-intensive industries in total exports of manufactured products, 1965–1990, by region (percentages)

Period	World	Developing countries Total	Asia	America	of which: Brazil	OECD Total	USA– Canada	EU	Japan
1965	29.5	38.2	21.3	76.2	49.9	29.1	27.0	24.1	29.2
1970	27.6	35.4	19.8	67.9	44.4	27.1	28.5	22.0	26.5
1975	26.6	26.0	17.0	48.0	21.6	26.6	24.3	23.8	29.6
1980	26.0	25.4	18.4	48.2	29.9	25.9	25.2	22.7	21.4
1985	22.5	22.5	15.7	45.3	38.5	22.3	20.0	21.9	14.1
1986	20.7	19.4	13.9	39.8	38.4	20.7	19.4	19.4	12.1
1987	20.5	18.4	13.2	40.7	34.9	20.6	20.5	19.0	11.7
1988	21.2	20.4	14.0	47.1	44.3	21.1	20.6	19.4	12.2
1989	21.3	20.0	13.7	47.6	44.3	21.3	21.5	19.2	11.9
1990	20.1	19.1	12.9	47.0	44.4	20.1	19.3	17.8	11.0

Note: Data for the EU (European Union) and USA and Canada excludes intra-EU and intra-USA–Canada trade. For analytical purposes and/or incomplete time series, the following countries are not included in the group of OECD countries: Austria, Iceland, Mexico, Norway and Turkey.

Source: Mollerus (1994), 'Environmental Standards: impact on SELA's competitiveness and market access', in *Trade and Environment, the International Debate*, SELA/UNCTAD.

4.2.5   Natural Resource and Energy Intensity

In Brazil, international competitiveness of sectors which use natural resources intensively tends to be high compared to sectors which make less intensive use of such resources. For example, in 1988 the Revealed Comparative Advantage Index of industrial sectors with a high Direct Natural Resource Coefficient (DNRC) was much higher than that of sectors with a low DNRC (see Box 4.1).[15]

Box 4.1   Natural resource intensity and export competitiveness

In the case of Brazil, there is a strong correlation between the intensity in the use of natural resources and export competitiveness. Ranking products in accordance with their Direct Natural Resource Coefficients (DNRCs), shows that the most natural-resource intensive products have in general achieved higher levels of international competitiveness. Indeed, the Revealed Comparative Advantage Index (RCAI) of the 10 to 20 products which make the most intensive use of natural resources is considerably higher than that of the 10 to 20 sectors which make the least intensive use of natural resources.

Revealed comparative advantage of products, ranked in accordance with their Direct Natural Resource Coefficient (DNRC)

Products, by DNRC	RCAI-1988	RCAI average 1980/88
10 highest	0.2555	0.2685
10 lowest	0.0306	0.0189
20 highest	0.2165	0.2499
20 lowest	0.1173	0.0803

Source: de Motta Veiga *et al.* (1995).

Data by the World Energy Council show that in Brazil industrial energy consumption per unit of GNP is high compared to most other countries. While the international trend is towards a reduction of energy consumption per unit of production, in Brazil this coefficient has remained relatively stable in the 1970s and 1980s. In these two decades, in Brazil the use of electricity consumption per unit of GNP increased considerably, reflecting a transformation in Brazil's energy grid. Electricity accounted for almost 50 per cent of industrial energy consumption in 1992, increasing from 32 per cent in 1975. It is to be noted that in Brazil around 87 per cent of electric power is generated by hydric resources. Thus, 'dirty' sources of energy, such as fuel-oil, fuel-wood and charcoal, are being replaced by cleaner sources of energy, such as hydro-electric power and natural gas.

It follows that while Brazilian industry is generally energy-intensive, the energy grid has been changing in favour of using clean and renewable sources of energy. Indeed, the availability of hydro-electricity is an important factor contributing to the comparative advantage of many industries. The report shows that this may be an important issue in the analysis of Brazil's vulnerability to external environmental requirements. For example, according to Brazilian industry, criteria regarding energy use in the context of certain European Union eco-labels have discriminated against Brazil by failing to take account of the characteristics of Brazil's own energy grid.

4.2.6   Vulnerability to External Environmental Requirements

The previous sections have pointed out that, because of certain characteristics, a relatively large share of Brazilian exports may *a priori* be expected to be vulnerable to external environmental requirements. This section complements that analysis by examining the importance and geographical distribution of Brazil's exports in sectors where environmental requirements are already emerging.[16] Such requirements have been identified by the UNCTAD secretariat. A preliminary estimate indicates that around 25 to 30 per cent of Brazil's exports to OECD countries belong to sectors where environmental requirements are already emerging (see Table 4.4).

Table 4.4   Brazil, 1993: exports of selected products which may be vulnerable to environmental requirements (millions of US dollars)

| Products | World | OECD countries | | | | Developing countries |
		Total	United States and Canada	European Union	Japan	
Total exports	38 679.4	21 372.4	8 479.5	9 957.5	2 313.0	15 928.7
Fish	191.6	166.9	100.0	18.3	48.3	24.7
Tuna	37.2	27.6	11.3	6.0	10.4	9.6
Shrimp	62.2	61.9	28.2	3.4	30.3	0.3
Fruit	286.6	239.8	111.3	109.8	0.5	0.7

Table 4.4   continued

| Products | World | OECD countries | | | | Developing countries |
		Total	United States and Canada	European Union	Japan	
Wood and wood products	837.8	619.6	255.6	325.9	16.0	211.6
Tropical timber	513.0	399.1	157.6	228.1	7.1	108.1
Fertilizers	45.9	14.1	14.0	..	0.1	31.9
Insecticides	161.9	76.0	42.5	27.9	0.5	84.8
Detergents	43.1	4.8	4.1	0.2	..	37.0
Paints	33.7	0.2	0.1	0.1	..	33.6
Certain other chemicals	229.1	129.0	75.5	23.0	24.9	96.3
Batteries	45.9	5.4	3.9	1.5	..	40.4
Asbestos	71.8	18.2	5.8	5.2	4.9	52.3
Plastics	675.9	177.5	81.5	85.7	0.5	491.3
Tyres	424.4	176.5	137.3	27.9	1.0	244.4
Paper and paper products	804.4	243.7	70.3	146.0	0.6	551.9
Textiles and clothing	1338.2	766.5	408.5	304.2	23.8	547.8
Leather/leather products	498.6	356.9	85.4	248.0	12.1	134.5
Footwear	1859.6	1731.4	1421.0	278.9	3.7	99.9
Cars	2807.2	632.1	319.3	278.8	0.8	2156.0
Products which may contain CFCs	1378.6	532.3	414.5	101.1	0.5	828.4
Refrigerators, etc.	164.0	10.9	4.6	1.9	..	151.1
Air-conditioners	55.2	29.9	28.0	1.5	..	24.2
All selected products	11780.8	6095.2	3324.9	2285.0	141.0	5569.6

Note: For analytical purposes and/or incomplete time series, the following countries are not included in the group of OECD countries: Austria, Iceland, Mexico, Norway and Turkey.

Source: UNCTAD, based on COMTRADE.

Table 4.5 Brazil, 1993: exports by commodity groups and markets (shares in percentages)

Commodity groups	World	OECD countries Total	United States and Canada	European Union	Japan	Developing countries
Total	100.0	55.3	21.9	25.7	6.0	41.2
Food and agricultural products	100.0	68.3	15.3	45.4	5.6	24.4
Food	100.0	67.7	14.5	46.1	5.1	24.2
Agricultural raw materials	100.0	72.6	22.3	39.4	9.9	25.8
Fuels	100.0	52.2	49.6	2.3	0.0	47.3
Ores and metals	100.0	71.1	8.5	38.3	23.9	25.9
Manufactured goods	100.0	46.4	26.9	14.7	3.1	52.1
Chemicals	100.0	44.0	17.6	18.2	6.6	52.7
Paper	100.0	33.6	12.0	18.4	0.1	64.9
Steel	100.0	29.7	16.0	5.8	7.0	69.6
Textiles and clothing	100.0	57.3	30.5	22.7	1.8	40.9
Leather	100.0	71.6	17.1	49.7	2.4	27.0
Footwear	100.0	93.1	76.4	15.0	0.2	5.4
Machinery and equipment	100.0	41.2	26.1	12.0	2.2	57.6

Note: For analytical purposes and/or incomplete time series, the following countries are not included in the group of OECD countries: Austria, Iceland, Mexico, Norway and Turkey.

Source: UNCTAD, based on COMTRADE.

The geographical distribution of exports is thus an important factor determining the vulnerability of Brazilian exports to external environmental regulations. For example, exports of sectors such as food products, in particular fruit and fish,[17] timber and timber products,[18] paper, textiles, and footwear are destined principally for the OECD countries. Tables 4.4 and 4.5 indicate, however, that the geographical distribution of Brazil's exports in other manufacturing sectors where environmental requirements are emerging in the OECD countries varies across sectors. In some cases (fertilizers, detergents, paints, batteries and products made from asbestos) exports go primarily to developing-country markets, which may reduce the vulnerability of these sectors to external environmental requirements. There has been a particularly strong growth of exports to Latin American countries as a result of trade liberalization and the ongoing process of economic integration in the context of MERCOSUL.

The value of exports to the OECD countries of products which are potentially affected by CFC policies,[19] represented US$726 million in 1989, and declined by 45 per cent between 1989 and 1992 (see Table 4.4 and Table 4.6).[20] It should be noted, however, that taking manufactured products as a whole the value of exports to the OECD countries also declined over the same period by 7 per cent. Exports of products which may contain CFCs to developing countries increased quickly in the early 1990s, but export growth was commensurate with that of the group of manufactured products as a whole. Overall, the share of the value of exports of products which may contain CFCs going to OECD markets declined from 59 per cent in 1989 to 39 per cent in 1993.

Table 4.6   Brazil, 1993: exports of products which may be subject to CFC policies* (millions of US dollars)

| Period | Exports of products which may contain ODSs | | | Exports of all manufactured products | | |
	World	OECD	Developing countries	World	OECD	Developing countries
1989	1282.2	726.2	544.6	18449.9	10703.3	7540.6
1990	1059.5	642.5	400.9	16259.5	9931.5	6128.8
1991	909.2	413.0	476.2	17323.6	9503.4	7625.1
1992	1047.3	398.2	637.6	20459.6	9914.5	10367.1
1993	1378.6	532.3	828.4	22735.1	10636.4	11843.4

Notes
For analytical purposes and/or incomplete time series, the following countries are not included in the group of OECD countries: Austria, Iceland, Mexico, Norway and Turkey.
*These are exports of products listed in Annex D of the Montreal Protocol which possibly contain ozone-depleting substances.

Source: UNCTAD, based on COMTRADE, and UNEP 'A note regarding the harmonized system customs code numbers for the products listed in Annex D of the Amended Montreal Protocol', UNEP/OzL.Pro.4/3, 28 May 1992.

4.3   SECTORAL STUDIES

FUNCEX carried out several case studies on specific sectors to analyse their vulnerability to domestic and external environmental requirements as well as to examine business strategies in response to environmental concerns. Such studies were largely based on surveys, using questionnaires and interviews with representatives of firms and industry associations. The sectors selected, that is, iron and steel, pig iron, and pulp and paper, have several common characteristics, such as (a) strong export growth during the 1980s and early 1990s; (b) intensive use of natural resources and energy; and (c) high pollution potential.

The case studies identify factors that determine the potential competitiveness impacts of environmental requirements at the firm level. These include:

(a) firm size and the share of exports in total output (smaller firms, particularly those which export a relatively small share of their output, tend to be less active in incorporating environmental factors in their business strategies). As most sectors are quite heterogeneous, that is in terms of firm size and level of technology used, the competitiveness effects of environmental requirements tend to be differentiated even within a particular sector. Furthermore, firms may differentiate products depending on whether they are exported or sold in the domestic market;
(b) the geographical destination of exports;
(c) patterns of competition in external markets. Competition on the basis of price tends to reduce the firm's ability to absorb cost increases resulting from environmental requirements;
(d) corporate structures – the more a company is vertically integrated, the greater its ability to control environmental factors throughout the product's life cycle tends to be.

All three sectors are vulnerable to environmental requirements, but the source and characteristics of such requirements vary from case to case. While external environmental requirements are relevant in the case of pulp and paper, in the other sectors environmental investments respond essentially to domestic environmental requirements. The sectoral studies further illustrate the characteristics of Brazil's exports, discussed in Section 4.2.

4.3.1 Pulp and Paper

The pulp industry and those subsectors of the paper industry which have achieved a high degree of international competitiveness (paper for printing, writing and packaging) are vulnerable to external environmental requirements for the following reasons: (a) a significant part of production is exported (around 40 per cent in the case of pulp and around 20 per cent in the case of paper); (b) a considerable share of exports goes to markets where environmental requirements are the most stringent; and (c) exports are concentrated in low-value-added products which compete in international markets on the basis of price.

Other subsectors of the paper industry may be less vulnerable, as exports go principally to markets where environmental requirements are less stringent (for example, special papers are exported principally to Latin American markets).

Within Brazil's pulp and paper industry, three types of firms can be distinguished: (a) large-scale producers of 'market' pulp; (b) integrated paper producers (owning plantations), which are also firms with large production capacities; and (c) a heterogeneous subsector of non-integrated paper producers, consisting largely of SMEs, many of which use recycled fibres. With regard to (b), the four largest integrated firms accounted for 39 per cent of total production of paper and 57 per cent of total production of pulp in 1992. The high and growing level of industrial concentration is associated with characteristics of the production process and investments made under Brazil's second National Development Plan, which aimed at an expansion of the production capacity of this industry and at modernization, supported by BNDES financing.

Large companies surveyed by FUNCEX, stated that a considerable share of their exports already had to comply with environmental requirements. However, they were able to comply with such requirements without significant adverse effects on their competitiveness. Several large firms stated that they had the capacity to produce, at customers request, ECF (elemental chlorine free) or TCF (totally chlorine free) pulp and paper.

Large producers had made significant environmental investments, to a large extent in response to domestic legislation, which was becoming more stringent. Smaller producers, however, would have greater difficulties in complying with stringent environmental requirements. In any case, both large and small firms remain vulnerable to increasingly stringent environmental requirements for two reasons. First, in the paper sector, consumer preferences for environment-friendly products are very relevant.[21] Secondly, a considerable portion of product and process technology is embodied in the equipment manufactured by a limited number of producers, which implies that adaptation to environmental standards may require large investments.

Concerns were expressed over recycling requirements and eco-labelling. Recycling requirements could significantly affect the competitiveness of pulp producers and integrated paper producers. It is to be noted that the competitiveness of integrated firms is to a large extent based on quickly growing eucalyptus. Indeed, eucalyptus takes approximately seven years to reach maturity, while species used by Brazil's major competitors may take 20 to 30 years. This makes Brazilian fibre some 45 per cent cheaper than North American and Canadian fibres. Recycling has not been well developed in Brazil. Among the explanatory factors are the quality of the forest base, the relatively low level of domestic paper consumption and lack of infrastructure, for example in terms of collection systems.

It follows that, in the case of Brazil, it may be more efficient from both an economic and environmental point of view to use virgin pulp rather than recycled materials in pulp and paper production. Environmental requirements emerging from external markets, for example in the context of eco-labelling, may thus be inappropriate in the context of domestic environmental conditions and priorities (see also Box 4.2).

4.3.2   Iron and Steel

Certain factors make the iron and steel industry vulnerable to environmental requirements, although vulnerability is lower than in the case of the pulp and paper industry. The iron and steel industry uses natural resources intensively and production is potentially highly polluting. Moreover, some segments of Brazil's iron and steel industry use charcoal; consequently the deforestation issue is of relevance for specific parts of the sector. It should also be mentioned, however, that given Brazil's energy grid, CO_2 emissions are, in general, lower than in most other countries. A survey conducted by FUNCEX reveals that the sector has not as yet faced external environmental requirements: among other reasons this is because there are no product-related environmental standards and regulations. Environmental requirements are of domestic origin. According to the survey, improved environmental management would imply higher energy efficiency, tighter pollution control and increased recycling; the Brazilian iron and steel industry considers that it is able to adjust to high standards.

An analysis of this sector illustrates many of the characteristics of Brazil's exports described in Section 4.2. Brazil's iron and steel industry has achieved high technological standards during the reduction phase, but such standards are relatively low during the final stages of processing. Consequently, Brazil's production and exports are concentrated in basic and semi-finished products, that is, low-value-added products. International competitiveness is based on price and hence any external influence which may force up the costs of production may seriously harm the competitiveness of Brazilian exports.

According to FUNCEX, between 1980 and 1992, around US\$1.3 billion were spent on environmental investments.[22] The Brazilian Steel Institute holds that environmental investments accounted for 20 per cent of total investments by the iron and steel sector in the period 1986 to 1992. Efforts to control pollution and to resolve environmental problems were being made essentially in response to domestic environmental policies and increased environmental awareness, resulting in the fuller incorporation of environment-related factors in corporate strategies. According to FUNCEX, the privatization of state-owned steel plants also contributed to this process.[23]

Environmental policies have focused on the reduction of air and water pollution and on avoiding deforestation. Legislation introduced in the State of

Minas Gerais in the early 1990s prescribed that by 1998 all charcoal consumed must originate from non-natural forests. This legislation forced charcoal-consuming steelmills either to invest in reforestation or to reduce the use of charcoal by converting their blast furnaces to coal (see section on pig iron below).

Another issue of concern to the iron and steel industry involves the implementation of domestic legislation regarding imports of scrap (IBAMA) as well as internationally agreed measures concerning trade in scrap metals (The Basel Convention). Only around 10 per cent of Brazil's total output of raw steel comes from companies which operate using scrap metal. In addition, as shown in Table 4.7, imports account for only a small portion of the total supply of scrap metals.

Table 4.7   Brazil, 1983–1992: supply of iron and steel scrap (10^3 ton)

Year	Consumption	Plant generated scrap	Purchases on the market	Imports
1983	5567	2667	2894	–
1984	6324	2965	3651	31
1985	6998	3629	3423	104
1986	7198	3718	3491	491
1987	7319	4013	3213	138
1988	7676	4242	3409	87
1989	8032	4654	3417	342
1990	6574	3248	2878	113
1991	5714	3155	2545	89
1992	6086	3482	2660	99

Source: Brazilian Steel Institute, IBS.

Industry is nevertheless concerned over the possible effects of measures restricting trade in scrap metals. Indeed, industry resorts to imports of scrap to make up for fluctuations in domestic supply. In the short run, an increase in exports coupled with a reduction in domestic steel consumption may result in shortage of domestically generated scrap. Second, in the medium term and the long run, a possible upsurge in Brazilian steel production could induce a considerable increase in the demand for steel scrap. In both cases, trade restrictions could adversely affect the sector's competitiveness.

After the adoption of Annex VII by the Fourth Conference of the Parties to the Basel Convention in February 1998, which contains waste considered hazardous by the Convention and subject to the multilateral export ban from OECD to non-OECD countries pursuant to decision III/I of the Convention, it is now clear that clean, uncontaminated iron and steel scrap and most ferrous-bearing residues will not be affected by such trade restrictions. Ferrous-bearing residues in dispersable form, however, still run the risk of being considered hazardous by the national legislation of Brazil and other trading nations. The latter particularly concerns the European Union which might resort to trade restrictions on such scrap material under the EU Regulation 120/97, which amends Council Regulation No. 259/93 on the supervision and control of shipments of waste within, into and out of the European Community.

4.3.3 Pig Iron

Brazil is an important producer and exporter of pig iron. Charcoal is used as the principal source of energy for approximately one-third of pig iron production. Independent producers (producing pig iron only) account for 20 per cent of total production, an important share of which is exported.

The independent pig iron industry consists of 78 small and medium-sized firms, with total revenues of US$490 million in 1992. The State of Minas Gerais accounts for almost 90 per cent of production. The sector emerged in the early 1970s, taking advantage of the abundant supply of iron ore and charcoal, as well as low labour costs. The cheap supply of charcoal was largely due to the expansion of agricultural frontiers which resulted in intensive forest clearing. The installation of new firms was also spurred by the fact that due to the relatively simple technologies and modest investment requirements there were no significant barriers to entry in this sector.

As a result of domestic pressures and increased awareness of environmental effects of deforestation, in the early 1990s the State of Minas Gerais introduced legislation prescribing that by 1998 all charcoal consumed must originate from non-natural or sustainable managed forests. As charcoal consumption accounts for as much as approximately 70 per cent of the production cost of pig iron, such legislation has very significant effects on competitiveness. According to sources from the pig iron sector, the costs of charcoal from reforestation projects amount to approximately US$25 per m³, compared to only US$19 to US$20 per m³ for charcoal from native forests. In addition, annual investments in reforestation projects required to comply with the law would exceed the annual sales revenues of the sector. Some steelmills were already closing down.

The legislation has nevertheless been supported by industry, which has agreed to move towards more stringent environmental standards following the gradual approach set out in the law. In addition, fiscal incentives and programmes aimed at supporting the financing of forest plantations (for example PROFLORESTA, as well as lines of financing provided by the World Bank) help to alleviate competitiveness effects. The case study on pig iron shows that stringent environmental standards have been introduced in response to domestic environmental concerns, despite their significant adverse effects on competitiveness. Positive measures, such as those mentioned above may have contributed to this outcome.

4.4 EFFECTS OF ECO-LABELLING ON BRAZILIAN EXPORTS

4.4.1 Vulnerability to Eco-labelling

Eco-labelling in the developed countries has caused concern to Brazilian industry. Attention has been generated, for example, by eco-labels for tissue products, developed under the programme of the European Union, in particular because the criteria may result in discrimination against the Brazilian pulp industry. Brazil is also potentially affected by eco-labels in other product groups. Several of the product categories for which criteria are being set under the eco-labelling programme of the European Union are of export interest to Brazil. Examples are given in Table 4.8.

Table 4.8   Brazil, 1993: exports of products earmarked for eco-labelling in the European Union

| | Brazilian exports | | |
| | World (US$ millions) (1) | European Union (US$ millions) (2) | Share EU/World (percentage) (2)/(1) |
Product category			
Tissue paper	28.9	3.5	12.1
Copying and writing paper	40.1	7.4	18.5
T-shirts	108.0	44.3	41.0
Bed linen	51.9	12.0	23.1
Footwear	278.9	1 859.6	15.0
Ceramics[1]	149.9	19.2	12.8
Lamps	42.7	7.5	17.6
Furniture[1]	191.1	120.3	63.0
Materials used (themselves not directly subject to eco-labelling)			
Wood pulp	717.6	259.7	36.2
Leather	401.9	188.1	46.8

Note: [1] Included in national eco-labelling programmes.

Source: UNCTAD, based on COMTRADE, and 'A statistical overview of selected eco-labelling schemes', TD/B/WG.6/MISC.5, 2 June 1995.

FUNCEX analysed the potential effects on Brazilian exports of European Union eco-labels in three sectors: tissue products, certain textile products (T-shirts and bed linen) and footwear (based on the national criteria for a footwear eco-label in the Netherlands). FUNCEX focused its analysis on an examination of the structure and export strategies of firms in the corresponding sectors in Brazil, and, taking into account these characteristics, a consideration of the degree of difficulties that Brazilian firms could encounter if they were to apply for an eco-label, based on interviews with representatives of firms and industry associations.

The characteristics of the export sector are different for each of the three product groups analysed. Brazil's pulp and integrated paper industry consists of large firms which have achieved a high level of vertical integration and have their own plantation forests. While the textile industry is very heterogeneous in terms of scale and technologies used, exports of T-shirts and bed linen to the European Union are concentrated in a small number of large firms. Conversely, in the case of footwear large firms account for most production, while exporters consist of large as well as small and medium-sized firms.

Brazil's exports of tissue products are relatively small and exports account for only a minor part of total production. Eco-labelling in tissue products, however, may have significant effects on exports of pulp. Production and exports of pulp are heavily concentrated in large firms. Indeed, the major exporter of eucalyptus pulp accounted for 55 per cent of total Brazilian exports in 1992. Exports accounted for almost 90 per cent of this firm's sales in 1993 and around one-third of its exports went to the European Union.

Brazil's textile exports are strongly concentrated in a relatively small number of companies. Indeed, five large firms located in the State of Santa Caterina account for the major part of exports of T-shirts and bed linen to the European Union. The two largest T-shirt exporters earmark just over 50 per cent of their total exports for Western Europe, principally Germany: in 1993 this represented $56 million. These two exporters accounted for 80 per cent of total Brazilian exports of T-shirts world-wide in 1993. The three largest companies accounted for 65 per cent of total Brazilian exports of bed linen in 1993.

With regard to footwear, exporters consist of large, small and medium-sized firms. The footwear sector is characterized by its concentration in two regional centres in southern Brazil: Novo Hamburgo in the state of Rio Grande do Sul (women's footwear) and Franca in the state of São Paulo (men's footwear). This regional polarization of production has attracted manufacturers of input materials and equipment, while spurring the development of a technological and information infrastructure in these production centres. In addition to underwriting the participation of small and medium-sized companies on the international market, this structuring has endowed Brazil's footwear exporters with flexibility in adapting to constantly changing rules and conditions for competing in global markets. The number of exporters increased from 294 in 1975 to 487 in 1992.

4.4.2 Eco-labelling Criteria

For all three product categories, the eco-labelling criteria being developed in the European Union relate principally to processes and production methods (PPMs). In addition, an important part of the criteria refer to the materials used: pulp (in the case of tissue products, see Box 4.2), cotton (textile products, see Box 4.3) and leather (footwear, see Box 4.4).

According to FUNCEX, among the principal difficulties that companies are likely to encounter in complying with the criteria are the following: (a) the need to certify the environmental attributes of inputs and the relationship with suppliers of input materials, (b) outdated equipment, (c) higher product prices in a market where competition is price-based, and (d) lack of market stimulation, linked to the fact that, in Brazil, the domestic market for 'environment-friendly' products is very small.

Box 4.2   Eco-labels for tissue products

Eco-labelling criteria for tissue products, proposed under the European Union eco-labelling programme, have been criticized by Brazilian industry.

Brazilian exporters have alleged that the emphasis on recycling in determining criteria regarding the consumption of renewable resources discriminates against Brazilian producers which use wood from plantation forestry. Indeed, fast growing eucalyptus and mastery of forest management technologies provide Brazilian industry with an important comparative advantage, which is further strengthened by economies of scale and the supply of renewable energy resources.

Brazilian industry has also alleged that the criteria related to SO_2 emissions in the production process are of little or no relevance since acid rain is not a major environmental problem in the location of production. They have further pointed out that calculations made to determine whether the criteria regarding the consumption of non-renewable energy resources are met result in discrimination against Brazilian producers, who depend largely on hydro-electricity.

Source: de Motta Veiga *et al.* (1994).

Box 4.3   Eco-labels for T-shirts and bed linen

Brazil's exports of textiles are concentrated in intermediate or finished products using natural fibres, particularly cotton. The specialization and competitive edge of Brazil in cotton products is also proven by the level of utilization of its export quotas under the Multifibre Agreement. Indeed, exports of cotton threads to the European Union have been affected as Brazil regularly filled its quotas. Quotas for cotton-knit shirts and T-shirts, brushed or smooth, have also been increasingly used. This characteristic makes the sector particularly sensitive to life-cycle analyses of products using environmental criteria related to the production and use of cotton fibres.

Criteria for eco-labels for T-shirts and bed linen developed under the eco-labelling programme of the European Union refer to environmental effects at different stages of the product's life cycle, in particular those related to cotton growing and the manufacturing of fabrics. Consequently, most criteria are PPM-related, referring, for example, to efficiency in the use of energy and water and the treatment of waste-water. There are specific criteria concerning the use of pesticides and chemicals in cotton growing and the use of dyes or chemicals in the manufacturing process, in most cases to address local environmental effects at the location of production. Only a few criteria are clearly product-related. A group of criteria has been developed regarding chemical residues in final products.

Five large firms located in the State of Santa Caterina account for the major part of exports of T-shirts and bed linen to the European Union. These large producers are already making adjustments to comply with environmental requirements of European importers. For example, one firm, exporting bed linen, stated that 50 percent of the value of recent investments had been prompted by environmental requirements.

Four of the five companies interviewed had information on the European Union eco-labels from their European clients. These large firms stated that they already complied with a number of the draft criteria for the EU labels for T-shirts and bed linen. However, some of them would have certain difficulties in complying with specific criteria. Among these criteria the following were mentioned by one or several firms: criteria related to pesticides and chemicals during cotton growing; the use of dyes, pigments and carriers during the manufacturing process; waste-water parameters; noise; cotton dust; and residue values in final products.

While large firms with commercial links with markets where environmental requirements are stringent may be in a position to comply with a number of the eco-labelling criteria, SMEs are likely to have much greater difficulties.

Source: de Motta Veiga *et al.* (1994).

Box 4.4   Eco-labelling for footwear

Brazil, the world's fourth largest footwear producer, exports almost two-thirds of the leather shoes it produces. Most exports of footwear, representing US$1.9 billion in 1993, go to the OECD markets (93 per cent of the value of total footwear exports in 1993). The European Union, where environmental requirements appear to be emerging, represented a market of almost US$300 million in 1993. Mandatory environmental requirements in Europe consist basically of restrictions on the use of pentachlorophenol (PCP) and other chemicals. The use of PCP as a leather preservative has already been banned in Brazil. A survey conducted by FUNCEX reveals that some companies may find certain difficulties in exporting to the European Union, in particular to Germany, because of restrictions on the use of PVC in footwear. Companies are aware of substitutes for PVC, but according to some sources, such substitutes may increase the cost of materials by at least 20 per cent.

In the Netherlands, the Stichting Milieukeur (SMK – Dutch Foundation for Eco-labelling) has developed a national eco-label for footwear, which became effective on 1 March 1994. The SMK has also been appointed as the 'lead competent body' for establishing draft criteria for a European Union eco-label (the European Flower) for shoes.

Only some of the criteria developed by the SMK are product-related. These include a long list of quality and performance ('functional') requirements, which are principally aimed at increasing the reparability and durability of shoes. One criterion refers to the 'energy content' of shoes, aimed at reducing the consumption of energy and raw materials. Other criteria, referring to materials, are clearly PPM-related. In the case of leather such criteria refer, for example, to chromium emissions into water, emission of organic solvents, and the treatment of waste water.

Interviews with the Technological Centre for Footwear, Leather and Similar Products (CTCAA) reveal that Brazilian footwear producers would, technically speaking, be in a position to comply with most eco-labelling criteria. However, the production cost of shoes which comply with the eco-labelling criteria would be substantially higher than that of conventional products.

However, the question of whether or not shoes comply with the eco-labelling criteria depends basically on the environmental quality of materials used, in particular leather, and many of the corresponding criteria are PPM-related. With a view to securing supply of raw materials, a number of footwear producers have become vertically integrated by purchasing leather tanneries (a process unrelated to environmental requirements). Such firms may be in a better position to ascertain the environmental attributes of their raw materials.

Source: de Motta Veiga *et al.* (1994).

With regard to (a), textile producers, for example, consider that it would be difficult to comply with criteria limiting the use of pesticides and chemicals during cotton growing. In Brazil itself the use of pesticides in cotton growing is low and cotton is almost completely harvested by hand. However, large-scale imports of cotton into Brazil are increasing rapidly and it is difficult for textile producers to certify that imported cotton is pesticide-free. Similarly, footwear producers are aware that most of the difficulties in meeting eco-labelling criteria arise from the fact that this would require changes in the production process of leather.[24]

The relationship between producers of finished goods and sectors producing input materials, such as chemicals and leather, is also an important factor. In the case of textiles, compliance with the criteria related to the use of chemical input materials depends to a large extent on the market power and negotiating capabilities of textile companies. Large firms often exert pressure on chemical industries[25] to supply – either through local production or imports – the input materials required in the European countries; they are unwilling to pay higher prices for these input materials, as this would affect the competitiveness of their prices on foreign markets. SMEs do not have this power. In this context, the pulp and paper industry, which has achieved a high level of vertical integration, is in a better position to control the environmental attributes of input materials.

With regard to (b), for major export companies investments in modernization of equipment are a prerequisite for participation in the international market. As they export to markets that are more environmentally demanding, their growth strategies, together with incentives to make additional investments in modernization and environmental management, increase and may become economically profitable. Nevertheless, it should be noted that even for these companies, compliance with certain requirements, for example with respect to waste-water treatment, may prove difficult. Criteria where compliance demands investments in new machinery are those to which small and medium-sized producers may well find the greatest difficulties in adaptation.

With regard to (c), footwear producers, for example, perceive that incurring the additional costs in adjustments required to comply with eco-labelling criteria would reduce the competitiveness of their products *vis-à-vis* other exporters who focus their competitiveness on price, principally suppliers from other developing countries, in particular China. They also think that market conditions will not allow them to recover the additional costs associated with the required adjustments.

Concerning (d), the FUNCEX studies point out that as there is no significant domestic demand for environment-friendly products, the domestic market does not help firms to recover incremental costs of production. This factor is the most relevant in the case of textiles, as exports are relatively small compared to the domestic market. Pulp and leather footwear, however, are produced principally for export.

4.4.3 Conclusions

Eco-labelling in the developed countries is emerging in several sectors of export interest to Brazil. The degree of vulnerability varies from sector to sector, depending on factors such as product coverage, the formulation and implementation of such schemes, aspects related to the consumer market as well as production structures in Brazil.

It is often mentioned that as eco-labels are voluntary, their trade impacts may be relatively small compared to the effects of mandatory requirements. Indeed, in this context Brazilian exporters of footwear appear relatively unconcerned over eco-labels; as they compete on the basis of price they perceive that their market shares will not be affected. Pulp exporters, however, are more concerned over eco-labels; issues such as recycling and deforestation are important factors in the context of consumer preferences and buying policies of importers in the developed countries.

Case studies carried out by FUNCEX indicate that eco-labels, in particular those which are based on a life-cycle approach, may result in discrimination against Brazilian exports and undermine comparative advantage.[26] The capacity of firms to adapt to eco-labelling requirements varies from sector to sector, and is dependent on the size of the company and the weight of exports – in particular to the European Union and other export markets where eco-labelling is applied – in the company's growth strategy. Given the high compliance costs, for the large majority of small and medium-sized companies in Brazil it would be very difficult to qualify for eco-labels while maintaining export competitiveness. Even for major export companies, the cost of compliance has been considered high, principally when this involves new investments in fixed assets. In the case of the textile and footwear industries testing and certification costs may also be particularly high. In addition, the eco-labelling process tends to lack transparency. FUNCEX also recommended initiatives at the international and national levels to mitigate potential negative effects of eco-labels on Brazilian exports, which are presented in Box 4.5.

4.5 CONCLUSIONS AND RECOMMENDATIONS

4.5.1 Conclusions

An analysis of the characteristics of Brazilian exports suggests that increasingly stringent environmental requirements emerging from external markets may

Box 4.5   Eco-labelling in Brazil

Currently there are two different proposals for setting up eco-labelling programmes in Brazil. The Brazilian Technical Standards Association (ABNT) has proposed to set up a Brazilian Green Seal programme; in addition, the Brazilian Forest Development Society has proposed the Forest Raw Material Origin Certificate (CERFLOR).

The Green Seal programme
The Green Seal programme is being developed under the administration of FINEP, a government agency which funds studies and projects. It has received funding from the government and the World Bank. The basic objectives of the programme are (a) to create awareness and educate consumers in the domestic market; and (b) to help exporters to meet environmental requirements emerging from external markets. While the first objective requires the programme to be well attuned to national conditions, the second objective calls for stringent criteria with a view to facilitating mutual recognition with eco-labelling programmes in the OECD countries.

At a workshop held in Rio de Janeiro in June 1993, 10 groups of products were suggested for eco-labelling: paper, leather and footwear, household appliances, CFC-free aerosols, car batteries, biodegradable detergents, lightbulbs, wooden furniture, packaging, cosmetics and toiletries. It was suggested that criteria should be based on a life cycle approach.

The implementation of the programme has been delayed, in particular because lack of funding has prevented ABNT from carrying out its functions in the field of coordination and implementation.

The CERFLOR forest products certification programme
Plans to develop the CERFLOR programme have been inspired by three factors:

(a)   difficulties faced by exporters of mahogany and tropical hardwoods;
(b)   external requirements faced by exporters of pulp and paper (for example, companies such as Aracruz Celulosa have received visits from representatives of foreign companies, such as Proctor and Gamble and Kodak in order to review environmental management);
(c)   European Union eco-labels based on life-cycle analysis.

At the time of drafting, both programmes were facing difficulties. One problem relates to the differences in environmental requirements in the domestic and the principal external markets. On the one hand, the domestic market currently may not respond to eco-labels and may not generate sufficient incentives for companies to improve the environmental quality of products. On the other hand, large exporters, which may be in a position to comply with the criteria of eco-labelling programmes in their major markets, may prefer to try to obtain the eco-labels of foreign programmes directly, rather than aiming at mutual recognition.

Source: de Motta Veiga *et al.* (1994).

have a potentially adverse impact on Brazil's export performance. The FUNCEX studies attribute the vulnerability of Brazilian exports to external environmental requirements to three factors: (a) the high natural resource and energy intensity of exports; (b) other characteristics of exports, in particular the fact that a large share of exports, especially the most dynamic export sectors, consist of homogeneous products, with little possibilities for product differentiation, which are competing in international markets on the basis of price factors; and (c) the high share of exports going to markets where environmental requirements are more stringent.

With regard to (b) – other characteristics of exports – FUNCEX points out that environmental requirements might adversely affect export competitiveness, for the following reasons in particular:

(a) certain external environmental requirements, which are inappropriate given domestic resource endowments, may reduce comparative advantage (an example can be found in certain European Union eco-labelling criteria for tissue products);
(b) large-scale production tends to increase investment requirements;
(c) the relationships between manufacturers of final products and suppliers of raw materials and intermediate goods may complicate the former's compliance with environmental requirements. In the case of Brazil, within the context of a rather closed economy, the government had played a major role in such relationships. Producers of final products may find it difficult to impose specific environmental requirements on suppliers of raw materials and intermediate products, in particular when compliance requires significant new investments. A notable exception is the pulp industry, which is vertically integrated and includes the ownership of plantation forests;
(d) competition on the basis of price makes Brazilian exporters, who normally are price-takers, vulnerable to any environmental requirement resulting in cost increases;
(e) as in the case of homogeneous products, the capacity for product differentiation is limited, Brazilian producers generally find it difficult to recover increased costs of environmental improvements through price premiums. In addition, since in Brazil itself the demand for 'environment-friendly' products is insignificant, the domestic market does not allow firms to recover incremental costs of production.

The vulnerability to environmental requirements is further illustrated on the basis of case studies of specific sectors; pulp and paper, iron and steel, and pig iron. Environmental requirements are especially relevant in the case of the pulp and paper industry. The sector is concerned in particular about recycling requirements and the use of voluntary instruments such as eco-labelling. The iron and steel industry may be relatively less affected by external environmental requirements. There are no significant product-related requirements in this sector and, in any case, the European Union (where, in general, environmental requirements tend to be the most stringent) is a relatively small export market for Brazil. Domestic environmental requirements tend to be more important. One issue of concern to the steel industry, however, is the effects of the Basel Convention on international trade in scrap. While in general only a small share of scrap used for recycling is supplied by imports, a reduction in domestic consumption of iron and steel products and, consequently, in the output of semi-integrated mills may create problems for the recycling industry if imports of scrap were to be restricted.

Brazilian industry may be more vulnerable to voluntary requirements related to inputs and PPMs than to mandatory product regulations. As the application of PPM-related mandatory standards to imported products is not allowed under WTO rules, eco-labelling and other voluntary instruments are growing in importance. In this context, two characteristics of eco-labelling were highlighted in the FUNCEX studies. On the one hand, as eco-labels are voluntary, they may be less of a threat than mandatory requirements. On the other hand, as eco-labels involve an analysis of the entire life cycle of the product, they embody a massive potential for discrimination between imported and domestic products based on the assessment of the various uses of inputs, as well as PPMs.

It should nevertheless be noted that improved environmental management responds largely to domestic requirements, as has been illustrated in the case of the forestry policy in the State of Minas Gerais. Sectoral studies indicate that a large portion of new investments consists of environmental investments, a trend that has been supported by policies of financial institutions such as the BNDES.

4.5.2 Recommendations

The FUNCEX studies indicate that improved environmental management is taking place in response to both external and domestic environmental requirements. Firms which are exposed to international markets may find it easier to adapt to increasingly stringent environmental requirements. Larger exporters, who have direct contacts with foreign clients and possess the financial and technological means to invest in environmental improvements, often use best environmental practices. It should be noted, however, that industrial sectors in developing countries tend to be quite heterogeneous. Small and medium-sized firms tend to have more difficulties in obtaining information and in adjusting to environmental requirements in external markets. Capacity-building efforts may help promote a process whereby the know-how and experience acquired by larger firms is transmitted to smaller firms.

The studies contain a number of recommendations, most of which refer to eco-labelling. Reducing the vulnerability of Brazilian exports to eco-labelling schemes would basically involve the following initiatives at the international level:

(a)   the adoption of non-discriminatory criteria and parameters as well as a decision-making process compatible with the provisions of the World Trade Organization (WTO); and

(b)   the development of multilateral initiatives leading to consensus on the preparation of guidelines for formulating and implementing national and regional eco-labelling schemes, which would serve as a basis for mutual recognition among different national schemes.

At the national level, the following elements are crucial:

(a)   increased awareness, within export sectors, of eco-labelling initiatives in the major export markets, as well as of their own production processes, including the systematic preparation and dissemination of technical data on the use of raw materials, other inputs and manufacturing processes;

(b)   broader fora for discussion and negotiation between exporters of finished goods and sectors producing input materials, seeking the establishment of mechanisms for cooperation that also lead to the modernization of the latter with a consequent reduction in vulnerability attributable to specific characteristics of Brazil's production structure;

(c)   development of a national eco-labelling scheme (see Box 4.5 on Brazil's Green Seal Project), technical cooperation with countries that have already implemented eco-labelling schemes, and the exploration of mutual recognition with other schemes; and

(d)   joint efforts by the government and the private sector to assess the initiatives under way in the European Union, and seeking in multilateral fora the compliance of eco-labelling schemes with the WTO Agreement on Technical Barriers to Trade.

FUNCEX also proposes further studies aimed at improving the understanding of trade and environment linkages, by analysing in particular:

(a)   the effects of specific environmental policies, standards and regulations on Brazil's exports (such as the study carried out on eco-labelling). It would in particular be worthwhile to analyse the trade and competitiveness effects of Multilateral Environmental Agreements;

(b)   possible changes induced by the trade liberalization process on the environmental strategies and performance of Brazilian industry; and

(c)   the effects of environmental requirements – both domestic and foreign – on the relationship between manufacturers of finished products and suppliers of raw materials and intermediate goods.

In addition, it would be worthwhile to analyse factors which motivate the emergence of specific environmental requirements in the OECD countries in sectors which compete with imports originating in Brazil. The case studies indicate that different requirements may emerge in different sectors. For example, the importance attached to recycling by the steel industry and the paper industry varies considerably. Therefore, it may be necessary to analyse the conditions of sectors in the countries where environmental requirements emerge, in particular as those conditions may explain the type of policy or instrument that is likely to be chosen.

NOTES

1.   A summary of this study was published in Brazil. See de Motta Veiga, Pedro (coordinator) (1994), 'Evidencias sobre as relacoes entre comercio e ambiente no Brasil', *Revista Brasileira de Comercio Exterior*, 41, October–December. (Only in Portuguese.)

2.   Brazil's exports are highly concentrated in natural-resource-intensive products and in sectors with large-scale or labour-intensive production processes. Although there has been an expansion of production and exports of high-value-added products, international competitiveness has been largely based on the relative abundance of natural resources (forests, water resources, mineral deposits) and agriculture.

3.   Manufacturing industries are responsible for around 60 per cent of emissions of organic matter and 100 per cent of the emissions of heavy metals in Brazil. See Serao da Motta, R. (1993), 'Politica de controle ambiental e competitividade', paper prepared for the *Study of the Competitiveness of Brazilian Industry*, Campinas.

4.   The National Environmental System consists of the Government Council (with representatives of all ministries); an advisory and executive council (CONAMA, made up of representatives of the States, the Central Government, non-government organizations and environmental experts); a Central Agency forming a bureau under the presidency (SEMAN) and an Executive Agency (IBAMA). SEMAN has been substituted by the Ministry for the Environment, Water Resources and the Amazon Region. The National Environment System also includes other government agencies involved with environmental preservation as well as the environmental bureaux of the states and municipalities. In order to provide financial support to the National Environment Policy, the National Environment Fund was set up, administered by the National Environment System.

5.   The Law established the basis for public-sector policies, which are largely based on command and control measures such as (a) environmental standards and regulations; (b) land use control (zoning and the establishment of protected areas); (c) environmental impact studies; and (d) penalties. According to the FUNCEX study, the use of economic instruments is poorly developed.

6.   For example, Decree 9927 of 6 July 1990.

7. For example, the II Industrial Pollution Control Project developed by the State of Sao Paulo and Brazil's National Pollution Abatement Programme.

8. The FUNCEX study mentions that at the time of drafting, BNDES loans for environmental protection were offered at annual interest rates of 6.5 per cent, lower than the average BNDES rate of 9.4 per cent and well below prevailing market rates.

9. Gazeta Mercantil, 6 June 1994.

10. *Ibid.*

11. FUNCEX (1994), 'Os Esquemas de Ecolabelling na União Européia eseus Impactos sobre as Expertações Brasileras', mimeo, report prepared for UNCTAD, Rio de Janiero.

12. Indeed, the average export price index (basis 1980 = 100) for all exports fell to 89.5 in 1993. Export prices declined for all major groups of products (basic, semi-manufactured and manufactured goods), in particular for semi-manufactured (the index stood at 65.4 in 1993) and manufactured products (the index fell to 85.6).

13. Pollution-intensive industries are identified on the basis of data on pollution abatement expenditures reported by United States manufacturers, published in *Manufacturers' Pollution Abatement Capital Expenditures and Operating Costs (1988)*, Department of Commerce, Bureau of the Census, Industry Division, Washington DC, 20233. See also Low, P. and A. Yeats (1992), in *International Trade and the Environment*, World Bank Discussion Papers, No. 159. A major shortcoming of these data is that they refer to the United States and are not necessarily valid for Brazil. Seroa de Motta has identified 'dirty industries', based on data on the level of 'remaining' water and air pollution for Brazilian industries.

14. Contrary to trends in world trade, the participation of pollution-intensive industries in exports from American developing countries has remained high. Indeed, while the share of these industries in world trade fell from 19.0 per cent in 1965 to 15.7 per cent in 1990, over the same period their share in exports from Latin America and the Caribbean increased from 10.7 per cent to 19.1 per cent. See Mollerus, R. (1994), 'Environmental Standards: Impact on SELA's Competitiveness and Market Access', in *Trade and Environment, the International Debate*, SELA/UNCTAD.

15. Nonnenberg, M.J.B. (1991), 'Ventagens Comparativas Reveladas, Custo Relativo de Fatores e Intensidade de Recursos Naturais: Resultados para o Brasil – 1980/88', IPEA, Texto para Discussao No 214, IPEA, Rio de Janeiro.

16. This section thus provides a preliminary indication of the incidence of environment-related measures, with different degrees of stringency, in Brazilian exports; it does not analyse their real impact on trade or export competitiveness.

17. In addition to phytosanitary measures, exports of shrimp are potentially affected by the threat of trade restrictions under United States' laws.

18. Exports to the OECD markets of timber and timber products are generally vulnerable to environment-related measures and consumer concerns related to deforestation, even though several studies have indicated that exports do not contribute significantly to deforestation in Brazil. The total value of exports of wood and wood products amounted to US$838 million in 1993. Of this, US$500 million could be classified as tropical timber, approximately 80 per cent of which goes to the OECD markets, in particular the European Union and the United States. Concerns over deforestation sometimes affect other sectors, such as pulp and paper, even though these sectors obtain their timber from planted rather than from natural tropical forests.

19. Multilaterally agreed targets to control the use of chlorofluorocarbons (CFCs) and other ozone-depleting substances (ODSs) have been negotiated in the framework of the Montreal Protocol on Substances that Deplete the Ozone Layer. The Multilateral Fund of the Montreal

Protocol provides financial assistance to developing countries to assist them in phasing out CFCs. A number of countries, in particular in the OECD area, have designed product policies using a range of policy instruments such as product standards, taxes and charges, eco-labelling, voluntary industry agreements and government procurement guidelines, to reduce the *use* of controlled substances and to complement policies aimed directly at the control of these substances. Thus, product policies and a shift in consumer preferences away from CFC-containing to CFC-free products imply that countries exporting to the OECD markets have to accelerate a shift to CFC-free technologies (independent from their own commitments under the Montreal Protocol) for products such as air-conditioners and refrigerators. This may, in principle, have some effects on trade, depending on the cost of technology switching. See UNCTAD, 'Newly emerging environmental, policies with a possible trade effect: a preliminary discussion' (TD/B/WG.6/9, 28 August 1995). In the case of Brazil, the value of exports of air-conditioners and refrigerators is relatively small. In addition, these products are exported mainly to other developing countries.

20. In 1993, exports recovered in line with an overall recovery of exports of manufactured products to the OECD markets.

21. According to Brazilian producers, consumers and environmental NGOs in the developed countries sometimes link Brazil's pulp and paper production with the deforestation issue, even though the sector obtains its raw materials from plantation forests.

22. The sector would need to invest another US$500 million to achieve the highest possible pollution abatement rates, taking into account the technological and commercial constraints of firms.

23. The National Steel Company (Compania Nacional de Siderurgia, CSN), located in the city of Volta Redonda, was privatized in 1993. CSN has scheduled to spend some US$100 million in environmental clean-up and health care projects. Some US$58 million will be used to compensate the city of Volta Redonda for environmental damage caused by operation of the CSN plant in this location. This sum will be used for environmental control programmes, clean-up of slums and health care programmes. Source: de Motta Veiga, P., M. Reis Castilho and G. Ferraz Filho (1995), 'Relationships between trade and the environment: the Brazilian case', study carried out under the joint UNCTAD/UNDP project on Reconciliation of Environmental and Trade Policies (INT/92/207), July.

24. Historically, the relationship between the footwear and leather sectors in Brazil has been characterized by a low level of cooperation. Companies in the footwear sector responded to this situation through verticalization (purchase of tanneries) and increased imports from neighbouring countries, in particular Argentina and Uruguay. In turn, this has prompted the leather sector to modernize, which could over the medium term streamline compliance with eco-labelling requirements.

25. Chemicals were supplied to the textile industry by a small group of transnational companies (TNCs) with plants in Brazil. Their production in Brazil depended on the characteristics of local demand, which was generally not very exigent with regard to quality and environmental criteria. This meant that chemical companies continued to produce in Brazil chemicals that were no longer used in Europe or the United States, or even banned in these countries.

26. FUNCEX also makes the point that establishing eco-labelling criteria for emissions contributing to environmental effects addressed by Multilateral Environmental Agreements (MEAs) may raise certain questions. In the first place, criteria which are established unilaterally by the eco-labelling programme of the importing country may not take account of internationally agreed targets set for different groups of countries. Such targets are negotiated by governments and tend to be set at the country level, taking into account the common but differentiated responsibilities of all countries. In the second place, whereas MEAs tend to set rights and obligations at the country level, eco-labels are granted to products. Commitments at the country level may not translate into uniform standards for all companies or production units in the country concerned. Indeed, through systems such as tradable permits and offsets,

governments and industry are trying to reduce emissions where such reduction is the most cost-effective. It would thus appear inappropriate to associate environmental disadvantages to unlabelled products originating in a country or region which as a whole complies with internationally agreed targets.

5. China

5.1 INTRODUCTION

A case study was conducted in China to examine the linkages between trade, the environment and development. The study was conducted by a research team consisting of Lu Ruishu, Xia Youfu, Li Jinchang, Zhang Jie and Lu Yaobing.[1]

The study examined the impact of environmental regulations on trade, as well as the effects of trade liberalization on the environment, focusing primarily on the impact at the firm level. Besides summarizing the results obtained by the study, this chapter incorporates other studies/research conducted on the subject of interlinkages between trade, the environment and development.

5.2 SPECIFIC PROBLEMS OF CHINA

General Trends in the Economy

China has been a largely planned economy, based on centrally planned targets of economic performance. The process of reform has been gradual and, until the beginning of the 1990s, recurrent debates about how to handle the balance between planning and the market had been a constant feature of China's liberalization. Since 1992, China's development goal has been shifting increasingly towards a 'socialist market', where markets play the primary resource allocation role.[2]

Although uneven, China's economic performance during the post-1978 reform period has been impressive. Enhanced trade performance and increased trade flows have been key to a high growth rate in the economy. As Table 5.1 indicates, the economy grew by as much as 13.4 per cent in 1993. However, inflation increased steadily over the period 1990 to 1994, leading to concerns of overheating in the economy. The current policy emphasis is therefore on macroeconomic stability, and on sustaining the prevailing rates of growth in trade and Foreign Direct Investment (FDI) flows, rather than on further accelerated growth.

However, the introduction of stringent environmental requirements in OECD markets could serve as a potential obstruction to sustained growth in trade. These issues are discussed in greater detail below.

Table 5.1   Economic indicators in China, 1990–1994

Economic indicators	1990	1991	1992	1993	1994
Real GNP growth (%)	4.1	8.2	13.0	13.4	11.8
Consumer Price Inflation (%)	3.1	3.4	6.4	14.7	24.1
Population (millions)	1139	1156	1173	1185	n/a
Exchange Rate (average-Rmb:$)	4.8	5.3	5.5	5.8	8.6

Source: The Economist Intelligence Unit, Country Report on China, 2nd quarter, 1995.

A large and expanding population has been another primary preoccupation in China. Estimated at 1.185 billion (see Table 5.1), China contains over 35 per cent of Asia's population. China has made remarkable progress in countering this challenge too. It has reduced the population growth rate with the help of an incentive system for effective family planning. The one-child campaign is still strictly implemented in urban areas, and other policies, such as emphasis on elevating the status of women, providing old-age security and maternal-child health services have been used to strengthen the programme.[3]

Composition of Exports and Imports

Reforms in China's trade regime have resulted in a boom, especially in the export sector. However, although trade grew over the period 1979–84, the most impressive growth has been observed since 1985. In 1983, total trade was US$43.6 billion, which increased sharply to almost US$70 billion within the next two years.[4]

Exports began to grow at the high rate of 20 per cent per annum. In fact, China's exports have grown faster than those of most other Newly Industrializing Economies (NIEs), such as Malaysia. Institutional decentralization, depreciation of the real effective exchange rate, and Foreign Direct Investment (FDI) all appear to have contributed to this strong export performance.[5]

Before the reform process began, China's exports comprised primarily crude petroleum and non-staple foods. Increased openness has resulted in a change in the structure of exports. Traditional export items, such as foods, agricultural raw materials and petroleum have declined progressively, from 52 per cent in 1975 to about 18 per cent in 1990.[6] On the other hand, the share of manufactured goods has increased from 46 per cent in 1965[7] to 82 per cent in 1994 (see Table 5.2). Most of this increase occurred between 1985 and 1990, when textiles and machinery began to be an increasingly important component of exports from China.

Table 5.2   China: total exports and imports by main commodity groups, 1985–1993

Commodity groups	1985	1990	1991	1992	1993	1994
Imports						
(in value)						
Total	39795.2	53345.1	63790.6	80585.3	103959.0	115613.0
Food and agr. prod.	4202.1	7719.5	7607.4	7649.3	6049.0	9960.4
Fuels	161.9	1272.2	2113.1	3609.5	5856.0	4080.2
Ores and metals	2104.8	1562.9	2089.8	3824.4	3988.8	3901.8
Manufactured goods of	31046.1	42506.0	51763.4	64908.2	87336.6	96924.1
which:						
Chemicals	4158.6	6669.9	9307.8	11083.8	9610.2	11969.0
Machinery and equipment	15498.3	21513.4	25664.9	30728.8	44468.2	51384.7
Textiles and clothing	1516.2	5474.1	7037.5	8189.5	8341.4	10146.1
(Shares in percentages)						
Food and agr. prod.	10.6	14.5	11.9	9.5	5.8	8.6
Fuels	0.4	2.4	3.3	4.5	5.6	3.5
Ores and metals	5.3	2.9	3.3	4.7	3.8	3.4
Manufactured goods	78.0	79.7	81.1	80.5	84.0	83.8
of which:						
Chemicals	10.4	12.5	14.6	13.8	9.2	10.4
Machinery and equipment	38.9	40.3	40.2	38.1	42.8	44.4
Textiles and clothing	3.8	10.3	11.0	10.2	8.0	8.8
Exports						
(in value)						
Total	25632.2	62091.4	71842.5	84940.1	91744.0	121006.3
Food and agr. prod.	5853.7	10048.8	10881.0	11577.4	11827.6	14768.1
Fuels	658.7	1323.3	1227.0	1436.7	1514.1	2246.0
Ores and metals	6634.7	5237.4	4753.7	4694.7	4112.0	4072.2
Manufactured goods of	9315.9	44310.6	54244.0	66794.9	73894.9	99555.9
which:		16888.6	20258.8	25415.9	27286.4	35736.0
Chemicals	4987.6	10833.0	13908.1	13172.6	15220.4	21830.4
Machinery and equipment	719.8	1444.4	2122.7	4373.4	5422.8	6430.0
Textiles and clothing	1280.5	3750.2	3848.9	4308.6	4576.2	6176.4
(Shares in percentages)						
Food and agr. prod.	22.8	16.2	15.1	13.6	12.9	12.2
Fuels	2.6	2.1	1.7	1.7	1.7	1.9
Ores and metals	25.9	8.4	6.6	5.5	4.5	3.4
Manufactured goods of	36.3	71.4	75.5	78.6	80.5	82.3
which:	19.5	27.2	28.2	29.9	29.7	29.5
Chemicals	2.8	17.4	19.4	15.5	16.6	18.0
Machinery and equipment	1.0	3.5	4.2	5.1	5.9	5.3
Textiles and clothing	5.0	6.0	5.4	5.1	5.0	5.1

Note: Food and agriculture products consist of SITC 0+1+2+4 less (27+28): Fuels consist of SITC 3; Ores & Metals consist of SITC 27+28+68; Manufactured products consist of SITC 5+6+7+8 less 68.

Source: UNCTAD, COMTRADE.

Manufactured goods have also increased in significance in the case of imports. During the period 1985–94, these have grown from 78 per cent to 84 per cent of all imports. This increase has occurred due to the growing need for machinery in the process of expanding export production. For instance, in 1992 exports based on imported materials accounted for close to 64 per cent of all of China's manufactured exports.[8]

5.3   DOMESTIC ENVIRONMENT AND ENVIRONMENTAL REGULATIONS

Growing industrialization and a growing population have heightened the environmental stress in China. This is manifested in the increased levels of air pollution, agricultural degradation, coastal degradation, and water quality and quantity problems.

As a result the government has begun to treat environmental pollution and ecological degradation as an important national concern. It is perceived by the government that environmental protection can only be carried out in light of the specific conditions of the nation's economic development, while also accepting that the pace of environmental protection must be commensurate with economic growth.[9]

Stringent measures have been established, with the aim of adhering to three basic principles: intensive management; prevention first; and the polluter pays principle. The process of environmental protection has required the intense involvement of central and local governments, as well as that of private enterprises.

China has promulgated and enforced the Environmental Protection Law, first implemented in 1979, and later amended in 1989.[10] Efforts have been made to gradually promote an integrated environmental system of unified management, with an increased level of coordination between different sectors and the agencies of environmental protection at varying levels. Many other laws pertain to marine protection, air, water and noise pollution prevention. In addition, an environment protection strategy has been adopted in industry, agriculture and other sectors, so that environmental protection is being integrated with expansion in production.

Emphasis is also placed on energy exploitation and technological innovation in areas of pollution control. The government has set up and reinforced environmental monitoring and information networks in an attempt to keep abreast of the latest developments in the quality of the environment and the state of pollution. Educating the masses on the issue of environmental protection has also become an important priority for the Chinese Government.

According to the study, the formulation and enforcement of strict environmental regulations has had a positive impact on several firms. Several examples are quoted where the government has urged exporters to invest in research and development in the area of environmental protection, along with investments in state of the art, environmentally friendly technology. The study emphasizes that adhering to environmentally friendly technologies and methods of production has led to improvements in the quality of exports, while also increasing the efficiency and profits of these firms. An example is provided in Box 5.1.

Box 5.1   The impact of cleaner production on a major firm

An example of the impact of cleaner production is the firm Zhouzhou, one of the world's largest producers of tungsten and tungsten intermediate products. Before 1984, this firm had engaged in environmentally damaging production. Upon censure from the government, the firm began employing environmentally friendly practices, integrating this aspect into their management strategy. Despite resource shortage, the firm invested close to US$4.3 million to reduce environmental pollution, while also controlling the emission of poisonous dust. Since then, no industrial deaths have been reported in this firm. At the same time, the firm's export value has increased, accounting for close to US$8 million in 1990, its reputation improving on account of the new practices established.

5.4   EFFECTS OF ENVIRONMENTAL REGULATIONS ON CHINA'S EXPORTS

5.4.1   Negative Effects of External Environmental Regulations

As stated in Section 5.2, China's exports have been growing dramatically in recent years. A large proportion of these exports go to developing countries, with Hong Kong, South Korea and Singapore accounting for almost 33 per cent of exports in 1994.[11] Close to half of all exports are directed at OECD countries. Among these, the main importers of Chinese goods are Japan and the United States, accounting for about 18 per cent of the export market each (see Table 5.3), whereas the European Union comprises about 12 per cent of exports from China.

Reconciling trade and the environment

Table 5.3   China: exports by commodity groups and markets, 1994 (millions of US dollars)

Commodity groups	World	OECD countries[1]				Developing countries
		Total	United States and Canada	European Union	Japan	
Total	121006.3	62199.3	21474.6	14607.7	21578.6	57875.3
Food & agriculture products	14768.1	7039.8	614.9	1503.8	4655.9	7540.8
Ores & metals	2246.0	969.5	160.9	240.6	534.1	1234.4
Manufactured goods	99555.9	51859.5	20300.6	12698.7	14671.3	47171.1
of which:						
Chemicals	6176.4	3049.3	636.1	1408.0	772.0	3016.7
Textiles & clothing	35736.0	16512.0	3960.1	3226.5	7497.8	19081.7
Machinery & equipment	21830.4	10967.1	4918.5	2856.4	2555.5	10712.0

Notes
See Table 1.
[1] OECD does not include Austria, Iceland, Mexico, Norway and Turkey.

Source: UNCTAD, COMTRADE.

Several products, for example fish products, are vulnerable to external environmental regulations as these are exported largely to the OECD countries (see Table 5.5). Tuna and shrimps are sensitive, since close to 90 per cent of their exports are directed at OECD countries. Shrimps are sensitive to regulations in Japan, to which more than half of shrimp production is exported. Japan's laws with respect to this product relate mostly to pesticide and antibiotic content. If traces of these elements are detected, the shrimps are likely to be rejected. Hence, if China does not adapt to these regulations, it may lose a large market for its shrimp exports.

Tuna is also potentially vulnerable to external regulations, since almost 90 per cent of China's exports go to the OECD countries. The United States, one of the major importers of tuna, has established the Marine Mammal Protection Act (MMPA), which stipulates the use of certain devices to protect dolphins, which are often caught along with the tuna. Since more than 30 per cent of China's tuna exports go to the United States, one can expect this product to be vulnerable to the MMPA, especially as China is attempting to capture a larger share of the tuna market.

The chemical residue content in agricultural products has affected the exports from this sector. Frozen chicken, for example, is losing its international market because exporters have been unable to eliminate the chemical residues present in this product. Vermicelli exports have been encountering problems too, on account of small worms being present in the vermicelli material.

While little information is available on manufactured goods, these too are potentially vulnerable since almost 85 per cent go to the OECD. The most important manufactured export from China, textiles, finds a significant market in the OECD with close to half of all textile exports being absorbed by this market in 1993.

Several external regulations could potentially harm textile exports to the OECD, for instance regulations pertaining to chemical content. In nations such as Germany, it is also expected that suppliers or traders will need to provide a declaration that certain chemicals are not present in their merchandise. The declaration will be binding, and will allow German importers to reject goods demonstrating traces of the chemicals without legal recourse for the Chinese textile exporter.

Although exact compliance costs of adapting to external environmental regulations are not available, these do seem to be a subject of concern in China, since textiles are such a major export item. If one examines the relative proportion of exports to the OECD versus developing countries, it appears that during the period 1985–1992, textiles exports have begun to focus increasingly on developing countries (see Table 5.4). This perhaps demonstrates a shift in the marketing of the product away from the nations with stricter environmental regulations.

Table 5.4   Textile exports from China, 1985–1992

Years	Exports to OECD (percentage of total)	Exports to developing countries (percentage of total)
1985	42.4	53.4
1986	48.2	46.3
1987	45.6	49.6
1988	39.0	60.8
1989	38.7	61.2
1990	37.5	62.4
1991	35.2	64.7
1992	36.3	63.5

Source: COMTRADE, UNCTAD.

Problems with the domestic environment are affecting textile exports. Serious water pollution has harmed the dyeing process, as a result of which only plain cloth can be exported. Water pollution also hampers the quality of the product. Therefore exporters are prevented from benefiting from higher value-added production and exports.

If dyes were to be used, several external environmental regulations would inhibit exports. For example, the use of certain dyestuffs, such as cobalt blue and sulphur black, has been banned in several OECD countries. Complying with stipulations regarding the toxic content of dyes may prove to be expensive and difficult.

The export of leather and leather products has also encountered some obstructions. The pentachlorophenol (PCP) content in Chinese leather has been considered too high in several European countries. Since over 60 per cent of leather products, and close to 78 per cent of footwear went to OECD countries (see Table 5.5) the limits on the use of PCP in leather has affected Chinese exports of this product. Leather exports are also potentially affected by regulations regarding dyestuffs.

Exporters face domestic environmental regulations in the light of local priorities and domestic environmental concerns. Therefore, the increase in costs owing to compliance with such regulations appears justifiable. However, if they also have to comply with external environmental Product and Process Methods (PPM) related regulations, their costs are likely to increase even further, thereby impacting on competitiveness, especially since most exports from China tend to compete in the OECD market largely on account of their low prices. This then raises the question of the desirability of enforcing such external regulations, especially since the laws established in China reflect their domestic environmental concerns.

Another conclusion which can be drawn from the above discussion is that China has, so far, been very successful at exporting light manufactured goods. The policy focus is shifting towards promoting higher-value-added products, exports of which will increasingly be required to bring in foreign exchange. Such a development strategy might face obstacles due to the increasing external regulations on higher-value-added products in OECD nations.

5.4.2   The Role of Small and Medium-sized Enterprises in Exports

The composition of China's exports has gradually shifted towards labour-intensive manufactures, growing from roughly one-third to as high as 75 per cent between 1965 and 1990.[12] With the growth in this form of exports, the SME (small and medium-sized enterprises) sector has also expanded.[13]

Today, SMEs in China are involved in providing a wide range of products and services in the export sector. In the case of machinery and electronic products, for example, one state alone has 313 factories engaged in export-oriented production. Some provinces have small enterprises established and

Table 5.5   *China, 1993: exports of products which are vulnerable to environmental requirements (millions of US dollars)*

Product	World	OECD[1]	USA	EU	Japan	Developing countries
Fish	1541.7	1240.5	204.3	50.9	954.5	300
Tuna	101.0	90.6	33.7	12.3	35.8	10.4
Shrimps and PR	453.7	398.4	116.8	23.7	245.7	55.3
Flowers	2.3	0.5	0.0	0.3	0.2	1.8
Fruits	1478.9	910.7	62.5	202.7	601.0	552.9
Beverages	231.2	25.8	8.2	6.2	9.5	200.4
Asbestos	11.9	2.2	0.1	0.4	1.7	9.1
Chemicals	258.2	140.0	23.9	65.8	42.8	115.4
Fertilizers	46.5	10.5	0.7	0.2	9.0	28.6
Paints	59.3	5.5	1.0	1.5	2.6	52.3
Cosmetics	121.9	21.6	6.5	4.1	9.3	93.4
Detergents	62.5	4.8	1.6	0.7	0.5	43.3
Lubrication	34.2	8.0	2.4	3.3	1.2	24.1
Insecticides	372.6	175.8	23.0	107.7	29.1	187.2
Plastics and products	178.5	1041.8	547.4	268.5	134.1	731.4
Tyres	199.4	49.1	27.3	12.6	2.2	140.2
Leather[2]	3357.6	2142.5	908.9	683.4	385.5	1211.7
Footware	5053.8	3920.5	2798.1	592.4	336.7	1126.4
Wood and products	764.5	523.0	90.0	110.6	304.1	239.8
Tropical timber	168.8	113.0	1.5	7.0	104.3	55.5
Paper & products	482.9	129.3	49.6	28.2	40.1	341.2
Textiles and products	25043.0	12079.7	3286.2	2576.2	4931.9	12865.5
Boilers	8.6	1.0	0.0	0.4	0.0	7.4
Air-conditioners	31.6	3.1	0.1	2.3	0.4	28.4
Freezers	56.0	25.5	12.9	10.4	1.5	28.6
Appliances	855.2	569.8	300.6	194.9	26.6	284.4
Batteries	300.3	46.8	15.9	25.4	1.0	251.9
Cars	393.2	134.3	104.5	9.4	15.7	244.5
Televisions	761.3	411.1	139.9	140.9	75.3	333.0
Lamps	267.1	110.3	39.4	55.1	6.6	155.5
Dyes and pigments	247.3	77.4	26.1	36.7	9.2	168.2
Total	43829.5	23811.1	8681.1	5181.2	7932.4	19766.6
Total (as percentage of all exports)	47.8	49.7	51.1	44.2	50.3	46.2

Notes
[1] OECD does not include Austria, Iceland, Mexico, Norway and Turkey.
[2] Leather does not include footware.

Source: UNCTAD, COMTRADE.

operated by larger enterprises. SMEs are involved in the processing of supplied materials, assembling supplied parts and in related trades. In one province there are over 18 000 such export-oriented SMEs.[14]

According to the study, the unchecked production of export-oriented rural SMEs has had a significant impact on the environment in China. These enterprises have been developing rapidly, and are characterized by a high average production density of pollution discharge and low levels of pollution control. Levels of industrial wastes are high, and only about 15 per cent of these are treated. The rate of eliminating smoke and dust from waste gas is only around 14 per cent. At the same time, many rural SMEs are mainly using old methods of coking, lead smelting and arsenic smelting, resulting in increased pollution.

So far, this segment of exporters have encountered few domestic environmental regulations. However, the government is attempting to include these enterprises in the process of cleaning up the domestic environment. Regulating SMEs may prove to be expensive, as they may only be able to pay part of the cost. If SMEs also have to adhere to external environmental regulations then their competitiveness on the international market may be affected.

Insufficient information prevents SMEs from making long- or even medium-term marketing plans. SMEs attempt to adjust to the prevailing environmental regulations in external markets[15] and are vulnerable to changes in regulations.

Another area of difficulty is the low level of technology available to many Chinese SMEs. According to the study, a large number of products exported by SMEs are unable to retain their market on account of their inability to meet environmental and health standards. A case in point is the production of light industrial goods and food products where market access problems have occurred due to their inability to meet the safety and hygiene standards required by importing countries.

5.4.3   Opportunities Offered by Emerging Environmental Regulations

China is attempting to develop a niche in the market for green foods. Since 1990, efforts have been made to formulate regulations for quality supervision and management. Successful experiments have also been undertaken in selling green foods within the country, to test the product for the external market, and the country has now begun to export green foods on the international market. According to the study, green foods have a price premium of 5 to 10 per cent, and efforts are being made to capture this premium as much as possible.

Another area where opportunities exist in this context is the export of environmentally friendly technologies. These are beginning to find a market in developing countries, where they are considered convenient, easy to use, and economical. For instance, Chinese water treatment equipment and noise control equipment have been exported to Pakistan, India, Malaysia, Indonesia and Thailand. The market for such products is large and growing, and there still exists the possibility of further expansion for Chinese exports. Countries are also beginning to show an interest in environmentally friendly equipment and inputs in agriculture and forestry management.

5.5   MULTILATERAL ENVIRONMENTAL AGREEMENTS

5.5.1   The Montreal Protocol

China has signed the Montreal Protocol. The agreement is of great significance to China because, unlike most developing countries, it is a producer of chlorofluorocarbons (CFCs). It also produces halons and methyl chloroform, and uses methyl bromide, mainly for commodity treatment of in-country stocks of grains, pulses and timber.[16]

The foam sector is the largest user in China of ozone-depleting substances (ODSs), accounting for 37 per cent of total consumption, and use is projected to grow at 6 per cent per annum if unchecked. Another important user of ODSs, the refrigeration and air-conditioning sector, is projected to have an unconstrained growth rate of 8 per cent per annum.[17]

Within China, a policy framework has been established to encourage the use of substitute technologies. For instance, a permit and quota system has been established, according to which government permission will be required for ODS manufacture, based on environmental impact assessment. In addition, incentives and taxes have been introduced to encourage the development of domestically applicable technologies.

In some cases, these have yielded success. For instance, effective phosphine-based substitutes are being used as an alternative to methyl bromide. At the firm level too, some progress has been made. For instance, one refrigerator factory has made improvements in foaming and freezing agents. As a result the freon content has been reduced to almost half of its original level, and exports to the European Union have increased.

In fact information on exports of refrigerators and freezers indicates that exports from China have been consistently on the rise since 1987 (see Table 5.6). Exports to OECD countries have been growing especially rapidly. However, this rise in exports is perhaps not so much on account of the CFC-free technology being introduced as the low prices offered by Chinese exporters of refrigerators and freezers. According to the study, adjustment to the Montreal Protocol remains a problem for most producers. The enterprises often do not have the ability to invest in research and development to acquire new ODS-free technology.

Table 5.6   China's refrigerator exports, 1987–1994

Year	Value (in million US$)	Exports to OECD countries	Exports to developing countries
1987	4.3	0.1	4.0
1988	15.8	0.7	15.0
1989	15.9	4.9	10.7
1990	18.7	6.3	12.2
1991	27.7	14.1	12.3
1992	47.3	18.8	27.5
1993	56.0	25.5	28.6
1994	59.0	27.0	30.5

Source: COMTRADE, UNCTAD.

Another challenge to phasing out ODSs is the growing imports of CFCs and HCFCs to China. During the period 1989–93 the average annual growth rate of imports of ODSs to China was close to 30 per cent.[18] According to the study, foreign investors, particularly those from Hong Kong, have been shifting their CFC-based production to one province in China. It was found that more than 20 enterprises in this province have been using significant quantities of CFCs and that during the period 1988–90 these enterprises have expanded their operations considerably in the region.

It has been estimated that the cost of ODS phase-out in China will be approximately US$1.4 billion.[19] China is also seeking US$ 660 million as compensation for the higher cost of substitute refrigerants.[20] In fact, it has agreed to speed up its phase-out of ODSs provided sufficient funds and appropriate cost-effective technologies are transferred in accordance with the provisions of the Protocol.

5.5.2   The Basel Convention

China is also a signatory to the Basel Convention on the movement of hazardous wastes. It has totally prohibited the import of hazardous wastes for disposal within the area of its national jurisdiction. According to the study, the unchecked import of harmful and toxic wastes has affected the environment and the health of a large number of people. The garbage imported includes old electrical equipment and cables, old ships, and scrap iron (see Table 5.7).

As for the sources of the imported wastes, over 53 per cent comes from a small number of developed countries. For example, the United Kingdom exported to China approximately 1353 tons of hazardous wastes in 1991, 7315 tons in

1992, and 4186 tons in 1993. Other significant exporters of waste to China include Japan, the United States and Hong Kong (see Table 5.8).

Table 5.7   Imports of some prohibited wastes into China, 1992–1993

Type of waste	Quantity (in 10000 tons)	Value (in US$10000)
Slag, dross and other scrap	7.3	29.7
Ash and slag of metals and their chemical components	4.8	123.1
Other slag and mine ash	18.4	1890.6
Wastes of leather	5.0	2255.6
Wasted thread	1.9	161.3

Source: Youfu, 1995.[21]

Table 5.8   The chief sources of imported wastes into China, 1993

Country	Quantity (percentage of total)	Value (percentage of total)
Japan	26.98	23.41
USA	14.24	16.59
Hong Kong	10.69	7.49
Russia	8.30	7.93
Germany	3.59	3.32
United Kingdom	1.81	1.93
Netherlands	1.61	1.74
Singapore	1.29	4.14
Italy	0.98	0.88

Source: Youfou, 1995.[22]

Several examples of the import of hazardous wastes are provided by the study. In early 1989, an American company attempted to seek stacking areas for its domestic waste in Shanghai, Ningbo, Haikou and other coastal cities. The government has taken a strong stand and refused permission to such applications.

Old ships have also been imported into China for dismantling purposes. These come primarily from the United States, Japan, Western Europe and Hong Kong and many contain harmful animal and plant residues. The dismantling process has also proved environmentally unfriendly. It generally leads to wastes like iron rust, electric welding, and greasy dirt, all of which heavily pollute the beaches.

It was reported to the Basel Secretariat that in September 1993 over 1200 tons of hazardous waste from the Republic of Korea entered a Chinese port without obtaining prior permission from the National Environmental Protection Agency of China. Through negotiations with Korea, the waste was sent back, but it took close to six months for this to be done,[23] thus harming the environment during the interim period.

In 1991, the government issued a notification of stricter control on the transfer of harmful waste materials into China, and tighter quarantine laws. There have also been regulations for the prevention of pollution caused by ship dismantling. Until now, however, the country has been unable to enforce quarantine effectively. Some institutions exist which have limited expertise in the assessment of disposal capabilities, although they are far from being adequately equipped to handle the quantity of waste which enters the country.

5.6   THE IMPACT OF ECONOMIC REFORM ON THE ENVIRONMENT

5.6.1   The Impact of Trade Liberalization

As Section 5.2 indicates, China's exports have grown rapidly over the last fifteen years. The reform process has had both positive and negative impacts on the environment in China. The significant contribution of liberalization has been through the dissemination of technology and benefits accruing to SMEs due to joint ventures.

Increased exports have enabled the country to earn enough foreign exchange to import environmentally friendly technology. An example of the environment benefiting from increased exports is the Shengyang Organic Chemical Plant, where increased foreign exchange earnings permitted the firm to invest in pollution control devices so that it could recycle its acid- and phenol-laden waste water. At the same time the plant's productivity increased, resulting in increased profits.

Greater exposure to environmentally friendly technology in OECD markets has also been conducive to cleaner methods of production. Increased imports have also had some beneficial impacts on the environment. China's import of environmentally friendly equipment and technology has been increasing alongside the import of more efficient power plants, mining machinery, metallurgical and casting equipment, and light industrial machinery. Such imports have aimed to reduce raw material and energy consumption, while also reducing the pollution level caused during production. The import of environmentally sensitive products, such as paper, pulp, and timber have had a beneficial impact on the environment in China, reducing the pollution and deforestation levels.

Increased demand for agricultural exports has led to the application of methods such as crop rotation in order to increase the productivity of agricultural land. This also enhances the ecological balance of the country. Examples of such an improvement have been noticed in the production of phoenix trees and grains, and in that of mushrooms and bamboo. For instance, rotating mushrooms with bamboo has increased the production of bamboo, while also increasing the productivity and export volumes of mushrooms.

Another area where economic liberalization has been beneficial to the environment is in some rural SMEs. There are several examples of export-oriented enterprises where rural-based suppliers have cooperated with the manufacturing units to reduce pollution with the help of more efficient and environmentally friendly technology provided by the latter. As a result, some SMEs were benefiting from the increased export activity of the country. An examples is where there was found to be coordination between plants to set up production lines in a way that substantially reduced pollution while enhancing productivity. The Dyestuff Plant in the Yuhong District of Shengyang jointly with the Shengyang Paint Plant transformed three workshops into a production line in 1987. This has almost eliminated the previously severe pollution, increased profits and allowed entry into international markets, leading to increased export earnings.

However, the detrimental effects of the expansion of liberalization seem to be even more significant. Negative impacts on the environment have been felt principally due to loss of biodiversity and the depletion of natural resources.

The unchecked export of wild animals has affected biodiversity in China. In the case of frog legs, for instance, the increase in exports has led to a proliferation of insect pests, affecting several crops, which in turn has required the extensive use of pesticide causing an increase in pesticide residues in products. Similar effects have been found in the case of snake and weasel skin exports, where the killing of these animals has resulted in the uncontrolled growth of the mouse population.

Productivity levels in wild animal related activities can be very low resulting in the killing of a large number of animals in order to earn little foreign exchange. For example, one ton of wild fowl and game requires about 1500 hares, or 1000 pheasants. During 1981–85, 340 tons of wild fowl and game were processed in the Baoji District of Shanxi Province earning only $0.7 million in foreign exchange.

The export of wild plants has also had an impact on the environment in China. One example is 'facai', which grows on the border of deserts and has an important sand fixation role. It has found a large export market in the post-liberalization era and the unchecked uprooting of this plant has led to serious desertification of over 200 km^2 around Erlianhaote City. In other cases increased exports have resulted in rapid reduction and even extinction of species. Increasing licorice root production in Inner Mongolia, Xinjiang and Ningxia has resulted in damage to grassland and a reduction in reserves to 40 per cent of the 1983 level. Rare medicinal herbs have been damaged even more seriously with species such as ginseng, eucommia ulmoides and gastrodia elata being pushed to the brink of extinction. The list of 354 wild plants which are on the verge of extinction in China includes over 100 species which have a medicinal value.

Increased demand for mineral resources has also led to their excessive extraction, thereby harming the natural resource level in the country. Typical cases are tungsten ores, antimony, tin and molybdenum, where expanding exports have led to serious depletion of these natural resources. The exploitation of one ton of mineral ores results in the loss of 1400 tons of surface soil in some parts of the country such as the southern part of Jiangxi. The concentration and refinement of metals produce toxicants which are detrimental to the environment. The exploitation of rare ores, mercury, and rare metals (especially arsenic and cadmium) has resulted in serious pollution of the environment by toxicant or radioactive by-products.

5.6.2   The Impact of FDI on the Environment

As in the case of export growth, the impact of FDI on the environment has been both positive and negative. In the Chinese context, it has been found that the investment share of firms in environment protection was higher in the case of FDI enterprises (2.27 per cent) than for domestic enterprises (0.94 per cent). In addition, the former tend to use more efficient technology and equipment, thereby reducing the consumption of energy and raw materials.

It was found, for example, that the output value as a proportion of energy consumption is 0.73 tons per 10 000 yuan for foreign enterprises, whereas it is 0.351 tons per 10 000 yuan for their Chinese counterparts. In the case of water consumption, it was found that the rate of recycling waste water was about 29 per cent for domestic firms, while it was over 68 per cent for the FDI enterprises. At the same time, some foreign firms have also invested in green foods and other environmentally friendly products, such as recyclable plastics.

However, under the pressure of the rising cost of environmental protection in their parent country, or in other developed countries, some foreign firms have diverted their highly polluting industries to China, thereby affecting the Chinese environment. Industries related to the pesticide DDT, a long-cycle toxic pesticide, and asbestos are only two of the environmentally unfriendly products produced by foreign firms in China. In 1991, for example, over 36 per cent of all FDI was invested in highly polluting industries[24] including the printing, dyeing and electroplating industries (see Table 5.9).

Table 5.9   Foreign investment in highly polluting industries in China

Industry	1991 Quantity	Value	1992 Quantity	Value
Printing and dyeing	188	18484	635	80558
Electroplating	38	2287	62	11082
Hazardous waste*	69	5381	195	14968
Controlled matters **	171	31078	1148	101411

Notes
* Refers to foreign firms which registered to import wastes.
** The production and consumption of controlled matters are prohibited by developed countries after 1996.

Source: Youfou, 1995.[25]

Besides a heavy concentration of investments in polluting sectors, much of foreign investment is on such a small scale that environmental management becomes very difficult. This is especially true since many foreign investors set up joint ventures with China's township factories, which are largely unaffected by the enforcement of environmental regulations.[26]

While it is true that some foreign firms tend to have superior technology, it has been found that the equipment used is often obsolete, and leads to high energy consumption and heavy pollution. Foreign firms sometimes have difficulties meeting the domestic requirements in terms of environmental protection. The machines can sometimes be so old that they are strictly prohibited in the parent company.[27] A survey of foreign firms in the special economic zone of Guandong reveals that only 28.4 per cent of these enterprises have the facilities to defend against dust and toxins.[28]

5.7   CONCLUSIONS AND RECOMMENDATIONS

5.7.1   Conclusions

China is an example of a nation where the impacts of environmental degradation on the economy are already being felt. Besides loss in productivity from the soil, the country has experienced severe water shortage as well as rapidly rising urbanization. It would appear that the trade-off between high growth rates in the economy and environmental protection are already being experienced.

While elaborate mechanisms, involving local and central governments, have been established to reduce pollution on a polluter pays basis, pollution, poor infrastructure in basic environmental protection and heavy population pressure continue to remain major problems for China.

As well as adhering to domestic regulations on environmental protection, firms in the export market are now having to adhere to those established by the importing markets. Their prices will rise as a result, and may lead to a loss in competitiveness among exporters. This is especially the case in textile, fish and agricultural products, where China was found to be vulnerable to external environmental regulations. This takes on a greater significance because much of the competitiveness among Chinese exports is derived from the low prices of the products.

Multilateral Environmental Agreements, in particular, the Montreal Protocol and the Basel Convention, have been of concern to China. As a result of the Montreal Protocol, most exporters are having difficulties in switching to non-ODS-based production despite efforts to aid technological adaptation. At the same time, problems have been encountered with the migration of ODS-using firms from Hong Kong.

The Basel Convention has also been of significance to China. Imports of hazardous wastes have been harmful for the environment and the health of the Chinese. While strict regulations have been established in the context of the import of hazardous wastes, the actual monitoring has not been entirely effective due to the lack of capacity in this area.

Trade liberalization has led to both positive and negative impacts on the environment in China. On the positive side, it provides export firms with a greater financial ability to invest in environmentally sound technologies, while also exposing them to environmentally friendly methods of production. The liberalization of imports has reinforced this aspect, since eco-friendly technologies can now be imported with greater ease. The importing of products such as pulp and paper has eased some of the pressure on local resources.

On the negative side, liberalization has also led to the production of eco-unfriendly products for export, which have resulted in loss of biodiversity and a depletion of the country's natural resources.

The impact of FDI on the environment has also been both positive and negative. The presence of foreign firms has led to the dissemination of environmentally friendly technology and methods of production. However, some of these firms have used obsolete and inefficient machinery which has harmed the environment in China. Several cases have been reported where highly polluting production has been carried out by foreign firms in the post-liberalization era.

5.7.2 Recommendations

Efforts should be made to study the experience of exporters to derive an understanding of the trade barriers arising from external environmental regulations. The government should then follow policies with a more holistic approach, including environmental considerations. It has been suggested that the best approach would be to eliminate pollution in the course of production, rather than following end-of-pipe methods, which are less effective and may also be more expensive.

In the context of the international market, green products should be promoted in a proactive manner. This is especially true for the agriculture sector, where Chinese enterprises have not yet been able to capture the price premiums associated with environmentally friendly production. Such an approach would also help to upgrade the hygiene level in production for domestic use.

The government should concentrate on a few firms where environmental protection and the development of green products can be the focus. Here, advanced technology and production methods should be fostered so that production for the world market can be in accordance with external regulations. In the medium term, such a model could be replicated in small and medium-sized firms, in areas where the external regulations would be compatible with domestic environmental priorities.

Another area where efforts should be concentrated is the development of environmentally friendly technologies. Besides promoting the growth of eco-friendly production, these could also be exported to developing countries, where a substantial market exists for low-cost environmentally friendly technology. In the short run, efforts must be made to promote environmentally friendly technologies on the international market.

In order to protect the domestic environment, production and export of highly polluting products must be strictly limited. Efforts should be aimed at upgrading technology and improving production efficiency so that the domestic environment does not suffer on account of export growth. Where an export harms domestic biodiversity, the government should limit these exports and, if possible, ban them.

Attempts should also be made to base production on waste recycling. Some firms in China have succeeded in producing sodium fluosilicate from waste pluori gas, which has been used for domestic consumption as well as for export purposes. A model should be made of such successful efforts so that these can be replicated on a larger scale.

It is important to encourage the import of advanced technology and environmentally friendly technology, with a view to reducing energy and raw material consumption while also reducing the pollution level in the country.

On the other hand, imports should be discouraged when they pertain to hazardous wastes. Building infrastructure and the ability of personnel to identify and monitor the import of hazardous wastes is essential. In this regard, the international community should assist by providing a high level of training so that monitoring and quarantine issues can be handled effectively in China.

Similarly, with respect to FDI, authorization should be provided for investment only after it has been established that the enterprise will carry out low pollution activities. It has also been suggested that the government should press for a letter of responsibility which would encourage foreign firms to minimize their pollution levels in China. Alongside this, further incentives should be provided to those firms whose production or technology can be a source of learning for domestic firms in the area of environmental protection.

Serious law enforcement is another issue requiring urgent attention in China. It may be useful to set up a legal system, involving a police force, courts for enforcing environmentally oriented regulations, and so on. This would also involve widespread information dissemination in which local governments could coordinate with central government for greater effectiveness.

On the international front, technical assistance should be provided to nations such as China for environment protection and monitoring the import of hazardous wastes. It is also necessary to increase research aimed at counteracting the environmental pollution of township enterprises, including export-oriented enterprises and those with foreign firm involvement.

It is also essential for China that there be a strengthening of the exchange of environmental protection technologies between developing countries. To this end, an environmentally sound technology development fund should be established.

NOTES

1. Ruishu, L., X. Youfou, L. Jinchang, Z. Jie and L. Yaobing (1993), 'Environmental protection and foreign trade development in China', study prepared for the United Nations Conference on Trade and Development, Geneva.

2. This information is based on The World Bank (1993), 'China updating economic memorandum: managing rapid growth and transition', Report No. 11932-CHA, 30 June.

3. World Resources Institute (WRI) (1995), *World Resources: People and the Environment*, New York: Oxford University Press.

4. This information is based on The World Bank (1993), 'China foreign trade reform: meeting the challenge of the 1990s', Report No 11568-CHA, 18 June.

5. *Ibid.*

6. *Ibid.*

7. *Ibid.*

8. *Ibid.*

9. *National Report of the People's Republic of China on Environment and Development* (1992), China Environmental Science Press.

10. *Ibid.*

11. Economist Intelligence Unit (1995), '*Country Report on China*', 2nd Quarter, London.

12. *Ibid.*

13. Economic and Social Commission for Asia and the Pacific (ESCAP) (1995), '*Expansion of Manufactured Exports from SMEs in ESCAP Region*', Vol.II: National Studies, ESCAP, New York. Most of the information on SMEs is based on this report.

14. *Ibid.*

15. ESCAP, op.cit.

16. United Nations Environment Programme (1995), '*Technology and Economic Assessment Panel: Report to the Parties*', Nairobi, Kenya.

17. The Montreal Secretariat (1995), *Summary of China's Country Programme for the Phaseout of ODS*, Montreal.

18. United Nations Conference on Trade and Development (UNCTAD) (1995) 'The policy debate on trade, environment and development', UNCTAD, TD/B/WG.6/10/Add.1.

19. The Montreal Secretariat (1995), op.cit.

20. WRI (1995), op.cit.

21. Youfou, X. (1995), 'Study on China's control measures to the transfer of foreign wastes and pollution intensive industries through trade and investment', paper prepared for the Working Group on Trade and Environment, Winnipeg, Canada.

22. *Ibid.*

23. United Nations Environment Programme (1995), 'Note by the secretariat for the third meeting of the Conference of the Parties to the Basel Convention', Geneva, September.

24. Youfou (1995), op.cit.

25. *Ibid.*

26. *Ibid.*

27. *Ibid.*

28. *Ibid.*

6. Colombia

6.1 INTRODUCTION

A study on trade and environment linkages in Colombia was completed in 1994. The study, funded by the Government of Colombia, was conducted by a small research team, working under the coordination of the National Planning Department. Building on the study, a number of other empirical studies were subsequently carried out in Colombia under UNCTAD's programme of technical cooperation in the field of trade and environment. These studies, which provide a first appraisal of the theme Trade and the Environment from Colombia's perspective, cover a large range of issues. This chapter provides a synthesis of the following studies:

(a) D. Gaviria, R. Gomez, L. Ho and A. Soto, *'Reconciliation of Trade and Environment Policies: the Case Study of Colombia'*. National Planning Office, Universidad Externado de Colombia and Ministry of Foreign Trade, Bogotá, May 1994.

(b) L. Ho, D. Gaviria, X. Barrera and R. Sánchez, *'The Potential Impact of European Union Eco-labelling Programme on Colombian textile exports'*. Paper prepared for the UNCTAD seminar on Eco-labelling and International Trade, Geneva, 28–29 June 1994.

(c) E. Uribe and Y. Medina, *'La Pequeña y mediana industria y su relación con las regulaciones y las instituciones ambientales en Colombia'*. Bogotá, June 1995.

Trade and environment linkages in Colombia should be considered in the context of developments in domestic policies as well as of international developments. With regard to domestic policies, since the beginning of the 1990s, Colombia has embarked upon a process of economic liberalization. Greater openness is expected to intensify linkages between external and domestic environmental policies and the international competitiveness of Colombia's industry. Of key importance to the study are the effects of domestic and external environmental policies, standards and regulations on the international competitiveness of Colombia's exports and on its development process.

During the economic liberalization process, economic growth has been based principally on rapidly increasing imports and production of non-tradable goods. Thus, the Colombian study pays considerable attention to the possible links between import liberalization and the environment. Secondly, Colombia is strengthening its environmental policies and institutions. Currently, environmental regulations in Colombia are generally quite stringent, but enforcement is difficult. One of the key issues in environmental policy-making in Colombia is the issue of the balance between achieving a higher level of enforcement of environmental laws and maintaining export competitiveness. To do this, policy-makers must ensure that environmental regulations becomes better attuned to local environmental and developmental conditions and priorities while manufacturers respond to changes in external environmental regulations.

As for international developments, the implementation of the results of the Uruguay Round provides Colombia with improved access to developed country markets through the reduction of tariff and non-tariff obstacles to trade. A key question is whether environmental requirements could potentially erode gains in market access (for example, in products such as fruit and textiles). With regard to international environmental issues, factors such as the trade and competitiveness effects of rights and obligations under Multilateral Environmental Agreements, such as the Montreal Protocol on Substances that Deplete the Ozone Layer or measures which may be contemplated under the Framework Convention on Climate Change, are relevant and are addressed in this chapter.

This chapter also addresses structural factors which are of particular interest in the context of the development problem, such as the special circumstances of small and medium-size enterprises and the expansion of production of primary products, which are produced almost entirely for export.

6.2 STRUCTURE OF INTERNATIONAL TRADE

In recent years, Colombia's foreign trade has grown considerably, largely as a result of an economic liberalization process initiated in the late 1980s. A large share of exports goes to OECD countries, the United States being the most important export market. However, regional markets such as the Andean Group and the recently consolidated G-3 (Colombia, Mexico and Venezuela) represent an important trade potential and are indeed growing in importance. Venezuela is Colombia's second largest export market (representing 10 per cent of the value of total exports in 1993).

Colombia's exports are also becoming increasingly diversified in terms of product composition. The share of food and other agricultural products in total exports decreased from 76.5 per cent in 1980 to 34.4 per cent in 1993, while that of manufactured products went up from 19.6 to 39.8 per cent over the same period (see Table 6.1). There was a sharp increase in the exports of fuels (in particular oil and gas) in the 1980s.

Table 6.1   Colombia: total exports and imports by main commodity groups, 1975–1993 (millions of US dollars)

Commodity groups	1975	1980	1985	1990	1991	1992	1993
Imports							
(in value)							
Total	1494.8	4662.6	4130.7	5588.5	4967.0	6683.9	9840.8
Foods and agr. products	203.7	678.4	554.4	592.9	507.3	858.2	996.1
Fuels	15.3	567.7	484.4	337.3	300.8	365.9	377.3
Ores and metals	54.1	147.0	129.0	193.4	193.0	247.6	269.8
Manufactured goods	1214.0	3236.8	2872.2	4278.7	3806.7	4968.6	7489.2
(share in percentages)							
Total	100.0	100.0	100.0	100.0	100.0	100.0	100.0
Foods and agr. products	13.6	14.6	13.4	10.6	10.2	12.8	10.1
Fuels	1.0	12.2	11.7	6.0	6.1	5.5	3.8
Ores and metals	3.6	3.2	3.1	3.5	3.9	3.7	2.7
Manufactured goods	81.2	69.4	69.5	76.6	76.6	74.3	76.1
Exports							
(in value)							
Total	1646.9	3945.0	3551.9	6765.0	7268.6	6915.8	7454.7
Foods and agr. products	1050.5	3019.7	2302.0	2513.4	2735.4	2724.7	2562.5
Fuels	105.6	112.4	578.3	2495.8	2091.0	1969.0	1888.3
Ores and metals	3.2	9.3	14.7	11.4	20.2	17.7	30.9
Manufactured goods	305.5	775.1	601.2	1698.9	2421.2	2202.9	2970.2
(share in percentages)							
Total	100.0	100.0	100.0	100.0	100.0	100.0	100.0
Foods and agr. products	71.7	76.5	64.8	37.2	37.6	39.4	34.4
Fuels	7.2	2.8	16.3	36.9	28.8	28.5	25.3
Ores and metals	0.2	0.2	0.4	0.2	0.3	0.3	0.4
Manufactured goods	20.9	19.6	16.9	25.1	33.3	31.9	39.8

Note: For analytical purposes and/or incomplete time series, the following countries are not included in the group of OECD countries: Austria, Iceland, Mexico, Norway and Turkey.

Source: UNCTAD, based on COMTRADE.

With trade liberalization, imports have been increasing rapidly, the industrial sector being the principal importer. Imports of agricultural, fisheries and forestry products have also increased significantly.

6.3 DOMESTIC ENVIRONMENTAL POLICY-MAKING

Although Colombia covers less than 1 per cent of the earth's land surface, it is very rich in natural resources and possesses 10 per cent of the world's species (flora and fauna). In fact, Colombia is second only to Brazil in terms of the total number of species living within its borders.

Colombia possesses large hydrological resources. The country's aquatic resources are highly valuable as a source for food, energy and wildlife. However, 40 per cent of the population has no access to a supply of water for domestic use.[1] The environmental infrastructure for the treatment of waste water and solid waste is insufficient. The rapid process of urbanization and industrialization has been one of the many causes of environmental deterioration in Colombia.[2]

6.3.1 Environmental Legislation in Colombia

Environmental policies, standards and institutions in Colombia are being strengthened, in particular through Law 99 of 1993 which, *inter alia*, created the Ministry of the Environment and the 'National Environmental System'. Law 99 also called for the liquidation of the Colombian Institute of Renewable Natural Resources and Environmental Resources (INDIRENA), decentralization of environmental policies through the restructuring of the Autonomous Regional Corporations and the creation of new environmental authorities in cities of over one million inhabitants, public participation, as well as the creation of sources of financing for environmental management. As a result of these reforms, environmental policy-making is going through a period of transition.

Environmental regulations in Colombia are generally based on stringent standards, but enforcement is difficult. A general problem is that most relevant environmental regulations are based on foreign standards, which ignore the economic, social and environmental conditions of Colombia. New environmental standards are being developed on the basis of a comprehensive study undertaken over a period of several years.

6.3.2 Environmental Legislation and Competitiveness

In order to assess Colombian industry's awareness of domestic and external environmental requirements, as well as its ability to comply with them, a questionnaire was sent to exporters and business associations from different types of industry.[3] The research team received 74 answers. More than 100 additional interviews were conducted.

The survey revealed that awareness about environmental requirements emerged to a greater extent from domestic rather than from external environmental requirements. About one-third of the respondents had experience with domestic environmental requirements and pressures. Of these, 24 per cent felt that compliance with domestic environmental standards affected their competitiveness positively, and only 4 per cent said such requirements affected their competitiveness negatively (the remainder did not know). Half of the respondents thought that the recent creation of the Colombian Ministry of the Environment[4] and the consolidation of national environmental policies, norms and institutions would affect their competitiveness positively (8 per cent thought these factors would affect them negatively and 38 per cent did not know).

6.4   ECONOMIC IMPACT OF EXTERNAL ENVIRONMENTAL POLICIES, STANDARDS AND REGULATIONS ON COLOMBIAN EXPORTS

This chapter analyses the significance for Colombian exports of existing external environmental requirements in general, based on the survey mentioned above, which covers various sectors. In addition, it examines the economic effects of specific environmental policy measures, such as the German Packaging Ordinance, eco-labelling programmes, and United States trade measures related to tuna and shrimps. It also reflects on trading opportunities for environment-friendly products.

Given the product composition and geographical distribution of Colombian exports (see Table 6.2), only a relatively small proportion of exports are already affected by environmental requirements in the OECD markets. Environmental requirements in sectors which constitute Colombia's traditional exports, such as coffee, are scarce or non-existent. Non-traditional exports to European countries, where new environmental requirements are emerging in sectors such as textiles, are relatively small. Indeed, in 1993 only around 9 per cent of the exports of manufactured products went to the European Union (this share was less than 6 per cent in the case of textiles and only 11 per cent for leather and leather products). A large share of Colombian exports goes to the United States (40 per cent of the value of total exports in 1993) and Central and South American markets. To a large extent this explains why two-thirds of the respondents to the survey conducted among industries and industry associations were not aware of environmental requirements emerging from export markets.

However, the survey indicated that in specific sectors, such as fruit, external environmental policies, standards and regulations had at times resulted in a more significant adverse impact on the competitiveness of firms. Fruit exports, representing US$463 million in 1993, had to comply with environmentally related requirements regarding inputs and packaging, and some exporters reported associated cost increases, ranging from 1 to 15 per cent. Fruit exporters were concerned that environmental standards were becoming more stringent, especially those in the United States (around 86 per cent of Colombia's fruit exports went to this market in 1993), for example, with regard to the use of pesticides.

Table 6.2   Colombia: exports by commodity groups and markets, 1993 (millions of US dollars)

Commodity groups	World	Selected OECD countries Total	United States and Canada	European Union	Japan	Developing countries
Total	7 454.7	5 143.0	3 074.8	1 660.3	238.0	2 157.3
Food and agricultural products	2 562.5	2 157.7	898.0	1 049.2	113.2	322.2
Food	2 134.6	1 779.0	592.4	984.5	111.9	278.6
Agricultural raw materials	427.9	378.7	305.7	64.6	1.3	43.5
Fuels	1 888.3	1 550.5	1 184.0	353.7	7.7	303.4
Ores and metals	30.9	20.7	16.8	0.3	3.6	10.2
Manufactured goods	2 970.2	1 412.0	974.1	256.9	113.4	1 520.8
Chemicals	419.8	43.7	30.2	11.3	0.1	373.2
Textiles and clothing	766.5	420.1	354.5	62.1	..	344.5
Leather	85.3	43.6	24.8	18.3	0.4	37.1
Footwear	78.6	28.9	22.3	5.2	1.1	49.6
Machinery and equipment	438.5	205.7	190.3	10.9	0.8	211.0
Other manufactured products	1 181.5	670.0	352.0	149.1	111.0	505.4

Note: For analytical purposes and/or incomplete time series, the following countries are not included in the group of OECD countries: Austria, Iceland, Mexico, Norway and Turkey.

Source: UNCTAD, based on COMTRADE.

Exports of fish and crustaceans are also vulnerable to external environmental regulations. For example, exports of tuna and shrimp are vulnerable to unilateral trade actions under United States environmental laws. Concern has also been expressed about the possible effects of eco-labelling initiatives in sectors such as flowers, as well as campaigns by certain non-governmental organizations (NGOs) concerning sectors such as coal and flowers. While these campaigns may have had little effects on sales, the Colombian Association of Flower Growers (ASCOFLORES) was reportedly worried that such campaigns might put pressures on European governments not to prolong certain tariff preferences granted to Colombia. As far as coal exports are concerned, campaigns had been advanced by British unions against a Colombian mine, even though the mining company in question reportedly complied with environmental norms and adhered to international environmental standards. Thus, certain NGO campaigns raise the issue of accountability, as imprecise and incorrect campaigns could prejudice the foreign trade of another country.[5]

The survey did not find many instances where environmental requirements emerging in sectors such as leather and textiles had significantly affected Colombian exports.[6] However, some textile exporters stated that they were unable to meet the requirements of their German importers to substitute certain dyes which were not allowed under private eco-labelling schemes in Germany. The Colombian exporters concerned had decided to bypass such requirements by diverting exports to other markets. However, given the importance of the German market, in the longer run they planned to adjust their production processes to the requirements of this market.

6.4.1 Unilateral Trade Restrictions

In Colombia there is concern that unilateral measures by developed countries may at least in part be attributed to commercial interests in the importing countries, and that they may force developing countries to invest in measures which are less relevant than others, given domestic environmental conditions and priorities. Colombia has been affected by unilateral trade measures imposed by the United States. Such measures are particularly relevant in the context of the trade and environment debate, as they involve the issue of process and production methods, known as PPMs (relating to marine resources). According to the study, an embargo on tuna fish resulted in significant income losses.

Tuna and dolphins
As a condition for access to the United States tuna market, Colombian purse seiners fishing in the Pacific Ocean have to comply with certain requirements (to use certain devices, to engage in certain manoeuvres to rescue dolphins and to carry observers on board). The research team estimated the corresponding compliance costs, as well as the loss in revenues resulting from a United States embargo on imports of Colombian tuna fish under the Marine Mammal Protection Act (MMPA).

Compliance costs per fleet (which varied depending on its size and the number of annual fishing expeditions) were estimated at between US$72000 and 107000 in terms of investment requirements, and an additional US$16000 to 20000 in annual operation costs. For large exporters, compliance costs represented approximately 2.5 per cent of the total annual operation costs.[7] For small exporters of tuna, however, compliance costs could be much higher.

Alleging that two Colombian fleets had not complied with the MMPA requirements and considering that the country had therefore violated the dolphin safety dispositions, in March 1992 the United States placed an embargo on all imports of Colombian tuna fish. The embargo became effective in March 1993.

While it was difficult to determine the precise economic effects of the embargo (tuna fish exporters were reluctant to disclose information on income losses), its impact was certainly substantial. The United States was the primary export market for Colombian tuna fish, representing 32 per cent of the total exported volume in 1992. According to one estimate, provided by the National Fishing Agency, INPA, the embargo reduced Colombian tuna fish production by 20 000 tons, representing a loss of US$20 million.[8]

According to the study, this measure was questionable on several grounds. First, it was considered a unilateral and extraterritorial application of a United States domestic environmental policy, which was in violation of international trade rules. Secondly, it was considered a non-tariff barrier (NTB), in particular since even when the Colombian fishing vessels had adopted the required measures, the United States had continued to apply the embargo for a considerable time (the embargo was lifted only in May 1994). Thirdly, it was considered that the embargo was unnecessary and that the prescribed 'dolphin safe' methods were ineffective or even counterproductive from an environmental point of view. For example, while measures to protect dolphins when fishing for tuna may protect dolphins, they may endanger other species and hence have other ecological costs.

Shrimps and turtles
As a condition for access to the United States shrimp market, the US Government generally requires shrimp trawlers to use Turtle Excluding Devices (TEDs), to minimize the by-catch of turtles. In May 1993, the US State Department required installation of TEDs on Colombian trawlers (on 30 per cent of Colombian vessels initially and subsequently on all commercial vessels, to obtain 1994 certification). If Colombia had failed to obtain the necessary certification, United States' shrimp imports from Colombia would have been embargoed.

TEDs are manufactured and installed in Colombia, using the specifications provided by the United States government, at a cost of US$100 to US$400 per net. Since a fishing vessel typically operates four nets, the cost per vessel ranges from US$400 to US$1600. The Colombian case study makes no mention of possible losses in productivity as a result of the use of TEDs.[9]

According to the study, as in the case of tuna, this measure was questionable on the grounds that it was a unilateral and extraterritorial application of a domestic environmental law of the United States and because it was not necessary from an environmental point of view. A 1992 study by INPA had revealed that only very few marine turtles were captured in shrimp fishing. In fact, the real danger to turtles may arise from other sources which are not addressed by the international community.

6.4.2   Packaging Requirements

The questionnaire and follow-up interviews gave some indication of the possible effects of emerging external standards and regulations in the area of packaging, in particular in Germany, on Colombian exports.

In certain sectors, for example the fruit industry, significant compliance costs were reported. Perhaps more importantly, packaging requirements had created uncertainty, in particular with regard to the type of packaging materials that would be acceptable to importers. Many Colombian export firms had little understanding of what exactly was required, and did not know where such information could be obtained. For example, Colombian banana exporters stated that they had insufficient information and reported uncertainty relating to the permitted use of staples and glue in packaging materials. The problem of the lack of precise and timely information was aggravated by the differences in requirements among importing countries.

Colombian exporters had at times incurred costs, delayed decisions or shifted to other materials because of perceptions rather than precise information regarding the requirements in the importing countries. New packaging policies had, in some cases, induced exporters to substitute certain materials for others. The reason was that importers preferred materials which were more easily recyclable, given existing recycling facilities in the importing country. At times, the preference for easily recyclable materials had also created obstacles for packaging using a mixture of different materials. In general, however, initial problems with new packaging requirements had been resolved after some time.

According to the National Federation of Coffee Growers (FEDECAFE), it appeared initially that the Packaging Ordinance would not allow the use of jute, which was not considered easily recyclable. There was concern that jute sacks would have to be re-exported to Colombia, as it was feared that incineration would be allowed only in exceptional cases under German legislation. Exporters had started to shift to plastics as a packaging material. However, the German Ministry for the Environment confirmed that recycling facilities for jute, as well as a market for recycled jute, existed in Germany.[10] Colombian coffee exporters confirmed that jute packaging had indeed been accepted in the German market. For economic reasons, however, exporters had started to use metal containers.

FEDECAFE nevertheless feared that packaging requirements in external markets created potential problems for exporters of processed (roasted and ground) coffee. Unlike the green variety, processed coffee was packed in aluminum packages with a plastic lining. Although the exporters had not yet been required to implement any changes, it was feared that there could be a conflict between environment-related packaging requirements and product-quality requirements.

Conversely, ASCOFLORES, the association of Colombian flower producers, stated that producers had not been forced to implement major modifications to comply with the Packaging Ordinance. Some of the changes that had been made included: reduction in the amount of packaging material; elimination of staples, hooks, other metals, and rubber; as well as the use of uniform packaging materials for all kind of flowers, to facilitate recycling. According to ASCOFLORES, packaging accounted for only 7 per cent of total production costs of flowers and as adjustments had been minor, compliance costs had not been significant. Moreover, most of the costs on the German side had been absorbed by the importer. ASCOFLORES had not heard of cases where flower exports had been rejected on account of packaging conditions.

6.4.3 Eco-labelling

Eco-labelling has generated some concern and interest in Colombia. The research team conducted two studies on the possible effects of the introduction of a European Union eco-label for certain textile products on Colombian exports (see Box 6.1). Preliminary work has been undertaken in Colombia to analyse the feasibility of establishing a national eco-labelling programme (see Box 6.2).

Given the composition of Colombia's exports by products and markets of destination, *a priori* it is to be expected that only a relatively small portion of Colombia's exports is potentially affected by eco-labelling in the developed countries. Considering the major export products, it would appear that coffee, oil, carbon, precious stones and chemicals are not probable candidates for inclusion in eco-labelling programmes. There is concern, however, that flowers might become exposed to the effects of eco-labelling in Europe. With regard to the other major export products, eco-labelling potentially affects leather (as a material used for the production of shoes) and textiles. Colombian exporters of bananas have been contemplating the advantages and disadvantages (from a commercial point of view) of private eco-labels, in particular in the framework of the SMART Banana programme sponsored by the Rainforest Alliance.

As mentioned above, two studies were undertaken on the possible competitiveness effects of a European Union eco-label for certain textile products (T-shirts and bed linen) on Colombian exporters. The first study was undertaken for UNCTAD in 1994. More recently, a follow-up study was carried out for the International Trade Centre (ITC). In both cases the research team interviewed representatives of a number of textile firms. In general, large firms were selected. The results were generally compatible with similar studies undertaken in other countries, such as Brazil (see Box 6.1).

Box 6.1   European Union eco-labels for textiles and Colombian exports

Information on the possible effects of eco-labelling for textile products (T-shirts and bed linen) in the European Union was obtained from three sources: (a) the larger survey based on a questionnaire and follow-up interviews (9 of the 74 respondents were textile producers; all of them relatively large firms); (b) more recent interviews with representatives of textile firms in Medellin and Bogota; and (c) meetings with several large textile industries, organized by ASCOLTEX (the association of textile producers).

Textile producers had made some investments in pollution control in response to national legislation. In fact, four out of nine had invested resources in environmental protection. National legislation, however, emphasized end-of-pipe air and water pollution control, as distinct from requirements regarding energy consumption and the use of chemical inputs. Although Colombian producers had not yet made significant investments in response to external environmental requirements, they were conscious that such requirements were becoming more stringent; they feared this might have an adverse effect on their competitiveness (the average share of exports in their total production was 28 per cent).

Although all firms surveyed considered that they were close to meeting many of the eco-labelling criteria, other criteria would be difficult to meet, for example those with regard to the use of chemicals or certain waste water and noise standards. Relatively large cost increases would arise from the need to monitor residue values in final products. Colombian producers questioned the scientific justification for the very stringent limit values set for a number of criteria. They also perceived verification procedures to be a major difficulty. Firms stated that compliance costs exceeded the expected commercial benefits of an eco-label by far. Meeting eco-labelling criteria would be particularly difficult for SMEs.

Source: Ho *et al*. (1994).

In the more recent series of interviews, however, the research team found greater awareness of eco-labelling than in earlier interviews, with entrepreneurs showing a better understanding of eco-labelling programmes as well as a more

Box 6.2   Proposals for a Colombian eco-labelling programme

Colombia is developing a national eco-labelling programme. While modelled on the programmes of Germany and other European countries, the Colombian programme will take domestic conditions into account. The project is spearheaded by the Colombian Ministries of the Environment and Foreign Trade, with the technical support of the National Planning Department. The objectives are:

(a) to promote environmental conservation in several sectors, addressing a variety of aspects, including emissions, energy use, and natural resource exploitation;
(b) to provide the domestic industry with means and incentives to increase its competitiveness through the implementation of environmental strategies; and
(c) to assist Colombian export firms in penetrating external markets.

The programme is thus being designed to address both domestic environmental and export concerns. Specific products to be covered have not yet been defined, but the programme will probably begin working with industries interested in promoting eco-labelling schemes, such as flowers and detergents. According to the study, interest among Colombian companies was large. The national flower association (ASCOFLORES) is developing its own eco-labelling programme.

Discussions focus on issues such as (a) whether the label should focus primarily on the product or take its entire life cycle into account; and (b) how stringent the criteria should be, in particular as compared to existing legislation. Colombian legislation is stringent at present, but enforcement is difficult and the level of compliance is low. There are also a number of environmental problems, such as ground water pollution, which are not covered by existing laws or standards. Verification is also an important issue. Difficulties could arise from the scarcity of qualified laboratories and institutions which could independently assess compliance with the criteria.

Source: Ho *et al.* (1994).

positive attitude towards eco-labels. Firms expressed support for a national eco-labelling programme and some of them expressed an interest in eventually applying for eco-labels used in the developed countries. However, the study mentions that Colombian industry and government remain concerned about the possible discriminatory effects of eco-labelling and the risk that eco-labels may be used for protectionist purposes. In this context, it was considered suspicious that eco-labels in the developed countries are emerging in sectors which are subject to import competition from developing countries, such as leather, textiles and flowers, rather than in sectors with potentially more harmful environmental effects (see Box 6.2).

6.4.4   Trading Opportunities for Environment-friendly Products

In Colombia there is interest in exploring trading opportunities for environment-friendly products. However, the study notes that, in general, current world demand for such products is still small. In most cases, shifting to environment-friendly production processes (and the losses in productivity that such shifts often imply), in order to gain access to small markets for environment-friendly products would not appear, under the current circumstances, justified from a commercial point of view. Consumers in developed countries are not willing to pay a sufficiently high price to allow cost internalization in the developing countries. In addition, access to environmentally sound technologies required to supply markets for environment-friendly products has generally not been forthcoming. There may also be a trade-off between consumer demands for 'perfect' products (for example in terms of size and presentation) which often requires the use of chemicals, and pressures to reduce the use of pesticides and fertilizers.

A market niche exists for environment-friendly coffee. As a major exporter of coffee, Colombia has of course an interest in emerging markets for environment-friendly coffee, including organically grown coffee. The growth in the world market for organically grown coffee has largely been fuelled by price premiums. For example, in March 1994 the price of organically grown coffee was quoted at US$1.26 per pound, versus 90 cents for regular coffee. Colombia's participation in the world market for organically grown coffee is, however, small (Colombia exports only around 52 tons per year). According to the study, there is only an incipient and marginal market for environment-friendly coffee.

The production of organically grown coffee faces other constraints. For example, certification is difficult to obtain and expensive. Certification costs can amount to more than US$30000, including annual fees and fees for hiring an expert visitor. Colombia has to rely on a few international certifiers, because national certifiers are not recognized by international buyers. This limits the viability of individual initiatives and therefore the only option for producers is to undertake joint efforts. In addition to certification problems, entering the market for organically grown coffee is largely dependent on price differentials. While, per unit of output, organically grown coffee production is cheaper than traditional and high-input coffee production, the organically grown coffee business involves an economic risk, and experience shows that when prices for regular coffee are high, producers often switch back to regular coffee production.

6.5 THE CASE OF SMALL AND MEDIUM-SIZE ENTERPRISES

Experience from other country case studies shows that firm size is an important factor in the ability of firms to adjust to environmental requirements. In general, small and medium-size enterprises (SMEs) have greater difficulties in complying with domestic and external environmental requirements than large firms.

In Colombia, SMEs contribute around 40 per cent to total manufacturing production and 50 per cent of its national employment.[11] As a result of their low level of technological development and their characteristics as an 'informal sector', SMEs' contribution to total industrial pollution is relatively high.[12]

Most SMEs are located around the major urban centres, in particular Bogota (34 per cent of all SMEs), Cali, Medellin and Bucaramanga. It has been estimated that 37 per cent of SMEs are located in urban areas not suitable for manufacturing activities. This situation is particularly relevant for family-run enterprises which are often located in areas with deficient public services and infrastructure, thus making it difficult for firms to attain higher productivity levels.

General problems of SMEs are related to their limited management capacities, technological obsolescence, insufficient quality control, insufficient access to information, inadequate credit facilities and, more importantly, inadequate infrastructural facilities. The low level of awareness and lack of information on environmental questions further complicates compliance with environmental requirements.

In 1992, the Corporation for Socio-economic and Technological Research of Colombia (CINSET) carried out a study on the environmental problems of SMEs, based on a representative sample of 802 firms. The study found that all SMEs had problems with the treatment of wastes generated in the production process. The study also found a low level of compliance with environmental standards and regulations. The principal environmental problems and the percentage of firms in the sample affected by such problems are shown in Table 6.3.

Despite their important contribution to manufacturing production and to industrial pollution, the participation of SMEs in the formulation of economic and environmental policies is very limited. Environmental policies in Colombia, which focus on direct control instruments, do not pay attention to the special circumstances of SMEs. However, the response of different SMEs to environmental policies was found to vary from sector to sector.

Table 6.3   Colombia: environmental problems of SMEs

Environmental problem	Portion of the sample (per cent)
Lack of any environmental management	64
Inadequate treatment of solid wastes	54
Inadequate treatment of liquid wastes	41
Inadequate treatment of gaseous wastes	41
Occupational risks as a result of inappropriate environmental conditions	30

Source: CINSET.

In the leather sector, for example, it was found that it may be very difficult for SMEs to comply with certain environmental standards and requirements. In Colombia, the leather processing and footwear industry obtains its materials largely from the independent tanning sector, a large part of which consists of small, artisan firms using outdated technologies. One area with many micro-enterprises is the San Benito neighbourhood in Bogotá, where 313 enterprises are located. According to a UNIDO study, none of the micro-enterprises in this area complied with effluent treatment standards.

The UNIDO study proposed that a common effluent treatment system, at an estimated investment cost of US$ 6.2 million and annual operational costs of US$2 million, be established to deal with the problem.[13] It is estimated that annual sales of the San Benito sector are in the order of US$18 million, whereas annual profits are estimated at US$5.4 million. Consequently, tanners would have to spend over 100 per cent of their estimated annual profits to meet the investment requirements, whereas operational costs of effluent treatment would reduce estimated profits by 40 per cent (operational costs alone would increase production costs by as much as 16 per cent).

Another case study on the bricks sector showed that there may be a trade-off between higher variable and higher fixed costs. In Colombia, SMEs supply between 20 and 25 per cent of the domestic market. The principal environmental impacts of the sector are caused by atmospheric emissions. In 1993, an association of small producers (PROTUGRES) presented an environmental action plan. PROTUGRES was developing three pilot programmes aimed at the substitution of coal as the source of energy used by the industry for: (a) the combination of 'crudo de castilla'[14] with gasoline; (b) the combination of coal and coke; and (c) propane gas.

The first process, using a combination of crudo de castilla (73 per cent) with gasoline (27 per cent) requires an investment of US$35000 per oven. The resulting variable costs would be US$470 per oven. The second process is based on a combination of coal (20 per cent) and coke (80 per cent). This process does not require any investment, but variable costs would increase from US$560 to 900 per oven, or by 90 per cent. While this process would have better environmental effects, the substantial cost increase would rule out this option, unless regulations were implemented and strictly enforced on all firms. The third process, based on the use of propane gas, was clearly the most environment-friendly. However, this process would require an investment of approximately US$40000 per oven and variable costs would be as high as US$1520 per oven. It could nevertheless be expected that variable costs may decrease significantly if the ongoing programmes to promote the large-scale use of natural gas, following the discovery of important natural gas reserves, were to be successful. Since natural gas was three times as inexpensive as propane gas, in the longer run variable costs could be reduced to US$500 per oven. Processes based on the use of gas would therefore be the most appropriate from both an environmental and economic point of view, provided that government support could be provided to promote the large-scale use of gas.

Another sector examined by the study is that of printing, where environmental effects primarily arise from effluent resulting from cleaning of the printing equipment. The level of pollution depends to a large degree on the technology used. For example, modern technologies based on automatic cleaning consumed only 30 per cent as much water, and discharge much less waste compared to obsolete technologies.[15]

While the volume of effluent generated by each firm is small, and a common effluent treatment system would not be very expensive (requiring an investment of approximately US$20000 and annual operational costs of US$8000), the geographical dispersion of SMEs would complicate the use of such a system. An alternative to the use of a common effluent treatment system consists in promoting the use of more environment-friendly inputs and biodegradable cleaning materials. However, such materials were 30 per cent more expensive than conventional materials.[16]

The study concludes by pointing to the diversity of the competitiveness effects of compliance with environmental standards for the different sectors in Colombia. It points out that in all the three sectors reviewed, environmental problems arise because of different reasons. For example, in the printing press sector the environmental impact arises more because of the lack of city planning, as it is the dispersion in the location of enterprises which makes it difficult to make joint investments and there is a lack of control on the part of environmental authorities. In the case of the brick industry, government intervention is needed to support the efforts of the brick industry to comply with environmental standards. In the case of leather industries, research is required in order to look for more cost-effective options. Thus solutions would have to be variable.

6.6   TRADE AND COMPETITIVENESS EFFECTS OF MULTILATERAL ENVIRONMENTAL AGREEMENTS

Colombia is a party to all major Multilateral Environmental Agreements (MEAs). The Colombian case study includes a preliminary analysis of the trade and competitiveness effects of the Montreal Protocol on the Substances that Deplete the Ozone Layer. A study was also undertaken on the possible effects of an internationally agreed carbon tax to reduce the consumption of fossil fuels. Such a tax could become relevant in the context of the Climate Change Convention.

6.6.1   The Montreal Protocol

As an 'Article 5' Party to the Montreal Protocol (MP), Colombia is entitled to a 10-year grace period to implement its obligations under the Protocol. However, Colombia, which ratified both the London and Copenhagen amendments to the Protocol, anticipated the phase-out of the consumption of chlorofluorocarbons (CFCs) by 1996 (Colombia committed itself to phase out the consumption of halon 1211 and halon 1311 by 1994 and of CFC-11, CFC-12 and methyl chloroform by 1996). Colombia does not produce any of the substances controlled by the Montreal Protocol, and ozone-depleting substances (ODSs) used are imported from the United States, the United Kingdom, Germany and Venezuela. The strategy for the phase-out of the consumption of ODSs has been presented to the MP's Multilateral Fund.

Based on an analysis by the government and the private sector, the possible trade and competitiveness effects of the Montreal Protocol can be grouped as follows: (a) effects on larger firms which have access to the Multilateral Fund; (b) effects on small and medium-size firms, which, according to the study, generally cannot access the Fund; and (c) effects on industries which rely on refrigeration, such as flowers, bananas and meat processing.[17]

With regard to (a), the country programme indicates that Colombia needs US$55 million from the Multilateral Fund to accomplish the objectives of the MP, of which US$18 million was needed in 1994. Projects for a total amount of US$8 million were approved in 1994. New projects will be prepared for funding by the Multilateral Fund. The Multilateral Fund had enabled larger firms to adapt technologies while remaining competitive.

With regard to (b), it should be noted that around 30 per cent of ODS users in Colombia are small firms. In practice, such firms may find it difficult to access the grants from the Multilateral Fund. As a result, the competitiveness of these small firms could be substantially affected by the MP.[18] There is thus a need to conduct studies to determine the costs of projects for small firms.

With regard to (c), industries which rely on CFCs for refrigeration[19] could be significantly affected by the MP. The study reports that it was expected that the supply of ODSs would be reduced significantly in 1995 because two-thirds of the ODS-producing plants in the United States and 100 per cent of those in Europe would close down. It was feared that a sharp reduction in supply would cause an increase in the price of ODS, and thus in the refrigeration costs of these industries. It was difficult to predict the corresponding effects on the industries concerned. Some of the potentially affected industries, such as the flower industry, were concerned over possible economic effects of the MP.[20]

6.6.2   Economic Effects of a Carbon Tax

A study on the possible effects of a carbon tax imposed on the energy sector in Colombia was commissioned from the research institute FEDESARROLLO. The institute developed a model, based on an analysis conducted in the United States by the American Petroleum Institute, to simulate the effects of an internationally agreed tax levied on the carbon content of fossil fuels. The model assumes that such taxes are levied at the point of production rather than on consumption. For different tax levels, ranging from US$ 10 to 100 per ton, the study analyses the effects of corresponding price changes for each of the major fuels (coal, gas and oil) on demand and tax revenues, as well as the effects on the major energy consumers in Colombia.

Given the existing differences between prices in the domestic market and export prices, relative price increases (in percentage terms) following the implementation of a carbon tax will be different for domestically consumed and exported energy. For example, a US$10 carbon tax on coal was estimated to result in an increase in the domestic market price of coal of 34 per cent compared to a 16 per cent increase in its export price. Domestic prices of oil and gas would increase by 4 and 8 per cent, respectively (see Table 6.4). Higher levels of carbon taxes would of course lead to larger price increases. Given the parameters used in the model, the estimated price increases following a US$20 carbon tax would simply be twice as high as those mentioned above.

Both external and domestic users will react to these price increases by changing the volume and composition of their energy consumption. It is estimated that a US$10 per ton carbon tax will cause declines of 17 and 7 per cent in the volumes of domestic demand and exports, respectively. Such reductions might be tolerable for the Colombian economy, but at higher tax

levels the impact on the demand for coal would become disruptive. At higher
levels of carbon taxes, exports of coal, representing US$622 million in 1992 (see
Table 6.4), could be significantly affected.

Table 6.4   Estimated effects in Colombia of a carbon tax of US$10 per ton

Model results	Simulation model		
	Type of Energy		
	Coal	Oil	Gas
Domestic price increase (percentage)	34	4	8
Export price increase (percentage)	16	7	n/a
Tax revenues (US$ millions)	141	213	24
On domestic sales	42	144	24
On exports	99	69	–
Memorandum items (1992):	Coal (tons)	Oil (barrels)	Gas (cubic feet)
Production (in millions)	23.2	159.6	143.9
Domestic consumption (in millions)	6.9	108.0	143.9
Exports (in millions)	16.3	51.6	0.0
Exports (value, in US$ millions)	622.0	920.0	–

Source: Gavaria, D., R. Gomez, L. Ho and A. Soto, 'Reconciliation of trade and environment
policies: the case study of Colombia', 1994.

The estimated impact of a carbon tax on domestic industry varies widely from
sector to sector, depending on the intensity of the use of fossil fuels. The
largest consumer of coal is the cement industry that has annual purchases of more
than one million tons. Other large consumers are the integrated stone, glass and
ceramics industries. The two industries most directly affected by the tax (cement
and stone, glass and ceramics) are relatively small in terms of their contribution
to GDP, compared to other energy-intensive industries. Nevertheless, since these
sectors contribute significantly to exports and employment, concerns about
international competitiveness are especially relevant. The cement industry is of
course an important supplier to the domestic construction industry. The largest
consumers of oil and its derivatives are the food, beverages and tobacco
industries, with an annual consumption of more than 1.2 million barrels.
Although a carbon tax would have a smaller impact on the price of oil than on
the price of coal, the effects on these industries could nevertheless be substantial,
and competitiveness could be severely affected.

On the basis of this preliminary analysis, the study concludes that carbon tax
rates above the 10 dollar level could be disruptive to energy markets and to
consumers. The immediate policy implication was that such taxes would either

have to be phased in over a long time period, or that the tax would have to incorporate some provisions to mitigate its effects, especially on the coal market. At a US$10 per ton tax level, the economic impact of the tax was more manageable, especially if tax revenues accrued to Colombia.

6.7 IMPACT OF TRADE AND TRADE LIBERALIZATION ON THE COLOMBIAN ENVIRONMENT

The research team reviewed a number of studies carried out in Colombia on the impact of trade liberalization on the environment. One study, commissioned from the Andes University (Universidad de Los Andes), examined the relationship

Box 6.3   Dirty industry migration

Reviewing the Colombian experience, aided by studies which had been undertaken by FEDESARROLLO, the research team rejects the hypothesis that industries with high pollution-abatement costs would relocate from developed to developing countries to take advantage of lower environmental compliance costs in the developing countries. First, although the level of enforcement of environmental regulations in Colombia is admittedly low, environmental legislation is nevertheless quite stringent. Transnational corporations (TNCs) are unlikely to invest in Colombia to take advantage of existing weak enforcement. The creation of the Ministry of the Environment in 1993 has reinforced the expectation that enforcement of environmental legislation will be strengthened. Secondly, the FEDESARROLLO studies indicate that other factors would make Colombia an improbable candidate for relocation of dirty industries.

A survey of the transfer of environmentally sound technologies also failed to lend support to the hypothesis regarding dirty industry migration. None of the subsidiaries of TNCs appeared to have been established in Colombia to take advantage of lower stringency of environmental regulations. The majority of the subsidiaries had been established to sell in the Colombian and/or other Latin American markets. In addition, most subsidiaries declared that they would not need to make any significant adjustment in their production process if environmental standards of the OECD countries were implemented in Colombia.

between trade policy and industrial pollution. The research team also drew on existing studies on the relationship between trade liberalization and recycling, and on the question of dirty industry migration (see Box 6.3). Several case studies were carried out on the environmental effects of export expansion.

6.7.1   Trade Liberalization and Industrial Pollution

In order to examine the linkages between trade liberalization and the environmental impact of industrial production, the Andes University compared index numbers of pollution intensity by industrial sector with indicators of revealed comparative advantage (at the 4-digit level of the Standard Industrial Trade Classification, SITC). Index numbers on pollution intensity per sector were based on data collected by the US Environmental Protection Agency regarding emissions of 320 toxic substances.[21]

Ranking industrial sectors in accordance with these two sets of index numbers did not show any significant correlation between pollution intensity and international competitiveness. In the case of only a few sectors did high pollution intensity coincide with a relatively high degree of revealed comparative advantage. These were for cotton products, leather tanning, printing and publishing, woven and final textile products, certain articles of wood and petroleum refining.

The study further examined trends in average pollution intensity over several periods which differed from each other in terms of trade liberalization. The results indicated that the average pollution intensity of industrial production, after having decreased slightly during the 1979–1981 period of import liberalization, increased over the 1982–1992 period, which included the recent liberalization process. Thus, no significant correlation was found between trade liberalization and average changes in pollution intensity.

With regard to exports, however, the share of the 21 most polluting industrial sectors in total industrial exports declined from 66 per cent of total manufactured exports in 1985 to 46 per cent in 1990 and 41 per cent in 1991.

6.7.2   Environmental Impact of Imports

As indicated in Table 6.1, Colombian imports have been growing substantially in recent years. The environmental effects of increased imports are difficult to assess. On the one hand there are scale effects, for example, increased imports of automobiles result in greater consumption of fossil fuels thus contributing to atmospheric emissions and other adverse environmental effects. Similarly, increased imports of electric machinery contribute to increased energy use. On the other hand, there are technology effects. Increased imports of capital goods and technologies, and stronger import competition facilitate technological progress, thus contributing to reduced environmental impact per unit. Import liberalization has had important effects on recycling in Colombia. It has made it no longer profitable to recycle domestic paper and this has had serious consequences for industry and employment. The conclusions of an ELSAM Consultants' study into these effects are contained in Box 6.4.

It is particularly difficult to ascertain the environmental effects of imports of agricultural products into Colombia. During the initial phase of trade liberalization, agricultural imports soared (see Table 6.1), producing unintended impacts in terms of the reorientation of agricultural activities, displacement of workers and other factors. The liberalization strategy in the agricultural sector has been redefined because of the large social and economic impacts it was producing.

In some cases, imports appeared to be displacing polluting and inefficient domestic industries. For example, the basic iron and steel industry, which has traditionally been a heavily protected, inefficient, and polluting activity, lost economic importance as a result of the trade liberalization policies in Colombia. Although the iron and steel industry continued to be protected, trade liberalization resulted in a 25 per cent increase in iron and steel imports between 1989 and 1993. Exports fell by 90 per cent during this same period. With the decrease in iron and steel production, the environmental impact of this industry was reduced. In addition, imports of capital goods reflected a process of technological innovation and industrial conversion.

The study further notes that the environmental effects of imports were rarely controlled by the government. In general, the Colombian Government did not control the toxicity or environmental impact of certain imports, such as pesticides, which were restricted in their countries of origin. As a result, Colombia largely relied on exporting countries to prevent exports of polluting and toxic products. This, however, did not provide adequate protection: for example, vinylum chloride (monomer), which is prohibited in the United States and other developed countries, has been exported to Colombia.

6.7.3 Environmental Effects of Export Expansion of Selected Primary Products

Case studies on shrimps and on a number of agricultural products which are produced almost entirely for export (bananas, flowers and coffee), indicate that there are environmental impacts associated with increased production to satisfy growing international demand. For each of these agricultural products, the area under cultivation has increased significantly over the last 20 years. Monoculture, combined with market forces, has stimulated high-input and capital-intensive production methods. Efforts are under way to shift to more

Box 6.4   Import liberalization and domestic recycling

Due to the economic liberalization process, an increased volume of recyclable waste material has been imported into Colombia. These imported materials, which are generally sold at relatively low prices, compete with domestic recyclable waste. The establishment of regional free trade zones with other Latin American countries has also resulted in an increased influx of cheap materials, exerting a strong downward pressure on the price of domestic recyclable materials.

One study by ECSAM Consultants Ltd. concludes that competition from imported materials has created a disincentive for domestic recycling of paper and cardboard waste. According to the study, these materials constituted 30 per cent of domestic waste by weight, compared to only 3 per cent for glass and 2 per cent for plastics (50 per cent of domestic waste comes from biodegradable food residues). In recent years, significant volumes of paper waste collected in the United States (especially from New York), Central America and Venezuela had been exported to Colombia.

While the sanitary landfill of Doña Juana in Bogotá received 3000 tons of paper and cardboard daily, the paper industry had begun to import almost 30 per cent of the material used for recycling. The largest paper companies in Colombia (among them Smurfit-Cartón de Colombia, Colpapel, Cartón América and Papel Familia) had designed eight investment projects involving the use of recycled paper, but a large part of the materials would come from abroad, rather than from domestic waste.

The Colombian paper industry preferred imported over domestic recyclable paper waste because of the high quality and low prices of imported materials. According to one company, Cartón de Colombia, it was easier and cheaper to import higher quality paper material from the United States than to acquire materials on the domestic market. As a result of increased imports, it was no longer profitable to recycle domestic paper.

The study claims that the social effects were also severe, as the people involved in waste collection, sorting and related activities came from a marginal and economically vulnerable sector of the society. Liberalization had reduced the principal source of income for 50 000 Colombian families, or about 200 000 people. Large and small recycling projects implemented within cities and municipalities became economically unfeasible, resulting in their bankruptcy and failure. According to the study, economic liberalization has thus contributed to resolving other countries trash problems to the detriment of the Colombian environment and society.

Source: ECSAM Consultants Ltd. 'Effects of Economic Liberalization on Material Recycling', Bogotá, 1993.

environment-friendly production processes, but such efforts may be hampered by economic and developmental constraints.

Shrimps are Colombia's major marine resource export item. Colombia occupies only a small part of the world shrimp market, but exports increased rapidly until recent years. Shrimps are mainly harvested in the Pacific Ocean and around 95 per cent of the production is exported, representing US$77 million in 1993. The United States is the principal export market (US$40 million in 1993).

International demand for shrimp may have resulted in overexploitation.[22] Shrimp production in the Pacific Ocean peaked in 1989, but fell afterwards. Exports of crustaceans in general have likewise fallen in recent years. The steep rise and subsequent decline in the production of specific types of shrimp suggest possible overexploitation. Indeed, in recent years harvests have largely exceeded the maximum sustainable and potential yields established by the national fishing agency, INPA. In recent years INPA has established annual bans on the capture, exploitation, processing and commercialization of white shrimps and other species.

According to the study, Colombian coffee is a clear example of a situation where international market forces have shaped the nature of the production process used in export-oriented sectors in developing countries. In Colombia, coffee was traditionally produced in a sustainable way. However, a sharp increase in world coffee prices, caused by a frost affecting Brazilian plantations in the mid-1970s, induced a technological change towards high-input coffee production systems. These high-input systems have environmental impacts, but the shift has been justified on economic grounds.

Currently, approximately 30 per cent of Colombia's coffee is produced under the traditional system, which generally meets the criteria of sustainable development.[23] For the remaining 70 per cent of production, reverting to traditional sustainable agroforestry coffee plantations would be possible under two scenarios: (a) the price premium and market size for environment-friendly coffee would have to be large enough to compensate for losses in productivity; or (b) the cost of inputs (fertilizers, pesticides) used in high-input systems would have to increase to a point where the traditional low-input systems, despite lower productivity, would be the best option from an economic point of view.

In Colombia, bananas are produced almost entirely for export. The area under banana cultivation has increased rapidly since the 1970s. Environmental impacts are, to a large extent, due to the production of bananas as a monoculture. Mass production, induced by strong international demand, has led to two types of environmental impacts: (a) deforestation and the elimination of native species, and consequently (b) decreased resistance to pests and diseases, requiring the application of (highly toxic) agrochemicals. The use of agrochemicals has also increased in response to international market requirements related to the appearance of the product (size, colour, and so on).

The banana sector produces considerable volumes of (organic and non-organic) solid waste. Efforts are under way to resolve or mitigate such problems. For example, 60 per cent of the banana producers in Uraba hire labourers to collect plastic ropes used to support the banana plant. These ropes are then used to make hammocks, rugs, tapestries, and so on, or are recycled in the major cities. Other farmers, however, find this practice too expensive. Research is also under way into substitutes for agrochemicals and into decomposition of organic waste.

Despite efforts to mitigate the environmental impacts of banana production, the industry is driven by international demand and competitiveness considerations. The industry is conscious of ecological impacts and is undertaking efforts to use cleaner production processes. However, addressing the major environmental concerns in most cases requires costly measures.

6.8　　CONCLUSIONS AND RECOMMENDATIONS

In Colombia, industrial awareness of environmental requirements has emerged to a greater extent from national environmental legislation than from external requirements. Colombia has enacted stringent environmental laws, but enforcement has been difficult. With the creation of the Ministry of the Environment, environmental policies are expected to become better attuned to local environmental and economic conditions and better enforced. Special measures are needed to assist SMEs in meeting environmental requirements.

So far, Colombian exporters have faced relatively few environmental requirements emerging from external markets, which can largely be explained by the composition and geographical distribution of Colombia's exports. Where environmental requirements have emerged, Colombian exporters have generally been able to adapt their products without major difficulties. In specific sectors, such as fruit, the effects of external environmental requirements have been more significant.

Although relatively few exporters have direct experience with external environmental demands, awareness of environmental factors is growing. Industry expects that environmental requirements will become more stringent in the future. A major concern of exporters relates to the lack of timely and precise information. Unintended adverse trade effects of environmental policies should be avoided or mitigated through improved transparency, and multilateral and bilateral cooperation.

The Colombian Government is especially concerned about unilateral measures with extraterritorial application. As a result of unilateral measures by the

United States, in one year the tuna industry lost 20 per cent of its revenues, or US$20 million.

Colombian industry, as well as the government, is also concerned over the lack of transparency and objectivity in eco-labelling schemes, even though Colombian exporters have not yet been significantly affected by this instrument. The developed countries' use of eco-labels in sectors where they find strong import competition, such as flowers, textiles and footwear, is considered suspicious and it is feared that eco-labels may be used for protectionist purposes. Eco-labelling and other voluntary measures should be non-discriminatory, transparent and based on an open process. Transparency should include the participation of developing countries in the design of criteria in product categories of export interest to them.

Multilateral cooperative approaches have to be preferred over trade restrictions, from both an economic and environmental point of view. For example, the Multilateral Fund under the Montreal Protocol has assisted larger Colombian firms in phasing out the use of ODSs. However, smaller firms have in practice not been able to benefit from the Multilateral Fund and their competitiveness could be seriously affected. There is a need for additional funds and more flexible operation of the Multilateral Fund in favour of small firms.

Trade liberalization has resulted in both positive and negative environmental impacts. It has not been possible to establish any link between trade policy and average pollution intensity of industrial production. During the recent period of economic liberalization, there has been a large influx of potentially contaminating products, such as cars and pesticides. On the other hand, there has been a continuous increase in imports of new technologies, facilitating technological modernization and industrial conversion which are expected to generate positive environmental impacts. Some polluting industries which used to be protected against import competition, such as iron and steel, have lost economic significance. On the other hand, imports of cheap waste paper have significantly affected recycling of domestic waste, resulting in adverse environmental and socioeconomic effects.

Case studies on shrimp and a series of agricultural products which are produced almost exclusively for export (bananas, flowers and coffee) indicate that production expansion in response to international demand has resulted in adverse environmental impacts. Such adverse effects are due to the technologies used, in particular monoculture and high-input production technologies.

There is sometimes a contradiction between product quality and environmental requirements. For example, markets compel banana and flower producers to produce high-quality products in terms of size and colour. However, achieving such product quality frequently requires the use of fertilizers and pesticides.

While Colombia is exploring trading opportunities for environment-friendly products, the small size of the market and the existence of other difficulties, such as high certification costs, indicate that such opportunities could make only a relatively small (albeit important) contribution to mitigating negative environmental effects. More far-reaching measures are needed aimed at ensuring that consumers in developed countries pay the environmental costs associated with their consumption patterns.

Possible adverse environmental effects of trade liberalization and export expansion should not be used as an argument against trade liberalization. Such effects should be addressed through appropriate environmental policies, based on the conditions and priorities of the producing countries, as well as policies aimed at allowing developing countries to incorporate to a greater degree environmental costs into export prices.

NOTES

1. Presidencia de la República, Departamento Nacional de Planeación, 'El Salto Social. Bases para el Plan Nacional de Desarrollo 1994–1998'.

2. E. Uribe (1994), 'Competitiveness and market access: trade and environment issues', presentation at the Workshop on Trade, Environment and Sustainable Development in the Americas, Ottawa, 18–19 October.

3. The questionnaire was distributed by the Department of National Planning (DNP), the Ministry of Foreign Trade, ANALDEX and ACOPLASTICOS to various export sectors.

4. By Law 99 of 22 December 1993.

5. Manuel Rodriguez Becerra, 'Some annotations on sustainable development: trade and the environment. The impact of trade-related policies on export competitiveness and market access', presentation at UNCTAD's Trade and Development Board at the first part of its forty-first session.

6. Restrictions on the use of pentachlorophenol (PCP) in Germany and other European markets had little or no effects, simply because Colombian industry generally did not use PCP.

7. Total operation costs of a large tuna fishing vessel (more than 400 tons of gross registry) for 70 days (making four fishing trips) amounted to approximately US$1.3 million.

8. *El Espectador*, 'Colombian tuna embargo is raised', 13 May 1994, p. 2-B.

9. Recently, the United States imposed an embargo on imports of shrimp from Trinidad and Tobago following the discovery that some trawlers, despite being equipped with TEDs, had removed these devices at sea. Press reports from Trinidad and Tobago indicate that according to some trawlers TEDs had reduced the shrimp catch by 30 per cent. The same reports, however, also quote studies indicating that there should be no reduction in the shrimp catch. Press reports also pointed out that the embargo had detrimental effects on the local shrimp industry. Because of the embargo, for many trawlers it was no longer profitable to initiate fishing expeditions. Local press reports, 22 and 23 May 1995.

10. The Ministry recognized that jute, if processed with vegetable oils (as was the case in Colombia), was a natural and environment-friendly product.

11. In Colombia, micro-enterprises and small and medium-size industries (SMIs) are defined by Law 78 of 1988. Micro-enterprises are independent economic units of a family type, in the

manufacturing, sales, construction or services sector, which employ no more than 20 persons, and with assets of no more than 15 million pesos (approximately US$39 000 in 1988). SMIs are manufacturing enterprises, which employ no more than 199 persons, and with assets of no more than 300 million pesos (approximately US$781 000 in 1988). For reasons of consistency with other reports, the term small and medium-size enterprises (SMEs), rather than SMIs, is used in this report.

12. E. Uribe and Y. Medina (1995), 'La Pequeña y mediana industria y su relación con las regulaciones y las instituciones ambientales en Colombia', Bogotá, June.

13. UNIDO (1994) 'Asistencia de la Zona Industrial de Curtiembres de San Benito, Colombia', July.

14. A heavy hydro carbide with a high content of sulphur and heavy metals, which is a residual of the oil-refinery process.

15. Solid waste (paper waste, zinc plates and photographic negatives) are generally donated or sold for recycling and cause less environmental impact.

16. Environment-friendly tintas (without heavy metals) cost US$8 per kilo. Conventional materials cost US$5.6 per kilo. E. Uribe and Y. Medina, op. cit.

17. In addition, according to the Country Programme, the government would forgo revenues from duties collected on imports of ODSs of an estimated US$184 000. Nevertheless, a large part of this loss in government revenues could probably be compensated for by import duties collected on substitute substances.

18. However, it should be noted that special provisions are being designed for small users, that is, SMEs, for example through providing funds to foundations which can then channel investments to SMEs. See UNCTAD (1995) 'The policy debate on trade, environment and development', report TD/B/WG.6/10, Geneva, 12 September.

19. In accordance with the strategy set out in the MP, refrigeration and air-conditioning equipment that had an important fraction of their life-span remaining would be serviced and maintained, whenever possible, through recycling of CFC-12 and CFC-11 or HCFC-22, thus allowing the reduction and eventual elimination of imports of these ODSs, in accordance with the chronogram set out in the MP. If recycling were not possible, equipment would have to be adapted for operation with substitute substances authorized by the Protocol.

20. However, it is to be noted that at the Executive Session of the Montreal Protocol held in the second half of August 1995, it was reported that the supply of CFCs may actually exceed the demand for it.

21. Data were collected on emissions of 320 toxic substances into the air, water and land and the solid wastes from 15 000 plants in all industrial sectors of the United States in 1987. LINHUM is the Lineal Indicator of Sharp Toxicity against Human Health and the Ecosystem.

22. Increasing world demand for shrimp coupled with diminishing yields induced fishermen to turn to less sustainable production methods, depleting the resource even further. Around 1985, fishermen started to use electronic nets. The use of these nets, which were produced in an artisan fashion at a relatively low cost, spread rapidly. In the period 1984–1988, the number of fishing boats increased five times, while shrimp production diminished by 50 per cent. The use of electronic nets led INPA to establish annual bans.

23. According to the study, FEDECAFE has not tried to market this coffee as sustainable, as it fears that this may affect the marketability of the remaining coffee production.

7. Costa Rica

7.1 INTRODUCTION

This chapter summarizes the main results of a national study analysing the relationship between trade and the environment in Costa Rica. The research was initiated to detect possible environmental effects caused by the expansion of trade as well as trade problems stemming from stricter environmental regulations. The study was conducted by the International Center on Economic Policy of the National University of Costa Rica (*Universidad Nacional*) with the support of the Ministry of Foreign Trade of Costa Rica. The research team consisted of Carlos Conejo (coordinator), Rafael Díaz, Edgar Fürst, Eduardo Gitli and Leiner Vargas.

The research was carried out between July 1995 and December 1996 using the following methods: (a) a review of a large number of laws, bulletins and documents concerning trade and the environment; (b) interviews with officials of relevant public and private institutions; (c) the distribution of a questionnaire, with the support of the Chamber of Industry, to 39 firms, to obtain their views; (d) visits to firms; and (e) case studies undertaken on three sectors.

The study analyses trade and environment linkages in the case of Costa Rica, including case studies on bananas, coffee and forestry products; some trade and economic effects of Multilateral Environmental Agreements; and Costa Rica's experience with some innovative mechanisms for financing, such as Debt-for-Nature swaps (see Box 7.1) and joint implementation.

7.2 THE IMPORTANCE OF TRADE IN THE COSTA RICAN ECONOMY

Three key periods can be identified in the evolution of Costa Rican trade in recent years. The first is characterized by crisis and economic destabilization (1980–1984) in which Central America experienced a severe decline in trade. The second consisted of the promotion of exports with a slow opening of the economy (1985–1990). The third consisted of the opening of the economy, the continued promotion of exports and the reconstruction of integrated regional trade (1991–1996).

Box 7.1   Debt-for-Nature swaps

In the framework of programmes for the reconversion of external debt managed by the Central Bank of Costa Rica (BCCR), *Debt-for-Nature swaps* emerged in Costa Rica in 1987. Such programmes have received financial support from the Governments of the Netherlands and Sweden.

The BCCR authorized the first project in 1987. The corresponding debt had a face value of US$11.7 million. In the period 1987–1990 Costa Rica received funding of US$16.5 which allowed it to buy external debt documents for a face value of US$96.5. In exchange, the BCCR emitted the equivalent of US$51.7 in *Bonos de Estabilizacion Monetaria (BEM)*, denominated in local currency. The following projects have been approved (in millions of US dollars):

Project	Year	Grant	Face value	BEM	Percentage of face value
Purchase and scientific management of forests	1987	4.4	11.0	7.33	67
Purchase of land and protection of National Parks	1987	0.9	5.4	4.05	75
Purchase of land and protection of National Parks	1988	0.8	5.6	1.68	30
Reforestation, forest management and protection of forest areas	1989	5.0	39.2	11.75	30
Purchase of land and protection of National Parks	1990	3.5	24.5	17.15	70
Purchase of land and protection of National Parks	1990	1.9	10.8	9.75	90
Total		16.5	96.5	51.71	54

Debt-for-Nature projects became less attractive in the early 1990s, on account of several factors:

(a) new norms established by the BCCR;
(b) the BCCR's priority in reducing the monetary supply with a view to combating inflation. One way to achieve this was to reduce the emission of BEM;
(c) the higher value of Costa Rican debt in the secondary markets for foreign debt titles. In particular, following the renegotiation of the external debt under the Brady Plan, the price of Costa Rican debt titles increased significantly, achieving ratios of between 45 and 63 per cent of their face value.

This resulted in stagnation of the Debt-for-Nature programmes in the early 1990s. However, renewed interest in the programme has emerged recently, particularly with regard to bilateral debts.

In summary, the Debt-for-Nature programme has strengthened the conservation of National Parks, particularly by facilitating the purchase of lands and the establishment of programmes to administrate and protect the corresponding areas.

After a period of recession and substantial reduction in trade (1980–1984), the export sector grew at an average yearly rate of 9 per cent between 1984 and 1995. The non-traditional export sector, which grew at an average annual rate of 14 per cent during this period, was the largest contributor to the surge in exports.

The country's total exports in recent years are presented in Table 7.1. This shows that coffee and bananas continue to be an important base of international trade in Costa Rica, in spite of the growth which some non-traditional products have experienced.

Table 7.1   Costa Rica: total exports, 1990–1995 (millions of US dollars)

Products	1990	1991	1992	1993	1994	1995	Percentage change 94/95
Traditional exports	666.5	766.0	802.1	846.6	957.1	1122.2	17.2
Bananas	317.0	402.9	491.5	536.7	569.9	620.8	8.9
Coffee	245.4	263.6	201.6	203.2	310.2	406.9	31.2
Meat	46.2	58.8	4.3	67.0	24.9	46.1	85.1
Sugar	33.5	21.4	28.1	28.9	48.3	42.8	−11.3
Others	24.4	19.3	39.6	10.8	3.8	5.6	45.5
Non-traditional exports	702.9	729.6	905.6	1132.6	1184.5	1375.5	16.1
Livestock/Fish	51.7	52.9	93.3	141.7	97.5	108.3	11.0
Timber & derivs	25.6	20.9	23.9	33.4	32.9	36.8	11.8
Agriculture[1]	153.4	167.5	194.0	239.6	284.8	335.7	17.9
Food ind.	50.2	48.9	137.3	163.0	173.2	229.6	32.6
Industrial	447.6	460.3	481.0	588.2	629.1	701.9	11.6
Sub-totals	1369.4	1495.6	1707.7	1979.2	2141.6	2497.6	16.6
Textiles: TAR[2]	81.2	94.5	109.0	115.6	116.9	126.5	8.2
Textiles: FZ[2]	25.4	40.3	58.0	79.0	93.5	142.1	52.0
Total exports	1476.0	1630.4	1874.7	2173.8	2352.0	2766.2	17.6

Notes
[1] This includes the category of timber and its derivatives.
[2] Textiles divided into those related to Temporary Admission Regime and Free Zones

Source: CENPRO.

Imports have increased significantly in recent years (see Table 7.2). Between 1985 and 1994 the average annual growth was 9.5 per cent, increasing to 3.2 million dollars in 1995, almost three times the 1985 level. The main imports are raw materials for industry, perishable consumer goods and capital goods for industry, which shows that the industrial sector depends heavily on imports.

Table 7.2   Costa Rica: composition of imports (millions of US dollars)

Category	1985	1990	1991	1992	1993	1994
Raw material for industry	467.1	745.6	710.7	861.3	941.7	933.6
Raw material for farming	69.7	86.7	97.6	110.9	117.1	44.6
Perishable consumer goods	149.3	328.9	330.0	407.8	492.9	460.7
Non-perishable consumer goods	52.7	132.3	109.3	148.8	329.4	256.2
Capital goods for industry	147.7	337.5	285.1	393.9	511.9	361.9
Capital goods for farming	9.3	10.6	8.5	12.2	15.9	24.6
Capital goods for transport	71.4	119.4	100.8	148.4	193.6	131.2
Construction material	28.3	63.5	72.3	85.7	93.0	97.1
Fuels and lubricants	89.9	149.5	153.1	159.7	174.1	169.9
Others	12.7	15.7	9.0	10.6	15.1	7.1
Total	1 098.1	1 989.7	1 876.4	2 439.3	2 884.7	2 486.9

Source: Central Bank of Costa Rica.

North America is the main destination of Costa Rican exports representing between 41 per cent and 44 per cent of the total exports (see Table 7.3). The United States is Costa Rica's main trading partner. The European Union is the second most important market receiving about 30 per cent of the exports while Central America represents approximately 16 per cent of Costa Rica's exports.

Table 7.3   Costa Rica: exports by economic regions (millions of US dollars)

Economic region	1994	%	1995	%
North America	998.3	44	1 062.1	41
Central America	360.7	16	427.6	16
South America	58.9	3	76.0	3
Caribbean	71.7	3	83.2	3
European Union	682.9	30	805.7	31
EFTA	16.8	1	22.0	1
Asia	44.8	2	115.8	4
Others	24.4	1	31.7	1
Total	2 258.5	100	2 624.1	100

Source: CENPRO, Department of Economic Studies.

7.3　THE EFFECT OF INTERNATIONAL ENVIRONMENTAL REQUIREMENTS ON COSTA RICA'S EXPORTS

For the Costa Rican economy, whose export supply depends heavily on products based on natural resources, increasingly frequent restrictions on trade for environmental reasons are perceived as a potential threat. An analysis of the exports of Costa Rica indicates their potential vulnerability to the establishment and widespread use in different international markets of environmental norms.

According to the calculations in this study, 40% of the exports of Costa Rica are potentially susceptible to environmental restrictions in their destination market, whereas 16 per cent are *directly susceptible*.[1] Some of the main restrictions which may be mentioned include: (a) standards and regulations related to the composition of the product; (b) making the producer responsible for recycling or waste treatment; (c) eco-labelling programmes; and (d) ensuring the reuse and recycling of certain products. This suggests the need for the government to develop a more active response in the area of national legislation, and control and implementation of norms and regulations. This is in order to stimulate the adjustment of national production to international markets, to facilitate its competitiveness and to adjust to the demands of environmentally stricter countries.

In some cases, Costa Rican exports were restricted due to the environmental production regulations in the importing countries. In particular, tuna, shrimp, meat and calamondin were restricted, although not blocked entirely in each case.

7.3.1　Perceived Effects of the Main Environmental Regulations

To analyse the economic impact of the main environmental regulations on the national productive sector, a questionnaire was distributed to 250 firms affiliated to the Chamber of Industry in Costa Rica; 39 firms responded. This survey showed that national producers are not very familiar with the existence of international environmental norms. Ten of the firms consulted (26 per cent) said that they had no information on the subject. This can be explained partly because the majority of the exports from Costa Rica go to the United States and Central America, where there are less environmental requirements concerning traded products than in the European Union. Nevertheless, there is an increasing awareness of the necessity of following stricter environmental standards, in order to be competitive in the future.

The firms were more concerned with the fulfilment of *national* environmental standards, particularly Law No. 7310 regulating the handling of liquid waste, and the Organic Law of the Environment, passed in 1995, which requires the presentation of an environmental impact study for all projects affecting the environment.

Based on the information obtained in the survey, it can be inferred that in Costa Rica environmental requirements are not as yet an important factor in accessing external markets. Indeed, 84 per cent of the respondents (34 firms) said that they had not encountered any limitations to market entry for environmental reasons. However, it must be emphasized that the small and medium-sized firms complained the most about the possible adverse effects on competitiveness of compliance with new environmental standards.

Of the 39 firms consulted, 31 said that they had introduced some type of initiative to reduce the environmental impact generated. Some of the main actions include treating sewage, the introduction of new technology, reforestation, and recycling waste. The study showed that the cost of compliance with the environmental norms is relatively low, since in the majority of the cases it is under 2 per cent of the total operating costs.

The entrepreneur's main concern is gaining the acceptance of products in foreign markets. This concern seems proactive rather than defensive. A large percentage of Costa Rican entrepreneurs are quite aware of the fact that in the future fulfilling environmental regulations will play an important role in their accessing of foreign markets.

7.3.2   Empirical Evidence of the Environmental Restrictions on Trade

In this research some restrictions on Costa Rican exports were detected, based on environmental protection measures established in developed countries. Although these restrictions have not led to a significant reduction in exports, it is important to point them out since they show how vulnerable certain national products are to environmental norms. The main cases are the following:

Shrimp
In 1995 the United Stated passed a law which requires those who export shrimp to that country to use 'Turtle Exclusion Devices' (TEDs) to protect sea turtles. Since nearly half of Costa Rica's shrimp exports go to the United States, it is necessary to be familiar with and apply its environmental regulations. Although there are no studies which quantify the economic impact of the use of TEDs, it is estimated that the loss of foreign currency for the country would be almost US$2000000. Another element to consider is the possible loss of competitiveness in other markets where the use of TEDs is not required.

Tuna
Tuna fishing in Costa Rica is carried out by Mexican and Venezuelan ships, since the country does not have a national fishing fleet. The national canning

companies buy tuna from these ships. Thus, Costa Rica has suffered the effects of the tuna embargo which the United States placed upon Mexico, and which is considered a secondary embargo. The economic effects of this embargo have not been quantified, but are believed to be significant. Efforts are being made to eliminate the embargo since the data from the International Tropical Tuna Commission (*Comision Internacional del Atún Tropical, CIAT*) show that the killing of dolphins due to tuna fishing in Costa Rica has been reduced substantially.

Beef
Towards the end of the 1980s a publicity campaign in Miami claimed that with every hamburger consumed, Costa Rica was becoming more and more deforested. The campaign was promoted by Miami environmentalist groups supported by meat producers in the area. There was so much pressure that the Miami Burger King decided temporarily to stop importing beef from Costa Rica. Although this did not have a serious effect on exports because these restrictions were soon lifted, it showed how vulnerable some export products are to environmental criteria.

Calamondin
The calamondin, a type of ornamental citrus, began to be produced by a national firm and exported to Europe, as part of the promotion of non-traditional exports. However, in 1993, the European Union prohibited the entry of these plants into Europe, based on the new regulations on sanitary measures. This was particularly due to the potential risk of the plants carrying the *Citrus Tristeza* virus which affects citrus plantations. Although the firm was able to prove that the plants were not carrying the virus, the European Union refused to reopen the exports citing the potential threat of the virus. Some perceive this action to be based on trade protectionist grounds rather than environmental grounds.

7.4   MULTILATERAL ENVIRONMENTAL AGREEMENTS

While complying with the main Multilateral Environmental Agreements (MEAs) may represent costs to other developing countries, in the case of Costa Rica they have been perceived as a source of new opportunities. For example, in the context of climate change, Costa Rica has been active in developing joint implementation programmes, particularly in the framework of the United States Initiative on Joint Implementation (see Section 7.5.3 on forestry). Costa Rica, in 1995, was one of the first developing countries to develop a national inventory of greenhouse gases.

Costa Rica has also been at the vanguard of policies aimed at the conservation and sustainable use of biodiversity, for example through the activities of the

National Institute for Biodiversity (INBio). There is an interest in exploring the potential of bioprospecting[2] to act as an incentive for conservation and sustainable development, for example by building partnerships with firms from developed countries, in particular regarding access to and diffusion of technology, finance and capacity-building. A much debated example is the agreement between INBio and Merck Sharp, signed in October 1991 with a total value of US$1 million. Cooperation arrangements have subsequently been established with the British Technology Group (BTG) and Cornell-Bristol Myers Squibb. However, it is recognized that there are still many uncertainties. For example, INBio has found problems in determining the value of potential biodiversity services, an issue which needs to be further examined. Therefore, Costa Rica has adopted a prudent approach towards signing bioprospecting contracts with a view to avoiding arrangements which bring little benefit to the country (see Box 7.2).

7.4.1 The Montreal Protocol

The objective of the Montreal Protocol is to control the trade, use and production of substances which harm the ozone layer, particularly CFCs and freon. Industrialized countries had to eliminate the production and use of CFCs by 1997. Developing countries, however, have ten more years to meet the regulations of the Protocol.

The annual *per capita* consumption of CFCs in Costa Rica is approximately 0.1 kg (mainly due to refrigeration) which places the country in the 'low freon-consumption' category, allowing it longer time to substitute the CFCs.

Costa Rica ratified the Montreal Protocol on 8 May 1991, under Law No. 7223, but a law to regulate its application has not yet been approved. A mechanism has been established to keep a record of the importers and the quantities of the imported substances.

A programme has been established to reduce the use of CFCs through: (a) a national freon recovery and recycling plan which includes improving maintenance techniques and recycling CFCs; (b) changing the use of refrigerants in domestic appliances.

Atlas Electrica, a refrigerator manufacturer in Costa Rica, has presented an industrial reconversion project for US$500 000 to the Multilateral Fund. The firm does not consider the cost of reconversion to be too high and expects to recover part of the investment through the process of recycling freon.

The Protocol has contributed to making importers and consumers of CFCs aware of the need to be prepared to substitute these substances. The use of CFCs and halogens such as propellent gases in *aerosols* have been prohibited. However, those consulted believe that it did not have a significant impact, since in this case, they may be easily replaced by hydrocarbons or carbon dioxide.

Box 7.2   Conservation and use of biodiversity

Costa Rica, with an area of 51 100 km^2 (20 000 square miles), has a varied topography and a diversity of microclimates, and is one of the biologically wealthiest countries in the world, per square kilometre. It is estimated that 5% of all the species existing in the world can be found in Costa Rica (WRI-INBio, 1994: 71). Therefore, a need exists to have adequate mechanisms for their use and conservation.

One of the most outstanding conservation efforts in the country has been made by the National Biodiversity Institute (*Instituto Nacional de Biodiversidad, INBio*). The most important and controversial area in this field has been the chemical and pharmaceutical prospecting of the country's biotic resources which could feasibly be used for the development of new commercial products. In this sense, one of the best-known agreements has been that of *INBio-Merck Sharp Convention*, in which *INBio* has promised to provide extracts of plants, insects and environmental samples for two years. In turn, *Merck* has promised to pay one million dollars, provide laboratory equipment, train national personnel and pay 10% of any profits made.

Although the Convention does offer benefits for the country, there still are some aspects subject to further analysis, such as: (a) the low value-added which this activity generates since the more sophisticated part of the process is done outside the country; (b) the legal-institutional competence of *INBio* to use national patrimony, since the samples are extracted from National Parks; and (c) the adequate establishment of the monetary value of the commercial use of public goods.

The contract with *Merck* has been extended. In addition, along these same lines, agreements of cooperation have been signed with *British Technology Group (BTG)*, which is interested in isolating nematicide substances to combat nematodes on banana plantations; and with *Cornell-Bristol Myers Squibb*, which is interested in isolating pharmaceutical substances in insects and anthropoids.

Another *INBio* project which is important to mention is the *Inventory of the Biodiversity of All the Taxa*. The objective is to find and classify all of the species which live in the same natural site, particularly in the Guanacaste Conservation Area, with an area of 120 000 ha. At present, *INBio* only has partial financing for the task.

The products which could potentially be affected by the Montreal Protocol are those which require refrigeration during transport, such as bananas, fruit, flowers, plants and meat. These products represent an important portion of the country's total exports and steps should be taken for the substitution of CFCs, in order to minimize the long-term effects of their phase-out.

Even if there are no specific data available on the expected effect of the Montreal Protocol in particular sectors such as electrical appliances and refrigeration, it is estimated that the overall cost of reconversion required will be no more than five million dollars.

7.4.2 CITES

The International Convention on the Trade of Endangered Species (CITES), signed in Washington in March 1973, was ratified by Costa Rica in 1975. However, the convention was actually applied in 1992 when the Law for Wildlife Conservation (Law 7317; 7 December 1992) was passed, and the necessary legal framework was created to enforce CITES in Costa Rica.[3]

In order to have effective operation of CITES, basic equipment and a broad training programme for customs officials are required to be able to detect the types of species leaving the country. However, according to the sources consulted in this study, basic control of exports exists only at the Juan Santamaría airport (the country's main exit port). Although other customs points are of less importance, they could be allowing the exit of some species.

It is important to emphasize that Law 7317 states that all imports and exports of wildlife species should pay a 5% tax, which supports the activities of the office in charge of administering CITES. Some orchid dealers have complained that this tax reduces their competitiveness. They feel that it should not apply to re-exports, as they import small plants from the Netherlands, which they develop for about two years and then export to the United States.

Within CITES, orchids are the most sought after plants in the country, particularly the purple orchid known as *Guaria Morada* (*Cattleya skinnery*). Since this plant is highly coveted by orchid collectors, some nursery owners have reproduced it for commercial purposes. This has caused a significant increase in the quantity of plants existing in Costa Rica to the extent that the CITES authorities in the country decided to move it from Annex I (endangered species) to Annex II (species which are not endangered, but which could be in the future). Thus, it could be concluded that in this case market mechanisms have promoted the conservation of the *Guaria Morada* in the country.

There are no precise estimates in the country of the amount of trade of products covered under CITES. However, it can be said to represent an insignificant percentage of Costa Rica's total exports. Thus, the commercial effect of the application of CITES is limited. Nevertheless, the environmental effect could be considered very valuable, given the country's biological wealth. Experts believe that CITES has contributed to reducing illegal trade in a number of species that were in danger of extinction, although it is recognized that there is still illegal trade.

7.4.3 The Basel Convention

The objective of the Basel Convention, signed in 1989, is to reduce the generation of dangerous waste, to promote their deposit as near as possible to the place where they are generated and to demand the environmentally safe handling of all dangerous waste.

Costa Rica ratified the Basel Convention on 8 August 1991, under Law 149. However, the enforcement mechanism is still lacking because regulations have not yet been passed.

Two products which have faced import regulations in Costa Rica are used tyres and burnt oil from ships, used in highway construction. Although burnt ship oil is not regulated by the Basel Convention, but rather by Marpol, which Costa Rica has not signed, the framework of the Basel Convention is used to apply this regulation.

No data exist on the commercial effects of the Basel Convention. However, the people consulted in this study feel that they would be quite low and argue that the environmental effect of the Basel Convention is very positive, since it protects the country from possible contamination which could have serious unforeseen consequences.

The Ministry of Health is the entity responsible for the administration of the Basel Convention in Costa Rica. The government has difficulty in adequately monitoring the fulfilment of the Basel Convention due to the lack of institutional development (laboratories, customs authorities and personnel).

7.5 CASE STUDIES

Bananas, coffee and forestry were chosen for study because, besides being important for Costa Rican trade, they are sensitive from the environmental viewpoint. Analysis was made of the vulnerability of these sectors to environmental requirements, both nationally and internationally, by visiting the main organizations and producers in each sector and by identifying the firms' familiarity with these requirements as well as their responses to them.

7.5.1 Bananas

The history of the banana in Costa Rica dates back to the 19th century. Throughout the 20th century it has been one of the main export products of the national economy. At present, Costa Rica is the second largest exporter of bananas in the world and has the highest productivity per hectare cultivated. The banana, after tourism, is the main generator of foreign currency.

The main environmental effects of banana production include pollution due to the use of pesticides, contamination from plastic waste, the loss of biodiversity, and deforestation. The use of large quantities of pesticides is indispensable, since the moist tropics are favourable for a disease known as *Sigatoka Negra*. As a matter of fact, Costa Rica is the main importer *per capita* of pesticides in Central America, of which nearly 45% is used for banana production (see Box 7.3 on imports and use of pesticides in Costa Rica).

It is important to point out that although Costa Rican banana production has been questioned because of its high consumption of agrochemicals, the banana has not faced any problems on international markets because of toxic residue on the fruit, except on one occasion.

One of the effects of the use of agrochemicals in this country was the sterilization of hundreds of banana workers which occurred with the application of Nemagon in the 1970s. There has also been much comment on the frequent intoxication suffered by labourers on banana plantations, which have been connected to several deaths. However, it should be emphasized that in the last few years the incidence of intoxication has decreased significantly.

Some of the steps which have been taken in Costa Rica to reduce the environmental effect of agrochemicals include: establishing adequate warehouses to store agrochemicals; periodic medical check-ups for the workers handling agrochemicals; strict control of the dosage applied; and the use of other pesticides as a substitute for those which are more toxic.[4] Moreover, a research programme is being conducted to produce plants which are resistant to *Sigatoka*. It is expected that in three or four years lines will be selected for commercial use which will require a significant reduction in the application of agrochemicals.

The use of plastic bags was introduced in the 1960s and has become standard practice as a way of protecting the fruit from being attacked by insects and a way of accelerating the ripening process. This generates about 67 kg/ha per year of plastic waste which takes a long time to biodegrade. Polypropylene used in tying the plants generates about 80 kg/ha per year of waste.

Two recycling plants for plastic waste have been constructed. A substantial amount of plastic waste is recycled and is mainly used to produce construction materials. The problem of recycling plastic is that the polyethylene which is produced is of a very low density which prevents the manufacture of new plastic bags.

One of the most criticized aspects of banana production has been its deforestation of primary forests and along riverbanks. Although national laws prohibit the cutting down of trees along riverbanks, the rivers which cross banana plantations are completely deforested.

Box 7. 3   Import and use of pesticides

Costa Rica is the largest importer *per capita* of pesticides in Central America and one of the largest *per capita* in the world. This can be explained in part because: (a) Costa Rica is the world's second largest banana producer (an activity which requires almost half of the pesticides used in the country); (b) Costa Rica is one of the countries with the highest level of productivity of coffee per hectare in the world (this is achieved by using a technological package with a high amount of pesticides); (c) in the last few years the export of non-traditional products (flowers, ornamental plants, pineapples, melons) has been intensified (significant quantities of agrochemicals are applied on these products); and d) farm input which the country imports is tax exempt.

This high consumption of pesticides is not surprising if we consider that the price of land and man hours in Costa Rica are up to double those of other countries of the region. The farmers' need for maximization leads them to concentrate on the production operation, using a pesticide-intensive combination of factors.

National legislation permits the import of any pesticide as long as its use is not prohibited in the country which it is exported from, whether or not there are restrictions on it in other countries. Moreover, in Costa Rica a restricted pesticide only needs approval from the Ministry of Agriculture regarding the interests of using it in the country for it to change from restricted to authorized. This explains why pesticides are used in Costa Rica which are restricted or prohibited in other countries. In addition, some pesticides restricted in Costa Rica are imported in large quantities.

It should be stressed that in the last few years training programmes have been promoted on the handling and use of pesticides, and on their harmful effects. These programmes have been supported by the Chamber of Farm Input, the Ministry of Education and some associations of farm producers. However, these efforts are still insufficient. Another area in which greater efforts should be made is in the processing and use of data, since the country does not have an information system to process and keep up to date information on the import and use of pesticides by product, active ingredient and country of origin.

It must be stressed that the banana industry has made some progress in reforestation, mainly on the new farms which were planted in the mid-1980s. In addition, in the early 1990s, a reforestation programme was started on several plantations. However, the magnitude of this progress is still being debated.

It is difficult to determine precisely the real cost of adapting to the new environmental norms in banana production due to the varying levels of environmental deterioration of the plantation at the beginning of the process, and the varying productivity of particular plantations. However, producers as well as representatives of CORBANA estimate that the cost is relatively low. According to initial calculations, it is believed that meeting the environmental norms will cost no more than 4 per cent of the total production costs. In many cases, it is much less.

It should be noted that the banana producers have not reported facing serious trade restrictions for not complying with the environmental norms established by the export markets. On the other hand, they have not experienced the positive effects of complying, such as better prices or new markets. Nevertheless, some producers are taking precautions due to the threat of losing certain markets, particularly in the European Union where there is increasing interest in restricting the entry of products which are not environmentally friendly.

In 1992 the ECO-O.K. seal began to be used in Costa Rica. It emerged as a joint initiative of the Rainforest Alliance, United States and the AMBIO foundation, Costa Rica. The objective of this seal is to offer a certification system to banana producers interested in applying an environmentally friendly production system. One firm, EARTH, consider that the production costs of certified bananas are about 2 per cent higher than those of conventional bananas. Although niche markets for certified bananas exist in Europe and the United States, none of the companies exporting certified bananas is reported to receive a price premium. However, firms consider that if in the future these norms are required in the export markets, the producers will have a competitive advantage which is perhaps the main reason why national producers are applying stricter environmental norms in banana production.

There are, however, certain factors limiting the use of the ECO-O.K. label. First, there may be trade-offs between environmental quality and other product quality factors. Second, the three largest exporters buy bananas from various plantations and it is difficult to distinguish bananas from certified plantations from those which are not certified.

The company which has shown most interest in ECO-O.K. is Chiquita, which certifies or is in the process of certifying production from 14 of its 29 plantations. However, Chiquita is not using the ECO-O.K. label, because only part of its production is certified.

There is a new initiative for producing organic bananas, mainly sold as a paste. Also small-scale efforts are being made to export dehydrated organic bananas. In addition, one farm produces and exports organic bananas to be consumed fresh on the European market. Nevertheless, there is still little knowledge as to the real feasibility of promoting organic banana production in the country on a large scale.

7.5.2   Coffee

Since the second half of the 19th century, coffee has been a dominant export product in Costa Rica. It continues to be one of the country's main export products although it has become increasingly less important as a percentage of total exports, which is due mainly to the instability of international prices and to the growth of other export activities.

The environmental effects of coffee production are caused by production at the farm and industrial level. The negative environmental impacts of farm production have been increasing due to the development of technological packages which improve the productivity per hectare, but require the intensive use of agrochemicals and erosion-prone cultivation techniques. Direct environmental effects are intoxications and the pollution of water with nitrates from the use of nitrogenous fertilizers. The best-known risks for human health are methaemoglobinaemia, or the blue baby syndrome, and gastric cancer. In Costa Rica this situation should be analysed carefully since 56 per cent of the area where coffee is grown is in the Central Valley, the most highly populated area of the country.

In coffee processing, the environmental effects are related to the generation of both liquid and solid waste which has mainly been disposed of in rivers and streams. Regulations which do address these problems do not stem from pressure from international markets, but rather they reflect national concern.

In farm production, the Ministry of Agriculture and Cattle Raising is the entity which defines the use of agrochemicals. The Ministry restricted and finally prohibited the use of lead arsenate on these plantations after the appearance of high concentrations of this agrochemical in coffee exported to Germany in the 1970s. However, control mechanisms still have not been established with respect to possible water pollution.

With respect to the processing phase, a timetable for a three-stage plan has been established to treat sewage in processing plants which is expected to substantially reduce liquid and solid waste.

The study has shown that the costs which the processing firms must bear to fulfil the environmental regulations are relatively higher for the smaller firms. This is particularly the case in the first stage where the costs of the investments required to reduce one-third of the use of water are relatively independent of the size of the plant.

The work necessary for stages two and three, which involves the introduction of depulping and anaerobic treatment of dissolved material, is very costly. In the case of a large coffee processing plant (over 96 000 pounds per year), the cost of this work is calculated at $220 000 which equals 5.5 per cent of the estimated costs of the plant. However, when access to credit is available, completion of the three-stage plan is financially feasible.

An alternative to traditionally produced coffee is organic coffee which does not require a cultivation system using agrochemicals. Producers can adapt to this system in two ways: (a) by beginning a new plantation with an organic system; or (b) by applying organic techniques to existing plantations, with a 3-year transition period to comply with the conditions for certification.

In 1993, there were 17 organic coffee producers in Costa Rica representing less than 1 per cent of the total production. The study shows that there is still interest in moving into organic production although certain obstacles have limited the growth of this activity.

When international coffee prices practically doubled between 1993 and 1994, many of the producers in the transition process to organic coffee production decided to apply agrochemicals to their plantations again, in order to increase short-term productivity.

The productivity level of organic coffee is lower than that of conventional coffee. There are no up-to-date studies on the different options for the application of organic technology, which makes it difficult to evaluate the degree of profitability of this activity.

The certification costs for an average small organic coffee farm of 3 hectares with a production of 25 600 pounds per hectare are 4.5 per cent of the total income (calculated for the 1995–1996 harvest). In the case of a production of 12 800 pounds, certification costs would be 9 per cent of the total income. In Costa Rica these costs have generally been borne by the processing plants which are also in charge of marketing the product. The national producers have received a premium of as much as 20 per cent.

7.5.3 Forestry

Costa Rica is recognized internationally for its efforts towards the conservation of the biodiversity of its flora and fauna. The establishment of the National Parks began in the 1970s and at present, about 25 per cent of the country belongs to National Parks and Protected Areas.

Nevertheless, the country has experienced a high rate of deforestation in the past few decades. In 1950, 72 per cent of the country was covered with natural vegetation, but this was reduced to 49 per cent in 1983, and further to 35 per cent in 1994.

Reforestation has been subsidized by the Costa Rican Government. Since the end of the 1970s, different types of incentives were established, such as tax exemptions, soft credits and grants for planted areas.[5] However, the government has been lacking the institutional capacity to adequately monitor the reforestation programmes. Although no reliable record exists, it is estimated that only 60 per cent of these projects are in good condition.

When analysing the environmental effects of the forestry sector, the production chain as a whole should be considered, not only the process of making the finished product. The first stage in the forestry industry is the extraction of the timber, which implies deforestation causing the following adverse environmental effects: soil erosion, a loss of biodiversity, the destruction of natural beauty and reduction in the water supply. The second stage is the milling of the timber. The environmental effects in this stage are related to the use of chemical products to 'cure' the wood, such as formaldehyde, which have toxic effects. The third stage is the manufacture of the finished products which requires the frequent use of chemical products such as solvents, paints, varnishes and aerosols. There is a potential risk of polluting rivers and affecting people and animals due to the inappropriate use of these products.

The export of timber represents less than 2 per cent of the country's total exports most of which go to the United States. Very little is sold to the European Union which may be the reason why only one of the firms surveyed faced environmental trade restrictions to market access.

Preliminary studies have shown that up until now national consumers do not seem to be willing to pay more for certified wood products. Although in international markets a possible premium may be foreseen, it is not clear if this incentive will be enough to prompt producers to readjust their productive processes to access markets for certified products. Currently, only the largest forestry projects are certified by the Green Cross seal. The people interviewed for this study felt that forestry certification is very costly and not profitable for firms with less than 500 hectares.

Forests do not only supply wood but also generate tourism, particularly eco-tourism, which has grown significantly in recent years and has become a main source of foreign currency. Also, with the Convention on Climate Change and the emergence of the Initiative of Joint Implementation, Costa Rica has been able to capture foreign currency as compensation for the service of carbon sequestration. Costa Rica has made important progress in national biodiversity prospecting and it is expected to be a source of economic benefits in the future.

Costa Rica is one of the leading countries in the development of Joint Implementation projects. In 1995 an office was established for evaluation of projects and their presentation to the Ministry of Environment and Energy (MINAE) for final approval. In addition, in 1994 Costa Rica and the United States signed the Declaration of Intentions for Bilateral Development, Cooperation and

Joint Implementation. This is a declaration which supports the bilateral efforts of the private sector to reduce the emissions of greenhouse gases. The United States Initiative for Joint Implementation (USIJI) has approved eight joint implementation projects with Costa Rica, three of which are already being carried out. The country has also signed an agreement with Norway, which is interested in supporting this initiative. It is expected that the initiatives for joint implementation will evolve towards the establishment of a stock market, where the rights for the emission of greenhouse gases will be negotiated. How this market will operate is still to be defined, including types of valuation, certification, verification and control of the projects. Since this is a novel initiative, it should be subject to permanent evaluation to determine the costs and benefits which it implies for the country, as well as their distribution.

In 1996, a new Forestry Law was passed with the intention of strengthening the protection of the National Parks as well as privately owned primary and secondary forests. In addition, a system of subsidies for reforestation and sustainable forest management was established. The law permits the export of logs, which previously had been prohibited, if they come from plantations, and this has aroused a great deal of debate in the country.

7.6   CONCLUSIONS AND AGENDA

7.6.1   General Conclusion

In the study no direct cause-and-effect relationship was found between the different macroeconomic policies in recent years and the levels of pollution or environmental deterioration. The latter are the result of both the economic growth pattern which prevailed over recent decades and the entire process of economic growth in the last few years. Some environmental problems have been addressed through measures which focus on conservation of environmental resources and mitigation of environmental problems. Nevertheless, the current level of environmental degradation still poses a threat to the sustainability of the productive sector.

The study detected a pattern of industrial growth with a distinct tendency towards the development of environmentally harmful industries. Although more research is needed, it appears that this pattern is not directly related to the economic and export promotion policies, and that the rate of increase of industrial pollution is not higher than that of production. It is recommended that more in-depth research is undertaken in those sectors which have a higher growth in their pollution indicators, such as foods, beverages and tobacco; paper, printing and publishers; and chemical industries.

There were less cases of actual export restrictions found in Costa Rica than in other national studies. In general, firms said that they had not been seriously affected by environmental regulations, although small businesses had some difficulties adapting to new environmental norms. Only in one case, in the fishing sector, was a decrease in competitive advantage experienced as a result of costly technological changes induced by environmental measures in the export market.

Of the 39 industrial firms consulted, 56 per cent consider that the sector has inadequate information systems on the environmental standards in international markets. This is partly related to the fewer environmental requirements in Costa Rica's main export markets, the United States and Central America. However, a group of export products, which represents around 40 per cent of the total value, is potentially susceptible to being affected by environmental regulations. As world trade is becoming increasingly more environmentally conscious, and geographical specialization of the economies continues, concern remains over the lack of institutional capacity to prevent and respond to environmentally based export restrictions.

A considerable national effort has been made in recent years to improve and update the institutional framework regarding the environment, but it is premature to evaluate the success of these efforts. Environmental conservation stems from both conservation and economic interests, as it has positive effects on tourism, investment and the promotion of exports.

Most of the concrete actions carried out to internalize the costs of controlling pollution have been more a product of social pressure (expressed in governmental regulations of a domestic nature) than direct restrictions on trade. The most outstanding cases are coffee, bananas and some industrial products.

Efforts have been made by producers, with the support of the NGOs and technical cooperation from other countries, to take advantage of new environmentally conscious niches opening up in the foreign market. Some of these efforts have had positive results, particularly in the case of organic coffee. Nevertheless, there is still some doubt as to the real dimension of the markets, the most suitable (and least costly) certification mechanisms, price differentials and marketing structures. Moreover, small producers who are environmentally friendly do not have much information and control over their product marketing.

Although the application of Multilateral Environmental Agreements implies potential costs for some of the member countries, in Costa Rica they have been perceived as generators of new opportunities. In particular, the Convention on Climate Change has been declared a priority for the national development strategy and the country benefits from the United States Initiative for Joint Implementation (USIJI).

The sustainable use of the wealth of national biodiversity is also creating an increasing number of opportunities for new areas of specialization. The novelty of the issue and the lack of national scientific capacity has made it necessary to train scientists and to establish an adequate regulatory framework in this area. The latter is difficult as no criteria exist yet to determine the true market value of biodiversity and to identify the real beneficiaries.

7.6.2 Conclusions on Case Studies

Banana producers have not yet experienced serious environmental restrictions in international markets. The main pressure has been at the national level. However, the producers are interested in introducing environmental norms to avoid the possible establishment of restrictions on access to certain markets in the future.

The production of organic bananas has recently become increasingly important in Costa Rica. The possibility of a larger export quota for the European Union, which is the product's main market, should be considered. More research is needed to determine the technical and economic feasibility of organic bananas on a large scale.

Based on this study, it can be concluded that the national coffee sector has not faced serious environmental restrictions in international markets. However, national environmental norms do affect the sector because the environmental problems in the coffee industry are mainly domestic.

The main environmental effect of coffee production in the country is water pollution. A three-stage plan has been developed to address the problem of waste produced by processing. It is estimated that the changes which should be introduced by the coffee processing plants to satisfy the environmental norms require an investment representing 5.5 per cent of the total cost of the plant.

In Costa Rica the production of organic coffee began in 1990 and currently accounts for less than 1 per cent of Costa Rica's total coffee production. Development of this sector has been slow due to uncertainty about the level of the premium, the scarce knowledge of this activity, certification costs and the lack of information to access markets. It will be necessary to conduct studies in order to determine: (a) the functions of production and real production costs as well as the behaviour of prices to determine profitability patterns and producer's response; and (b) what institutional improvements would be required to promote production.

The case of Costa Rica has shown that it is easier to apply certification programmes in large-scale forestry projects for two reasons: (a) it provides the opportunity to respond to the environmental requirements of the market on a large scale; and (b) because the large-scale option reduces certification costs per hectare. However, the situation is completely different for small producers, for whom the high certification cost per hectare practically prevents them from participating in the traditional forestry certification systems. Given the high number of small forest owners in the country, certification programmes should be promoted for organized groups of producers to reduce costs.

7.6.3 Agenda

- In-depth studies should be encouraged regarding the production–certification–marketing circuit of organic products. These studies should contain not only marketing aspects but also analysis of productivity and costs. When the conventional form of the product has difficulties accessing the markets, the possibility of negotiating openings for organic or ecologically sustainable production should be explored.

- Specific studies should be undertaken regarding pollution caused by the reduction of import barriers for products which have a direct potential for pollution (automobiles, fuels, agrochemicals, products with CFCs, products with non-biodegradable packaging, and others).

- Studies on the regulation and use of agrochemical products should be conducted.

- It is suggested that the government establish an efficient, up-to-date information system with statistics on imports and on the use of pesticides in the country.

- The Harmonized System of Merchandise Classification should differentiate between organic products to facilitate their marketing.

- It is suggested that UNCTAD keep an inventory of bilateral or multilateral negotiations on the subject of biodiversity. At the same time, it is important for UNCTAD and the World Organization for Intellectual Property Rights (*Organisation mondiale de la propriété intellectuelle, OMPI*) to prepare technical assistance projects for Costa Rica. This task should be carried out in cooperation with the Convention on Biodiversity. As part of the project, activities should be designed which improve the scientific and institutional capabilities.

- It is recommended that together with UNCTAD, the Framework Agreement on Climate Change conduct an extensive study on bilateral and multilateral negotiations regarding greenhouse gases in Joint Implementation programmes. The study should address both the global and local dimensions of such programmes. From a global perspective, pollution should be controlled at its origin. At the local level, benefiting from environmental resources could considerably enhance development.

- Biodiversity is a complex topic and its treatment is facing a series of unknowns. One of them is the establishment of mechanisms to evaluate potential biodiversity services. Another aspect is the Intellectual Property Rights on Biodiversity. These are areas where Costa Rica requires further research and advice from multilateral organizations.

NOTES

1. *Directly susceptible* exports are those which are destined for a market where that product has received some type of restriction, whereas *potentially susceptible* exports are those for which there is a some type of restriction in a market other than the one to which they are destined.

2. The systematic evaluation of biological material in the search for economically valuable discoveries.

3. The administration of CITES is under the control of the Ministry of Environment and Energy, in a small office composed of a CITES representative, an authority of flora, another on fauna, and basic administrative support. This office is also supported by scientific authorities on the subject, which in Costa Rica is made up of the National University of Costa Rica, the University of Costa Rica and the Association of Biologists.

4. It is important to mention that at one point European importers required the elimination of the use of staples to seal the boxes of bananas. This was easily solved by replacing the staples with glue.

5. The country has invested nearly $100 million in forestry incentives, with which 123 000 hectares have been reforested and around 22 000 hectares of primary forest have been managed.

8. India

8.1 INTRODUCTION

The Marrakesh agreement has opened up new opportunities for Indian exports, particularly in the areas of textiles and certain agricultural items.[1] However, in India, there is growing concern that the benefits of freer access to the OECD market may be undermined by non-tariff barriers in the form of stringent and sometimes arbitrary environment-related regulations. Export growth could also lead to increased pressures on the environment at home, but domestic environmental problems may or may not correspond to ecological preoccupations in developed nations. Given scarce funds, there may be a trade-off between addressing developmental issues and domestic ecological concerns, and investments in environmental improvements in response to external environmental regulations.

Two case studies were carried out to examine the linkages between trade and the environment from the perspective of India. The first study conducted by Jyoti Parikh, V.K Sharma and Manoj Panda at the Indira Gandhi Institute of Development Research, surveyed 30 representatives from pertinent industries, export promotion councils and government organizations in order to gain an understanding of the level of awareness of eco-standards among manufacturers and exporters, and the cost of compliance with external regulations on Indian exports.

The second study, carried out by Vasantha Bharucha, examined readily available reports/papers on the issue, as well as conducting a detailed questionnaire-based survey and holding discussions with a number of industry representatives and institutions in relevant sectors. The sectors surveyed were tea, dyes, agricultural products and processed foods, marine products, leather, textiles, and the refrigeration and air-conditioning industry. This chapter presents a synthesis of the two studies, while also drawing on other sources on this subject.[2]

The main conclusion emanating from the studies is that compliance with external eco-standards often necessitated the import of inputs and technology which were likely to raise the price of the final output. Since competitiveness of many Indian exports is based on price factors, such a price rise could hamper India's competitiveness in several sectors under study.

However, both studies were of the opinion that Indian exporters would be better off complying with the environmental requirements in the near future to avoid the possibility of losing a significant market for their products. This, according to the studies, was achievable through a well-defined policy structure to address issues relating to trade, development and the environment.

8.2 SPECIFIC PROBLEMS OF INDIA

The importation of raw materials and capital goods, coupled with poor foreign exchange earnings in India, has resulted in a chronic balance of payment problem. Low investment levels, and the consequent unemployment and domestic inefficiency were some other features of the Indian economy.

These, among other factors, pushed India towards a substantial change in policy in 1991. Liberalizing the economy entailed the aggressive export promotion of a variety of goods and incentives to attract Foreign Direct Investment (FDI). In 1993, the exchange rate was made convertible on the trade account, a major deviation from the entirely regulated exchange rate system of the past. Of particular relevance in the context of trade and environment linkages is a significant reduction in tariffs on many capital goods and inputs, which may permit the import of eco-friendly technologies and inputs at prices which don't significantly harm competitiveness.

The forces of liberalization have unleashed several factors which are relevant to the issue of trade and environment. Exporters, while interacting with the OECD market, are exposed to eco-technology as well as regulations. If they are successful at acquiring the eco-technology and adapting to these eco-standards, it would afford them the possibility of earning premium prices.

On the other hand, complying with the regulations may involve adopting production and process methods which raise the price of the final product, making it uncompetitive in the international market. In addition such a price rise will make the product unattractive for the domestic consumer. Exporters will then depend exclusively on the export market to recover the cost incurred in making environmental improvements.

8.3 DOMESTIC REGULATION

The environmental concerns and priorities of a low-income nation like India with mass poverty are very different from those in developed countries. While problems of global warming, ozone layer depletion and loss of biological diversity are emphasized by the industrialized world, the concerns in India centre around poverty alleviation and development. The immediate ecological concerns which need addressing here are contaminated drinking water, inadequate sanitation facilities, and smoky indoor air.

In accordance with its priorities, the government's focus has largely been on domestic sustainable development. For instance, benzidine dyes have been banned here because of local concerns about their effects on health, rather than through overseas pressures, although this would also benefit the export of dyes to OECD markets.

Concern for the local environment has led to several environmental regulations like the Water Act of 1974, the Air (Prevention and Control of Pollution) Act of 1981, and the Environment (Protection) Act of 1986. The Ministry of Environment and Forests is the enforcing authority which also implements changes in the regulations as and when necessary.

Some other regulations kept in view the needs of the environment locally, as well as international ecological concerns. The leather sector, for instance (Box 8.1), has come under heavy regulation from the government owing to both domestic concerns, as well as those of importers of Indian leather. For instance, the government has made compulsory provisions for effluent treatment in new tanneries. Common effluent treatment (CET) plants are being set up. Another regulation in this sector has been the ban of pentachrolophenol (PCP), which is used as a preservative for raw hides and skins.

In the area of agricultural production too, domestic regulations have been aimed largely at both local consumers and the international market. Although pesticides and chemicals are perceived as essential for increasing the productivity level in the agriculture sector, the government is attempting to curb the use of those chemicals which are deemed harmful to health. This aspect of domestic regulation is discussed in greater detail in the following section.

8.4   EFFECTS OF ENVIRONMENTAL REGULATIONS ON TRADE

For several decades, the Indian government has emphasized growth through import substitution, involving the import of capital goods. Machinery has therefore been a major import in this country. Besides machinery, fuels, manufactured goods, food and agricultural produce have been main imports (see Table 8.1).

Food and agriculture also form an important part of exports from India. Recently, attempts have been made to widen the range of exports, resulting in the promotion of high-value-added items such as processed agro and marine

Box 8.1   The Indian leather industry

The leather industry is one of the oldest and fastest growing industries in India. However, the potential environmental impact of the leather industry is widely acknowledged. In addition to the traditional problems of air and water pollution, there are other concerns like chemical safety, contamination of land and ground water, inadequate provision for solid waste and sludge disposal, and spills and accidents involving chemical substances. In one state, Tamil Nadu, workers suffered from skin disorders because of poor safety measures.

Considerable technical development has occurred in the recent past, and relatively less polluting tanning processes are now available. However, many obstacles remain in the way of widespread and effective introduction of these technologies, the most significant being high capital costs and maintenance costs. The government is beginning to play an active role in setting up common effluent treatment (CET) plants. In some cases, joint collaborations are being set up. For instance, UNIDO have set up CET plants in Tamil Nadu jointly with several Indian institutions, with the aim of treating effluents from a cluster of about 100 tanneries.

In the northern city of Kanpur, which has the largest concentration of leather processing in India, large amounts of waste get discharged into the river Ganga. To address this ecological problem, an ambitious Indo–Dutch collaboration is underway. As a part of this project, tanners, the Indian government and the Dutch government will contribute financially. The idea is that composite wastes from tanneries are mixed with domestic sewage, and jointly treated to reduce the Biological Oxygen Demand (BOD) load.

Even with such collaborations the cost incurred for setting up effluent plants and the cost of operation are very high. One study estimated the cost of treatment of waste water for the 500 000 tonnes of skin and hide India processed each year to be over US$15 million. This is an additional burden on Indian tanneries, which is likely to be reflected in the price of the final output. For exporters, particularly those producing at a small and medium scale, these price hikes, to meet variable costs and to adapt to external eco-stipulations, may affect their competitiveness.

products in the export basket. This is perhaps reflected in the growth in the food and agriculture segment of exports in the last three years. India has also successfully exported textiles, food and agricultural products, and leather. In 1993, for instance, these three items accounted for close to half of all exports, in value terms (see Table 8.1).

Table 8.1   India: total exports and imports by main commodity groups, 1975–1993 (millions of US dollars)

Commodity groups	1975	1980	1985	1990	1991	1992	1993
Imports							
(in value)							
Total	6289.5	13818.7	16223.6	23798.7	19509.1	24206.0	23058.3
Food and agricultural							
products	1750.9	1482.4	1920.3	1720.4	1135.3	1825.2	1508.5
Fuels	1418.6	6167.6	4297.8	6495.9	5839.7	7215.4	6290.9
Ores and metals	983.3	1835.2	3378.0	4189.8	2637.9	3479.7	4356.6
Manufactured goods	2836.1	5346.9	8824.3	12185.8	9736.0	12065.3	12351.9
(share in percentages)							
Total	100.0	100.0	100.0	100.0	100.0	100.0	100.0
Food and agricultural							
products	27.8	10.7	11.8	7.2	5.8	7.5	6.6
Fuels	22.6	44.6	26.5	27.3	29.9	29.8	27.3
Ores and metals	15.6	13.3	20.8	17.6	13.5	14.4	18.9
Manufactured goods	45.1	38.7	54.4	51.2	49.9	49.8	53.6
Exports							
(in value)							
Total	4354.8	7510.6	8949.5	17858.8	17873.0	20679.4	22206.5
Food and agricultural							
products	1817.0	2490.9	2522.3	3505.4	3361.0	3675.9	4167.2
Fuels	192.4	403.7	533.5	832.3	650.9	623.1	540.8
Ores and metals	792.2	1730.7	1947.2	4711.9	5060.8	6036.3	5893.5
Manufactured goods	1953.0	4404.3	5200.2	12624.1	12875.5	15202.6	16377.4
(share in percentage)							
Total	100.0	100.0	100.0	100.0	100.0	100.0	100.0
Food and agricultural							
products	41.7	33.2	28.2	19.6	18.8	17.8	18.8
Fuels	4.4	5.4	6.0	4.7	3.6	3.0	2.4
Ores and metals	18.2	23.0	21.8	26.4	28.3	29.2	26.5
Manufactured goods	44.8	58.6	58.1	70.7	72.0	73.5	73.8

Source: COMTRADE, UNCTAD.

After the disintegration of the USSR, India has turned increasingly to the OECD as its export market. In 1993, for instance, this market accounted for 57 per cent of India's exports. The main products absorbed by this market are leather, textiles, and food and agricultural products (see Table 8.2).

Table 8.2   India: exports by commodity groups and markets, 1993 (millions of US dollars)

Commodity groups	World	OECD countries Total	United States and Canada	European Union	Japan	Developing countries
Total	22 206.5	12 389.5	4 215.3	5 797.4	1 740.2	8 018.6
Food and agricultural products	4 167.2	1 871.7	465.9	867.3	494.7	1 878.6
Leather	540.8	416.7	53.2	334.1	7.5	93.5
Textiles	5 893.5	4 297.6	1 362.7	2 404.7	208.3	1 251.7
Manufactured goods	16 377.4	9 776.4	3 604.5	4 665.3	941.7	5 654.0
Metals	821.9	448.7	15.9	127.9	294.0	349.2
Chemicals	1 632.8	710.8	201.8	412.9	39.1	705.6

Source: COMTRADE, UNCTAD.

Of these, textiles have the highest export value to this market, representing 73 per cent of total textile exports in 1993. Another product of significance in this context was leather, where 85 per cent of exports went to the developed countries. Marine products are also an important export to the OECD, accounting for 83 per cent of India's total exports of these products. This sector is of particular importance to India's trade relationship with Japan, as marine products account for 21 per cent of India's exports to that country. Dyes and pigments, and fruit and vegetables are largely absorbed by the OECD (see Table 8.3).

Table 8.3   Regional market shares in India's export of sensitive products, 1993 (in percentage terms)

Commodity groups	World	OECD countries Total	United States and Canada	European Union	Japan	Developing countries
Total	100.0	57.0	18.0	26.1	7.8	36.1
Marine products	100.0	82.9	12.4	24.8	45.2	16.9
Fruits	100.0	65.5	27.9	26.8	5.1	31.9
Vegetables	100.0	75.7	21.4	32.9	3.3	20.6
Leather and leather products	100.0	84.8	17.1	58.9	1.5	11.7
Footwear	100.0	79.6	29.0	45.5	0.8	8.2
Textiles	100.0	73.3	20.5	39.6	3.6	22.8
Dyes and pigments	100.0	60.1	21.2	32.4	1.6	39.3

Source: COMTRADE, UNCTAD.

The importance of the OECD in India's exports makes it vulnerable to the eco-regulations established by this market. The extent of vulnerability of these products will be determined by the cost of compliance involved and access to technology required in the process.

8.4.1   Mandatory External Regulations

Whether or not mandatory external regulations affect the market for Indian exports will be determined by the cost of compliance and level of technological upgrading involved. The following section summarizes the findings of the studies in this regard, while also discussing the efforts being made, both by individual firms and the government, to comply with the regulations. The section focuses on German laws, largely because this one country accounts for about 69 per cent of all sensitive exports. Among sensitive products, about 16 per cent of leather products (except footwear) and as much as 47 per cent of textiles go to Germany.

Dyes

Regulations on dyestuffs affect both the textile and the leather sector directly, since both these sectors have encountered cost increases in an attempt to conform to eco-standards related to this intermediate product. The use of certain dyestuffs such as Cobalt Blue and Sulphur Black has been banned in external markets. Complying with stipulations regarding the pH level of the dyes may be difficult and expensive.

In the case of Sulphur Black, a by-product of maize starch has been identified as a viable substitute. For Cobalt Blue, however, changes in the manufacturing process were found to require a heavy investment of over US$ 13 million,[3] owing mainly to the upgrading of technology, particularly the establishment of secondary treatment plants in order to obtain the requisite quality, and investment in automation control instruments for monitoring purposes. Such adjustments were found to be close to impossible for the small-scale producers of dyes, which form a significant portion of dyestuff suppliers.

Switching to non-benzidene dyes also implies higher costs. One study estimated that the cost of Direct Black 38 dye was about $3 per kg, whereas Direct Black 22, which is non-benzidene, was priced at $8–10 per kg. In the case of textiles, raw materials, of which dyes are a significant cost, accounts for about 60 per cent of the cost of production.[4] Therefore regulations pertaining to dyes are likely to increase costs of the final output.

The adjustments required to comply with external regulations are likely to be particularly high for the small and medium-sized enterprises (SMEs). While exact numbers on their contribution to exports in the dyestuff industry are not available, one study does estimate that over 60 per cent of production is by small-scale enterprises.[5] One can therefore extrapolate that an important part of exports comes from small-scale units. To the extent that this segment contributes to exports, it will be particularly affected by external eco-regulation, because the unit compliance costs are likely to be higher than those for larger-scale enterprises.

Leather

Leather is one of the most seriously hit sectors among Indian exports. Besides stipulations on dyes, several other regulations inhibit its performance on the international market. Germany in particular, have banned the use of PCP, while in the EU, the threshold level in this regard is 1000 ppm. Germany also limits the use of formaldehyde. The use of environmentally friendly chemicals has become mandatory, restricting the process by which leather may be manufactured.[6]

Presently, most of the tanneries are resorting to the use of an imported substitute, BUSAN 30, which is acceptable to the external market. On average, the price of this substitute is ten times higher than the price of PCP.[7] Even though all chemical inputs together account for about 10 per cent of costs, complying with the eco-regulation is likely to affect the competitiveness of Indian leather.

One of the studies[8] reported that adhering to stringent external standards in dyestuffs would require the import of BUSAN 30. While the cost of compliance in this regard was difficult to estimate, it was felt that the cost of the tests alone could increase the price of shoes by \$3–\$4 per pair.[9] At the same time, a concern was expressed that even among imported dyes, the exact composition was not always known. Therefore, even incurring this extra cost would not necessarily guarantee entry into the more stringently regulated OECD markets. Overall, exporters stated that the cost of replacing all chemicals with eco-friendly ones raised total costs by 10 to 15 per cent.[10]

While the cost of compliance to the standards and testing costs are high, they are particularly onerous for the SMEs, which are responsible for about 70 per cent of the total leather exports from India.[11] Considering that these units face problems of accessing finance and technology to begin with, they are likely to be most affected by the external eco-regulations prevailing in the leather sector.

Textiles and ready-made garments

In addition to the stipulations pertaining to dyes, several other regulations are also imposed on textiles and garments being exported to the OECD markets. Statutory measures require that consumers are protected by compulsory labelling concerning formaldehyde. In addition, a ban has been issued on the use of some substances which have been identified as carcinogenic or allergenic.

As in the case of leather, an important part of ready-made garment exports come from SMEs. According to one estimate, this segment contributes as much as 63 per cent to the total exports from this sector.[12] Hence, a high proportion of the industry will face severe difficulties in complying with external regulations with respect to the quality of dyes in textiles, as well as regulations pertaining to other chemicals.

Considering that about 40 per cent of India's textiles go to the European Union, the steep compliance cost is likely to reduce the volume of India's textile export to this market, where competitiveness is determined by the ability to sell at lower prices (see Table 8.3). Therefore, the potential gain from the textile negotiations concluded at Marrakesh may be diminished by compliance with the eco-regulations in question.

Furthermore, German authorities have begun subjecting garments from India to extensive tests for traces of certain chemicals. It is expected that producers, suppliers or traders will now have to provide a declaration that these chemicals are not present in their merchandise. The declaration will be binding and allow German importers to reject goods demonstrating traces of these chemicals without any legal recourse for the Indian exporter.

Tea

Indian teas have been affected by the developed countries' preoccupation with pesticide content. Germany, for example, has made complaints about the high residue levels of Ethion, Tetradifon and Heptachlor in Indian teas. Complaints have also been received from other OECD importers about Assam, Terai and Booras teas containing high levels of Bicofol.

After studying the impact of eco-regulations on Indian tea exports, the government has banned 12 hazardous pesticides, including DDT, and has restricted the use of some less hazardous, but still harmful pesticides. Steps are also being taken to encourage organic farming, so that Indian tea and agro-products become more acceptable on the international market, while also benefiting the domestic consumer.

While the government has been attempting to regulate tea production, problems remain in the area of testing. Government officials contacted in the study stated that, while imposing bans on pesticides and issuing guidelines for tea growing were possible, lack of testing facilities was an important barrier to attaining eco-friendly production of tea.

Although figures on incremental cost were not available for the tea industry, exporters did state that adopting eco-standards on a large scale would increase the cost of production significantly enough to affect their world market for this product. This is particularly true in CTC and orthodox tea, where India's main competitors, China and Sri Lanka, have reported that they are unaffected by these eco-standards. Considering that India's competitiveness in this market depends on its ability to sell at low prices, complying with eco-regulations may imply a loss of market share. Complying may be more rewarding for high-value Darjeeling tea. Being a premium tea, it is more likely that the cost increase owing to compliance will be met with a price rise.

Food processing

Both Japan and the EU have strict regulations in this sector. In Japan, the Food Sanitation Law prohibits the import of many citrus fruits from India such as carambola, pomegranate, passion fruit, and so on. The Residue Standards of Agro Chemicals Law, applicable to nuts, sets limits to the extent of use of at least 22 pesticides.

Agricultural products also come under strict supervision in the EU where all imported food products are liable for inspection at the first point of entry for compliance with the food laws pertaining to the country of entry. The regulations in the EU also stipulate conditions regarding the labelling of packaging materials used in the imported products.

In one state in India, attempts were made to substitute DDT with the more eco-friendly pesticide, Malathion. The resulting cost of adopting the more acceptable pesticide was found to be four times the original cost, increasing substantially the burden on government support programmes. At the same time, the adjustment to eco-friendly production in this sector will have to be rapid to fully exploit the potential for enhanced agro-exports in the post-Uruguay-Round period.

Dramatic reductions in pesticide content of food production are also difficult from the point of view of development and growth. In India, great emphasis is placed on increasing the productivity of horticultural products, which is achieved through the extensive use of pesticides. Achieving lower costs through pesticide use are, however, not compatible with the requirements of importing markets in the OECD. If organic farming is pursued, in accordance with international eco-standards, the price competitiveness of Indian agro-products is likely to be seriously affected.

Marine products

Marine products are another environmentally sensitive group of products (see Box 8.2). The EU, especially Germany, has taken the lead in defining environmental product standards related to fish and fish products. The most important standard relates to the cadmium, mercury and lead content in the fish exported to OECD countries. The EU directive has also imposed process standards requiring hygiene during handling, processing and storage of marine products.

Box 8.2   The experience of exporters in the seafood industry

---

Detailed interviews with several exporters handling fish and shellfish exports, and information obtained from the Marine Products Export Development Authority (MPEDA), revealed that exporters were aware of bacteriological requirements. Standards for pesticides and heavy metal residues have not posed a major problem for Indian marine exports.

Because India uses mainly small craft, Indian fishing has not come under international criticism for being wasteful and a threat to endangered marine species like the blue whale and the dolphin. In addition, marine products are exported predominantly to the EU and Japan, where the Marine Mammal Protection Act is not applicable (see Table 8.3).

For packaging, most exports in the marine sector are sent out in bulk packages. Exporters do not seem to have encountered censure on environmental grounds. The type and material of packaging is decided according to the specific requirements of the importer, and the industry regularly collaborates with institutions such as The Indian Institute of Packaging for available testing facilities.

Exporters were, however, of the opinion that if the industry moved towards the production of higher-value-added marine products, and as the scale of operations increased in this sector, meeting external regulations would become increasingly difficult.

Japan's laws with respect to shrimps, a major export from India, pertain mostly to the level of pesticide and antibiotics contained in the exported fish. All types of antibiotics, and oxolinic acid and oxytetracyclines are banned; even though there is no fixed limit, if traces of the above are detected the shrimp consignment is liable to be rejected. Similarly, if traces of pesticides including DDT, Aldrin and Heptachlor are detected, the consignment will be subject to bans.

To promote Indian seafood in the international market, the government has introduced several regulations aimed at quality control and standardization in private processing facilities. Frozen fish and fishery products are subject to quality control and inspection prior to export, depending upon the stipulations made by the importer. Without a certificate of inspection, the export of frozen marine products is prohibited.

Exporters of these products stated that a long waiting time for testing and certification could lead to compromises on the freshness of the export. Since marine products are perishable items, there is a trade-off involved in testing for eco-friendliness and perishability of the product.

Packaging

Regulations concerning packaging materials, product charges, deposit–refund systems and take-back obligations have been put in place in OECD countries. The most comprehensive legislation existing today appears to be the German Packaging Ordinance, which holds manufacturers and distributors responsible for taking back used packaging.

Most Indian exporters are subject to these packaging laws if they are exporting to OECD nations, since all exports involve packaging. Furthermore, packaging materials which are of relevance to India, for instance jute, may be affected by the newly enacted packaging regulations, mainly because German consumers are not sufficiently familiar with it.

Recently, bulk drugs were not accepted into Germany because the plastic containers were made of non-recyclable materials.[13] Exporters are making serious attempts to conform to the standards stipulated for packaging in order to avoid such problems.

In the textile sector, packaging materials, such as polyvinylchloride (PVC) and high density polyethylene are being replaced by cardboard. Similarly, stiffeners in yarn bundles and garments are being replaced by cardboard. Exporters interviewed stated that the incremental cost of changeover to environmentally friendly packaging was 2 per cent to 3 per cent of packaging costs.[14]

Packaging laws in the OECD also affect the leather industry since this sector uses packaging materials both for individual pairs of shoes and for bulk packaging. Some exporters comment that for leather and leather products, the cost of packaging to a stringently regulated market such as Germany was twice the usual packaging cost to tanners.[15]

8.4.2 Voluntary Measures

Along with statutory eco-standards, criteria are also being set in importing countries, through eco-labelling. In the EU, several labelling systems exist which apply to the final output as well as the process and production method itself. Such criteria relate to the pesticide content in cotton and chemical usage in bleaching, dyeing and finishing.

Several factors hinder Indian textile exporters in complying with eco-criteria in the OECD market. For one, the loss of productivity associated with growing organic cotton may not be compensated for by the price premium associated with eco-friendly textile production. The case of organic cotton growing, like that of organic food crops discussed in the section on food processing, reflects a trade-off between productivity and eco-friendliness.

The cost factor remains a significant barrier to compliance with eco-labelling. Exporters were of the opinion that the standards prescribed in the OECD would involve importing a number of chemicals, while also requiring additional know-how. These were estimated to increase fixed costs by 10 per cent and variable costs by 15 per cent.[16]

Such costs are particularly onerous for small and medium-sized enterprises. Even among larger exporters, complying with the prevailing eco-criteria may not be sufficient to justify the cost because the market fetching price premiums is only about 25 per cent of the European market, while the competition to capture this market is intense. Hence, the incremental cost of adherence to eco-criteria may not be recouped.

At the same time, if production lines are adjusted to accommodate such methods of production, the price hike in the final product may affect the rest of the international demand for Indian textiles, which depends significantly on its price competitiveness. Exporters interviewed in one of the studies felt that such a price rise would severely affect the rest of their market.[17] It would also be impossible for small exporters, who, as stated earlier, contribute substantially to the textile sector, to meet the costs involved in making the above adjustments. Therefore, the problem of compliance with eco-labels in the textile sector seems very serious.

For leather products, the Indian industry felt that eco-labelling would act as a non-tariff barrier because of the cost elevation involved in subscribing to the label. At the same time, exporters felt that not doing so could affect about 50 per cent of their leather exports.[18]

Exporters of leather also felt that there had been lost opportunities owing to the implementation of eco-labels without adequate opportunities for exporters, such as those in India, to adjust to these. At the same time, the lack of technical and financial assistance to help leather exporters to benefit from the opportunities offered by price premiums in this sector acted as another barrier. A case in point is the technology for testing. While efforts are being concentrated on developing a number of testing facilities, with collaboration between the Indo-German Export Promotion Project and the Central Leather Research Institute, significant progress remains to be made.

Indian leather exports are rendered even more vulnerable because of the high costs of verification of compliance with the eco-criteria in different importing countries. In the case of footwear, for example, a rough estimate of the incremental costs of adjustment indicates that the cost of compliance with eco-labelling would be about 33 per cent of the present export price, affecting India's price competitiveness directly.[19]

The Indian Government is also attempting a voluntary system of eco-labelling, known as the Ecomark. The criteria for obtaining this label are currently being established, and collaboration with a British labelling agency is under way to make India's Ecomark rigorous enough to gain acceptability in the international market.

8.4.3 Response to External Regulations

Part of the vulnerability of exporters is simply due to the lack of knowledge about rules. One of the studies indicated that nearly all the big exporters were quite familiar with environment-related product standards in the OECD market. Exporters to Germany, in particular, were well informed, especially those in the textile and leather sectors. Information regarding eco-regulations and labelling came mostly from the importer.

The larger exporters were found to be in a better position to adapt to international regulations. A case in point was a firm in the automobile industry. Telco, a car exporter to the European Union, upgraded all its existing technology and ensured that all the component manufacturers did the same. All the information was supplied by a technical consultant, while the changes were carried out by the firm alone.[20]

Among small exporters, however, the awareness and adaptability was generally lower. In the Indian context, the handicaps experienced by such exporters is of significance because they contribute significantly to exports. In 1991–92, for example, the share of SMEs' exports to total exports was almost 32 per cent (see Table 8.4). This share has also been rising over time. In the year 1991–92, for instance, it increased by 43.7 per cent in one year. These figures suggest that this segment of the export sector is substantial and growing. Problems affecting the export sector are likely to hit SMEs more significantly because of their inability to acquire information and the lack of financial backing to adapt to the external eco-regulations in importing markets.

If the environment-related standards did not bind SMEs immediately, they had close to no knowledge of it, making their exports more vulnerable in the long run. The dye industry seemed to suffer from this problem. A distinct gap existed between the larger, organized dye producers and the smaller ones.

In the leather sector, too, the small-scale sector tanneries were found to have low awareness of eco-regulations. In fact, it was difficult to convince them to adopt the cost-effective common effluent treatment. The government had to intervene in this regard.

The questionnaire revealed that lack of dissemination of information through a centralized agency acted as a barrier for the small-scale producers. Attempts are being made by the Bureau of Indian Standards to provide corrective measures in the form of providing relevant details to smaller manufacturers and exporters.

Awareness of and adaptability to external eco-regulations are essential for further growth. Several sectors are vulnerable to these regulations, but have not yet been affected by them in a significant manner. However, as the scale of operations rises, exports are likely to become more immediately affected. In such a situation, firms are better off taking precautionary measures, even if the cost of adjustment is high.

Table 8.4   Trends in the export contribution of SMEs in India, 1981–1992

Year	SME share of total exports	Growth rate in SME share of total exports (percentage)
1981–82	26.5	26.0
1982–83	22.9	–1.2
1983–84	21.9	5.8
1984–85	22.1	17.4
1985–86	25.4	8.9
1986–87	28.9	31.6
1987–88	27.8	20.0
1988–89	27.0	25.5
1989–90	27.6	38.9
1990–91	29.7	26.7
1991–92	31.7	43.7

Source: ESCAP, 1995.[21]

8.5   MULTILATERAL ENVIRONMENTAL AGREEMENTS

Besides eco-standards in importing countries, India's growth and development will also be affected by the Multilateral Environmental Agreements (MEAs) in which it participates. It is a signatory to the Basel Convention and Montreal Protocol and its subsequent London amendment.

Although India is a signatory to the Basel convention on the Transboundary Movement of Hazardous Wastes and their Disposal, it opposes the ban on the importation of scrap. The use of recycled scrap proves to be more eco-friendly while also being more cost-effective than the production of virgin metal. In fact, according to the Indian Non-Ferrous Metals Manufacturers' Association, 45 per cent of India's metallurgical industry is based on the recycling of scrap in about 5000 plants employing close to half a million people.[22] Importing scrap is therefore of great importance in the Indian context. It is therefore clear that if a ban is imposed on the importation of scrap, the metallurgical industry will be significantly harmed.

In addition, India strongly advocates international monitoring of boundaries to prevent the illegal importation of hazardous materials which can damage its environment and result in loss of productivity and competitiveness. In this context, it is also of the opinion that exporters should be held liable for illegally dumping hazardous wastes, and provisions be made for compensating the damage.

Under the Montreal agreement, India has agreed to phase out the production and use of CFCs by the year 2006, having received a grace period of ten years since it is a small consumer of CFCs (the annual per capita consumption of this gas was about 11 g per person in 1990). As part of the London Amendment, India is also obliged to ban exports of controlled substances to countries which are not party to the Montreal Protocol. It has also ratified the gradual phase-out of carbon tetrachloride and other fully halogenated CFCs, methyl chloroform and HCFCs over time. So far, information is available only on the impact of the phase-out of CFCs.

For India, the phase-out of CFCs takes on a greater significance because, unlike many developing countries, it is a producer of this substance. The competitiveness effects will also be felt by the manufacturers of products using the controlled substance. R&D costs will also rise, as will the cost of the final products such as refrigerators and air-conditioners. Indirectly, industries such as agricultural and marine products would also be affected because of their large-scale use of refrigeration.

Adjustment costs

Adjustment costs were calculated in terms of costs incurred by producers of CFCs, industries which use CFC as an input, and consumers of final products. Expenditure on Research and Development geared towards the discovery of potential substitutes for CFCs are another adjustment cost taken into account.

A Task Force established by the government has assessed the incremental costs of adhering to the Montreal Protocol. Besides this report, two other studies have carried out estimates of adjustment costs, envisaging two scenarios, one where the phase-out would take place early, and the other, where it would occur towards the end of the phase-out period. An early phase-out would mean replacing CFCs as soon as possible, instead of using the installed capacity until all plants are paid off. A later phase-out, on the other hand, would imply unconstrained growth of CFC production and consumption until the final date of phasing out.

Table 8.5   Adjustment cost for India in implementing the Montreal Protocol (in million US$ net present value)

Source	Early phase-out				Late phase-out			
	P	U	C	T*	P	U	C	T*
World Bank[23]	192	68	60	320	82	50	350	482
MEF[24]	120	40	147	307	43	37	62	703
Task Force[25]	–	–	–	1400	–	–	–	2450

*Note   * P represents producers; U users; C consumers; T total.

As can be seen from Table 8.5, the cost of adjustment is higher for the producer in the case of an early phase-out, because their investment outlays in CFC technologies will not be fully recovered. Costs will also have to be borne because the capacity for CFC production is greater than domestic demand. Not being able to export CFCs to Article 5.1 countries will mean that this excess capacity will have to be shut down. Alternatively, in view of the capacity available for exports, it may be necessary to bring out adjustments early and identify indigenous substitutes. This, however, would also prove to be an expensive exercise, adding to the cost of adjustment. In addition, some of the units have not even finished paying for their investment yet. Shutting down or investing in new technology would increase the burden of adjustment, although Research and Development costs are lower in the short run. The additional cost to users and consumers of the final product will be small.

On the other hand, if a late phase-out occurs, the consumer bears a greater burden, because while the producer of CFCs would have written off his investment, the users of this substance and consumers of the final products will be unable to recharge their CFC-using refrigerators and other products after 2010.

Overall, the estimates conclude that late phase-out is more expensive than an early phase-out. This is mainly because the number of consumers, who will bear the greater burden of the late phase-out, greatly outweigh the number of producers of the controlled substance. In a tropical climate like India's, the need for air-conditioners, refrigerators and water coolers is greater than in a cooler country.

In addition, with developments in horticulture, aquaculture, and floriculture especially for exports, cold storage chains become increasingly important. The growth of this section of the economy is projected to be high in the coming years, increasing the demand for refrigeration.

While it is felt that the fund established by the Montreal Protocol will help to pay for the cost of adjustments, the study of India shows that even the amount required by this one country is higher than the total of US$278 million[26] that the Fund has approved for project development.

At the firm level, it was found that the transition to intermediate substitutes was very expensive. Besides acquiring the substitute chemicals, firms also have to acquire suitable technology for these substitutes. In addition, substitute chemicals do not operate with the same efficiency as CFCs. As a result, even where tie-ups had been possible, exporters felt that the cost of adjusting to HCFC was 30 to 35 per cent of the current price of refrigerators.

Firms were generally of the opinion that the basic system design necessary for switching to the intermediate technology is not available at present in India. Thus, firms had to rely on tie-ups with foreign companies. However, where no joint venture was possible, acquisition of technology was very difficult, because foreign companies were reportedly unwilling to share HCFC technology.[27] In general, the only technology available to India is the CFC technology, which is not useful even in the medium term. Acquiring appropriate technology for long-term use is out of the question because it has not been developed, even internationally.

Another technological barrier is that CFC-free new technology may not be suited to the tropical conditions in India. On this subject, information and testing facilities are difficult to access. Emphasis must be laid on Research and Development for identifying indigenous substitutes, which are suitable for Indian conditions. The overall cost of compliance will also depend on the technology used by the firms. According to one study, developing indigenous technology would be the most cost effective option for India in the long run.

8.6 EFFECTS OF ENVIRONMENTAL REGULATIONS ON INDIA'S EXPORTS

Economic liberalization has led to the expansion of production for export. However, production for export still comprises only a small proportion of the overall production for the large domestic market, making it difficult to conclude that exportables contribute significantly to the environmental damage in the country.

One study did attempt to analyse the average CO_2 emission caused by production for export, as compared to that caused by production for domestic consumption.[28] In doing so, the study took into account indirect or 'embodied' exports, namely, those outputs which are purchased by other Indian industries and then used as inputs in the production of exportables. In this context, electricity turned out to be a very significant polluter.

Sectors under study were leather, chemicals, marine products, cotton textiles, tea and coffee, mining and electricity. An exact correlation between production for export and level of CO_2 emission could not be established. For some products, such as leather and electricity, the proportion of export production to total production was the same as the proportion of emission caused by export production to that caused by total production. In several other sectors, such as chemicals, mining and marine products, the percentage contribution of the exports to emissions was lower than the percentage of output going towards exports. Tea and coffee, on the other hand, demonstrated a higher than proportionate emission level. Therefore, no exact correlation across sectors could be established between environmental damage and production for export.

When considering the greenhouse gas emissions of all the above sectors combined, the study found that exports accounted for 9.8 per cent of carbon dioxide emissions in the country while they constituted about 8.7 per cent of the total output in the country, demonstrating that export production is only slightly more carbon intensive than overall production in the country.

The discussion on the impact of export production on the environment also concluded that of the ecological damage which is attributable to exports, most is local in nature, and can therefore be solved by government intervention in accordance with the developmental priorities in India. Thus, given the differences in environmental priorities, the resource scarcity and the local nature of the impact of export production, the most desirable environmental management may be achieved when trade is decoupled from the environment.

8.7   CONCLUSIONS AND RECOMMENDATIONS

8.7.1   Conclusions

The studies concluded that external eco-regulations and eco-labelling are beginning to affect Indian exports. Sectors most significantly affected include textiles, leather, dyes and food products. As the scale of operations in marine exports rises, these too are likely to become increasingly sensitive to external regulations.

Complying with external standards has been difficult in the sensitive sectors mainly because of the cost involved. Changes to accommodate eco-friendly inputs and technology were found to affect the price of the final product. In addition, complying with eco-standards sometimes involved changing the production line, leading to an additional price rise. Because most Indian exports compete on the basis of low price, such a price rise is likely to hamper their competitiveness.

Complying with voluntary labelling too was found to affect Indian exports. While conforming with labels has associated price premiums, the market for eco-friendly products was small, and tough competition existed to capture this segment. Hence, while the cost of compliance was high, higher returns were not assured.

The cost of compliance with eco-regulations and eco-stipulations was found to affect the SMEs most seriously. In the case of India, these contribute significantly to the exports of the sensitive sectors. Approximately 70 per cent of leather exports from India, for instance, come from SMEs. Exporters in this segment are the worst off because they are unable to access information about external regulations. Given their scale of operations, access to eco-friendly inputs and technology is also very difficult. Government intervention and support in this sector is thus required.

Besides external regulations, MEAs are also important for India. The Montreal Protocol is likely to affect India in particular, mainly because, unlike most developing countries, India is a producer of CFCs. Adhering to this agreement would therefore affect producers, user industries and consumers. It was concluded that in the case of an early phase-out, the major cost of the switchover would be borne by producers of CFCs. A late phase-out would affect users and consumers of final goods more significantly. Overall, the cost involved in an early phase-out was found to be lower than the cost of a late phase-out.

In addition to the cost of phase-out, lack of access to technology was found to be a major preoccupation in the context of the Montreal Protocol. Exporters felt that foreign firms possessing the phase-out technology were unwilling to share it. At the same time, this technology did not take into account the climatic conditions prevailing in India. Hence, exporters felt that Research and Development efforts were required to discover technology which, while adhering to the Montreal Protocol, would also be suited to Indian conditions.

On the question of the impact of trade liberalization on the environment, the relationship was not clear. This was mainly because exports comprise only a small portion of the GDP in India, making it difficult to isolate the impact of production for exports and production for the domestic market.

8.7.2 Recommendations

Like many developing countries, India faces a dilemma. Urgent budgetary claims relating to education, health and infrastructure will have to be balanced with the eco-concerns of importers that could, nonetheless, negatively affect exports and retard India's development process.

In order to cope with the problems arising out of eco-regulations, a concerted policy structure is required so that compliance with these can take place without compromising on domestic development priorities. For this, proactive measures would be required on the domestic and the international level.

Positive measures at the domestic level
The participation of the corporate sector should be encouraged, as those affected by external regulations and MEAs often find feasible solutions. Taking the

example of the phasing out of CFCs, it was found that while the government is still deliberating over what phase-out strategy to adopt, many Indian refrigeration and air-conditioning manufacturers have already begun the process of adjustment.

However, some activities cannot be carried out by individual firms for lack of funds and technology. Information dissemination is a case in point. Creating awareness of regulations, voluntary labels and available eco-friendly technology, would require government intervention. The government could involve exporters' councils. These would serve as a link between the government and the exporter. In order to fulfil such a function, however, the councils need to be strengthened so that they are made aware of the latest developments on markets, prices, technology, raw materials, new processes and new regulations on the environment. In addition, they will have to develop analytical skills in assessing the changes and formulating their strategies in the face of continuously changing markets.

Export councils should also be delegated to collect information from exporters and participate in international trade negotiations, along with the government, so that the concerns of exporters with regard to stringent and changing regulations are addressed effectively.

Besides information and negotiation, other issues also require government intervention. Testing for compliance with environmental regulations is one such area. While it is clear that testing the quality and the degree of eco-friendliness of the product is desirable, the technology to do so has been inaccessible to firms domestically. In such a case, the government should provide financial assistance, while also facilitating foreign collaborations for the purpose of testing.

In the case of the dyestuff industry, government intervention would also be desirable. This is particularly true because a significant portion of the output comes from SMEs. A number of these firms have requested that government assist them in establishing common treatment plants, as the cost of establishing these facilities is quite high. Since even a common plant is expensive, both state and central governments have begun to fund CET plants.

This policy would, however, only be viable if the units are located in close physical proximity. If they are scattered across a region, another solution would have to be found. One option may be to encourage, through subsidies and other incentives, the use of organic chemicals, so that the pollution level can be minimized.

If eco-friendly techniques are used in the production process, these must be marketed aggressively to attract attention in the international market. To this end, a joint effort between exporters, export promotion councils and the government would be ideal.

The government should take a proactive stand in areas where the domestic ecological concerns and those of major export markets coincide. The government has already intervened in the case of benzidine content in dyes, and excessive pesticide use in tea and other agricultural products. A similar pro-active stand is required in other areas which are of both local and external ecological concern.

Positive measures at the international level

Importing countries should assume responsibilities with regard to the imposition of eco-regulations. In order to prevent the formulation of arbitrary standards, the country should study the impact of regulations on domestic producers and exporters. Regulations should be developed in consultation with India, particularly if it is a significant supplier of the product.

It has also been argued in one study that the burden of justifying regulations on environment and health grounds, for instance, should rest on the importing country and that the arguments should be available for open debate.[29]

On the issue of changing regulations, exporters have noted, particularly in the area of leather exports, that there is a lag between the law coming into effect, and effective information dissemination. The importing country must give sufficiently early notice to exporters, so that they are in a position to learn about the new regulation and respond to it effectively.

If the regulation creates technological barriers, help from developed countries would be extremely useful. The technology required for carrying out eco-friendly production and the techniques to test for eco-friendliness are so varied that even with governmental intervention, the costs involved may be too high for exporters to remain competitive. Some coordination between OECD nations would be helpful, as would the provision of financial assistance for testing facilities. Indo-German and Indo-Dutch collaborations in the leather sector are already underway, and similar efforts need to be made in other sectors.

Where sales of technology are required, caution must be exercised, however. The technology purchased should be attuned to the comparative advantage that Indian exporters enjoy based on their own processing methods, labour costs and environmental assimilative capacity.

In sectors where technological cooperation is not possible, or the technology for eco-friendly production has not been devised even in OECD countries, it would be essential to provide financial and technical assistance to research institutes which are equipped to carry out the relevant research. Some organizations, such as the Indian Institute of Packaging, are already involved in such activities. These should be identified and fortified, and efforts should be made to encourage innovations in the area of eco-friendly technology which is suitable for India.

In order to facilitate compliance with external eco-regulations, cooperation between the importing nations and countries like India must take place. Thus, negotiations regarding the stringency of regulations must be held. At a domestic level, rigorous information dissemination, and eco-friendly production and packaging in line with its comparative advantage, can help India gain in the long run in terms of a cleaner environment and an expanded export market.

NOTES

1. Some items in which India might have an advantage are certain varieties of rice, cotton, tobacco, tea, coffee, banana, and pepper. This information is based on information provided in Nayyar, D. and A. Sen, (1994), 'International trade and the agricultural sector in India', *Economic and Political Weekly*, Bombay.

2. Other works used in this summary are chapters from *Trade, Environment and Sustainable Development: A South Asian Perspective*, UNCTAD. The works referred to in particular are Jhamtani, R.C., 'Making Trade and Environment Policies Compatible'; Jha, A., 'Protection of the Environment, Trade and India's Leather Exports'; Achanta, A. *et al.*, 'The Transfer of Environmentally Sound Technologies'.

3. Bharucha, V. (1997), 'The Impact of Environmental Standards and Regulations set in Foreign Markets on India's Exports', in V. Jha, G. Hewison and M. Underhills (eds), *Trade, Environment and Sustainable Development: A South Asian Perspective*, London: Macmillan Press, pp. 123–42.

4. *Ibid.*

5. *Ibid.*

6. Dyes used in the production of leather and leather products also come under strict scrutiny in OECD nations. The specifics are discussed in the section on dyes.

7. Bharucha, op. cit.

8. *Ibid.*

9. *Ibid.*

10. Parikh, J.K., V.K. Sharma, U. Ghosh and M.K. Panda (1994), 'Trade and environment linkages: a case study of India', report prepared for United Nations Conference on Trade and Development, August.

11. Bharucha, op. cit.

12. This estimate is based on data provided by ESCAP, 1995 and Parikh *et al.*, 1994.

13. Bharucha, op. cit.

14. Parikh *et al.*, op. cit.

15. *Ibid.*

16. Bharucha, op. cit.

17. *Ibid.*

18. *Ibid.*

19. *Ibid.*

20. Achanta, A., P. Dadhich, P. Ghosh and L. Noronha (1997), 'The Transfer of Environmentally Sound Technology with Special Reference to India', in V. Jha, G. Hewison and M. Underhill

(eds), *Trade, Environment and Sustainable Development: A South Asian Perspective*, London: Macmillan Press, pp. 185–202.

21. ESCAP (1995), *Expansion of Manufactured Exports by Small and Medium Enterprises (SMEs) in ESCAP Region, Vol.II: National Studies*, New York: United Nations.

22. Bidwai, P. (1995), 'Environment: India vacillates on toxic exports ban', *South–North Development Monitor – SUNS*, September.

23. Estimate of the World Bank, 1991.

24. Estimate of the Ministry of Environment and Forestry, India.

25. Estimate of the Task Force Report, Government of India.

26. COWI Consult. & Goss Gilroy Inc. (1995), 'Study on the financial mechanism of the Montreal Protocol', United Nations Environment Programme.

27. Bharucha, op. cit.

28. Parikh *et al.*, op. cit.

29. Parikh, J. (1993), 'GATT talks: the green angle', *The Economic Times*, 4 December.

9.   Malaysia

9.1   INTRODUCTION

This chapter provides a synthesis of the report 'Trade and Environment Linkages: a Malaysian Case Study' carried out by a research team from the Institute of Strategic and International Studies (ISIS), Kuala Lumpur, Malaysia, in May 1995.[1] It describes aspects of Malaysia's trade, development and environment policies, and national efforts to integrate these with a view to achieving sustainable development. The ISIS study analyses trade and environment linkages on the basis of case studies on the Montreal Protocol on Substances that Deplete the Ozone Layer, timber exports, and pollution control in key industries such as electronics and palm oil. The palm oil case study draws on past studies to analyse the trade and welfare effects of environmental regulation in the country.

The Malaysian authorities regard strong economic growth as necessary to reduce and eradicate poverty, correct economic and social imbalances, and maintain social stability in a multiracial society. The government's stated aim is to reach the status of a fully developed country by the year 2020. The National Development Policy (NDP) provides a framework for economic development. Making economic development and environmental protection mutually supportive is a key issue.

9.2   TRADE, ENVIRONMENT AND DEVELOPMENT IN MALAYSIA

Malaysia has one of the fastest growing economies in the world. Its Gross Domestic Product (GDP) grew at an annual average of 6 per cent in the 1980s, and almost 9 per cent in the early 1990s. Economic development and infrastructure investments have brought tremendous improvements to environmental problems that are linked to poverty and low levels of development. Water supply, for instance, has improved significantly and now reaches 90 per cent of households, compared to only 55 per cent in 1980 and 42 per cent in 1970. A third of the population had no sanitation facilities in 1980, but this was reduced to 8.5 per cent by 1990.

However, with economic growth, some environmental problems have intensified. For example, agricultural activities and agro-based industries, such as the processing of palm oil and rubber, were major sources of water pollution in the 1970s and early 1980s. Air pollution, especially in large urban areas, has become a matter of concern. Rapid industrialization has also generated large volumes of solid wastes.

The Environmental Quality Act (EQA) reflected these concerns. This included regulations on crude palm oil (1977), rubber (1978), clean air (1978) scheduled wastes (1989), sewage and effluents (1979), lead concentrations in motor gasoline (1979), and motor vehicle noise (1987). In the case of forestry, the National Forestry Act (1984) provides the basis for environmental legislation.

9.2.1 National Development Policies

Malaysia's economic success is closely related to its national development policies.[2] For example, from 1986 to 1995 the 'Industrial Master Plan' (IMP) provided the framework for a more diversified and integrated manufacturing sector and an advanced industrial economy through promoting technological capability and competitiveness. Market forces played an essential role in ensuring allocative efficiency. The IMP coordinated the role of the government in supporting private sector led growth and achieved its aim of ensuring industrial growth and diversification.

Development and environmental objectives have been integrated within government policies. For the period 1991–2000, the Second Outline Perspective Plan (OPP2) aims to accelerate poverty eradication and correct social and economic imbalances within a rapidly expanding economy. The 'prudent management of natural resources and ecology as well as the preservation of natural beauty and a clean environment for the present and future generations' is an objective of the OPP2.[3]

The National Policy on the Environment also sets out principles and strategies necessary to harmonize economic development goals with environment imperatives. The Minister of Science, Technology and the Environment is a member of the National Development Council, chaired by the Prime Minister.

The importance of preserving the environment to ensure that growth and development are sustainable is also recognized in 'Vision 2020', which aims to transform Malaysia into a developed country by the year 2020, while ensuring sustainability and improving the quality of life.[4]

9.2.2 Trade Policies

Malaysia has an open and export-oriented economy. The export sector has contributed significantly to economic growth and its share of GDP increased from 50 per cent in 1970 to 81 per cent in 1990. Diversification has resulted in large changes in the composition of exports. For example, rubber and tin, which accounted for more than half the value of total exports in 1970, are now insignificant exports. Crude petroleum, palm oil and timber are now the most important commodities in terms of export values.

Table 9.1   Total exports and imports by main commodity groups, 1975–1993 (millions of US dollars)

Main product categories	1975	1980	1985	1990	1991	1992	1993
Imports								
(in value)								
Total	3524.6	10734.7	12515.1	27840.5	35182.8	39153.5	44416.5
Food and agricultural products	714.1	1474.2	1631.0	2403.0	2701.8	3022.4	3246.0
Fuels	423.7	1626.7	1515.5	1484.5	1549.1	1677.7	1662.2
Metals	184.7	427.4	366.3	1015.6	1208.4	1304.9	1552.6
Manufactured goods	2175.8	7144.9	8960.5	22872.3	29527.3	32908.4	37289.8
Electronics	354.8	1676.6	2702.4	6944.0	9355.5	10442.9	13359.9
(share in percentages)								
Total	100.0	100.0	100.0	100.0	100.0	100.0	100.0
Food and agricultural products	20.3	13.7	13.0	8.6	7.7	7.7	7.3
Fuels	12.0	15.2	12.1	5.3	4.4	4.3	3.7
Metals	5.2	4.0	2.9	3.6	3.4	3.3	3.5
Manufactured goods	61.7	66.6	71.6	82.2	83.9	84.0	84.0
Electronics	10.1	15.6	21.6	24.9	26.6	26.7	30.1
Exports								
(in value)								
Total	3846.6	12939.2	15632.4	29445.9	34300.4	40766.6	47103.1
Food and agricultural products	2205.7	5958.2	5600.5	7492.1	7523.3	8437.4	8565.4
Fuels	418.6	3198.5	4930.1	5389.2	5306.4	5260.8	4848.8
Metals	533.2	1318.5	831.4	611.7	526.1	626.3	582.8
Manufactured goods	664.4	2426.7	4247.4	15839.8	20794.2	26270.8	32809.0
Electronics	126.6	1281.4	2423.8	7828.2	9505.2	11429.8	14632.4
(share in percentages)								
Total	100.0	100.0	100.0	100.0	100.0	100.0	100.0
Food and agricultural products	57.3	46.0	35.8	25.4	21.9	20.7	18.2
Fuels	10.9	24.7	31.5	18.3	15.5	12.9	10.3
Metals	13.9	10.2	5.3	2.1	1.5	1.5	1.2
Manufactured goods	17.3	18.8	27.2	53.8	60.6	64.4	69.7
Electronics	3.3	9.9	15.5	26.6	27.7	28.0	31.1

Note: For analytical purposes and/or incomplete time series, the following countries are not included in the group of OECD countries: Austria, Iceland, Mexico, Norway and Turkey.

Source: UNCTAD based on COMTRADE.

The Government has encouraged the production and export of high-value-added products, *inter alia* through attracting foreign direct investment (FDI).[5] FDI is mainly concentrated in export-oriented industries such as electronics, chemicals, and basic metals. Manufactured products accounted for 70 per cent of the value of total exports in 1993, an increase from 17 per cent in 1975 (Table 9.1), with electronics accounting for more than 30 per cent.

The United States is Malaysia's single most important export market (Table 9.2) and electronics account for almost half of the value of total exports to this market. A high share of exports also go to ASEAN countries (28 per cent in 1993), in particular Singapore (22 per cent in 1993).

Table 9.2   Malaysia: exports by commodity groups and markets, 1993 (millions of US dollars)

Commodity groups	World	OECD countries Total	United States and Canada	European Union	Japan	Developing countries
Total	47 103.1	24 016.6	10 033.9	6 832.5	6 119.1	22 709.0
Food and agricultural products	8 565.4	3 510.9	435.9	1 353.7	1 471.8	5 000.1
Food	4 444.4	1 312.4	250.4	622.4	305.4	3 099.7
Agricultural raw materials	4 121.0	2 198.5	185.3	731.3	1 166.4	1 900.3
Fuels	4 848.8	1 798.5	57.2	1.8	1 680.6	3 045.4
Metals	582.8	246.9	23.7	65.0	141.9	333.9
Manufactured goods	32 809.0	18 403.6	9 504.3	5 386.4	2 807.3	14 103.6
Chemicals	1 007.2	320.2	69.6	84.9	123.7	674.3
Textiles and clothing	2 628.2	2 001.5	1 063.8	754.2	108.9	590.5
Footwear	115.4	39.5	5.0	28.1	1.4	69.3
Machinery and equipment	20 813.2	12 129.7	6 593.1	3 474.7	1 688.8	8 484.5
Electronics	14 632.4	8 910.6	4 887.5	2 559.4	1 281.8	5 675.5

Note: For analytical purposes and/or incomplete time series, the following countries are not included in the group of OECD countries: Austria, Iceland, Mexico, Norway.

Source: UNCTAD, based on COMTRADE.

9.2.3   Domestic Environmental Policy-making

While successfully implementing policies for achieving fast economic growth, Malaysia has also taken important steps to enhance environmental protection. The EQA was enacted in 1974, and the Division of Environment (now

Department of Environment, DOE) was established in 1975 to accomplish national goals in environmental protection.

The EQA requires licences for the use of certain sites, and for pollution at levels that exceed 'acceptable conditions'. These conditions are prescribed by the Minister of the Environment. Polluters are subject to prosecution and criminal sanction if emissions exceed levels corresponding to 'acceptable conditions'. A licence can be conditional.[6] The fee varies according to: (a) the class and location of premises; (b) the quantity of wastes discharged; (c) the pollutant or class of pollutants discharged; and (d) the existing level of pollution. An example of this for palm oil is contained in Section 9.6.1.

The installation of pollution abatement equipment as required by the EQA is subject to the Best Practicable Means (BPM) approach adopted by the DOE. Recognizing that some firms may face short-term difficulties in complying with environmental regulations and need time to adjust, the Clean Air Regulations, and the Sewage and Industrial Effluent Regulations allow for contravention licences to be granted if there are no 'known practicable means' to ensure compliance. The term 'practicable' may also cover an existing technology if its acquisition and subsequent adaptation is economically 'prohibitive'. ISIS points out that, contrary to some interpretations, contravention licences are not licences to pollute, but are instead interim measures to allow firms with short-term difficulties more time to install or upgrade pollution abatement equipment. An ISIS study, undertaken for the ASEAN secretariat, shows that the number of contravention licences has fallen steadily in recent years.[7]

Numerous regulations are enforced by the DOE under the EQA. Air, water and hazardous wastes are priorities for environmental management.[8] A mandatory system of Environmental Impact Assessment (EIA) was also introduced under the Environmental Quality (Prescribed Activities) (Environmental Impact Assessment) Order 1987. In a preventive approach to environmental management, EIA is required for a range of activities. In addition, there are programmes for environmental research and development.

9.3   THE IMPACT OF ENVIRONMENTAL REQUIREMENTS ON MALAYSIAN EXPORTS

9.3.1   Vulnerability to External Environmental Requirements

The vulnerability of exports to environmental requirements depends on many factors, such as the composition of products and markets, industrial structures, economic growth rates, level of development, and domestic and international facilitating policies. Malaysia's vulnerable export sectors include timber, textiles, air-conditioners and electronics. The value of these exports is shown in Table 9.3, based on data on emerging environmental policies, standards and regulations collected by the UNCTAD secretariat.[9]

Table 9.3   Malaysia, 1993: exports of selected products which may be vulnerable to environmental requirements (millions of US dollars)

Product	World	OECD countries Total	United States and Canada	European Union	Japan	Developing countries
Total exports	47 103.1	24 106.6	10 033.9	6 832.5	6 119.1	22 709.0
Fish	304.1	212.5	23.9	59.2	102.8	91.6
Tuna	26.0	20.1	6.1	0.3	11.3	5.8
Shrimp	125.5	111.1	14.8	48.7	27.5	13.9
Fruit	148.5	14.5	0.3	12.2	0.2	133.7
Wood and wood products	4 710.2	2 314.4	200.8	597.2	1 399.2	2 395.7
Fertilizers	75.0	34.1	4.7	0.0	3.6	38.9
Insecticides	36.5	9.7	9.0	0.1	0.1	26.4
Detergents	104.3	9.6	0.6	3.5	5.0	92.6
Paints	42.1	1.1	0.1	0.1	0.3	40.5
Batteries	29.3	6.6	2.5	2.6	0.3	22.5
Asbestos	10.7	4.0	0.2	0.9	1.3	6.6
Plastics	481.7	156.1	48.2	43.5	44.3	322.6
Tires	63.0	32.9	0.4	24.4	1.7	30.0
Paper and paper products	203.8	28.5	6.0	5.2	7.1	173.0
Textiles and clothing	1 975.6	1 385.7	633.6	544.2	95.4	573.8
Leather/leather products	53.6	27.2	9.7	11.4	3.8	26.4
Footwear	115.4	44.5	3.7	28.1	1.4	70.8
Cars	223.8	152.5	3.2	140.5	5.1	70.7
Products which may contain CFCs						
Refrigerators, etc.	13.3	0.3	0.1	0.1	0.0	12.7
Air-conditioners	622.6	198.8	32.9	47.3	103.6	406.9
All selected products	10 765.0	5 346.1	1 278.5	1 724.5	1 892.6	5 371.7
As a percentage of total exports	22.9	22.2	12.7	25.2	30.9	23.7

Note: For analytical purposes and/or incomplete time series, the following countries are not included in the group of OECD countries: Austria, Iceland, Mexico, Norway and Turkey.

Source: UNCTAD, based on COMTRADE.

Malaysia is firmly against the use of unilateral trade measures for environmental purposes. In a report prepared for the GATT Trade Policy Review Mechanism, the government points out that 'a major concern for Malaysia is the increasing use of unilateral measures for reasons of environment. Environment could and has been used as a convenient cover for protectionist motives. An even more dangerous trend is the use of unilateral measures such as eco-labelling to restrict imports of products to impose a country's own environmental standards on a third country, merely because it originates from a country with environmental policies and standards different from its own'.[10]

9.3.2　The Case of Tropical Timber

Timber was Malaysia's third largest commodity export in 1993, after petroleum and palm oil. Apart from 'commodity timber', Malaysia also exports timber products, such as plywood/veneer, mouldings and furniture. The manufacture of timber products is promoted, rather than the export of commodity timber. However, although forest utilization has facilitated the process of industrialization and poverty eradication, Malaysia's economic development has become much less dependent on its forest base.

The volume of commodity timber exports fell from 20.4 million m^3 in 1990 to 9.3 million m^3 in 1993 (Table 9.4). This was entirely due to a fall in log exports and can be attributed to both domestic and external policies. Domestic regulations on sustainable forest management[11] caused a reduction in logging areas and timber production. Log production fell from 50 million m^3 in 1991 to 37.3 million m^3 in 1993. Industrial and development policies also encouraged high-value-added manufactured exports. Commodity exports declined in importance, falling from 85 per cent of total exports in 1980 to 25 per cent in 1993.

External factors, in particular unilateral measures, also had adverse effects on exports. The ISIS study points out that unilateral measures are non-tariff barriers to trade, particularly when such measures only target tropical timber. Unilateral measures include bans or restrictions on the use of tropical timber, mandatory and voluntary labelling requirements, and campaigns.

The study lists Austria, Belgium, Germany, Hong Kong, the Netherlands, Switzerland and the United Kingdom among the countries and territories implementing or contemplating unilateral measures. Such measures have also been implemented by local authorities, including municipalities.[12] Austrian legislation on the labelling of tropical timber was eventually revoked when Malaysia took the issue to the GATT Council.

The effects of external environmental requirements depend largely on the geographical distribution of timber exports as well as Malaysia's response to external developments. In the case of sawn logs, Malaysia's principal export markets are Japan, the Republic of Korea and Taiwan (collectively accounting for 86 per cent of export value in 1993). These countries have not implemented environmental regulations affecting timber trade.

However, in the case of sawn timber, some of Malaysia's export markets (notably the Netherlands)[13] have or intend to implement measures which may affect trade in timber.

Table 9.4   Malaysia, 1980–1993: production and exports of timber

	1980	1985	1990	1991	1992	1993
Saw logs						
Production						
(thousand m³)	17916.3	30957.1	40100.9	49859.7	43510.9	37260.3
Exports						
Value (RM millions)	2618.2	2771.2	4041.2	4099.6	3851.4	2914.1
Volume (thousand m³)	15156.2	19630.5	20354.0	18318.0	17914.0	9288.0
Unit value (RU/m³)	172.2	141.2	198.5	212.2	215.0	313.8
Share of exports in production (volume), in percentages	84.6	63.4	50.8	46.5	41.2	24.9
Sawn timber						
Production						
(thousand m³)	6237.1	5574.7	8725.4	8802.8	9458.4	9224.2
Exports						
Value (RM millions)	1344.1	1136.8	3064.7	3008.3	3487.7	4545.0
Volume (thousand m³)	3245.2	2780.1	5222.0	5021.0	5392.0	5477.0
Unit value (RU/m³)	414.2	406.9	586.8	599.1	646.8	929.9
Share of exports in production (volume), in percentages	52.0	49.9	59.8	57.0	57.0	59.4

Malaysia has responded by organizing campaigns to oppose unilateral measures and by diversifying export markets, including by substituting markets where unilateral measures are emerging for other markets. Malaysia's policy of encouraging domestic higher-value-added activities could also be seen as a form of market substitution. In addition, production methods have sometimes been adapted to external market requirements. Timber certification is also increasingly seen as a marketing tool for access to green markets. The study suggests that, due in part to these responses, unilateral measures in overseas markets have not significantly affected Malaysia's timber exports.

International measures focus on eco-labelling and certification based on sustainable forest management.[14] Timber certification is seen by Malaysian industry as a useful marketing tool in greener markets, subject to the following conditions:[15]

(a) labelling must be applied to all types of timber. Temperate and boreal timber account for almost half of the world's forest cover and almost 90 per cent of world timber trade;

(b) labelling must be based on internationally agreed standards and criteria for sustainable development and not merely on standards developed by one or a few countries;

(c) all actions not consistent with the foregoing should be revoked or abrogated.

Malaysia has attempted, though so far unsuccessfully, to get the International Tropical Timber Organization (ITTO) to include temperate and boreal forests under the International Tropical Timber Agreement. The ITTO has set the target year of 2000 as a date beyond which all trade in tropical timber will be from sustainably managed forests.

9.4 MULTILATERAL ENVIRONMENTAL AGREEMENTS

9.4.1 The Montreal Protocol[16]

Under Article 5(1) of the Montreal Protocol on Substances that Deplete the Ozone Layer, Malaysia has a 10 year grace period for implementing commitments under the Protocol, as well as access to the Multilateral Fund. Malaysia has ratified the London and Copenhagen Amendments. Although Malaysia has until 2010 to phase out CFCs, halons and carbon tetrachloride, Malaysia aims to complete this by 2000.

Table 9.5 shows that ODS consumption (measured in ODP) has fallen since 1988. The use of halons has fallen drastically. Simultaneously, the production of electronics, air-conditioning and refrigerating equipment has steadily increased. As ODS consumption per unit of production has fallen considerably, this shows that measures undertaken to comply with the Protocol are effective. When acceding to the Protocol, Malaysia consumed close to 0.3 kg per capita. With high growth rates, particularly in sectors such as electronics, refrigerating and air-conditioning, Malaysia's per capita consumption would have exceeded this in the 1990s in a 'business as usual scenario'.

The study points out that, particularly as a result of the accelerated phase-out of ODS production in the developed countries, CFCs could become scarce and substitutes might not be readily available. In most cases substitutes are still significantly more expensive than ODSs used for the same purpose.[17] The study mentions that some Malaysian industries had reported difficulties in securing ODS supplies and costs had increased significantly for some. The

Table 9.5 Consumption of ODSs controlled by the Montreal Protocol (Annex A)

ODS	ODP	Period								
		1985	1986	1987	1988	1989	1990	1991	1992	1993
CFC11	1.0	353.0	576.0	810.0	998.0	834.0	1005.8	1120.2	1442.7	2045.9
CFC12	1.0	456.0	1064.0	1358.0	1645.0	1470.0	1381.2	1740.6	1306.0	1426.7
CFC113	0.8	119.0	684.0	376.0	1216.0	1381.0	1244.2	1210.6	836.8	189.5
CFC114	1.0	2.0	3.0	35.0	53.0	30.0	n.a.	n.a.	2.4	n.a.
CFC115	0.6	n.a.	n.a.	1.0	n.a.	5.5	1.8	n.a.	n.a.	n.a.
CFC Cons		940.0	2327.0	3080.0	3912.0	3720.5	3634.2	4071.4	3587.9	3662.1
ODP equiv		916.0	2190.0	2904.6	3669.0	3441.3	3384.2	3829.3	3420.5	3624.2
Halon 1211	3	71.0	150.0	198.0	270.0	246.0	221.3	56.1	193.7	90.6
Halon 1301	10	56.0	120.0	101.0	38.0	60.0	13.3	10.0	8.6	n.a.
Halon 2402	6						2.1			
Halon Cons		127.0	270.0	299.0	308.0	306.0	236.7	66.1	202.3	90.6
ODP equiv		773.0	1650.0	1604.0	1190.0	1338.0	809.5	268.3	666.6	271.8
Total Cons quantity		10670.0	2597.0	3379.0	4220.0	4026.5	3870.9	4137.5	3790.2	3752.7
ODP equiv		1689.0	3840.0	4508.6	4859.0	4779.3	4193.6	4097.6	4087.0	3896.0

Source: Malaysia, Department of the Environment.

average unit values of ODS imports for the period 1990 to 1993 are shown in Table 9.6.

Table 9.6   Malaysia, 1990–1993: imports of ozone-depleting substances (unit values)

	1990	1991	1992	1993
Unit values (RM/kg.)				
CFC11	4.395	4.163	3.790	4.341
CFC12	4.744	4.860	4.369	5.208
CFC113	5.811	5.094	5.290	6.684
CFC114	5.423	9.675	9.299	11.628
CFC115	6.247	5.324	5.354	13.189
Halon 1211	9.291	8.978	12.344	12.700
Halon 1301	11.370	13.302	14.308	23.265
Halon 2402	6.861	5.569	4.235	6.310

Note: US$1 is approximately RM 2.50.

Source: Malaysia, Department of Statistics, External Trade Statistics – Imports 1990–1993+.

Implementation of Malaysia's country programme

Malaysia is using a combination of approaches to achieve phase-out targets ahead of the granted time frame. The National Action Plan was prepared in 1991 with the involvement of industry. A National Steering Committee to control and monitor the use of ODSs and a Technical Advisory Committee for evaluating applications for CFC imports were established. The Customs Prohibition of Import and Export (CFCs and Halon) Order 1993 (Schedule II),[18] the Environmental Quality (Prohibition on the use of CFCs and Other Gases as Propellants and Blowing Agents) Order 1993,[19] and the Application Permit System under MITI 1994[20] were also introduced. Other measures include the Fire Services Department's order to restrict the use of halons, the Malaysian Industrial Development Authority guidelines to discourage the use of CFCs and DOE guidelines to assist enterprises in the phase-out programme.

Working groups under the National Steering Committee assisted in devising a national strategy. In certain sectors accelerated phase-out schedules were implemented. Individual agreements on phase-out dates were reached with all TNCs in Malaysia.

Investment incentives are also used. Fiscal measures include duty exemption for imports of non-ODS technology (particularly CFC and halon recovery technologies) and HCFC134a. There are also tax incentives for investments in environmentally friendly technologies.

Principal uses of ODSs and phase-out strategies

In Malaysia ODSs are mainly used in engineering and electronics, air-conditioners, refrigerators and the production of foam. Electronics accounted for 30 per cent of CFC consumption in 1993, compared to over 50 per cent in 1990. Consumption by air-conditioners and refrigerators increased from one-third in 1990 to 50 per cent in 1993 (Table 9.7).

CFC113 and methyl chloroform (MTC) are used in solvent cleaning. Carbon tetrachloride (CCl_4) is rarely used in Malaysia due to its known carcinogenicity. Numerous alternatives exist. In the electronics sector, the ODS phase-out is largely dependent on firms. While many large firms have already begun phasing out ODSs, small and medium-sized enterprises (SMEs) have yet to do so, due to financial considerations and application complexities.

While the consumption of CFC113 has declined rapidly (from 1441 tonnes ODSs in 1989 to 370 tonnes ODSs in 1993), that of MTC, which has a much lower ODP, has increased from 2348 tonnes in 1989 to 2620 tonnes in 1993. However, with the increasing availability of safer alternatives, MTC will eventually be phased out. According to the study, this will allow the industry to remain competitive, particularly as some developed countries are introducing labelling requirements.[21]

MITI's strategy for phasing out ODSs in solvent-cleaning includes promoting the 'work smart' concept and good housekeeping to minimize CFC leakage during processes; requiring chemical suppliers to prepare end-user awareness programmes and disseminate information on technology and substitutes for ODSs; assisting enterprises with ODS phase-out investment projects; identifying the remaining ODS users using the Application Permit System and other means, and encouraging them to phase out ODSs; and identifying SMEs which use ODS solvents and encouraging them to participate in phase-out projects.

In the foam sector, ODS use (principally CFC11 and CFC12) more than doubled between 1989 and 1993. In 1993 the government gazetted an Order under the EQA to prohibit the use of CFCs in foam making as of 1 January 1995 or 1 January 1999, depending on the type of foam manufactured. Numerous alternatives exist, and water blown CO_2 is the most common.

HCFC22 is used as a refrigerant in residential and small commercial air-conditioners. The sector's ODS consumption more than doubled between 1989 and 1993. No cost-effective alternatives exist and thus consumption is expected to further increase. There are no regulations prohibiting the use of ODSs in this sector.

CFC11 and CFC12 are used for refrigeration and large commercial air-conditioners. Consumption remained constant between 1989 and 1993 with a

Table 9.7 ODS consumption by sector (tonnes)

Sector	Substances	1989	%	1990	%	1991	%	1992	%	1993	%
Solvent cleaning	CFC113	1441	19.3	1244	15.1	1100	12.0	800	9.2	370	4.0
	MTC	2348	31.5	3057	37.2	2701	29.4	2829	32.4	2620	28.5
Foams	CFC11, 12	590	7.9	696	8.5	870	9.5	1088	12.5	1360	14.8
Car air-conditioning	CFC12	894	12.0	1012	12.3	1126	12.3	1171	13.4	1276	13.9
Residential and small commercial air-conditioning	HCFC22	1296	17.4	1309	15.9	2439	26.6	1809	20.7	2600	28.3
Residential and large commercial air-conditioning	CFC11, 12	485	6.5	320	3.9	378	4.1	435	5.0	495	5.4
Aerosols	CFC11, 12, 113, 114	180	2.4	350	4.3	300	3.2	300	3.4	300	3.3
Fire-fighting	Halons	201	2.7	207	2.5	231	2.5	263	3.0	137	1.5
Agriculture	Methyl bromide	24	0.3	28	0.3	33	0.4	30	0.3	30	0.3
Total		7459		8223		9178		8725		9188	

Source: ISIS, based on data provided by DOE, chemical suppliers, major users and chairmen of Working Groups.

30 per cent increase in the production of refrigerators. This was probably due to the availability of alternatives. In the refrigeration sector, CFCs were phased out in 1995. Meanwhile central air-conditioning manufacturers have switched to lower ODP HCFCs.

CFC12 is the main refrigerant in the mobile air-conditioning and refrigerated transport sector. Car air-conditioners consumed 1276 tonnes in 1993, an increase of 43 per cent from 1989. The target was to stabilize consumption at 800 tonnes per year from 1997. The Multilateral Fund of the Montreal Protocol has approved US$3.5 million to assist this sector in phasing out ODSs.[22] This requires new equipment and replacing substances in existing equipment. As new car models have been fitted with air-conditioners using HCFC134a, consumption of CFC12 in original equipment is expected to decline significantly. Fifty per cent of cars manufactured or locally assembled are already using non-ODS systems. Malaysian manufacturers were informed by their developing country suppliers that the availability of CFC12 could not be secured after 1995. As developed countries stopped producing CFC12 in 1995, alternatives were used to avoid critical shortages.

In Malaysia, halons 1301 and 121 are commonly used in the fire-fighting sector. When developed countries phased out halon production in 1993 this created a supply shortage in Malaysia and prices rocketed. CO_2 and chemical powders are substitutes. Other alternatives include water sprinklers, fine water mists and inert gas systems. Major chemical producers are also conducting research on substitutes for existing fire-fighting installations.

The aerosols sector includes insect sprays, personal care products, household products, medical products, automotive products, spray paints and industrial products. CFC11 and CFC12 are commonly used as propellants, and CFC113 and CFC114 as solvents. HCFC22 is used as a substitute for CFC11 and CFC12. Other alternatives include hydrocarbon propellants in insect sprays. It is estimated that 60 per cent of aerosol manufacturers, especially producers of insecticides, have converted to hydrocarbons. It is believed that some 20 to 30 small-scale producers still use ODSs.

In the agricultural sector, methyl bromide is used as a pesticide and in the export of agricultural products. It is used for commodity treatment (55 per cent), structure treatment (36 per cent), oil fumigation (5 per cent) and quarantine treatment (4 per cent).

Effects of CFC phase-out on the refrigeration and air-conditioning sectors

Effects on production of refrigerators and air-conditioners   The ISIS study indicates that input costs for refrigerators and air-conditioners have increased due to the accelerated phase-out of ODS production in the developed countries.

However, although Malaysia's production of refrigerators and air-conditioners continued to increase strongly, the proportion of input costs in output values remains constant. The study suggests that industries were able to shift increased production costs to consumers through higher prices, as well as develop productivity-enhancing technology.

Effects of ODS phase-out on exports of air-conditioners   Malaysia produces refrigerators for its domestic market.[23] Air-conditioners are, however, important exports (US$622 million in 1993), with two-thirds going to developed countries.

The ODS phase-out may affect exports through increased production and capital costs which may affect competitiveness, unless other producers face similar cost increases. In addition, if CFC-based products are phased out, firms that do not switch to ODS-free technologies and products may face a decline in exports.

Exports of air-conditioners to all countries have continued to increase strongly since 1986 (Table 9.8), suggesting that increases, if any, in production costs or changes in consumer preferences in the OECD countries have not, as yet, affected these Malaysian exports.

Table 9.8   Malaysia, 1981–1993: exports of air-conditioners

| Period | Value (millions of US dollars) | | | Shares (in percentages) | |
	Total	OECD countries	Developing countries	OECD countries	Developing countries
1981	34.2	16.4	17.8	47.9	52.1
1982	32.2	12.3	20.0	38.1	61.9
1983	25.8	6.2	19.5	24.1	75.8
1984	28.3	5.5	22.8	19.4	80.6
1985	31.8	9.4	22.4	29.6	70.4
1986	61.4	30.5	30.9	49.6	50.4
1987	120.6	70.0	50.6	58.1	41.9
1988	176.6	77.8	98.8	44.0	56.0
1989	226.7	115.9	110.6	51.1	48.8
1990	203.9	76.1	127.5	37.3	62.5
1991	403.8	218.0	185.4	54.0	45.9
1992	500.9	196.6	299.7	39.2	59.8
1993	622.6	198.8	406.9	31.9	65.4

Source: UNCTAD based on COMTRADE.

9.4.2   Basel Convention

Malaysia acceded to the Basel Convention on the Control of Transboundary Movements of Hazardous Wastes and their Disposal in 1993. The Ministry of Science, Technology and the Environment (MOSTE) and the DOE are national enquiry points. As required, the DOE has taken measures to distinguish wastes imported or exported for recovery and disposal. To enforce the Convention, control procedures were introduced under the Customs Act 1967, i.e. the Customs (Prohibition of Exports) (No. 2) Order 1993 and the Customs (Prohibition of Imports) (Amendment) (No. 3) Order 1993. These specify that any movement of toxic and hazardous wastes into or out of Malaysia must have prior written consent from the government.

Hazardous waste is a recent problem and the Scheduled Wastes Regulations were introduced only in 1989. The infrastructure and trained manpower for the safe handling of wastes are still lacking. Efforts to improve waste management focus on increased surveillance and enforcement, public awareness, education programmes and the creation of a centralized waste treatment facility (see below).

Malaysia does not allow the disposal of hazardous wastes in its territories. However, Malaysia is of the view that scrap metal and other recoverable non-hazardous wastes that have economic value should not be classified as 'waste' under the Convention.

9.4.3   CITES

Malaysia acceded to the Convention on International Trade in Endangered Species (CITES) in 1977. A National Steering Committee was established under MOSTE with the Department of Wildlife and National Parks as secretariat. The study notes that Malaysia is concerned that some countries are using conservation measures as disguised trade barriers. Efforts to include ramin, in the absence of substantive evidence, in the list of endangered species, are seen by Malaysia as a protectionistic measure.

9.5   ENVIRONMENTAL MANAGEMENT SYSTEMS: POSSIBLE EFFECTS OF THE ISO-14001 STANDARD ON MALAYSIAN EXPORTS

The study notes that environmental management systems (EMS), in particular the development of standards under the ISO 14000 series, have generated both interest and concern in Malaysia.[24] The principal concern is that should ISO

14001 certification become a *de facto* condition for doing business, Malaysian producers will face additional costs. These may be higher for Malaysian firms, in particular SMEs, than for their competitors in developed countries who are familiar with EMS. On the other hand, the continuous environmental improvements encouraged by ISO 14001 may induce cost savings, for example through a more efficient use of resources. ISO 14001 is also a basis for certifying a firm's EMS, which may lead to greater credibility with overseas clients and the government. With emphasis on self-regulation by industry, the government may also benefit from ISO 14001 as enforcement officers can concentrate on the most polluting industries. A National Committee on Environmental Standards and ISO 14001 has been established.

The potential effects of ISO 14001 on exports from Malaysia are difficult to predict. Any such effects are expected to occur principally in inter-firm transactions, particularly with overseas customers.[25] The closest analogue is perhaps the ISO 9000 series on quality management. Experience with ISO 9000 may shed light on the possible impact of ISO 14001. However, although quality is of direct importance to all firms, environmental concerns may only be significant in environmentally sensitive industries.[26] Thus, ISO 14001 may have relatively little effect on certain sectors.

The Standards and Industrial Research Institute of Malaysia (SIRIM) launched a pilot EMS programme in December 1995. The objectives were to improve understanding of the ISO 14001 standard and problems that may arise during its implementation, to assess the costs and benefits of implementing the standard, to gain EMS auditing experience and to determine training requirements. Thirty-two firms applied to join the programme, representing a broad range of sectors, such as rubber and rubber products, palm oil, and electrical, electronic, chemical and petrochemical industries. Participating companies with an EMS in place can receive trial audits free of charge. A few firms have been certificated under the scheme and others are in the process of becoming certificated.

Participation costs involve: (a) the added costs of implementing an EMS and (b) registration costs. With regard to (a), ISO 14001 requires firms to establish and maintain an EMS based on self-determined environmental policy and goals.[27] Compliance with all applicable domestic environmental regulations is a minimum requirement. DOE statistics demonstrate that the rate of compliance[28] with domestic environmental regulation varies from sector to sector. It may also vary according to firm size. ISO 14001 further expects participating firms to go beyond national environmental requirements, and to show a commitment to continuously improve the EMS. This may imply additional costs for firms in all sectors. At the same time, EMS may contribute to environmental improvements and economic benefits, for example through savings on input costs or improved business opportunities.

With regard to (b), securing and maintaining certification is expensive. In general, firms in developing countries may have to rely on the services of expensive consultancy firms in setting up an EMS. Registration fees may also be an important cost factor.

9.6   POLLUTION CONTROL IN KEY EXPORT SECTORS

9.6.1   The Palm Oil Industry

Malaysia is the world's largest producer of crude palm oil (CPO). Palm oil played a key role in government policies to reduce rural poverty and income disparities between ethnic groups.[29] Oil palms are grown in estates (55 per cent of the total area) or by smallholders (45 per cent) assisted by government land development schemes. In general, yields per hectare are higher in estates.

By 1975, CPO had also become the country's worst source of water pollution. Pollution caused by organic wastes from CPO mills was equivalent to pollution generated by a population of more than 10 million people. CPO production increased three fold between 1975 and 1985. The population equivalent of this would thus have increased to 33 million if effective abatement policies had not been implemented (assuming there is a linear relationship between production and levels of pollution). However, the equivalent fell to 0.08 million people in 1985 demonstrating the success of Malaysia's policies in this sector: high rates of growth were achieved simultaneously with significant environmental improvements. This has been cited as an example of where a trade-dependent industrializing nation has moved decisively against pollution in a key export industry.[30]

The pollution problem
In the CPO industry, pollution is caused by the discharge of palm oil mill effluents (POME) into watercourses. Although POME is easily degradable, the biological reaction depletes the oxygen in water and affects aquatic life. Water from polluted rivers and streams is also unsuitable for human consumption.[31] The POME problem was unique to Malaysia and no proven technological solution existed.

Pollution abatement
The government's first step was to pass the EQA in 1974 (see Section 9.2.3). As mentioned earlier, this authorized the DOE to attach licence conditions for pollution control taking into account economic costs.

The Environmental Quality (Prescribed Premises)(Crude Palm Oil) Regulations, imposed standards on POME and required CPO mills to apply for an operating licence annually. The standards were made increasingly stringent over four years.

There were several provisions to alleviate the burden of compliance. First, by phasing in the standards over four years, this allowed industry time to construct and gain experience in operating treatment facilities. Secondly, the licence fee varies according to levels of POME discharge[32] and consists of two parts: a flat processing fee and a variable effluent-related fee. Thirdly, mills could choose the least-cost option of either paying the cost of treating the POME to meet the standard, or paying the excess fee to discharge POME with a BOD concentration exceeding the standard. Fourthly, research and development is encouraged through fee waivers for mills conducting research on POME treatment.

Performance of the regulations
The regulations performed disappointingly in the first year. The DOE had expected the average daily discharge of BOD per CPO mill to go down from 220 to 25 tonnes. Although the average daily discharge was reduced significantly, it was still 125 tonnes. Many chose to pay the excess fee.

The DOE responded by making the standards more stringent, and mandatory. With strict enforcement, the average daily discharge of BOD was reduced to 60 tonnes per mill in the second year and continued to improve in succeeding years. Efforts to develop improved treatment technologies were given a boost in 1980 when the Palm Oil Research Institute of Malaysia (PORIM) was established. The development of various commercial by-products from POME (animal feed, fertilizers and biogas) also facilitated the reduction in BOD discharge.

Distribution of compliance costs
The distribution of compliance costs is key to determining competitiveness effects. Both CPO and refined palm oil (RPO) are sold in extremely competitive world markets. This prevented industry from passing on compliance costs to consumers in importing countries. Instead, they lowered the prices they paid farmers for fresh fruit bunches (FFBs). One study estimates that while the competitiveness effects on the RPO and CPO sectors were very small, the FFB growing sector (both smallholders and plantation owners) suffered significant losses in revenue. Thus, while environmental protection did not impair the competitiveness of the exporting sector, it significantly changed the distribution of returns to trade, affecting in particular producers of primary inputs.[33]

9.6.2   The Electronics Industry

The electronics industry is Malaysia's largest manufacturing sector in terms of output, export earnings and employment (Malaysia is the world's third largest producer of semiconductors). Output increased at an annual rate of 30% for the period 1988–1993, and the value of exports increased from US$1.3 billion in 1980 to US$14.6 billion in 1993.

FDI is important in this sector. Transnational Corporations (TNCs) have been encouraged to set up export-oriented industries. Malaysia created an attractive investment climate, including a ten year pioneer status incentive scheme[34] in selected sub-sectors of the industry, establishing Free Trade Zones (FTZs)[35] and Licensed Manufacturing Warehouse Facilities (LMWFs).[36]

With the government promoting local research and development, the industry, which initially concentrated on the assembly and testing of semiconductors (using imported technology and materials), grew to include electronic components, and consumer and industrial electronics. Although the components subsector has dominated, other subsectors have grown significantly in recent years.

For electronics, the environmental effects of production mainly relate to: (a) the use of ODSs for cleaning purposes; (b) atmospheric emissions; (c) the discharge of non-toxic effluent into watercourses; and (d) toxic wastes.

With regard to (a), with the ODS phase-out, CFC-based solvents are being replaced. Some producers are also switching to no-clean technology. These issues have been analysed in Section 9.4.

Concerning (b) and (c), the industry has achieved high rates of compliance with environmental regulations. Atmospheric emissions are controlled by the Environmental Quality (Clean Air) Regulations. DOE statistics reveal a high rate of compliance in this industrial sector (98 per cent in 1993) and compliance rates in the electronics subgroup (mostly TNCs with emission control equipment) may be even higher.

The Environmental Quality (Sewage and Industrial Effluent) Regulations 1979 set standards for effluents. Again statistics show a high rate of compliance by this sector (93 per cent in 1993).[37] In the electronics subsector, all plants have treatment facilities for non-toxic effluents.

With regard to (d), the electronics industry consumes large quantities of acids, alkalis and oil-dominated chemicals. These often result in wastes contaminated with toxic compounds from the production process, and toxic waste remains the most significant environmental problem. Due to a lack of treatment facilities, waste materials have been accumulating in industrial sites. Some are exported to countries such as the United States, the United Kingdom, Germany, Japan and Singapore, for treatment and eventual disposal. According to a conservative estimate in 1986, this resulted in an annual expenditure of US$150 million on waste management. However, the situation should improve with the construction of an Integrated Scheduled Waste Treatment and Disposal Facility (consisting of a storage facility, an incinerator and a landfill) by the government. This has been fully operational since June 1998.

9.7   CONCLUSIONS

The Malaysian experience demonstrates that active development strategies aimed at eradicating poverty and economic development can run parallel with, and are complementary to, efforts to increase quality of life through environmental management. The ISIS study clearly shows that improved environmental protection and increased pollution control are being achieved simultaneously with high rates of export-led economic growth.

Malaysia's success in promoting high rates of economic growth and enhanced environmental protection simultaneously is attributed to three factors: (a) technological development; (b) strong cooperation between the government and industry; and (c) availability of international sources of finance, such as the Multilateral Fund under the Montreal Protocol. Environmental problems associated with trade liberalization or expansion can be alleviated through efficient and effective domestic environmental policies and programmes. Furthermore, with appropriate policies at the national and international levels, the trade effects of environmental measures can be minimized and environmental policies need not result in adverse economic consequences for regulated sectors.

The ISIS study analyses important export sectors which are vulnerable to environmental requirements, including the use of unilateral measures. Malaysia is firmly against the use of unilateral trade measures for environmental purposes. The effects of measures such as eco-labelling and consumer preferences are difficult to assess. For example, although Malaysia's export earnings from timber have fallen drastically, this is partially the result of domestic industrial policies to promote domestic downstreaming activities as well as domestic environmental regulations.

The study suggests that the ODS phase-out has had relatively little effect on Malaysia's trade and competitiveness. This can be attributed to the close cooperation between government and industry in devising cost-effective approaches and incorporating sector-specific targets in the national ODS phase-out strategy; a combination of measures involving regulations, voluntary measures, investment incentives, capacity-building and technological development; industrial structure, in particular the predominance of TNC affiliates; and assistance from the Multilateral Fund under the Montreal Protocol. Sectors such as refrigerators and air-conditioners, could be affected by cost increases due to the accelerated CFC phase-out in developed countries. However, although input costs may have increased, their share of output values has remained relatively constant. Thus the study concludes that increased production costs could have led to higher finished product prices, or that technological changes could have increased productivity. Statistical evidence further demonstrates that Malaysia's production of refrigerators and air-conditioners has continued to increase, with exports of air-conditioners increasing sharply.

The ISIS study also shows that the environmental effects of rapidly increasing production can be controlled through appropriate national environmental policies. Malaysia's palm oil experience is cited as an example where a trade-dependent industrializing nation moved decisively against pollution in a key export industry.

The rapid expansion of the electronics industry could have created serious environmental problems if unchecked. However, this has been successfully controlled and regulated through the Environmental Quality Act. Compliance with regulations on air and water pollution has been high. The study attributes this to multinational companies installing adequate emission control equipment. The treatment and disposal of hazardous and toxic wastes, however, remains a problem, and is being resolved through the construction of a Central Waste Treatment Facility.

Perhaps the most fundamental economic consequence of any environmental measure is the immediate impact on production costs, product prices, and international competitiveness. The effect on trade and export competitiveness depends to a large extent on the ability to pass costs on to product prices. Case studies show that this is not possible in highly competitive markets such as palm oil. In less competitive sectors, such as refrigerators and air-conditioners, it is more likely that these costs can be incorporated into export prices.

ISIS suggests the following actions for achieving sustainable development objectives:

(a) integrating trade and environment policies;
(b) spatial and temporal differentiation of environmental standards;
(c) technical cooperation and the transfer of environmentally sound technologies; and
(d) institutional strengthening.

NOTES

1. The members of the research team were Rozali Mohamed Ali, Khalid Abdul Rahim, Helen Nesadurai, Norashikin Abdul Hamid, Norhayati Mustapha, Ong Hong Cheong, Ridzwan Othman and Adli Che Aad.

2. Malaysia's approach to industrial development is very similar to the post-war economic reconstruction strategies adopted by Japan and the Republic of Korea.

3. The Second Outline Perspective Plan, 1991–2000, p. 6.

4. Vision 2000 was first enunciated by Malaysia's Prime Minister, Dr Mahathir Mohamed in 1991.

5. Since 1968, the Malaysian Government has maintained a range of investment incentives for sectors such as manufacturing, agriculture and tourism. These were widely expanded in 1986, following the recession, as a means for promoting economic growth. Since 1987, 60

per cent of current investment in manufacturing consists of foreign capital, largely directed at export-oriented industries. According to a Trade Policy Review study by the GATT secretariat, the government is now more selective in encouraging investment. A recent review of the investment incentives structure brought changes intended to ensure the compatibility of investment flows with Malaysia's current stage of development. The present focus is on high technology, higher capital intensity and domestic value added, expanded linkage with domestic firms and environmental protection. See GATT, *Trade Policy Review: Malaysia*, Volume I, p. 49.

6. Vincent, J.R. (1993) 'Reducing effluents while raising affluence: water pollution abatement in Malaysia', Harvard Institute for International Development (HIID).

7. ISIS also points out that the authorities want to avoid granting contravention licences in the context of FDI. Indeed, foreign investors, and TNCs in particular, display high rates of compliance with environmental regulations. Their environmental control practices are frequently more stringent, and often follow a code of practice instituted by the parent company.

8. The Environmental Quality (Clean Air) Regulations 1978, the Environmental Quality (Sewage and Industrial Effluent) Regulations 1979 and the Environmental Quality (Scheduled Wastes) Regulations 1989.

9. The figures presented in the table are a preliminary indication of the value of exports which may be vulnerable to environment-related measures, with varying degrees of stringency. They do not analyse their real impact on trade or export competitiveness. For a discussion, see UNCTAD, 'Newly emerging environmental policies with a possible trade impact: a preliminary analysis: a statistical annex' (TD/B/WG.6/9/Add.1 of 6 November 1995).

10. GATT, *Trade Policy Review, Malaysia*, Vol. II. p. 34.

11. The National Conservation Strategy includes an action plan for sustainable forest management. This includes reducing logging areas, logging permits and licences; production quotas in accordance with ITTO recommendations; progressive reduction of annual coupes within the framework of Malaysia's 5-year Plans; stiffer penalties for illegal logging; stronger enforcement; and EIAs for forestry activities.

12. See, for example, Rubik, F. (1993) 'Product policy in support of environmental policy – case study Germany', IÖW.

13. An example of a voluntary agreement to restrict timber trade to sustainably produced timber is the Tropical Timber Covenant (CTH) in the Netherlands. A certification system covering all timber (not only tropical timber) may be established within the covenant in 1995. Stuurgroup convenant tropisch hout, Certificering van Duurzaam geproduceerd hout, April 1995.

14. In this context, the third session of the Commission on Sustainable Development (CSD) established an open-ended *ad hoc* Intergovernmental Panel on Forests to pursue consensus and formulate coordinated proposals to promote the management, conservation and sustainable development of all types of forests. Trade and environment issues related to forest products and services, including the issue of voluntary labelling and certification and its impact on developing countries, are among the priorities of the Panel.

15. Speech by Dr. Lim Keng Yaik, Minister of Primary Industries at the Seminar on Trade in Timber from Sustainable Managed Forests, organized by the Ministry of Primary Industries and the Malaysian Timber Industry Development Council, Kuala Lumpur, Malaysia, 5 to 6 April 1994.

16. The section on the Montreal Protocol in the ISIS study is based on interviews with officials from the DOE and MITI, supplemented with an examination of Malaysia's Country Programme, annual reports of major companies and industrial surveys conducted by the Malaysian Statistics Department.

17. In Malaysia, 1994 market prices (RM/kg) for ODS substitutes were reported to be as follows: R123 at an average price of 28.00 (substitute for CFC11, priced at 11.20); HC at 1.00 (substitute for CFC11 in aerosol, priced at 0.40); HCFC134a at 40.00 (alternative for CFC12, priced at 16.00); and R141b at 11.25 (substitute at 4.50).

18. The Customs Duty (Amendment) Order 1994 (Schedule II) was issued in 1995 to monitor the import of controlled substances listed in Annex C and Annex E of the Protocol. It also monitors trade with non-parties to the Protocol.

19. The Environmental Quality (Prohibition on the Use of Chlorofluorocarbons and Other Gases as Propellants and Blowing Agents) Order 1993 prohibits the use of controlled substance as propellants in aerosols and portable fire extinguishers (now in effect); as blowing agents for extruded polystyrene foam, thermoformed plastic packaging, moulded flexible polyurethane foam (now in effect); as blowing agents for rigid polyurethane foam (with effect from 1 January 1999); as propellants in pharmaceutical products (with effect from 1 January 1999); and the use of combustible petroleum gas or other combustibles as propellants in aerosols (with effect from 1 January 1999).

20. Companies intending to import ODS have to apply to MITI for a permit. An Advisory Committee (MITI, DOE, Customs and MIDA) sets import quotas for companies based on their historic use of controlled substances, and priority uses under the Country Programme.

21. For example, a United States labelling law is reported to have resulted in eliminating solvents used in the manufacture of electronic components and products traded in global markets, as US companies required suppliers to certify parts as CFC-free and assisted the suppliers in adopting new technology. See UNEP, Montreal Protocol of Substances that Deplete the Ozone Layer, 'Technology and economic assessment panel, report to the parties'. Part II: Economic and Financial Implications of Hydrochlorofluorocarbon Control Scenarios for Article 5(1) Countries, p. II-23. November 1995.

22. For data, see 'Information on implementation of projects and activities by agencies'.

23. Exports are modest (US$13 million in 1993) and those to developed countries are insignificant.

24. EMS are based on a set of voluntary rules that companies may adhere to in order to better control the environmental impact of their activities based on self-determined environmental policies and objectives. To avoid the proliferation of varying EMS standards, the ISO has developed an international standard on EMS (ISO 14001). See UNCTAD, TD/B/WG.6/9

25. Although a company could have numerous reasons for certifying to ISO 14001, for Malaysia and many other developing countries, demonstrating the company's environmental performance to its overseas customers is likely to be the most important driving force. See Henry, J. (1995) 'ISO 14000 Series Standard and its impact on industry', paper delivered at the Workshop on ISO 14000 and its Impact on Industry and Trade, Seoul, 29 November.

26. Since the customer is not subject to the environmental effects of the company using the standard and since environmental performance includes both objective and subjective measures, it is difficult to determine to what extent the customer's environmental needs have been satisfied. See Henry (1995), op. cit.

27. In general, SMEs may face more problems than large firms in establishing EMS. A number of investments required to fulfil the commitments to comply with applicable legislation to reduce pollution and to continuously improve environmental performance may not be economical on a small scale. Lack of information, lack of human resources, fear of additional bureaucracy and the costs involved in setting up the system and in certifying may be major bottlenecks for SMEs.

28. The DOE records the number of firms that comply or violate the EQA regulations as part of routine monitoring by regional offices. Thus, compliance rates are not based on the degree of compliance of individual firms.

29. To assist owners of small land parcels, several agencies, in particular the Federal Land Development Authority (FELDA), were established. FELDA's mission was to develop land and provide settlers with the infrastructure, land holdings, and technical assistance needed to raise crop yields and incomes. Although initially focused on rubber, by 1975 FELDA's activities concentrated on palm oil. Most settlers were ethnic Malays.

30. Khalid Abdul Rahim (1991), 'Internalization of externalities: who bears the cost of pollution control?', in *The Environmentalist* **11**, 19–25.

31. In 1982, palm oil alone accounted for 63 per cent of water pollution in terms of biochemical oxygen demand (BOD). However, by 1988, only 1 per cent of BOD was generated by palm oil mills. Over the same period, the share of BOD load generated by rubber mills also declined significantly: from 7.4 per cent to 1.1 per cent. Currently, domestic sewage is the main contributor to water pollution in Malaysia. See Khalid, A.R. and W.A. Mustafa (1992), 'External benefits of environmental regulation: resource recovery and the utilisation of effluent', *The Environmentalist*, **12** (4), 277–85.

32. The EQA authorized the DOE to vary the size of the licence fee, *inter alia* according to the quantity of waste discharged. This gave the DOE latitude to make the licence fee equivalent to a pollution tax: mills that polluted more would be taxed more via the higher licence fee.

33. A.R. Khalid and J.B. Braden (1993), 'Welfare effects of environmental regulation in an open economy: the case of Malaysian palm oil', *Journal of Agricultural Economics*, **44** (1), January.

34. Pioneer Status can be given to any company (foreign-owned or domestic) registered in Malaysia intending to participate in a promoted activity or to produce a promoted product. A company given Pioneer Status pays tax on only 30 per cent of its statutory income, for 5 years from a production date determined by MITI. GATT, *Trade Policy Review Malaysia*, Volume I, p. 110.

35. The main objective of FTZs is to provide facilities for manufacturing industries producing goods mainly for export. Any activity in an FTZ is subject to minimal customs control. FTZs are excluded from the Principal Customs Area (PCA). See GATT, *Trade Policy Review: Malaysia*, Volume I, p. 67.

36. Where the establishment of a Free Zone is neither practical nor desirable, the government may allow the setting up of LMWFs. Facilities are similar to factories operating in Free Zones. Companies normally approved for LMWFs are those which produce only for export. Companies exporting not less than 80 per cent of their production and which use mainly imported raw materials and components are also considered for approval of LMWFs. See GATT, *Trade Policy Review Malaysia*, Vol. I, p. 68.

37. In other manufacturing sectors, the lack of proper and efficient effluent treatment systems has been cited as a reason for non-compliance, particularly with respect to meeting heavy metal, COD (chemical oxygen demand) and BOD standards.

10.   The Philippines

10.1   INTRODUCTION

A research team from the Philippine Institute for Development Studies (PIDS) conducted a study on the links between trade and environment and the effects on the Philippine economy. This study titled 'Trade and Environment Linkages: The Case of the Philippines' was conducted by a research team consisting of Dr Ponciano Intal, Dr Erlinda Medalla, Dr Marian de los Angeles, Dr Danilo Israel, Virginia Pineda, Paul Quintos and Elizabeth Tan.[1]

Completed in 1994, the study provided a macroeconomic analysis of the interlinkages between trade and environment in the Philippines. It first identified the major sources of pollution and resource degradation in the economy, and proceeded to analyse the impact of internalization of environmental costs on the international competitiveness of different sectors. In addition, the study undertook a simulation exercise to examine the potential effects of trade liberalization on the domestic environment. The interaction between trade and the environment was also discussed in the context of sectors such as coconut, fisheries, forestry and textiles. This study has provided a basis for national discussions in the Philippines and for a number of articles presented at international conferences.[2]

10.2   SPECIFIC PROBLEMS OF THE PHILIPPINE ECONOMY

The performance of the Philippine economy has been dominated by intermittent balance of payment crises, which along with a high level of external debt and structural deficiencies in the economy meant that the country was hard hit by the world debt crisis of the early 1980s.

The effects of considerable external borrowing were exacerbated by the unproductive investment which occurred in the country during the late 1970s and early 1980s. The debt and economic crisis of 1983–1985 led to a sharp fall in demand, a decline in national income and a significant decrease in private and public savings. In addition, the Philippines' tariff structure and easier access to foreign exchange for intermediate inputs and capital goods made this phase of industrialization particularly import dependent. The ensuing growth of import-substituting industries could not be absorbed by the small domestic market. For these reasons, along with several other factors, this phase of industrialization was unable to lead the country towards sustained growth.

A system of peso overvaluation which penalized exports, weak backward linkages and a bias towards imported capital goods, along with the debt crisis, sharpened the need for major macroeconomic and structural policy reforms in the Philippines.

In addition to the country's economic crisis of 1983–1985, heightened pressure from the international donor community, and the economic successes of the more export-oriented economies in Asia, propelled the Philippines towards a more outward-oriented and financially stable economy.

By 1990, the Philippines succeeded in substantially reducing its external debt, mainly through debt rescheduling, debt buybacks, debt equity swaps and increased official development assistance. The country also undertook major trade, financial and fiscal reforms during the late 1980s and early 1990s. Tariff rates were reduced, the foreign exchange market was liberalized, the foreign equity restrictions on the Philippine industries were relaxed and the land lease period for foreign firms was lengthened in an attempt to attract Foreign Direct Investment (FDI).

Over time, the share of exports in GDP has increased. Exports occupied close to 30 per cent of GDP in 1990–1992, whereas they had occupied only 6 per cent of GDP during 1980–1985. During the 1970s and the 1980s, the commodity structure of Philippine exports also changed dramatically. The share in total exports of the country's traditional exports, mainly agriculture and resource-based products, declined markedly. The contribution of agriculture to total exports, for instance, declined from 67 per cent in 1970 to only about 17 per cent in 1993. Metals, too, have lost importance as their share in total exports fell from 13 per cent in 1975 to 4.5 per cent in 1993 (see Table 10.1).

Labour-intensive manufactures, especially textiles and semiconductors, have begun to play a more significant role in exports than traditional items. In 1993, for instance, semiconductors accounted for US$806 million and textiles for US$989 million (see Table 10.2). Other emerging exports are furniture and fixtures, chemicals, processed foods and fresh or simply processed fish. Overall, exports of manufactured goods accounted for almost US$4.7 billion in 1993, although this was less than the level in 1991 (see Table 10.1).

The changes in the commodity structure of imports, although less dramatic, have been influenced by the sharp fluctuations in the price of oil during the 1970s and 1980s, affecting the share of mineral fuels and lubricants in total imports. Among the goods which have shown a rising trend in imports during the period 1980–1993 have been capital and intermediate goods; for example, machinery and equipment imports increased from US$1203 million in 1975 to US$6087 million in 1993 (see Table 10.1). This trend may be explained, in part, by the increase in import requirements of the country's export of products such as garments and semiconductors, which are highly import intensive.

Table 10.1   Pilippines: total exports and imports by main commodity groups, 1975–1993 (millions of US dollars)

Commodity group	1975	1980	1985	1990	1991	1992	1993
Imports							
(in value)							
Total	3776.2	8294.6	5444.6	13040.4	12845.2	15464.9	18772.7
Food and agricultural products	512.6	826.5	704.4	1664.6	1421.1	1681.2	1886.7
Fuels	800.1	2354.8	1508.0	1939.5	1934.8	2147.4	2150.6
Ores and metals	76.2	250.6	87.6	445.9	606.4	501.9	537.7
Manufactured goods	2178.4	39417	2018.0	6931.0	8836.7	8617.3	11184.8
of which:							
Chemicals	442.7	814.2	645.2	1487.2	1500.4	1610.3	1804.6
Machinery and equipment	1202.7	1978.2	770.9	3385.3	4477.1	4363.5	6087.1
(share in percentages)							
Food and agricultural products	13.6	10.0	12.9	12.8	11.1	10.9	10.1
Fuels	21.2	28.4	27.7	14.9	15.1	13.9	11.5
Ores and metals	2.0	3.0	1.6	3.4	4.7	3.2	2.9
Manufactured goods	57.7	47.5	37.1	53.2	68.8	55.7	59.6
of which:							
Chemicals	11.7	9.8	11.9	11.4	11.7	10.4	9.6
Machinery and equipment	31.8	23.8	14.2	26.0	34.9	28.2	32.4
Exports							
(in value)							
Total	2216.2	5750.9	4588.8	8090.7	8838.3	9789.6	11212.1
Food and agricultural products	1492.6	2411.7	1459.7	1681.8	1791.9	1839.8	1914.5
Ores and metals	293.7	1183.1	490.0	661.8	637.6	569.2	500.1
Fuels	37.5	38.2	34.5	180.7	232.2	238.0	228.8
Manufactured goods	258.8	1213.2	1228.4	3063.4	6172.7	4041.8	4668.0
of which:							
Textiles and clothing	55.5	353.3	302.7	772.7	2008.6	972.1	989.0
Machinery and equipment	11.8	123.7	305.3	989.2	2479.5	1643.8	2092.0
Semiconductors	0.0	45.3	240.3	369.6	1375.1	593.5	805.6
(share in percentages)							
Food and agricultural products	67.4	41.9	31.8	20.8	20.3	18.8	17.1
Ores and metals	13.3	20.6	10.7	8.2	7.2	5.8	4.5
Fuels	1.7	0.7	0.8	2.2	2.6	2.4	2.0
Manufactured goods	11.7	21.1	26.8	37.9	69.8	41.3	41.6
of which:							
Textiles and clothing	2.5	6.1	6.6	9.6	22.7	9.9	8.8
Machinery and equipment	0.5	2.2	6.7	12.2	28.1	16.8	18.7
Semiconductors	0.0	0.8	5.2	4.6	15.6	6.1	7.2

Notes
Food and agriculture products consist of SITC 0+1+2+4 less (27+28); Fuels consist of SITC 3; Ores & Metals consist of SITC 27+28+68; Manufactured products consist of SITC 5+6+7+8 less 68.

Source: UNCTAD, COMTRADE.

Table 10.2   *Philippines: exports by commodity groups and markets, 1993 (millions of dollars)*

| Commodity group | World | OECD countries[1] | | | | Developing countries |
		Total	United States and Canada	European Union	Japan	
Total	11212.1	8413.4	4578.7	1834.6	1825.6	2693.3
Food and agricultural products	1914.5	1517.3	539.9	346.8	599.8	369.7
Ores and metals	500.1	267.6	2.8	6.3	257.1	231.2
Manufactured goods	4668.0	3493.4	1952.8	869.9	565.1	1109.1
of which:						
Textiles and Clothing	989.0	760.8	478.5	219.4	46.0	216.2
Furniture	159.0	145.0	89.5	38.3	10.8	13.0
Semiconductors	805.6	557.6	304.4	171.6	81.1	247.7
Machinery and equipment	2092.0	1554.4	909.1	308.4	308.8	527.5

Notes
See Table 10.1.
[1] OECD does not include Austria, Iceland, Mexico, Norway and Turkey.

Source: UNCTAD, COMTRADE.

10.3   DOMESTIC ENVIRONMENTAL PROBLEMS AND POLICY-MAKING

10.3.1   Domestic Regulations

In the last two decades, increasing water, air and sea pollution have become important concerns in the Philippines. Poverty, population pressure, poor economic and environmental policy implementation and several severe natural disasters have exacerbated the environmental stress. In addition, insufficient investment to redress the ecological deterioration has compounded the problem.

The rising resource and environmental stress is in some ways linked to the overall growth pattern of the Philippine economy. According to the study, the country's macroeconomic and industrial policies during the 1960s and 1970s were largely responsible for the unsatisfactory job creation in industry and agriculture. During this period there was a net transfer of resources out of agriculture, which discouraged private investments in this sector. In addition, the manufacturing sector became more capital intensive, resulting in a higher capital-to-output ratio during the 1970s.

This seems to suggest that the government was unable to pursue development according to the evolving comparative advantage. As a result, the Philippines continued to exploit its resource-intensive sectors rather than expanding the production and exports of manufactured products. Underpricing of natural resources and the poor implementation of resource protection measures were factors which contributed to the depletion of the country's renewable resources.

The study identified the following causes of environmental degradation in the country:

1. *Pricing failures* This is the most direct cause of environmental degradation; environmental costs of production and/or consumption are not internalized (for example, air and water pollution).
2. *Institutional failures* These exacerbate the problem of pricing failures because of poor property rights arrangements (use of public property in upland and urban areas), and open access to fugitive resources (fisheries, and so on).
3. *Government investment failures* This reflects the failure of governments and the private sector to invest in 'public good'. Activities such as municipal sanitation, sewerage facilities, and appropriately designed roads do not receive adequate funding, and increase the level of pollution. It also reflects the poor financial position of the government in light of the many demands on its budget.
4. *Excessive extraction of resources due to poverty, population pressure and high demand for Philippine exports* This is an important indirect source of environmental degradation in the country. Because of the failure to generate enough employment in the lowlands, millions of Filipinos have moved to the environmentally fragile uplands, thereby accelerating the problem of soil erosion in the country. The country's major cities, especially Metro Manila have serious problems of squatting and congestion. Poverty also prevents households from investing in sanitation facilities. At the same time, demand for Philippine resource-based exports such as aquaculture products has led to overfishing and resource depletion.

After recognizing the seriousness of environmental problems, the Philippine government adopted in 1989 the Philippine Strategy for Sustainable Development. This strategy addresses the problems of environmental and natural resource policies, the impact of population pressure, and issues pertaining to programmes and institutions in the context of trade and the environment.

In the forestry sector, for example, the government attempted to reduce deforestation by curtailing demand through the imposition of a log and lumber export ban, and the control of the trade in intra-country wood products. Since this was not successful, the focus shifted to rectifying the pricing failure. In 1990, the government switched from a specific tax to an *ad valorem* tax. As a result, government revenue increased by 15 times.

The main aim behind the change in policy was to discourage logging while also inducing greater efficiency in downstream industries. Underpricing of timber had resulted in an inefficient and large logging sector, and in downstream industries which were found to have low wood conversion ratios compared to downstream industries in other nations such as Japan. Higher forest charges were thus expected to result in the elimination of inefficient firms, thus reducing the size of the logging sector and inducing higher efficiency in downstream industries.

In order to better control resource extraction, the government enforced its regulations more strictly, often cancelling licences in cases of excessive felling. This policy resulted in a decrease in the number of holders of timber licence agreements and other land lease agreements by 50 per cent during the period 1980 to 1990. On the other hand, there appears to have been an increase in the number of industrial tree plantations and small-scale users, such as users of integrated social forestry lands.

Besides directly reducing deforestation, the change in policy was also aimed at generating revenues to finance forest management and rehabilitation activities. Recent investigation, however, has shown that channelling funds in this direction has not been feasible because of the general pressure on government revenues.

In the fisheries sector, the problem of defining property rights has been difficult to solve, mainly because of the open-access nature of the sector. In the case of the tuna industry, for instance, the rising number of fishermen and the increase in sophisticated gear and techniques are eventually expected to cause stock depletion.

Unsustainable fishing practices aggravated the overfishing problem, in addition to mangrove destruction and problems arising out of the flooding of inland and coastal aquaculture areas, sedimentation of coastal areas and deterioration of inland and marine water quality.

In an attempt to curb overfishing, the government reduced the average nominal import tariffs rate in the fisheries sector from 78 per cent to 40 per cent in 1980. This policy resulted in a sharp increase in imports, which helped reduce the pressure on the domestic resource base. In this regard, encouraging imports was considered an important step towards reducing the pressure on the dwindling fish stocks in the Philippines.

The government has introduced the Fisheries Sector Programme (FSP), which is financing ongoing studies aimed at ascertaining the appropriate level of economic rent that must be extracted from users of government-owned fishponds and finding ways to rehabilitate mangrove resources in some parts of the country. The FSP is also aiming to measure the economic rent that must be extracted from commercial fishermen to eventually bring fishing stocks back to a sustainable level.

Little concrete domestic policy to curtail overfishing is actually in place, however. Attempts are being made to implement the Local Government Code (LGC), as a result of which the participation of the local government and peoples' organizations in the management of local natural resources is expected to grow. It is expected that the LGC will lead to the quicker development of a system of property rights aimed at reducing resource exploitation substantially. In addition, endeavours are being made to implement the Coastal Resource Management (CRM) programmes which promote fishing efficiency and alternative employment opportunities for the coastal poor.

A study was launched by the Environmental and National Resource Accounting Project (ENRAP) to examine the relative sources of environmental damage. A macroeconomic analysis was performed, taking into account all the sectors of the Philippine economy. At the national level, the government and the household sectors were found to contribute to water pollution primarily through urban run-offs, and through household waste from inadequate sewage and drainage systems in many communities. The government also contributes to water pollution because of the soil erosion from public lands which have been deforested or otherwise unsustainably managed. The household sector contributes to air pollution through the burning of fuel and through personal transportation.

One striking feature of the Philippines is that in relative terms, the industrial sector is not a major source of environmental damage, and of air and water pollution. The ramifications of this fact are discussed in greater detail in the next section.

The above does not imply that the Philippines has enacted few environmental regulations. On the contrary, existing regulations, which are often based on United States standards, are among the most stringent in developing Asia. Their enforcement, however, may face difficulties. According to one study, an estimated 35 per cent of the medium and large industrial firms and most of the small firms do not comply with existing effluent regulations.[3] Stricter enforcement of existing environmental regulations would therefore serve the dual purpose of improving the domestic environment and of increasing the marketability of Philippine products in environmentally conscious consumer markets.

10.3.2 The Cost of Enforcing Environmental Regulations

In order to estimate the economic effects of internalizing environmental costs, the study identified the production and consumption externalities of different sectors, and estimated the contribution of each production activity to environmental pollution and off-site damages which resulted in resource degradation.

Internalizing environmental costs would involve substantial investment in pollution abatement, mainly in the purchase of Pollution Control Devices (PCDs). The discussion below pertains to total capital investments required to reduce emissions and effluents by 90 per cent of the current levels.

In accordance with the finding that the government and the household sectors are the largest polluters in the Philippines, the cost of pollution abatement is also highest for these sectors. For instance, among government expenditures, public administration and defence alone account for close to 35 per cent of total abatement cost. Households, which contribute significantly to the pollution level in the Philippines, would account for a little over 20 per cent of the total cost of abatement. Agriculture and fisheries would require another 15 per cent of the abatement expenditure.

In contrast, the manufacturing sector would require less than 6 per cent of abatement costs. For manufacturing as a whole, the investment requirement is equivalent to only about 1.6 per cent of manufacturing output. The relatively small share of this sector reflects the amount already invested in PCDs.

According to the study, this finding seems to indicate that industry has already invested in pollution abatement, particularly compared to the household and government sectors. An important implication is that in the context of environmental damage, emphasis must shift from 'dirty factories' to the government, household and agricultural sectors. The large, basic infrastructural needs of the Philippines, such as sewerage and drainage systems, have not been given due emphasis as imperatives to environmental protection.

The above findings also indicate that there may be higher environmental returns from investment in infrastructure rather than in industrial pollution abatement. This consideration must be borne in mind in the international debate. Excessive emphasis on industrial pollution may contribute little to improving the environment since it could result in insufficient effort being applied to the development of basic infrastructure as a primary condition for improving environmental protection.

10.3.3   Competitiveness Effects of Internalizing Environmental Costs

The implication of 'getting the prices right' through the imposition of pollution taxes or user charges, or alternatively, enforcing pollution laws, was investigated by using pollution control cost figures generated by the Environmental and National Resources Accounting Project (ENRAP). In addition, the potential effects on international competitiveness of undertaking more stringent pollution control were explored.

A major concern is that full cost pricing through the imposition of pollution taxes or user charges would make industries less competitive. In order to study the impact of environmental cost internalization on competitiveness, the study used a ratio of Domestic Resource Cost (DRC) and Official Exchange Rate (OER) to determine the level of competitiveness of a sector. The DRC refers to the value of domestic resources required to earn one unit of foreign exchange. In this case, environmental costs associated with a sector are added to the DRC estimation, and this is compared with the OER to indicate whether or not the cost of earning one unit of foreign exchange (including the cost of pollution abatement) is commensurate with the returns associated with it. Thus, while internalizing environmental costs, a ratio of DRC/OER below 1, signifies international competitiveness, whereas a ratio above 1 indicates the opposite.

Table 10.3   *Philippines: simulation of the impact of internalization on international competitiveness of selected sectors*

Sector	Environment cost (% of output values) Scenario I	Scenario II	DRC/OER[1] Scenario I	Scenario II
Commercial fishery	5	10	0.52	0.61
Aquaculture and other fishery activities	5	10	0.95	1.02
Coconut/copra	5	10	0.89	0.94
Processed coconut	5	10	1.14	1.36
Forestry	5	10	0.91	1.01
Textiles	0.67	–	1.07	–

Notes: [1]Represents the ratio of Domestic Resource Cost (DRC) / the Official Exchange Rate of the peso to the US dollar (OER).

Source: Intal *et al.*, op.cit.

For most of the industries listed in Table 10.3, when the environmental cost is 5 per cent of the output value, the DRC/OER ratio remains below 1, indicating that the product is still competitive on the international market. The results of the PIDS study therefore indicate that in most sectors, if environmental taxation is devised such that firms would opt to avoid payment of taxes and instead choose to invest an equivalent amount in pollution control, then the sector need not lose its export competitiveness in the long term.

In only two sectors would competitiveness be significantly hampered if environmental costs were internalized. In the case of forest and wood-based industries, which are already non-competitive, pollution abatement would further decrease competitiveness. Increasing wood imports is thus desirable to reduce resource pressure and encourage domestic wood processing. In the case of the textile sector, internalizing the cost of environmental damage would raise prices to an uncompetitive level. Since this has been a protected sector in the economy, internalizing environmental costs, which are equivalent to 0.67 per cent of the output value, would increase the ratio of DRC/OER to 1.07, thereby accentuating the uncompetitiveness of the product (see Table 10.3).

It appears from the previous section that compliance with Philippine environmental regulations can be achieved without substantially increasing costs in most industries. Considering that the eco-regulations in the Philippines are, to a large extent, based on standards in the United States, compliance with domestic standards may move the export sector closer to regulations prevailing in the OECD countries. An important implication of this is the need for greater enforcement of the prevailing regulations, rather than the need to enact more stringent regulations.

The above result must be qualified, however. Although the sectors at large may not lose their competitiveness, smaller firms are likely to have difficulties complying with the regulations. This may be mainly because economies of scale are significant in environmental investments. In addition, unlike large firms for which internally generated sources of financing tend to be available, small and medium-sized enterprises may find it difficult to gain access to capital for environmental investments due to low or negative private returns. Hence, according to the study, there is a need to grant more leeway to smaller firms in the course of enforcing regulations on domestic industry as a whole.

10.4   EFFECTS OF ENVIRONMENTAL REGULATIONS ON THE PHILIPPINES' EXPORTS

10.4.1   Impact of External Regulations on Exports

A significant portion of Philippine exports is directed to Japan, the United States and the European Union. In 1993, for instance, the OECD accounted for 75 per cent of total exports (see Table 10.4).

The fisheries sector appears to be the most vulnerable to external regulation, with over 87 per cent of exports being directed at the OECD. Of this, shrimp is the most prominent, because 96 per cent of exports are to the OECD. In particular, shrimps are sensitive to regulations in Japan, where more than half of this product is exported. Japan's laws with respect to shrimps relate mostly to pesticide and antibiotic content. If traces of certain pesticides are detected, then the shrimps are likely to be rejected. Hence, if the Philippines does not conform to these regulations, it could lose a huge market for its shrimps.

Table 10.4   *Philippines, 1993: exports of products which are vulnerable to environmental requirements (percentages)*

Product	World	OECD[1]	USA	EU	Japan	Developing countries
All	100.0	75.5	38.5	17.4	16.1	23.8
Fish	100.0	87.3	17.5	9.7	54.0	9.9
Tuna	100.0	88.2	21.4	28.6	21.7	3.2
Shrimps	100.0	96.2	11.6	0.0	83.5	3.8
Coconuts	100.0	88.4	41.4	27.3	1.9	11.3
Coconut products	100.0	88.1	43.2	40.6	3.5	11.3
Beverages	100.0	86.1	59.1	12.7	8.6	13.2
Leather products[2]	100.0	94.1	71.6	5.0	9.8	5.7
Footwear	100.0	87.8	33.5	40.5	7.6	11.4
Wood and products	100.0	77.6	18.6	32.5	21.9	22.0
Tropical timber	100.0	72.1	4.8	42.9	21.0	27.9
Paper and products	100.0	76.3	21.9	42.1	6.1	23.7
Textiles and products	100.0	76.2	44.3	23.0	4.1	23.0
All vulnerable products	100.0	75.7	29.9	18.2	23.5	22.5

Notes
[1] OECD does not include Austria, Iceland, Mexico, Norway and Turkey.
[2] Leather products except footwear.

Source: UNCTAD, COMTRADE.

Tuna is also potentially vulnerable to external regulations, because almost 90 per cent of Philippine exports is absorbed by the OECD. In one of the major importing markets for tuna, the United States, the Marine Mammal Protection Act (MMPA) stipulates the use of certain devices to protect dolphins, which are often caught along with the tuna. Since over 20 per cent of tuna exports go to the US, one can expect this segment to be vulnerable to the MMPA. In this context, there is a difference in values, because in a poor country such as the Philippines, dolphins have also been fished for commercial purposes.

Exports of coconut and processed products are subject to regulations on the aflatoxin content, which is considered potentially carcinogenic. In recent years, the European Union, in particular, has set stringent standards for coconut products, particularly copra meal and other feedstuff imports. A new standard, set in 1991, has reduced the permitted aflatoxin level to less than half of the initial level.

An analysis of the costs and benefits of reducing aflatoxin content was performed by the study. The results of the analysis indicated that drying the coconut by using the 'tapahan' method would help firms comply with the external regulation. It was found, however, that the estimated capital cost of employing this method was about 7 cents per kg of dried copra, while the operating cost was about 10 cents per kg. The total cost of drying copra using the tapahan method was therefore about 17 cents per kg. On the other hand, the estimated price premium associated with compliance was only about 10 cents per kg. There was thus a net cost associated with compliance with the external regulation on aflatoxin.

In the case of coconut oil exports, the main problem is the perceived nature of tropical oils as a source of fats and cholesterol. For instance, some organizations in importing countries pointed out the alleged role of tropical oils, including coconut oil, as likely causes of heart-related diseases and other ailments.

However, according to the study, the scientific evidence against coconut oil is tenuous. It is argued by the coconut industry that coconut oil does not have cholesterol since intensive scientific research shows that cholesterol is present only in animal oil.[4]

In the textile sector, outdated technology may hamper compliance with external environmental requirements. The Philippine textile sector was found to be obsolete in comparison with international standards in terms of the speed, variety and quality of production. To the extent that older technology tends to be less environmentally friendly, this sector has not sufficiently addressed ecological problems, despite attempts to boost textiles through policies such as export credits. Because this sector was protected through both import restrictions and high tariffs over a significant time period it had little incentive to improve its obsolete technology.

The study states that so far Philippine exports are not significantly affected by external eco-regulations. The experience with external regulations, until now, seems to indicate that the greatest impacts are likely to be on the prices of raw materials and on research and development costs.

10.4.2 Response of Philippine Exporters to External Regulations

The study conducted a questionnaire-based survey, which revealed that firms had little awareness of environmental regulations prevailing either domestically or internationally, although most of them stated that internalizing environmental costs would be useful for the Philippines.

Companies exporting to the OECD had a greater awareness of eco-regulations prevailing in these markets. Some exporters stated that if they did not comply with external requirements, they may still have the possibility of retaining some of the OECD market, although at lower prices.

Entrepreneurs could also divert production towards the domestic market. If such a market diversion were to occur, the Philippine economy would suffer, predominantly on account of the foreign exchange loss. This does not support the idea that lax environmental standards can serve as an implicit subsidy to exports. In the Philippine case, it would appear that lack of enforcement of strict eco-regulations may actually result in exporters becoming more inward looking, thereby reducing the country's capacity to export. Therefore, the enforcement of regulations in the Philippines would actually have a positive effect on the country's export growth.

10.5 MULTILATERAL ENVIRONMENTAL AGREEMENTS

The study expresses the view that in the case of the Philippines the trade and competitiveness effects of Multilateral Environmental Agreements (MEAs) have not yet been of great significance. The successful attempts at addressing global environmental problems, for instance the Montreal Protocol and CITES, relate to products (for example, refrigerators and endangered species) which do not feature significantly in Philippine exports. The Montreal Protocol may, however, affect industrial users of refrigeration equipment. This aspect is, however, not discussed in the study.

Efforts at regulating open-sea resources, including the 1989 Wellington Convention for the Prohibition of Fishing With Long Driftnets and the UN Moratorium on Driftnet Fishing are still tenuously monitored. Besides, the study points out that driftnet fishing is not practised in the Philippines to any significant degree.

Timber exports by the Philippines could be significantly affected by agreements based on principles of 'sustainable forest management'. For the Philippines, this could affect the timber trade and furniture exports, as the local sources of eco-friendly timber, grown through industrial plantation, are very limited and are likely to remain so because of the long gestation period involved.

10.6 IMPACT OF ECONOMIC OPENNESS ON THE ENVIRONMENT

Trade liberalization is a central component of the Philippine economic programme. *A priori*, it is difficult to determine the net effect of trade liberalization on the country's environment. On the one hand, trade liberalization encourages increased national income and poverty alleviation through increases in employment, including export-oriented labour-intensive activities. Increased employment should help retain people in urban areas, reducing the incentive to migrate to fragile lands, thereby relieving to some extent the population pressure which has been affecting the environment in the Philippines. Higher incomes also mean demand for better sanitation facilities and a higher tax base which could provide more funds for public projects. In addition, freer trade could lower the cost of imported pollution control technologies and eco-friendly inputs, thereby affecting the environment positively.

On the other hand, trade liberalization could imply an increase in the absolute pollution level because of the growth of the economy, including that of the highly polluting sectors. For instance, one view is that a devaluation of the national currency could also push the economy towards the production and export of products from highly polluting sectors. Hence, the exact impact of trade liberalization on the Philippine environment is not clear.

In order to further understand the link between trade liberalization and the environment, the study examined Philippine trade in terms of pollution intensity. A drop in highly polluting exports was evident among the agricultural and forest resource-intensive exports in the latter half of the 1970s (Box 10.1). This partially explains the decrease of their share in overall highly polluting exports from 51 per cent to 31 per cent between 1975 and 1980 (see Table 10.5). Highly polluting exports (primarily vegetable oils, fish and fish preparations, and preserved fruits) likewise declined substantially during the latter half of the 1980s, contributing once again to a drop in the proportion of highly polluting exports to total exports from 38 per cent in 1985 to 22 per cent in 1990.

In contrast, unskilled labour-intensive exports are found to be less polluting overall. Since this category of exports has grown most significantly during the last two decades, its low pollution intensity could explain the increase in the proportion of less polluting exports over the period 1975 to 1990 (see Table 10.5).

Overall, the discussion seems to suggest that over the past decade, as Philippine exports have shifted from natural resource-intensive to labour-intensive there has also been an apparent trend towards a lower pollution intensity of exports (see Table 10.5).

Table 10.5   Philippines: exports by pollution intensity, 1975–1990 (percentages)

Pollution intensity	1975	1980	1985	1990
Highly polluting	51.07	31.30	38.36	21.84
Polluting	18.20	26.70	18.20	22.34
Less polluting	30.73	42.00	43.44	55.82
Total	100.00	100.00	100.00	100.00

Source: Intal *et al.*, op. cit.

Box 10.1   The impact of trade restrictions on the forestry sector

The forestry sector is a good example of the manner in which trade-restrictive policies can affect the environment. While restrictions on log and lumber exports had been attempted for several reasons in the past, in the 1970s this policy was driven by economic rather than environmental considerations. The government encouraged higher value-added downstream activities in wood-processing activities in the hope of earning more foreign exchange, generating more employment, and using the already dwindling resources more efficiently. Thus, logging concessions and log export quotas were preferentially awarded to entrepreneurs interested in processing activity. Moreover, with an export ban in logs effectively pushing domestic prices down, the input costs for the processing industry were lowered, thereby providing considerable effective protection for this industry.

Nevertheless, the results were discouraging. Among lumber, plywood and veneer exports, only lumber displayed any substantial increase in volume of exports over the 1970s. The poor export performance has been partially attributed to the dwindling resource base in the country. According to the study, a more important factor was the high wastage rate in processing. It was reported in 1977 that sawmills operated at only 29 per cent of capacity, plywood mills at 35 per cent and veneer mills at 64 per cent. In addition, the ratio of DRC to OER in the forest-based industries indicates that sawmills, veneer and plywood industries are indeed inefficient. These firms were found to have low wood conversion rates. For instance, in the case of plywood, the industry was found to have a conversion rate of 43 per cent, as compared to that of Japan, which had a much higher conversion rate of 55 per cent.

While failing to propagate the downstream wood-processing industries, the restrictions on log exports meant forgone revenues, particularly in the light of the low conversion rates prevailing in the processing industries. According to the study, the loss in rent due to wastage during the period 1979–82 was calculated to be approximately $500 million. But the waste of the resource base was stated to be even greater than the loss in rent.

It follows that forestry trade restrictions as a tool for encouraging higher value-added exports and saving scarce resources were not successful in the forestry sector of the Philippines. At the same time, this policy was shown to be harmful to the environment.

In the case of imported products, there is a similar trend. Agriculture and forestry resource-intensive sectors, for example, have shown an increase in the proportion of non-polluting imports. Although mineral-intensive products are mostly highly polluting, these are compensated for by labour-intensive imports which have increased in the non-polluting category. Overall, there is an evident decline in the share of polluting imports in favour of non-polluting imports (see Table 10.6). Therefore, both exports and imports seem to be moving in the direction of less polluting commodities.

Table 10.6   Philippines: imports by pollution intensity, 1975–1990 (percentages)

Pollution intensity	1975	1980	1985	1990
Highly polluting	51.07	57.23	45.20	48.41
Polluting	37.06	30.27	31.22	26.22
Less polluting	11.24	12.50	23.58	25.37
Total	100.00	100.00	100.00	100.00

Source: Intal *et al.*, op. cit.

The PIDS team analysed the likely impact of trade liberalization on the Philippine environment. The Chunglee model, a multi-industry partial equilibrium model was used. In this context, trade liberalization is defined as tariff reduction with or without induced changes in the real exchange rate. The model, however, is static and assumes fixed input–output ratios and constant factor prices. The dynamic effects accruing from increased investment are, therefore, not taken into account. Because of its limitations, the simulation results are meant primarily to provide only rough indications of the direction of change in the economy and its probable impact on the environment.

Three main aspects are taken into account while analysing the impact of trade liberalization on the environment. First, the model attempts to evaluate whether or not tariff reduction encourages less polluting industries. The second aspect is whether or not the tariff reduction will increase the absolute level of pollution in the country. At the same time, the model also studies the impact of the real exchange rate on the relative incentives to the growth of industries manufacturing tradable products and the non-tradable sector.

It is hypothesized that the government implements a 50 per cent across-the-board reduction in tariffs. Table 10.7 summarizes the results. Two scenarios are presented, one where the real exchange rate changes, and the other where it does not. A dramatic reduction in tariffs without a corresponding change in real exchange rates will leave much of the Philippine agriculture and manufacturing sectors challenged by competition from imports. The impact is the greatest in capital-intensive import substitution industries, such as chemicals, machinery and basic metal products.

Table 10.7   Philippines: trade liberalization and the impact on the environment

Product description	Change in output (%) I[1]	II[2]	Pollution intensity[3]
Agriculture	−1.89	9.95	1.4474
Fishing	−0.90	11.18	0.0000
Logging and other forestry	7.69	21.89	5.1093
Mining	0.98	13.53	3 8189
Manufacturing of which:	−13.37	−3.04	0.3259
Food processing	−7.08	10.88	0.4245
Beverages and tobacco	−9.49	7.87	0.4582
Textiles and footwear	-9.09	8.37	0.2068
Wood and wood products	−5.42	12.94	0.6316
Chemical products	−25.31	−11.85	0.1071
Non-metallic mineral products	−23.79	−9.96	0.0918
Basic metals and metal products	−21.21	−6.74	0.2929
Machinery	−25.52	−12.11	0.1036
Other manufacturing	−10.95	6.05	0.0593
Total	−9.88	5.49	0.7922

Notes
[1] Refers to post reform scenario with 50% reduction in tariff and fixed exchange rate
[2] Refers to post reform scenario with 50% tariff reduction and flexible exchange rate
[3] Refers to the ratio of abatement cost or environmental damage costs to sector output.

Source: Intal *et al.*, op.cit.

The simulation model finds that trade liberalization with currency depreciation raises the national average pollution and environmental damage intensity of production. This is because of the reallocation of output towards logging, mining and agriculture which have large off-site environmental damages. Even in the manufacturing sector, there appears to be a reallocation of output towards the industries with higher pollution/environmental damage. Some such sectors are food processing, beverages, and wood products.

The overall results of the PIDS simulations based on the Chunglee model indicate that there could be a potential trade-off between trade liberalization and environmental protection. The study concludes that without the internalization of environmental costs and process changes, trade liberalization can lead to increased environmental stress. However, this model does not take into account the effects of increased income on the environment, which may alter the result.

10.7   CONCLUSIONS AND RECOMMENDATIONS

10.7.1   Conclusions

Environmental degradation and resource depletion in the Philippines are largely due to market and policy failures. Property rights over environmental goods and services are not well defined, and firms have generally failed to internalize costs. The government has also failed to appropriate the economic rent from the exploitation of the country's resources. This has allowed private agents to capture massive returns, thus widening the gap between private costs and social costs.

Partially as a result of resource depletion, the comparative advantage has shifted from resource-intensive sectors, including agricultural crops, fishery and mineral-based products, to labour-intensive products, which are less pollution-intensive. However, pollution-intensive production may yet increase in the future as the more developed countries increasingly specialize in the more skill-intensive service industries, leaving more space for developing countries in manufactures, which are typically more polluting than service industries.

The study analyses the possible impact of cost internalization on Philippine industries, and shows that most manufacturing industries can indeed bear the costs of incremental investments required to reduce emissions and effluents to reasonable levels. Running costs of pollution abatement will not amount to more than 2 per cent of output cost for most sectors in the economy. In a number of industries where the Philippines currently has an international market, the comparative advantage can be retained even with an environmental tax of up to 5 per cent of output.

However, environmental policy based on cost internalization will further lower the effective protection for domestic industry, implying that the incorporation of environmental costs in the export industries worsens further the already negligible or negative effective rate of protection, thus increasing the disincentive to export. This suggests that the imposition of cost internalization on exports needs to be tied to broader trade liberalization – a significant redirection of the country's trade towards a lower tariff regime and a lower exchange rate.

Trade liberalization is expected to have positive or negative effects on the environment by changing the relative effective rates of protection of the different industries which will have varying degrees of associated environmental damage. An across-the-board liberalization can be expected to encourage producers of tradables, including nature-based industries such as forestry, mining and agriculture, all of which are associated with large off-site environmental consequences. Another result emanating from the simulations is that when devaluation accompanies tariff cuts, the comparative advantage of these sectors is reinforced. Under such a policy scenario, other highly polluting sectors, such as food, beverages, tobacco and wood products, are encouraged.

A static analysis suggests a possible trade-off between trade liberalization and implied gains in efficiency and welfare, on the one hand, and environmental protection on the other. Such an argument, however, does not take into account the dynamic effects of increased competition resulting from freer trade. For example, state of the art resource-efficient technology which can bring its own ecological gains.

In addition, liberalizing trade, particularly the importation of those products which reduce the pressure on domestic resources, will help attenuate the resource depletion in the country. At the same time, trade liberalization exerts competitive pressures on downstream processing industries and thereby helps conserve scarce resources. It seems then that trade liberalization should take place in conjunction with environmental and natural resource management policies.

10.7.2 Recommendations

The failure to direct industrial development according to the country's evolving comparative advantage resulted in the country remaining trapped in resource-intensive sectors during the late 1960s and 1970s. Given the underpricing of natural resource extraction and the poor implementation of resource protection, the country's renewable resources were significantly depleted over time.

The challenge is to minimize conflicts between environmental protection and economic growth. Ideally, the policy structure should aim at heightening the symbiosis between the economy and the environment in production and consumption for improved quality of life, better distribution (among social classes) of opportunities for income generation, and increased funds for resource regeneration and environmental protection.

To maximize the economic benefits and indirect environmental benefits (through poverty reduction, for instance) of trade liberalization and expansion while also minimizing the direct negative impact on the environment, it is important to internalize environmental costs of production and consumption, and to improve property rights arrangements. In this regard, the government would have to modify or strengthen property rights in sectors characterized by open-access regimes. In addition, it is important that the government captures the economic rent or minimizes excessive private gains in the exploitation of public goods, while also ensuring that private agents bear the social cost of private activities. Any increase in government revenue would be useful for increasing its investment in resource regeneration (for instance, reforestation) and environmental protection (in cases such as sewerage and sanitation). The environment would also benefit from an increased awareness among citizens of the social impact of private activities.

Another sphere in which the government could intervene effectively would be in disseminating and promoting appropriate and sustainable technology. For example, the more rapid adoption and diffusion of state of the art technology would result in a higher quality capital stock that uses resources more efficiently. It would be particularly relevant to upgrade technology in sectors such as textiles, which have enjoyed high protection.

The study also emphasizes the importance of better enforcement of existing domestic environmental regulations. Besides cleaning up the environment, this would harmonize Philippine products with those in the OECD, and result in fewer additional compliance costs in meeting external eco-regulations.

The evidence presented suggests that with some special consideration for small firms in selected sectors, the economy can afford the incremental cost of internalizing environmental costs. A larger threat to competitiveness is the lax enforcement of environmental regulations. Incentives should be provided to exporters to make the environmental investments consistent with the high product standards in export markets.

Property rights are another area which needs serious policy planning. In the case of fisheries, for instance, a concerted effort is required. Because the fishing sector involves a large number of people and a vast geographic spread, better enforcement would require an improvement in the logistical complement (boats, personnel, salaries, fuel costs, and so on) alongside community-based resource management.

The participation of the coastal fishing community, which has an interest in limiting or rationalizing access to fishery resources, is paramount in identifying priority user groups and enforcing local laws specific to municipal fisheries. The aquaculture and marine-culture subsectors must be made to bear the high impact of production on the marine environment, for example by imposing high enough licence fees. Performance bonds can also be required to better induce investment in the necessary clean-up technology if pollution charges are not adequately effective.

Overall, increased economic openness is seen as a potentially important factor contributing to the correction of policy failures of the past. Given reasonably good environmental policy and management, international trade enhances opportunities for improving resource allocation, redressing resource constraints and raising economic growth prospects. It is important, therefore, to strengthen the economic and indirect environmental benefits of trade liberalization, through appropriate national policies, considering that cost internalization in the Philippines seems to be practicable without major adverse effects on export competitiveness, provided environmental investments are cost-effective (for instance, in the case of infrastructure), and that positive measures are implemented at the international level.

Policy initiatives at the domestic level must be supported at the international level, for instance through improved market access and prevention of trade barriers resulting from environmental policy. At the same time, trade restrictions must not be used to influence the environmental policies of other countries, in this case, the Philippines. There is a danger that unless the principles of international cooperation on trade and the environment are clear, the environment can become a subtle form of industrial protection in importing countries.

Finally, multilateral institutions and environmental organizations need to pay greater attention to the poor state of public investment in basic infrastructure, which may contribute more to environmental degradation than manufacturing industries. While domestic and international discussions have tended to highlight polluting industries, the basic infrastructure needs of a developing country have not been given due emphasis as imperatives to environmental protection. In view of the budgetary constraints facing most developing countries such as the Philippines, greater efforts should be concentrated on investing in the basic infrastructure required for environmental protection.

NOTES

1. Intal, P., E. Medalla, M. los Angeles, D. Israel, V. Pineda, P. Quintos and E. Tan (1994), 'Trade and environment linkages: the case of the Philippines', Philippine Institute of Development Studies.

2. For instance, Intal, P. *et al.* (1994), 'Trade, environment and development in the Philippines', paper presented at the Workshop on Trade and Environment in Asia–Pacific: Prospects for Regional Co-operation, East-West Centre, Honolulu, Hawaii, 22–25 September.

3. Montgomery Consulting Engineers (1992), *Environmental Management Strategy*, The World Bank–United Nations Development Project.

4. United Coconut Association of the Philippines (1989), 'The coconut oil crisis: the poisoning of America,' *Coconuts Today*, **VII**, December.

11. Poland

11.1 INTRODUCTION

A case study was conducted on trade, environment and development linkages by a research team at the Wroclaw Academy of Economics, Department of Economics. The research team consisted of Professor Dr Boguslaw Fiedor, Dr Stanislaw Czaja, Dr Andrzej Graczyk and Dr Jerzy Rymarczyk, and the study was completed in 1994. This chapter, prepared by the UNCTAD secretariat, summarizes and updates the findings of the study.

The study focuses on the trade and environment issues related to the market reforms that have been central to the economic changes in Poland during the period of transition to a market economy. In assessing the trade and environmental impacts, the study does not try to distinguish between these reforms and trade liberalization, something that would be very difficult to do since trade liberalization is an integral part of the overall reforms.

The transition to a market economy and the endeavour to join the European Union in the future represent a tremendous challenge for the Polish economy. The need to upgrade domestic environmental policies relatively quickly to correspond to those in the European Union further adds to the challenge. Short-term adjustment costs to the Polish economy may thus be significant; the long-term costs will depend on how Poland succeeds in the adaptation process.

The reasons for environmental damage in Poland are not trade-related. In fact, the state of the environment in Poland seems to vindicate the theory that closed economies are often more polluting than economies open to international trade.

11.2 BACKGROUND TO POLAND'S ECONOMY

For over forty years, the Polish economy was based on a centrally planned system whose major features included membership of the CMEA (Council for Mutual Economic Assistance), rapid industrialization with promotion of heavy industry, and foreign trade controls. The system resulted in the considerable isolation of the Polish economy from international markets, and, according to a recent GATT/WTO report, instead of letting the economy develop based on comparative advantage, produced a disproportionately large and diversified industrial sector dominated by state-owned enterprises operating at low levels of efficiency.[1] The political decision to concentrate on heavy, energy and raw material intensive industry was facilitated by Poland's abundant raw material deposits.

During the 1980s, many reforms took place, especially concerning Poland's foreign trade system and foreign investment regime. In 1990, Poland embarked on an all-encompassing economic reform programme that aimed at a transformation from a centrally planned economy to a full market economy. The most important elements of the programme relating to international trade were the introduction of internal convertibility of the Polish currency for current account transactions, and the passing of laws and regulations that practically eliminated most export and import restrictions and removed the state monopoly in foreign trade: that is, the introduction of liberal foreign trade.

The removal of the state monopoly in currency transactions enabled enterprises to maintain direct economic relations with foreign trading partners and thus uncovered the differences in domestic and world market prices. In order to achieve price comparability, it was also crucial to cancel subsidies on most goods and services. Poland's openness to free trade in goods was preceded by the removal of barriers preventing the flow of foreign capital into Poland. Some results of the reform programme are already to be seen in that domestic prices have become more in line with world prices. For example, between the end of 1989 and the beginning of 1992, the average domestic coal price experienced an 18-fold increase in nominal terms. During the same period, nominal gas prices increased 12 times for industrial users and 80 times for households. Also, the supply of goods has improved due to import liberalization, competition has strengthened and the private sector has expanded.[2] In 1995, Poland had the fastest growing economy in Europe, and the country attracted around US$6 billion worth of foreign direct investment between 1990 and mid-1995.[3] Poland's external debt has fallen substantially since it started reforming its economy. The Polish experience of debt is summarized in Box 11.1.

The transition process in foreign economic relations was and still is negatively influenced by many aspects of Poland's economic structure resulting from past central planning activities: domination of heavy industries, obsolete technology, low productivity and small innovation propensity.

Polish industry has also been characterized by high energy and raw material intensity leading to high direct pollution intensity, and by the poor quality of most goods and the consequent lack of competitiveness in international markets. Finally, Poland typically exports low value-added goods where competition is keen and international prices have been falling, making it difficult to pass on environmental costs in product prices.

High energy intensity is an important feature of the Polish economy with repercussions for trade and environment linkages.[4] Many factors have led to the

Box 11.1   Poland's external debt

When Poland started reforming its economic system it had a large external debt and was the world's fourth largest debtor country (after Brazil, Mexico and Argentina). However, after debt reductions agreed to in the Paris Club of official creditors and the London Club of commercial bank creditors, the remaining Polish debt stood in January 1995 at roughly US$1000 per capita.[1] Earning foreign currency through exports is an important avenue for Poland to service the debt. Also, debt-for-environment swaps, where creditor countries cancel a part of Polish debt if a corresponding amount of money is spent for environmental protection in Poland, have been concluded with the governments of the United States and France.

[1] 'In search of foreign finance', *Financial Times Survey, Poland*, 28 March 1995.

high energy intensity in Poland. These include the environmentally disadvantageous, energy-intensive industry structure; obsolete and energy-intensive industrial technology resulting in wastage and inefficiency; shortcomings in the common energy policy of the former CMEA; and low effectiveness of state environmental protection policy. In particular the consequences of the energy policy followed over four decades by the CMEA are of a very persistent character, and major infrastructure investments are needed to overcome the problems created by the system.

There have also been external phenomena that complicate Poland's foreign trade relations, such as the decay of the former USSR (which was Poland's most important trading partner) and the consequent virtual collapse of trade with it; the dissolution of the CMEA and the reunification of Germany. To Poland, all these events meant breaking off traditional links between Polish enterprises and partners from former CMEA countries which accounted for more than half of Polish foreign trade. This was particularly important because many goods that were produced for this market did not meet the requirements of other markets. However, among the economies in transition, Poland has been among the first to divert its exports to the European Union and other market economies.

The direction of Poland's foreign trade has indeed undergone a major reorientation towards market economies, especially the European Union. The share of trade with Central and Eastern European countries has declined while that of European Union countries has grown (see Table 11.1). Due to the enlargement of the European Union in 1995, the European Union now accounts for an even larger share of Polish trade. However, a noticeable growth of the import and export share of other areas, in particular Asia and North America, can also be observed.

Table 11.1   Regional changes in Polish foreign trade (share in percentage)

	1980	1985	1990	1991	1992	1993	1994
Exports							
European Union	22.8	22.6	46.7	55.5	57.9	63.5	62.6
Countries with economies in transition	52.4	40.7	22.1	16.8	15.4	9.6	14.5
Imports							
European Union	19.7	19.5	42.5	49.9	53.1	57.2	57.5
Countries with economies in transition	52.9	47.9	25.2	19.0	16.3	10.7	14.3

Sources: UNCTAD, based on COMTRADE database. For 1994, Central Statistical Office, Warsaw.

Particularly important to the gradual opening of the markets of highly developed countries to Poland is the 1991 Association Agreement with the European Union, aimed at establishing free trade in industrial goods and a partial liberalization of agricultural trade between the signatories before the year 2002. Poland's ultimate goal is to achieve full membership of the European Union.

11.3   DOMESTIC ENVIRONMENTAL POLICY-MAKING

11.3.1   State of the Environment

Some of the past economic activities have resulted in harmful impacts on the Polish environment. The state of the Polish environment is most critical in areas that Polish environmental statistics identify as environmentally hazardous regions. In 1990 such areas comprised 11 per cent of the country's area and included 35 per cent of the population. An overwhelming share of these regions are located near enterprises in the fuel-energy sector. However, at the same time, 27 per cent of the country was in a natural or close to natural state.[5]

When considering the state of the environment in Poland, it is necessary to emphasize the spatial concentration of many pollution sources. Although high spatial concentration is harmful for the environment, the local carrying capacity of which may be exceeded, the concentration may in some cases also be a positive feature in that it may facilitate cost-efficient cooperative pollution prevention investments.

Atmospheric air pollution in Poland is characterized by the domination of stationary source emissions; mainly burning hard coal and lignite in the energy sector. Coal-fired power plants account for about 70 per cent of sulphur dioxide emissions. Poland is also a large emitter of carbon dioxide (CO_2). The spatial distribution of air pollution in Poland is highly uneven due to the concentration of the major emission sources as well as the transboundary pollution to the southern and western territories. Large urban-industrial agglomerations are located in the most polluted areas. However, atmospheric emissions have recently been decreasing and, for example, there is now an ongoing programme funded by the Global Environment Facility (GEF) to switch from coal heating to gas and electric heating. This should result in significant improvements in local air quality in most big urban agglomerations.[6]

Transboundary air pollution is mainly received from Germany, Czech Republic and Slovakia. However, between 1992 and 1994 the import of air emissions (mostly SO_2) from Germany has noticeably decreased due to the technological reconstruction of power plants in the former East Germany. Air pollution from Polish sources, in turn, is transported by wind to, for example, Scandinavian countries. Studies in these countries have indicated that for receiving countries such as Finland and Sweden it may be more cost-effective to invest in air pollution prevention in Poland than in their own countries.

Over 40 per cent of towns and about 98 per cent of villages in Poland have no sewage treatment facilities. Many towns with a population exceeding 100 000 inhabitants do not possess municipal sewage treatment plants, and 52 per cent of industrial plants discharge waste water into their own sewage treatment facilities. Existing facilities, both municipal and industrial, are often out-of-date and overloaded. The lack of water resources in Poland is already becoming a serious impediment to the country's development. For example, there are difficulties in supplying some regions with drinking water. Since most surface water is polluted, there is a tendency to use good quality ground water for industrial purposes. Partly as a result of environmental policies and partly as a reflection of slowing economic activity, the pressures on water quality caused by household, municipal and industrial discharges have started to decrease.[7]

Almost all water from Polish territory runs into the Baltic Sea, and Poland is the largest contributor to Baltic Sea pollution. The Baltic Sea has suffered severe environmental damage: the seabed has become partly lifeless, and spawning grounds and some plankton species have decreased, which in turn has resulted in decreasing productivity of Baltic Sea fisheries. In order for Poland to reduce the pollution in the Baltic Sea from Polish rivers (a reduction of 50 per cent has been agreed to), cooperation with neighbouring countries in the framework of the Baltic Sea Convention is indispensable. For example, around 30 per cent of biological contaminants and 60 per cent of heavy metals discharged into the Baltic Sea by the Vistula and Odra rivers originate from sources outside Poland.

The forests in Poland have been among the most severely damaged in Europe, with 75 per cent of all trees in Poland showing some damage from atmospheric pollution.[8] Also, for 40 years the wood harvest level exceeded the cutting plan, which has led to a skewed age distribution of trees. A project for forest protection called Green Lungs of Europe is underway in collaboration with GEF.

Polish industry generates yearly around 120 million tons of waste, of which only 50 per cent is being used for economic purposes. The small utilization rate results mostly from the high share of post-flotation sludge in wastes, but also from a shortage of waste processing installations. A legislative process to introduce a bill on waste management and to establish recycling targets has been started. Although industrial waste still remains one of the major environmental challenges for Poland, the volume of such waste has recently been decreasing. However, at the same time, the volume of municipal waste has been increasing.

11.3.2 Environmental Legislation in Poland

With the economic reforms, liberalized foreign trade, and the increasing significance of OECD markets, Polish products have become more exposed to environmental requirements in the export markets as well as to world price levels for energy and raw materials. This has necessitated stricter domestic environmental policy measures and improved enforcement, resulting in likely improvements in environmental quality but also, in some cases, increased production costs. The responsibility for environmental administration and legislation lies mainly within the Ministry of Environmental Protection, Natural Resources and Forestry, although several other ministries and other authorities also deal with environmental issues within their specific domains.

In particular, major changes are taking place in Poland's domestic environmental policy-making as a result of the Association Agreement with the European Union that requires, *inter alia*, the convergence of Poland's environmental standards and regulations with those of the European Union in an anticipated time frame of 10 years.[9] The Polish Government has expressed its intention to move towards meeting European Union environmental standards and legal norms as soon as possible. According to Article 68 of the Association Agreement, Poland shall use its best endeavours to ensure that future legislation is compatible with European Union legislation. Thus Polish law is to be modified progressively and adapted to conform, first with the spirit of European Union directives, and, as far as possible, with their details whenever this does not entail excessive costs.[10] Bearing in mind Poland's goal of achieving full membership of the European Union, it will eventually have to harmonize its legislation with that of the European Union.

The subsidiarity principle of the European Union implies that Poland does not have to introduce into its national legislation all the detailed regulatory provisions of the European Union, but only those that would ensure implementation of the Union's objectives in the sphere of environmental protection and make Polish environmental legislation consistent with the main principles of European Union environmental policy.[11]

The main legal instruments used for environmental policy-making in the European Union include regulations, directives, decisions and recommendations, of which only regulations and directives are binding instruments of European Union law. Regulations are binding to member states as such. Directives are also binding as to their goals, but the ways of achieving those goals can be selected by the member state. Decisions are issued on individual matters and bind only the specific entity concerned (for example, an enterprise). Finally, recommendations have no binding power.

The most important environmental instruments of the European Union, with which Poland will have to ensure the compatibility of its existing and future legislation, include directives and regulations relating to the following:

- ambient air standards with respect to sulphur dioxide (SO_2), suspended dust, nitrogen oxides (NO_x) and lead;
- SO_2, NO_x and dust emissions by industrial facilities, thermal power plants, and existing and constructed municipal waste incinerators. Particularly important for Poland here is the directive on large combustion facilities that, in addition to setting limit values on emissions of individual facilities, also defines maximum emission levels for member countries;
- pollution emitted by mobile sources, including the directives on unleaded gasoline, car and truck fuel gas emissions, and catalytic converters;
- drinking water quality;
- industrial and municipal sewage treatment plants;
- reduction of surface water pollution by fertilizers and pesticides;
- solid waste disposal and management;
- the use, disposal and storage of hazardous/toxic wastes;
- packaging;
- Environmental Impact Assessment; and
- the availability of environmental information to the public.

The harmonization of Polish environmental legislation with that of the European Union, in particular emission technology and product standards, may have serious general economic consequences through increased environmental protection costs and impacts on the export competitiveness of specific sectors and enterprises. This is particularly true since the harmonization process is proceeding in parallel with the consolidation of many standards and norms within the European Union, which is expected to result in the introduction of more stringent standards. It is very likely that some Polish exporters will not be able to meet those standards in the short run and thereby may lose markets both in Poland and within the European Union.

The German Institut fuhr Wirtschaftsforschung (ifo) has estimated that the overall costs that Poland would have to bear in order to achieve environmental quality comparable to European Union standards would amount to around US$30 billion.[12] Taking an example from the energy sector, Polish analysts estimated that approximately US$5 to US$10 billion (depending on the emission abatement scale) would have to be spent to achieve the European Union emission standards for SO_2, NO_x and dusts from fuel combustion in the energy sector by 1998. This expenditure has not been implemented but some programmes have been undertaken and, as part of its accession strategy for the EU, an accelerated programme is being drawn up. Though these standards would be comparable to the European Union directive on large combustion facilities, they could still be insufficient in the context of planned total emission ceilings to be achieved by certain member countries by the years 1998 and 2003.

There are thus areas of environmental policy-making where the harmonization of Polish regulations with those of the European Union may be very costly and difficult. However, there are also areas where Polish regulations do not significantly diverge from their European Union counterparts or are stronger than the latter, but their enforcement may be relatively lax. It should also be noted that when Poland started its transition towards a market economy, it also adopted a new environmental policy based on the polluter pays principle and the concept of sustainable development. This facilitates the harmonization process in conceptual, legislative and cost terms.

11.3.3 Trade Impacts of Domestic Environmental Policy

The tightening of environmental standards is of particular significance to the energy sector, where power plants have to install fuel gas desulphurization facilities before the year 1999. Calculating production cost increments on the basis of German experience in implementing a similar programme, one can expect the production costs in thermal power plants to increase by 30 to 40 per cent. Should an overall technological reconstruction of Polish power plants take place, with both SO_2 and NO_x emission abatement, the cost increase would certainly be higher. For instance, the third largest power plant in Poland (located in the 'Black Triangle' area[13]), would need approximately US$1.2 billion to carry out such a modernization programme. This would result in a radical decline in

SO_2 and NO_x emissions but also a likely tripling of the current price of electricity generated by the power plant. This, in turn, would inevitably lead to the overall collapse of electricity exports by Tur\w which is the largest Polish electricity exporter.

Stricter emission standards and their improved enforcement may also influence the exports of hard coal (one of Poland's most important export products[14]) and hard coal-intensive products. This sector is already facing major financial difficulties; at current production and transport cost levels and with increasing supply from low-cost foreign competitors it is approaching the limit of export profitability. Also, strict enforcement of environmental standards and regulations could lead to limitations in hard coal extraction in some large and technologically outdated mines or even to the closing down of these mines. If all the current and proposed environmental standards and regulations were implemented and enforced it is estimated that Polish hard coal exports could fall from 23 million tons in 1993 to 7 to 10 million tons in the year 2000.

Also of importance are the new restrictive regulations concerning the emissions of air pollutants from cokeries. Modernization costs of cokeries (replacing wet coke quenching with the dry method) will be tremendous, but the modernization should bring considerable environmental improvements by reducing atmospheric air pollution by 80 to 90 per cent in a few years. Since Polish coking coal still remains cheaper than imported coal, it is likely that despite increased prices domestic buyers may continue buying it. The most important consequence of higher domestic coke prices will be the increased production costs of pig iron and the resulting higher prices of steel and steel products.

One of the underlying premises for the ten-year technological modernization programme in Polish metallurgy is the high energy, labour and pollution intensity of the sector. In the context of the restructuring programme, some of the country's 26 steel plants will be closed on technological and ecological grounds, and in some other plants production capacity will be reduced.[15] The implementation of the programme should result in reducing harmful environmental impacts by 70 to 80 per cent while steel production would be reduced by 5 million tons from the launching of the programme. At the same time, production costs are expected to decrease by US$20 to US$25 per tonne. This should enable the Polish metallurgy sector to retain its competitiveness in international markets.

The increase in electricity prices due to more rigid environmental standards would also influence production costs and prices of many energy-intensive goods and thus their export competitiveness. Therefore, exports of the following products might decrease: fertilizers, plastics, organic chemicals, products and semi-products made of non-alloy steel, rolled products, zinkified plates, low-processed copper products, cement, and some building materials. These products (together with electricity exports) currently account for an estimated 15 per cent of Polish exports. For some of these products, such as steel and copper metallurgy, cement products and electricity, substantial free production capacity exists. However, the tightening environmental standards may prevent these sectors from increasing their exports.

In the cement industry, a complete technological reconstruction will be implemented within ten years, leading to the abandonment of the energy-intensive wet technology. It is expected that this will not only enable the cement sector to reduce its energy intensity and cement and clinker-related dust emissions by 70 to 80 per cent, but also reduce production costs, help to avoid atmospheric emission fees, and increase export competitiveness.

11.4 EFFECTS OF EXTERNAL ENVIRONMENTAL REQUIREMENTS ON TRADE

11.4.1 Vulnerability to External Environmental Requirements

The composition of Polish exports is highly geared towards energy and raw material intensive products with polluting processes. This results in two-fold implications: first, exports are vulnerable to external environmental standards, and secondly, export production places a negative burden on the Polish environment.

Along with the economic reforms, as the trade regime has shifted from a centralized, partially barter system, to one of decentralized commercial trade, and as domestic prices were liberalized, Poland has seen a drop in exports of electrical and engineering goods and an increase in exports of 'light industry goods' (clothing, knitting and leather), wood and paper, and metallurgical goods. At the same time imports of almost all items have increased, particularly chemicals, wood and paper, food items and agricultural products. Table 11.2 shows the development of the composition of Poland's imports and exports in relative terms over the period 1980–1993.

The destination of exports also has a bearing on the vulnerability to external environmental requirements. Typically, in OECD markets and especially in the European Union environmental requirements are stricter than in many other markets. Within the European Union, Poland's two largest export markets are Germany and the Netherlands; both are countries with particularly strict environmental protection requirements. In 1994, private sector exports to Germany made up as much as 41.9 per cent of total private sector exports.[16] Table 11.3 shows Poland's exports in 1993 by commodity groups and markets.

Finally, to estimate the vulnerability of Polish exports to environmental regulations, it is necessary to look at the extent to which products sensitive to environmental requirements are exported to environmentally conscious markets.

The UNCTAD secretariat has identified some sectors sensitive to environmental regulations based on environmental regulations applicable in OECD markets for each sector. Table 11.4 shows the destination and value of Poland's exports in those identified sensitive product categories that are of most significant export interest to Poland. All in all, US$4804 million, or 34 per cent of total exports, were in products identified as sensitive to environmental regulations in 1993. In the OECD market, the share of exports which may already be facing environmental requirements was 39.8 per cent and in the European Union market this share was 42.2 per cent.

Table 11.2   Total Polish exports and imports by main commodity groups, 1980–1993 (share in percentage)

Commodity groups	1980	1985	1990	1991	1992	1993
Imports						
Food and agricultural products	19.1	15.4	10.7	15.1	14.1	13.5
Fuels	18.1	22.2	21.9	18.9	16.8	12.4
Ores and metals	5.7	5.6	4.5	2.5	3.3	3.0
Manufactured goods	51.0	56.1	62.4	61.1	64.2	69.5
Exports						
Food and agricultural products	8.9	11.2	15.3	17.9	18.0	14.3
Fuels	13.2	15.7	10.7	10.7	10.6	8.8
Ores and metals	7.2	8.1	9.3	9.0	11.3	8.9
Manufactured goods	60.7	62.0	58.3	54.5	59.0	66.1

Note: Food and agricultural products consist of SITC 0+1+2+4 less (27+28); fuels consist of SITC 3; ores and metals consist of SITC 27+28+68; manufactured products consist of SITC 5+6+7+8 less 68.

Source: UNCTAD, based on COMTRADE database.

Table 11.3   Poland: exports by commodity groups and markets, 1993 (millions of dollars)

Commodity groups	World	OECD countries[1] Total	United States and Canada	European Union	Countries with economies in transition	Developing countries
Total	14044.1	10124.6	452.5	8916.1	1353.6	1635.3
Food and agricultural products	2005.2	1399.9	61.2	1235.2	360.5	131.6
Food	1546.8	1024.8	59.9	892.6	353.0	115.8

Table 11.3   continued

Commodity groups	World	OECD countries[1] Total	United States and Canada	European Union	Countries with economies in transition	Developing countries
Agricultural raw materials	458.4	375.1	1.3	342.6	7.6	15.8
Fuels	1241.1	815.6	3.4	650.8	88.3	106.1
Ores and metals	1252.9	929.3	19.8	805.4	71.8	121.7
Manufactured goods	9279.2	6886.0	362.9	6180.1	780.4	1232.6
of which:						
Chemicals	948.3	535.4	37.7	450.9	198.6	127.1
Textiles and clothing	1885.1	1741.6	77.8	1599.1	72.3	44.7
Leather	122.6	118.6	0.4	116.9	1.5	0.2
Footwear	109.4	87.8	15.6	69.6	18.2	0.6
Machinery and equipment	2887.0	2010.9	131.0	1794.1	352.3	398.5
Other manufactured products	3326.8	2391.7	100.4	2149.5	137.5	661.5

Note: [1] Data for OECD do not include Austria, Iceland, Mexico, Norway, Turkey.

Source: UNCTAD, based on COMTRADE database.

Table 11.4   Poland: exports of selected goods sensitive to environmental regulations by destination, 1993 (millions of dollars)

Products	World	OECD countries[1] Total	United States and Canada	European Union	Countries with economies in transition	Developing countries
Textiles and textile products	1878.3	1756.7	70.6	1600.8	70.3	44.2
Cars	675.5	607.1	16.9	574.6	38.4	19.1
Wood and wood products	547.4	521.9	5.4	457.4	4.5	5.3
Fruit	391.5	296.7	0.7	243.4	81.6	28.1
Plastics and plastic products	196.2	154.8	0.5	139.2	21.3	9.7
Paper and paper products	145.8	97.9	0.8	85.3	9.0	29.4

Table 11.4　continued

Products	World	OECD countries[1]			Countries with economies in transition	Developing countries
		Total	United States and Canada	European Union		
Leather and leather products (excluding footwear)	117.2	113.6	0.6	103.1	2.3	0.5
Fertilizers	110.5	97.7	15.1	79.7	0.0	9.9
Footwear	109.4	89.2	14.8	69.6	18.2	0.6
Chemicals	105.4	46.9	0.1	38.3	2.8	45.0
Beverages	102.2	88.5	3.6	77.2	13.4	1.9
Appliances	91.2	82.5	0.4	73.0	1.9	4.6
Lamps	86.2	76.8	9.2	65.9	1.1	7.2
Fish	68.9	60.1	0.6	58.0	4.8	0.9
Tyres	66.1	56.5	2.3	51.2	4.3	5.0
Freezers	26.3	14.6	0.0	11.4	9.7	1.1
Cosmetics	17.6	5.2	0.1	4.4	10.9	0.2
Dyes and pigments	14.0	10.1	2.9	5.5	0.5	3.3
Insecticides	13.7	7.7	0.1	7.6	2.4	3.4
Shrimp and shrimp products	12.1	12.0	0.0	11.9	0.1	0.0
Batteries	11.7	1.9	0.0	1.4	7.8	2.5

Note:　[1] Data for OECD do not include Austria, Iceland, Mexico, Norway, Turkey.

Source:　UNCTAD, based on COMTRADE database.

11.4.2　Specific Requirements Affecting Poland's Exports

Regulatory measures

As can be seen from the vulnerability analysis above, the most important external environmental regulations potentially affecting Polish exports are those that exist in the European Union markets. However, through the Association Agreement, Poland is bound to the convergence of its environmental regulations with those of the European Union. Thus, the main external environmental regulations have already been or will be incorporated in domestic environmental policy-making (analysed in Section 11.3).

Voluntary instruments

Although voluntary instruments are in principle non-compulsory, they may in practice nevertheless have an impact on Polish exports. The most important voluntary measure with a potential impact on Poland's exports is the European Union eco-labelling scheme. In general, voluntary requirements in the European

Union markets (including consumer preferences) cannot, naturally, be under similar harmonization requirements to regulatory measures.

Table 11.5 shows that many of the categories for which criteria are being set under the eco-labelling programme of the European Union are of export interest to Poland. Further, the European Union is for Poland clearly the most important export market for these products.

According to one study, Polish producers are concerned over the potential impact of the European Union eco-labelling scheme on their exports.[17] Knowledge of the requirements, particularly those related to the life cycle of products, is weak among producers. Further, the difficult financial situation of many companies may prevent adaptation to the criteria. For companies in the most difficult financial circumstances, even the testing and other costs related to the application process may represent a critical obstacle.

Table 11.5　*Poland, 1993: exports of products earmarked for eco-labelling in the European Union (millions of US dollars)*

Product category	World	Exports to European Union (EU)	EU share of Polish exports (%)
Final products			
Tissue paper	14.4	9.8	68
Copying and writing paper	0.8	0.6	75
T-shirts	310.8	299.3	96
Bed linen	28.6	25.2	88
Footwear	109.4	69.6	64
Ceramics[1]	4.2	3.2	76
Lamps	87.1	66.3	76
Refrigerators[1]	14.8	10.7	72
Furniture[1]	470.2	397.0	84
Raw materials (themselves not directly subjected to eco-labelling)			
Wood pulp	28.7	15.3	53
Leather	61.6	58.8	95
Cotton	4.4	4.1	93

Note:　[1] Included in national eco-labelling programmes.

Source:　UNCTAD, based on COMTRADE database, and 'A Statistical Overview of Selected Eco-labelling Schemes', TD/B/WG.6/Misc.5, 2 June 1995.

Relevant ministries are now discussing setting up an eco-labelling scheme in Poland. This scheme would take the life-cycle approach and adopt essentially the same criteria as the European Union eco-labelling scheme, but allow for less stringent criteria for domestic manufacturers in the beginning. The main objectives of the planned scheme would be to help Polish producers to increase competitiveness in both domestic and international markets, to hamper the uncontrolled use of eco-labels in Poland, and to improve the ecological image of Polish commodities in the European Union markets. However, at present, very few Polish consumers are affected by eco-labels in their purchasing decisions. If prices of eco-labelled products include a premium these products may be less competitive in the domestic market.

11.4.3 Opportunities for Marketing Environmental Goods and Services

Tightening environmental standards and regulations in Poland promotes the development of sectors supplying environmental goods and services. Compared to other economies in transition, Poland started producing environmental protection technologies relatively early, and developed many original pollution control technologies that are often cheaper than environmental protection technologies from OECD countries. Assuming that other countries with economies in transition will intensify their efforts in the domain of environmental protection, environmental goods and services to this market may become an important export item for Poland.

Regarding Polish agricultural exports, the low consumption of fertilizers and pesticides (compared to the European Union average) and the abundance of relatively cheap manpower in the Polish rural population create potentially favourable conditions for the development of an environmentally friendly agricultural segment. The fact that even before the market reforms 80 per cent of agriculture in Poland was in the hands of small-scale private farmers has greatly facilitated the adaptation of the sector to market economy conditions.[18]

Although the market niche for environmentally friendly agricultural products in the European Union still remains small, it is expected to quickly expand. All the programmes of environmentally friendly agricultural development in Poland are to a significant extent based on export aspirations to the European Union market. However, considering that agricultural trade between Poland and the European Union is only partially liberalized under the Association Agreement, and that Polish producers have already found it difficult to compete against subsidized European Union agricultural products even in the domestic market, to what extent these aspirations can be achieved remains to be seen.

Further, exporting Polish 'green' agricultural products to developed countries would lead to confrontation with strong competition from other producers. This is especially the case considering the lack of necessary professional skills in Poland and strict regulations concerning such products in most Western countries. The study also notes that environmental pollution from past activities has resulted in the contamination of about 10 per cent of agricultural land in Poland.

The policy followed by some developed countries regarding the exportation of domestically prohibited pesticides to Poland, and their aggressive marketing there, may also become an obstacle for the development of environmentally friendly agriculture in Poland.[19] Many Polish farmers may purchase these pesticides because they are cheaper and because the farmers do not have sufficient information on their potential harmful environmental effects. Contamination of Polish soils and plants with such pesticides might set back the efforts of exporting environmentally friendly agricultural products to the European Union.

11.5 EFFECTS OF MULTILATERAL ENVIRONMENTAL AGREEMENTS ON TRADE

Multilateral Environmental Agreements (MEAs) have become an essential component of international cooperation in environmental protection. Poland is signatory to about 40 such agreements, although Poland's broader participation in these agreements started only after 1990. Regional environmental agreements to address regional problems, such as those concerning the Baltic Sea or the 'Black Triangle', also play an important role for Poland. Through participation in MEAs, Poland's environmental policy is integrated with that of the international community, including European Union member states.

Due to Poland's late participation in MEAs, it is as yet hard to find examples of their influence on Polish exports. Some agreements, like the Basel Convention, have already had direct impacts on the Polish economy. Others are anticipated to have an impact, like the Climate Change Convention which may reduce Poland's coal exports through discouraging the use of fossil fuels.

The Basel Convention on the Control of Transboundary Movements of Hazardous Wastes and their Disposal resulted in amendments to Polish legislation, introducing the prohibition of hazardous wastes' imports into Poland. The amendments allow the import of hazardous wastes to be used only for strictly defined economic purposes with individual permits and under certain conditions. Sectors particularly affected by restrictions in waste exports and imports are the forest products and metallurgical industries: import limitations in waste paper and scrap iron are likely to lead to price increases of these secondary materials in the domestic market and, ultimately, to increased production costs.[20]

As a signatory to the Montreal Protocol on Substances that Deplete the Ozone Layer, Poland must completely abandon the use of freons and halons by the year 2000. Poland does not produce these compounds but their domestic use accounts for 1 per cent of world consumption. Freons can be relatively easily eliminated from aerosol containers, but their removal from the production of polyurethane foams may cause temporary cost increases in the Polish furniture sector, thus weakening to some extent the export competitiveness of upholstered furniture.

It has also been suggested that Poland's commitment to cease the use of freons in refrigerators, freezers and freezing counters could bring about, at least in the short run, reductions in the exports of these products, since Poland does not have the technology to eliminate ozone-depleting gases and the import of such technology would place increased costs on the refrigerating industry. For the same reason, the production costs of frozen food (fruit, vegetables, meat and creamery products) could also increase. However, in the face of import competition, Polar, the domestic monopolistic manufacturer of refrigerators, freezers and washing machines, has been able to completely remove freons from its refrigerators. These refrigerators are now sold both in Poland and in European Union markets.

There are also a number of regional treaties that may influence Poland's structure of industrial and agricultural production and hence its foreign trade. The Convention on the Protection of the Marine Environment of the Baltic Sea Area requires the control and restriction of, *inter alia*, pollution from land-based sources into the Baltic Sea. In the context of the Baltic Sea Environmental Action Programme adopted in 1992, 119 'hot spots' will be addressed in a cooperative manner, of which 38 are in Poland. A large investment (in the region of US$8 billion) will be required to fulfil Poland's commitments to reduce the pollution load into the Baltic Sea. A programme of construction of 111 sewage treatment facilities at a cost of US$300 million is already in progress.

An important regional agreement for Poland is the cooperation with the Czech Republic, Germany and the European Union to reduce SO_2 emissions in the Black Triangle area. The area generates one-third of European SO_2 emissions, which has led to substantial forest damage. The agreement has resulted in reduced sulphur emissions from power stations, however, the costs of this are reflected in higher electricity prices and reduced electricity exports from Poland (see Section 11.3.3 on the Tur\w power plant). The long-run objective of the programme is compliance with European Union environmental standards in the region.

Finally, Poland has concluded or is concluding several bilateral environmental agreements with its neighbouring countries Germany, the Czech and Slovak Republics, Ukraine, Belarus, Lithuania and Russia. These agreements relate mainly to water management and nature protection.

11.6   EFFECTS OF TRADE POLICIES ON THE ENVIRONMENT

11.6.1   Trade Liberalization

In addition to the internal reforms that include trade liberalization, Poland has also been part of the international trade liberalization process. Poland has been a member of the General Agreement on Tariffs and Trade, participated fully in the Uruguay Round and is now a member of the World Trade Organization.

In general, it is expected that the market reforms taking place in Poland should improve the state of the environment, particularly in the longer term as inefficient and polluting companies are forced to close down. Also, the Association Agreement with the European Union and the consequent need to strengthen environmental requirements and their enforcement in Poland should result in a cleaner environment.

Imports
Environmentally friendly imported products can have a positive impact on the Polish environment in two ways: by replacing more polluting alternatives, and by forcing Polish suppliers to improve the environmental qualities of their products. A case in point has been the imports of cleaner petrols and engine oils.

Also, the access of Polish companies to cleaner technologies and resources is ameliorated by freer trade. The reforms opened new opportunities for Polish enterprises to buy machines, spare parts and raw materials abroad directly, without the compulsory intermediation of state owned foreign trade enterprises. Owing to the generally better quality and higher technological level of most imported goods, these imports became a significant contributing factor to the modernization of many Polish enterprises. However, this has also led to the displacement of domestic production by increased import competition.

The study also lists several cases where environmentally harmful products were exported to Poland by developed countries. Such products included, for example, domestically prohibited pesticides, asbestos and CFC-containing used refrigerators. Further, the increased imports of consumer products such as food and cosmetics have been accompanied by an inflow of packaging waste that is frequently difficult to recycle or reuse.

Theoretically, international trade makes it possible for a country to reduce local environmental pollution to an extent by importing goods whose production significantly damages the environment instead of producing them domestically. However, it seems that Poland is not receiving such relative environmental benefits through international trade. On the contrary, in 1990–1992, environmentally disadvantageous changes took place in Poland's industrial exports and imports. The share of pollution-intensive goods in total exports increased during the period. Simultaneously, industrial imports increasingly consisted of goods whose domestic manufacturing would not significantly damage the natural environment. As a consequence, one can speak of a special 'division of labour' between Poland and other countries, in particular European Union countries. To a growing extent, Poland is importing manufactured goods whose production does not cause major dangers to the environment, while in its exports, Poland is specializing in goods whose production significantly damages the natural environment.

Foreign direct investment
Capital available through foreign direct investment is crucially needed for the restructuring and modernization of the Polish economy. However, the study raises the question whether 'dirty industries' tend to migrate to Poland, especially since the Polish institutional and legal environmental framework is not yet fully developed. There are several examples of FDI into Poland that relate to the establishment of production lines for products that face several environmental regulations in the European Union: examples include polyurethane foams, PVC bottles, aluminium cans and phosphate-containing detergents. But there are also several examples where FDI has contributed to environmental improvements in Poland. The study concludes that FDI into Poland has been neither systematically negative nor positive for the domestic environment.

There is a problem related to privatization negotiations between the government and foreign investors, namely the division of economic liability for past contamination and the payment of any outstanding environmental fees and fines. As regards the costs of clean-up, two solutions have been used: the reduction of the selling price by clean-up costs, or the state assuming the liability for past contamination. The study reports that the latter solution has been more commonly used. In 1992, an interministerial committee was established to deal with environment-related issues in the capital privatization procedure.[21]

11.6.2   Environmental Impacts of Export Production

Environmental resources have been used very intensively in Poland; both as raw materials and as a recipient for pollution and wastes. The majority of pollution in Poland is generated by industry, primarily the fuel-energy, metallurgical, chemical and mineral industries. Some of the environmental damage may in the long run set constraints on economic growth, for example in the form of reduced productivity of agriculture and fisheries, lack of clean water, and health problems.

Hard coal, the extraction of which has major harmful environmental impacts, is one of Poland's most important export products. In the first half of the 1970s coal exports reached about 40 million tonnes and Poland became the second largest hard coal exporting country in the world. In the 1980s, despite radical political changes, a new programme of coal extraction development was designed. However, the implementation of the programme was impossible due to both the general economic difficulties of that time and the pressure of other emerging interest groups, including national and regional environmental groups. Hard coal exports thus fell during the whole period of economic reforms in Poland. Although the industry will be forced to undertake certain environmental protection activities in the future, it is highly desirable from the environmental point of view for Poland to decrease dependency on coal exports (see Box 11.2).

Box 11.2   Hard coal consumption in Poland

The Polish economy has a strong dependency on solid fuels consumption and has also been characterized by a very stable fuel mix structure for the past thirty years. Whereas in many developed countries there has been a remarkable absolute and relative increase in the utilization of crude oil, gas and non-conventional energy, the Polish economy has shown the quite opposite trend of a very high and almost constant solid fuel share (hard coal and lignite) of primary energy carriers.

It has been recognized in Poland that it would be necessary, both from an economic and environmental point of view, to reduce coal consumption and switch to increased gas consumption. However, the composition of Poland's fuel endowments (large coal deposits), and the lack of foreign currency to import fuels have in practice prevented adopting such a policy without the help of foreign aid. A natural factor that could accelerate the process of reducing coal dependency in the future is the gradual worsening of environmental conditions in hard coal mines, and the subsequent decrease in the price competitiveness of hard coal. Polish energy policy now aims at doubling gas consumption by the year 2000.

Within the metallurgical industry, hot rolled products, whose production is highly energy- and raw material-intensive, are major export products. A large proportion of the production of the chemical industry is also exported. Most chemical industry products such as organic chemicals, fertilizers and plastics are energy intensive, and their manufacture tends to be polluting especially in terms of effluent discharges. Thus, the production and export of chemical products contributes strongly to the pollution of the natural environment in Poland.

11.7   CONCLUSIONS AND RECOMMENDATIONS

The case of Poland is a clear and interesting example of how economic and environmental policies may be mutually reinforcing. On one hand, the past economic system produced both an inefficient economy and a polluted environment. On the other hand, the reforms now being undertaken in Poland should lead both to improved economic efficiency and a cleaner environment.

The need to harmonize a number of Poland's environmental standards with those of the European Union coincides with internal economic reforms and difficulties, accentuating the pressures facing the domestic economy. Harmonization costs may reach US$30 billion. The crucial question is therefore how Poland will succeed in undertaking economic transition and a simultaneous upgrading of environmental policies.

A cost-effective strategy should be developed for the harmonization of Polish environmental regulations with those of the European Union and their strengthened enforcement, paying attention to the general economic conditions of the Polish economy. In the harmonization process, Poland's environmental priorities must also be considered. Elements of such a cost-effective strategy might entail a broader use of economic tools, and a focus on pollution prevention, although clean-up of past pollution will also be needed. The European Union has also expressed its willingness to assist Poland financially, technologically and organizationally in its efforts to improve environmental protection, and funds for this purpose are available, for example, through the PHARE programme.

Implementing pricing reform and diverting production towards a less pronounced dependence on energy- and raw material-intensive goods are sound policies from the point of view of trade, environment and economic growth. New standards could be phased in gradually, accompanied by mitigating policies to minimize any undesired impacts of a rapid harmonization of environmental standards with the European Union.

It is also important to invest in the incomplete and overloaded environmental infrastructure in Poland. Such investments would complement those aimed at upgrading the technology used by individual firms.

Since Poland traditionally concentrated on pollution-intensive and raw-material-intensive heavy industries, there have been no incentives for innovation towards resource conservation, and new policies are needed to promote such environmentally friendly innovation. Foreign investment policy is one of the important instruments for supporting innovation and it could be directed at promoting the use of environmentally sound technologies. Also, an efficient mechanism for the development and diffusion of cleaner technologies should be developed.

As an economy in transition, Poland faces special difficulties regarding the implementation of Multilateral Environmental Agreements since it does not qualify for the assistance available under some of these agreements. Further, while economies in transition are trying to advance in their industrialization process, they must also simultaneously revise longstanding misallocations in economic structures.

At present, due to financial difficulties, many companies are forced to use polluting technology which is also technologically obsolete and economically inefficient. The restructuring of the Polish economy should result in an improved financial situation for Polish enterprises, thus enabling them to better comply with tighter environmental standards as well as meeting the obligations coming from MEAs. Such improvements should also enhance the export potential of these companies.

NOTES

1. *Trade Policy Review, Poland 1992*, Volume I, General Agreement on Tariffs and Trade, Geneva, 1993.

2. At the beginning of 1995, the share of private enterprises in total industrial production was more than 38 per cent, in construction almost 86 per cent, in retail trade about 89 per cent, in exports over 51 per cent and in imports 66 per cent. The private sector employed about 61 per cent of the total labour force in the economy and accounted for about 56 per cent of GDP. Central Office of Planning, (1995), 'Poland 1995. Information on the economic situation in the first quarter with short-term forecast', Warsaw, May.

3. 'Poland is rising at full speed', *Talouselama*, No. 28, 1995, Finnish only, and *Quarterly Report by Polish Foreign Direct Investment Agency*, Third Quarter, Warsaw, 1995. Note also that exports by companies with foreign participation have been showing an increase: their share in total exports rose from 10 per cent in 1992 to 16.4 per cent in 1993. In absolute figures the value of those exports rose more than twice. Foreign Trade Research Institute (1995), 'Foreign investments in Poland', Warsaw.

4. Poland's energy intensity (British Thermal Units/$1987 GNP) has been in the region of 76 374; this is the 7th highest figure in the world. World Resources Institute (1992), *The 1992 Information Please Environmental Almanac*, Boston: Houghton Mifflin Company.

5. OECD (1995), '*Environmental Performance Reviews, Poland*'.

6. However, the fact that the number of cars in Poland has more than doubled in the past six years has resulted in a considerable increase in harmful atmospheric emissions from mobile sources.

7. OECD, 1995.

8. World Resources Institute, 1992.

9. The Association Agreement notes that the task of combating the deterioration of the environment has been judged to be a priority among the Parties to the Agreement (Article 80).

10. OECD, 1995.

11. These include the polluter pays principle, the prevention principle, the public participation principle, the subsidiarity principle, and the principle on transboundary environmental protection.

12. Other estimates suggest a cumulative total of US$35 to US$50 billion. An estimate of the approximate time horizon for the task, given current efforts, can be made using the 1992 figure for environmental investment expenditure of the equivalent of US$1 billion. However, there is room to speed up the process of convergence, with increased cost-effectiveness of environmental expenditure and integration of environmental concerns in economic and sectoral policies (OECD, 1995).

13. The border region of Poland, Germany and the Czech Republic has been called the 'Black Triangle' due to significant air pollution in the region, particularly by SO_2 emissions.

14. In 1991, exports of coal, coke and briquettes accounted for 8.5 per cent of total exports.

15. Ministry of Industry and Trade (1993), 'Restructuring of the iron and steel industry in Poland in the years 1993–2002', Warsaw.

16. Foreign Trade Research Institute (1995), 'Selected data on Polish foreign trade', Warsaw.

17. This section is based on Dr Zbigniew Jakubczyk (1994) 'Ecolabelling schemes in Poland', presented to the UNCTAD Workshop on Eco-labelling and International Trade, Geneva, 28–29 June 1994. The study was funded by the International Development Research Center, Canada.

18. 'Living museum on the land', *Financial Times Survey, Poland*, 28 March 1995.

19. For example, in 1990 Poland received US$60 million worth of foreign aid in the form of pesticides, some of which were prohibited or strictly regulated in the donor countries.

20. Waste paper falls under the waste categories covered by the Basel Convention due to the de-inking sludge that is generated in the process of recycling waste paper.

21. It has been suggested that the prospect of high environmental costs (particularly those related to cleaning up past contamination) have inhibited foreign direct investment in Central and Eastern Europe. Zamparutti and Klavens (1993) 'Environment and Foreign Investment in Central and Eastern Europe: Results from a Survey of Western Corporations', *Environmental Policies and Industrial Competitiveness*, OECD.

12. Thailand

12.1 INTRODUCTION

A case study on trade and environment linkages in Thailand was conducted by a research team consisting of Dhira Phantumvanit (coordinator), Sitanon Jesdapipad, Sophia Wigzell, Natapon Buranakul and Rachanee Bowonwiwat of the Thailand Environmental Institute (TEI), Bangkok and completed in 1995. This chapter, prepared by the UNCTAD secretariat, summarizes and updates the findings of the study, and draws from the study 'Thailand's Trade and Environment' by the same authors.

Thailand is a country with a high growth and export-oriented economy. The study focuses on three kinds of trade and environment linkages in Thailand. First, regarding the effects of export production on the environment, few systematic effects on the Thai environment were found. Except for shrimp farming, there is no major production sector where exports are responsible for pollution. Rather, pollution is mainly a domestic issue caused by rapid growth. Second, foreign environmental regulations are important to Thai producers in the fishery sector and to small-scale companies in the textile sector. Larger and technologically advanced firms, such as the footwear industry, adapt to foreign regulations well. Third, multinational environmental agreements exert different effects on Thai exports. CITES has limited some trade opportunities in orchids, for instance. There are indications that the Montreal Protocol, which gives Thailand a grace period of 10 years for phase-out, made ODS-using production more attractive to multinational producers.

12.2 THAILAND'S ECONOMY AND THE RELEVANCE OF INTERNATIONAL TRADE

12.2.1 Structure of Trade

In the 1960s and early 1970s Thailand was an agrarian, less-developed economy. In 1970, the contribution of manufacturing to GDP corresponded to two-thirds of the contribution of agriculture.[1] The development strategy was import substitution.

After this initial emphasis on import substitution, a switch to export orientation followed, starting in the mid-1970s.[2] Since the mid-1980s Thailand has been one of the world's fastest growing economies with growth averaging over 11.5 per cent in the four years to 1990 and 8 per cent in the following four years. Real GNP increased four-fold between 1970 and 1990. In 1993 manufacturing contributed almost three times more than agriculture to GDP.

Export-oriented trade and investment policies in manufacturing led to staggering annual growth rates of exports between 1985 and 1991 of more than 25 per cent in real terms.[3] Investment was promoted by the Board of Investment (BOI) for domestic and foreign investors through the exemption or reduction of corporate income taxes and from import duties for machinery and raw materials. Section 12.6 elaborates on the environmental effects of export promotion.

Rapid growth was led by external demand. The share of exports in GDP increased continuously, from 15.6 per cent in 1960[4], to 20.4 per cent in 1980, to 28.1 per cent in 1990, and to 29.1 per cent in 1994. The growth of manufacturing and of manufacturing exports accounts for most of this. The share of manufacturing in GDP increased from 23 per cent in 1981 to 27 per cent in 1992. The importance of exports for growth are underlined by the increase of manufacturing exports as a share of merchandise exports, increasing from 32 per cent in 1980 to 60 per cent in 1990.[5] Growth corresponded to a rise in unit cost, with the consequence that manufacturing is now moving away from low value-added activities. Thailand has become a producer of more technology-intensive goods.[6]

In the early 1960s, primary commodities such as rice, rubber, tin, maize and sugar, as well as processed foods, made up more than 95 per cent of products exported. Food processing complemented the primary commodities significantly by adding value to goods exported. Since the early 1980s, the Thai export base has diversified, shifting the relative importance to higher value-added goods. Electrical apparatus and circuits (23.9 per cent), textile and footwear (20.1 per cent) and machinery (12.8 per cent) account for the major share of exports, followed by canned foods, jewellery, plastics, vehicles, rubber and sugar.[7] In addition, certain export markets are critical to certain products. For example, the EU imports more than 70 per cent of Thailand's cassava, while Japan imports almost all of Thailand's shrimp and more than 83 per cent of frozen chicken exports.

Japan and the United States remain Thailand's largest individual trading partners, with 21 per cent and 17.1 per cent of exports, respectively, in 1994. There has been some re-orientation of Thailand's exports away from Europe, which accounts for 14.9 per cent of exports, towards neighbouring Asia. The share of ASEAN countries and the East Asian NICs (Newly Industrializing Countries) has increased to over 25 per cent.[8]

After a period of import substitution and later a switch to export promotion, Thailand has changed its trade policy a third time in recent years. Export promotion had begun to expose constraints and had led to rising costs, eroding the external competitiveness of Thailand's labour-intensive agricultural and manufacturing base. Thus, since the early 1990s, Thailand has sought to move its economy towards a more neutral balance of incentives.

There has been a redirection of the investment incentives offered by the Board of Investment (BOI) away from export promotion to regional development, with all remaining export-related incentives to be phased out by 2002.

Trade liberalization constitutes the second element of Thailand's policy change in the 1990s. Thailand's level of average applied import tariffs is 30 per cent. Reductions negotiated under the Uruguay Round were to reduce tariffs to 17 per cent in 1997. Thailand's membership of ASEAN will also contribute to reduced protection. In 1993, ASEAN brought into operation the Common Effective Preferential Tariff (CEPT) as the core mechanism for implementing the Asian Free Trade Area (AFTA); by 2003 the average tariff on AFTA products is scheduled to be an estimated 2.45 per cent, compared to Thailand's current rate on AFTA imports of 19 per cent. Thailand is a member of the Asia-Pacific Economic Cooperation (APEC), whose members account for three-quarters of Thailand's external trade. APEC is to achieve free and open trade and investment in the region by 2020.

The effects of the new policy still have to be evaluated. On the one hand, opening up trade may lead towards a more diversified economy and balanced growth. On the other hand, the danger exists that with the liberalization of trade and the increasing importance of exports, Thailand becomes more heavily exposed to foreign measures limiting market access. For example, the environmental product measures set out in Section 12.4 show how increasingly important free trade and market access are, especially in Thailand's main export markets.

12.3   DOMESTIC ENVIRONMENTAL REGULATION

The rapid industrialization of the last thirty years has resulted in a number of serious environmental problems, including urban congestion, air and water pollution, deforestation, salinization, and soil erosion. In particular, the rapid growth of the Thai economy during the late 1980s and early 1990s has exacerbated the environmental problems associated with production. The various production sectors cause different pollution. Organic wastes are mainly produced by textile, food and beverage industries. Hazardous wastes come from the fast growing sectors of machinery, chemicals and basic metals. The centralization of production in the kingdom has concentrated most of the industry-related water and air pollution in the six provinces of the Bangkok Metropolitan Region (BMR).[9] Value added from manufacturing in the BMR increased from 71 per cent in 1981 to 75 per cent in 1989.[10] Rapid, unplanned urbanization and infrastructure bottlenecks in these provinces also have produced pollution problems from non-industrial sources. The main pollution problems in the BMR include air pollution with suspended particulate matter and lead, water pollution with organic and toxic wastes, and traffic congestion.

To combat the environmental deterioration from growth in the last years, several pieces of environmental legislation were introduced. The main environmental legislation in Thailand is the 1992 Enhancement and Conservation of National Environment Quality Act (NEQA). NEQA strengthens existing laws within a policy framework outlined in the Seventh National Economic and Social Development Plan. Central in the NEQA is the polluter pays principle, allowing, for example, the application of user charges on central treatment plants. The second important legal instrument is the 1992 Factories Act which demands that industries do not cause adverse effects on the environment. The Factories Act regulates several aspects of licensing of a plant and sets standards on a case-by-case basis. The Factories Act levies fines for non-compliance which can effectively close down a plant.[11]

Thailand's environmental problems are typical for a developing country. Because resources were extremely limited in the early stages of the development process, a decision had to be made whether to spend resources on cleaning up the environment or for development purposes. Thailand chose the later and considerably expanded its agricultural production, thereby deteriorating the environment. Consequently, on the one hand Thailand has successfully wiped out malnutrition over the last 10 years and on the other hand environmental deterioration in Thailand is mostly of domestic origin. However, there are cases where environmental problems can be attributed to export production, as elaborated in Section 12.6. The effects of foreign environmental measures on Thai trade will also be considered in the following section.

12.4   EFFECTS OF FOREIGN ENVIRONMENTAL REQUIREMENTS ON THAILAND'S EXPORTS

The study points out that environmental requirements in the importing countries are often perceived in Thailand as a threat to its export growth. The concentration of exports towards certain markets has made them vulnerable to the regulations in these markets which apply to imported goods. For instance, most shrimp go to Japan while most cassava and 70 per cent of Thai fruit exports go to the EU.

In general, however, thriving Thai exports have been flexible enough to adapt to foreign environmental regulations, often behaving pro-actively.

Table 12.1   Thai exports of sensitive products, 1993 (millions of US dollars)

Products	World	OECD	USA	EU	Japan	Developing countries
All exports	37 097.7	22 379.1	8 002.1	6 154.4	6 295.3	14 210.5
Fish	3 401.8	2 920.2	979.1	432.8	1 191.5	476.8
Tuna	702.4	613.8	255.5	147.4	93.6	85.6
Shrimps and prawns	1 957.2	1 766.8	686.4	193.6	727.4	189.7
Flowers	31.2	28.7	3.0	7.5	17.3	2.4
Fruit	890.2	726.2	12.4	620	80.4	163.5
Beverages	112.9	69.8	38.9	20.7	3.0	43.0
Asbestos	5.5	0.9	0.0	0.2	0.3	4.6
Chemicals	9.9	6.5	0.5	4.2	1.2	3.1
Fertilizers	2.9	0.0	0.0	0.0	0.0	2.6
Paints	89.9	1.6	0.0	0.2	0.1	83.0
Cosmetics	45.1	3.1	0.9	1.1	0.2	41.6
Detergents	19.4	3.2	0.4	0.3	1.4	16.0
Lubrication	12.5	2.6	0.1	0.4	2.0	8.4
Insecticides	19.4	7.9	0.7	4.3	1.9	10.1
Plastics and plastic products	1 558.2	351.5	87.7	124.7	85.0	1 189.0
Tyres	165.5	106.2	23.6	66.4	4.9	59.0
Leather and leather products (excluding footwear)	697.4	494.7	244.3	149.1	54.1	201.5
Footwear	1 035.0	837.8	346.0	391.3	25.0	193.9
Wood and wood products	290.9	244.2	85.3	82.4	59.3	46.5
Tropical timber	18.6	11.4	1.0	6.8	2.6	7.1
Paper and paper products	72.4	21.4	3.8	11.3	2.8	49.1
Textiles and textile products	5 182.0	2 973.1	1 143.3	1 086.6	437.7	2 168.2
Boilers	0.1	0.0	0.0	0.0	0.0	0.1
Air-conditioning	328.7	154.3	18.7	13.6	114.6	174.1
Freezers	172.4	76.5	0.6	9.3	60.2	93.5
Appliances	246.6	201.1	101.8	40.0	40.6	44.9
Batteries	48.9	10.0	0.2	5.6	2.5	38.3
Cars	395.0	117.5	19.0	53.3	13.0	266.7
Televisions	720.0	611.1	246.2	240.8	96.3	107.6
Lamps	48.2	25.4	14.4	3.0	4.2	20.0
Dyes and pigments	36.0	7.4	2.7	2.9	1.2	28.4
Total sensitive products	15 638.0	10 002.9	3 373.6	3 372.0	2 300.7	5 535.9
Sensitive products/all exports (%)	42.15	44.69	142.15	54.79	36.54	38.95

In analysing the potential vulnerability of Thailand's exports to foreign environmental requirements, it is necessary to consider the proportion of exports which is perceived to be environmentally sensitive in certain foreign markets. The UNCTAD secretariat has identified some sectors as particularly sensitive to environmental regulations (and sanitary and phytosanitary standards) based on environmental regulations applicable in OECD markets. Table 12.1 shows the destination and value of Thailand's exports in those product categories identified as sensitive.

In 1993, 42.2 per cent of total exports were in products identified as sensitive to foreign environmental regulations. The percentage of sensitive product exports is highest in Thai exports to the EU; 54.8 per cent of total exports were classified as sensitive. The share of Thai exports, classified as sensitive, to other parts of the world, is approximately 40 per cent. A number of environmental regulations or voluntary standards emerging in the EU, such as the EU eco-labelling programme, confirm that the EU is a particularly environmentally sensitive export destination.

Two product groups (fish, tuna and shrimp, and textiles and footwear) account for 80 per cent of all sensitive exports. Fish, tuna, shrimp and prawn alone account for approximately 40 per cent of all sensitive exports, with an especially high share going to Japan. Textiles and footwear account for another 40 per cent of sensitive exports, and plastics constitute 10 per cent. However, an important share of textiles and three-quarters of plastics exports go to developing countries, which seldom have trade-inhibiting environmental regulations. It seems that market access may be easier for Thai producers when trading with developing countries.

The analysis above provides a general picture which does not differentiate between the various trade-inhibiting effects for the separate product groups. TEI conducted several case studies on specific export sectors giving a more in-depth picture of trade-inhibiting effects of foreign environmental regulations.

12.4.1   Shrimp, Fish and Tuna

The Japanese government's 1991 Anti-Additive Import Regulation had an impact on Thai exports of shrimp and shellfish. The Regulation, a Sanitary and Phytosanitary (SPS) measure, requires that shrimp entering the Japanese market must be free from pesticide and antibiotic residues. Because nearly all Thai shrimp are exported to Japan, producers were forced to adapt. The shrimp industry and Thai government responded to this legislation by discouraging the use of antibiotics, or, at a minimum, by discouraging the application of antibiotics in aquaculture ponds during the three weeks before harvest.

In 1994, the Thai fishery industry was affected by a French SPS measure. The French Ministry for Agriculture, Health and Safety announced that imports of fishery products from all countries, except New Zealand, Canada, Chile, Argentina and the Faroe Islands, would be banned for health and safety reasons.

It was expected that 3 billion Baht of Thai fishery products would be affected. There are rumours that protection of the French fishery industry, rather than health and safety reasons, was the cause of the import ban.

The study concludes that the above mentioned Japanese regulation did not pose problems to Thai producers who adjusted to the regulation and whose exports are still growing. The French import ban however was considered arbitrary, not being applied equally to all countries. Also, the French regulation, by banning imports completely rather than setting a certain standard, gave Thai producers no opportunity to adjust.

The exports of canned tuna processed in Thailand are affected by US measures. Canned seafood, particularly canned tuna, is one of Thailand's largest export items. Exports amounting in 1994 to US$5 billion make Thailand the world's largest exporter of canned tuna. Eighty per cent of the raw tuna is from foreign suppliers.[12] In 1989, 45 per cent of exports went to the United States and a large portion to the European Union. There was some concern that the United States Marine Mammal Protection Act, which requires dolphin-safe fishing of tuna, may endanger Thai exports of tuna. The study finds that Thai producers have indeed changed their sources of raw tuna to comply with US restrictions. One Thai producer, having been accused of providing products that were not 'dolphin-safe', was compelled to undertake a publicity campaign to provide reassurance that it did not buy tuna from fishing boats whose practices endanger dolphins. The producer is funding a programme to test the feasibility of the use of fish-aggregating devices (FADs), which avoid killing dolphins when catching tuna.

As in the tuna case, a proactive stance was undertaken by Thai producers and by the government in other instances. In accordance with UN resolution 44/225, the United States banned imports of fish from any country using large-scale driftnets. Even though Thailand was not listed as a country using such fishing methods, it was accused by the 'Earth Island Institute' of using such methods. The Thai government subsequently held consultations with the Institute and laid down specifications on the length and depth of driftnets to be used in Thai waters such that they would not endanger living marine resources.

There are two other US acts banning imports of shrimp (and their products) which are caught by methods endangering sea turtles.[13] Under these laws 120 countries, including Thailand, are listed as using fishing methods endangering sea turtles. A complaint was presented before the WTO by India, Malaysia, Pakistan and Thailand against a ban on importation of shrimp and shrimp products from these countries imposed by the United States under Section 609 of US Public Law 101-62. Violations of GATT provisions as well as nullification and impairment of benefits were alleged. The 6 April 1998 WTO panel report ruled against the import ban on marine shrimp from certain countries and is now being appealed by the United States.

Overall, the Thai fishery industry may have only been slightly affected by the regulations listed above due to specific domestic circumstances. Indeed, Thailand imports a high percentage of raw fish for processing rather than catching it domestically. Processing industries are able to change suppliers in order not to endanger access to sensitive markets, which is easier than fishery fleets changing production methods.

12.4.2 Textiles

The textile industry was one of the main industries promoted in the early stages of industrialization. Even though export growth in other industries has been higher, the textile industry is still, besides electronics, the major Thai export sector. In 1995, Thai textile producers were faced with a German ban of Azo dyestuffs, which were found to be carcinogenic. Dyeing firms had to switch to substitutes which amounted to a cost increase of 5–20 per cent. Smaller producers have difficulty in absorbing the higher costs.

12.4.3 Eco-labelling and Packaging Requirements

Textiles are not only subject to mandatory requirements as shown above, but are also subject to 'softer' measures, namely eco-labelling programmes. With respect to one eco-label developed by the private sector for textiles in Germany, Thai producers are not inclined to comply. According to the study, they are concerned that the market niche for such products is not sufficiently large to justify any changes in product standards. When pressed to deliver eco-textiles, some producers said that they would prefer to switch to alternative markets, such as the Middle East.

The attitude of footwear producers towards eco-labelling is far more positive than that of textile producers. The study by Wigzell on eco-labelling suggests that the footwear industry is more modern and uses more advanced technological processes than the older textile industry. The footwear industry self-confidently asserts that if there is sufficient demand, producers will attempt to produce footwear that meets the labelling requirements. For instance, producers stopped using PCPs because this was requested by export markets.

The study concludes that up until now the impact of eco-labelling schemes in Thailand's key markets in North America, East Asia and Europe has been negligible. None of the Thai Promotion Offices in those countries reported Thai products which had either been granted or refused an eco-label. Nor did the majority of the eco-label criteria developed apply to products included among the main exports from Thailand.

The study states that compliance costs may become prohibitive if eco-labels proliferate and are based on a life-cycle analysis. Eco-labelling schemes for textiles currently exist in Canada, Japan, Scandinavia and the European Union.

Thailand has developed an eco-labelling scheme called 'Green Label', which applies criteria based on life-cycle analysis to products proposed for certification. There is another scheme for pesticide-free vegetables. Labelling in hotels and resorts has been developed for water and energy conservation, often in order to attract foreign tourists (eco-tourism). The study notes however that eco-labelling is still in its infancy. Developing a national scheme would help Thai producers acquire the necessary skills to comply with eco-labels in foreign markets, especially when the eco-label requirements are based on life-cycle analysis.

Packaging requirements pose some difficulties for Thai producers as well. The fisheries and frozen products processing sector has been affected by German 'Green Dot' legislation on the content of recycled plastic for packaging. The study finds that the cost of compliance has not been prohibitive, however, limited information on this German regulation scheme made compliance more difficult.

12.5 THE IMPACT OF MULTILATERAL ENVIRONMENTAL AGREEMENTS

12.5.1 The Montreal Protocol

Thailand qualifies for listing under Article 5 of the Montreal Protocol, which gives developing countries with ODS (ozone-depleting substance) consumption of less than 0.3 kg per capita a grace period to fulfil the requirements of the Protocol. Article 5 states that these countries are entitled to delay implementation of control measures for a period of ten years from the time the Protocol came into force, that is, until 1 January 1999, and qualify for phasing-out assistance. Thailand easily met these requirements with an ODS consumption of 0.05 kg per capita in the base year 1986, but since then consumption has increased drastically to 0.16 kg per capita in 1991 (Annex A substances: CFC and Halons).[14] If consumption continues to grow, Thailand will soon exceed the limits of Article 5.[15]

Imports of the most important ODSs, CFC113, CFC12 and CFC11, have increased three-fold from 1986 to 1991. Imports of 1,1,1-trichlorethane have doubled in the same period. Rising output and exports of products requiring the use of ODSs seem to be the major underlying cause. Exports in the electronics industry, for instance, have been increasing at rates of 7 to 10 per cent annually in the 1990s. In 1994, one-fifth of Thai exports were in electronics and electrical appliance goods, products which contain ODSs or utilize ODSs in production.

Solvent cleaning is responsible for 43 per cent of ODS consumption in Thailand. The most widely consumed ODS in Thailand is CFC113, of which 90 per cent is used for solvent cleaning in the manufacture of printed circuit boards and as a degreasing agent for metal parts and precision components. 1,1,1-trichlorethane is also used for solvent cleaning.

Air-conditioning is the second largest user of ODSs, responsible for 22 per cent of total ODS consumption. CFC12, the second most widely used ODS in Thailand, is used mainly for mobile air-conditioners. CFC11 is used for building-comfort cooling.

Refrigeration uses 11 per cent of ODSs, mainly CFC12 as a refrigerant and CFC11 as an appliance insulation foam.

Smaller quantities of Halon 1211 and Halon 1301 are used for fire-extinguishing purposes. CFC114, CFC115 and carbon tetrachloride are used in Thailand in the refrigeration, solvent cleaning, aerosols, and foam industries.

After ratifying the Protocol, the Thai government has launched a phase-out programme on a semi-voluntary basis in which all of the major firms participate. Further, the government has instituted an import licensing requirement for CFCs. A quota system allocates import shares to the ten largest CFC importers, controlling approximately 80 per cent of CFC imports.

Because a significant part of ODS consumption is by export industries, effects of the Montreal Protocol on producers are of concern. The study mentions positive as well as negative effects of the Protocol on producers. On the one hand, the study perceives the restrictions of the Protocol as a chance to enter new markets overseas. An example illustrates how new markets can be entered by using ozone-friendly technology. Sharp invested about 100 million Baht to replace CFC11 with C-pentane in refrigerators, a substance which is highly flammable and demands high expertise. The shift caused additional expense of 12 per cent of total cost. According to the study, the adjustment was successful for the company because the CFC-free refrigerator became a marketing success.

On the other hand, certain firms are forced to undergo costly adjustments. For instance, one firm had to undertake a complete phase-out because phase-out was mandatory for supplying its products to other companies.

The study interprets rising ODS imports as a sign of foreign firms taking advantage of Thailand's status under Article 5. Thailand is attracting production from countries which do not qualify for the grace period. The study mentions that shifting production to Thailand is especially easy since Thai production requiring the use of solvents is 97 per cent undertaken by Japanese, European, and US firms or is part of a joint venture with Thai firms.

The fact that Thailand may become a 'pollution-haven' for ozone-damaging production could undermine the success of the Protocol. Also, with rising use of ODS in Thailand, phasing out will be more difficult when the grace period ends. In consideration of the fact that plants owned by foreigners cause the most concerns, the Thai Department of Industrial Works (DIW) has entered into an agreement with the US Environmental Protection Agency (EPA) and the Japanese Ministry of International Trade and Industry (MITI) that encourages multinational companies to halt their use of CFCs as solvents in their Thai operations on the same schedule as adopted in their home operations. This project responds to the fact that solvents constitute 40 per cent of Thailand's use of CFCs and that up to 97 per cent of solvent use is by Japanese and US companies, and joint ventures.

As an Article 5 country, Thailand is eligible to receive financial assistance from the Multilateral Fund established by the amended Protocol in 1991. US$19 million has already been allocated, mostly to refrigerator and air-conditioner producers, and to the electronics industry for the development of alternative technologies. The study mentions that much of these funds is reallocated to the largest firms and that small and medium-scale industries may have problems obtaining or adapting to such technologies. Also, there is a lack of adaptation to permanent, ozone-friendly alternatives rather than interim chemical substances with adverse environmental impacts.

In sum, Thailand has not violated its commitments to the Montreal Protocol. But because Thailand is at the beginning of phase-out, no negative effects on production or on trade can be observed. Phase-out in Thailand may be easier because most ODS consumption is by multinational firms which have the necessary resources to undertake phase-out measures. However, there is still a lot to do. With only a few years before the end of the grace period, most of the refrigerators sold in Thailand still use CFCs and many exported products still contain CFCs or are produced using CFCs. Should the Protocol be expanded to include production process rules, Thailand's trade would be adversely affected.

Adverse effects on production are expected if companies delay their phase-out too far into the future for two reasons. First, with current growth rates of ODS use in Thailand, a delay will soon cause the Article-5 limit to be exceeded, leading to additional compliance costs for producers. A second factor making a delayed phase-out costly is the rising cost of CFCs as production falls and CFC-scarcity increases.

12.5.1 The Basel Convention

Thailand became a signatory to the Basel Convention on 22 March 1990 and ratified the Convention on 24 November 1997. Although the Convention has only recently been ratified, Thailand conducted various activities to reach its objectives. Order No. 45/2531 on hazardous wastes and the amended Order 41/2536 forces chemicals and other dangerous wastes to exit through the central port of the country. The government is preparing a licensing scheme and specific customs procedures for importers and exporters of wastes.

The study mentions that toxic waste imports have increased considerably in recent years, but supposes that imports should significantly decline because Thailand is now preparing to ban the import of hazardous wastes. It is difficult to obtain global and detailed figures on the waste trade because of widespread illegal trafficking of wastes. The study finds insufficient capacity for identifying and classifying hazardous materials at the port, as well as a serious lack of communication and coordination among various government agencies handling hazardous waste issues.

The National Environmental Board (NEB) is currently working on projects to regulate imports of wastes which are included in the Basel Convention. In 1993, the Environmental Board ordered a ban on importing used batteries, which are used in smelting factories. Further, the Board imposed a preliminary two-year import control on recycled plastics, working out definite orders and guidelines in the meantime.

12.5.3   CITES

Thailand ratified CITES in 1983 and was soon afterwards accused of not undertaking the necessary measures to effectively deal with the illegal trade of endangered species. Thailand became a platform for the illegal trade of protected species falling under CITES. These products were imported to be re-exported after being provided with 'papers' to make them legal trade items.[16] CITES sanctioned Thailand with a ban on all trade in CITES-relevant products.[17] The ban was lifted in 1992 after Thailand undertook the following measures. First, Thailand imposed the ban on itself, stopping most of the trade in endangered species. Second, Thailand passed the Law on Endangered Wild Flora and the Law on Plant Species. The Law on Plant Species was amended in 1995 to come into force in 1998, making export permits for species controlled under Appendix 2 mandatory. Similar measures exist for the fauna trade.

The commitment to CITES has affected Thailand's trade in orchid plants, which are exported in large numbers (on average 400–500 thousand plants per year). Under CITES, one whole family of orchids was prohibited from exportation. Prior to the CITES agreement wild orchids were exported. Artificially propagated orchids have partially replaced wild orchids in many export markets.

Another important issue facing Thai exports under CITES is the trade in crocodiles and crocodile products. Thailand is one of the most important crocodile breeding countries. Crocodiles and crocodile products have to be licensed for export and fall under the supervision of CITES. The impact of CITES on the Thai crocodile trade is hard to determine. A number of countries expanded their production of crocodiles considerably, increasing the supply on the world market, while market opportunities were limited. The United States imposed a total prohibition on imports of various CITES species, including crocodiles. There are rumours that the United States ban on crocodile imports was meant to protect domestic alligator producers, rather than save endangered species.

In the case of Thailand, CITES has been effective in reducing some forms of wide-scale endangered wildlife trade, such as the export of snakes and lady slipper orchids. However, legislation remains insufficient to limit illegal trade. Also, more could be done by taking such steps as levying substantial penalties for convicted trafficking, regularly patrolling wildlife markets, especially in border regions, and making regular inspections of registered and reputed wildlife owners. In order to curtail the wildlife trade, a much larger budget for increased manpower and training would be needed.

12.6 THE EFFECTS OF TRADE POLICIES AND EXPORT EXPANSION ON THE DOMESTIC ENVIRONMENT

Thailand's early export pattern, dominated by agriculture, put pressure on its natural resource base. This resulted in deforestation and long-term decline of soil fertility. In more recent times, exports have diversified. Manufactured products became the major export commodities (see Section 12.2). This diversification of exports was successfully supported by the investment promotion activities of the BOI. These activities were an attempt to attract domestic and foreign capital into a few selected sectors of export production. Since the early 1990s, the BOI has changed the export investment promotion strategy to promotion of investment in general.

Thai domestic and foreign investment promotion had mixed effects on the environment.[18] On the one hand, there is evidence that domestic and foreign investment promoted by the BOI was undertaken in relatively pollution-intensive (hazardous waste producing) sectors like electrical machinery, transportation equipment, metals and non-metal products, and chemicals. Some care should be taken, however, when using this evidence to evaluate the state of the environment. Pollution depends not only on the type of industry, but on the technique of production and how it is applied.

On the other hand, investment promotion by the BOI provided incentives for business expansion or relocation outside of Thailand's Bangkok Metropolitan Region (BMR). This eased environmental pressures in the BMR, which is the most seriously affected region. Within the BMR investment incentives were given for export production only, whereas in the intermediate area of 10 provinces a broader range of investment measures was subsidized. In the outer provinces, or 'Zone 3', subsidies were double those in the intermediate area and included subsidized infrastructure projects. Additionally, restrictions on foreign investment were eased in 1995. These measures supporting decentralization have born fruit. In 1995, almost 9 out of 10 investments approved by the BOI were in Zone 3.[19] Therefore, because of the various influences of export promotion, there does not appear to be any systematic effect of FDI on the environment.

12.6.1   Agriculture

The environmental effects of agricultural production for export are hard to separate from the effects of production for domestic use. The adverse effects of agriculture in Thailand have been felt over a long period of time. In the last thirty years the rapid expansion of the production of cash crops in the East, lower North and Northeast regions has been responsible, at least in part, for the rapid deforestation experienced in those regions, and in the Northeast in particular. This deforestation had significant short- and long-term effects on the local environment, including the loss of biodiversity and non-timber forest products, and an increase in soil erosion.

Additionally, it is difficult to identify clear links between the cultivation of a particular crop and its direct and indirect effects. However, damage can be traced to a single export product in the case of the large-scale production of tapioca in the northeastern part of the country.

The rural sector is currently changing towards greater diversification of crops and to non-farm activities. In many areas of the country formerly covered with paddies, rice is no longer produced. Some of the land has been devoted to other crops. But the more recent diversification is not without environmental problems. One example mentioned in the study is the production of ginger in Chiang Rai. Ginger requires new land for cultivation each season, making it very land demanding.

12.6.2   Coastal Aquaculture

Shrimp production helped to diversify Thai exports but caused concerns about detrimental effects on the environment. Besides the canning of tuna, shrimp production is the second major fishery item promoted for export by the Thai government. Due to strong overseas demand, production increased almost ten-fold between 1980 and 1990, and in the 1990s at rates of over 20 per cent annually. This made Thailand the most important shrimp-producing nation in the region, accounting for 15 per cent of world cultured shrimp. Most of the production is for export to Japan (also see Section 12.4).

Intensive shrimp cultivation in Thailand took off in 1986, as investors in similar production facilities in Taiwan and Japan shifted some of their production capacity to the relatively unexploited Thai coastline. Cultivation of shrimps is a relatively easy process at a low technological level. Thus, many local people have switched from fishing and rice cultivation to small-scale shrimp farms. In addition, the Thai government has actively supported shrimp cultivation in several coastal regions. Support included subsidized diesel, soft loans for the very capital-demanding shrimp farms and investment breaks. The study points out that government support was very successful in terms of the expansion of the industry, but did not contribute to the sustainability of the operations themselves.

One main environmental problem of shrimp production is land clearance. The area used for shrimp culture expanded by approximately 150 per cent from 1980 to 1990, and further in the 1990s. Although shrimp farming has been intensified, 42 per cent of total shrimp farming is undertaken on former forest lands. The clearance of mangrove forests, which are the centrepiece of coastal eco-systems, is particularly notable. It was estimated that between 1979 and 1986 alone, 38.3 per cent of total mangrove clearance was undertaken for coastal aquaculture purposes and mainly for shrimp farming. This corresponds to the clearance of 13 per cent of all mangrove forests. Another study finds that 64.3 per cent of mangrove clearance was undertaken for aquaculture.

A second concern is saltwater intrusion into freshwater aquifers, and shrimp pond effluent discharges. The abstraction of freshwater from underground aquifers for intensive farming in Thailand has resulted in salt water intrusion and salinization of freshwater aquifers. With intensive shrimp culture, shrimp pond effluents pollute freshwater supplies. Effluents are from salt water and contain living and dead bacteria and plankton, antibiotics, and shrimp parts.

In 1991, the Thai government reacted to these concerns with a set of rules. Shrimp farmers have to be registered and shrimp farms over 8 ha require waste water treatment according to set criteria. Water pollution is limited by a regulation setting a maximum BOD concentration on released waste water. Releasing salt water into farming areas or into freshwater resources is also forbidden. However, enforcement of the rules seems to be a problem. Rules are not applied in the same manner to all producers, giving preferential treatment to local companies. A second source of concern is that the water treatment technologies demanded by the government are not always the most efficient ones.

12.6.3 Timber

The timber industry is closely linked to the environmental problems of intensive agricultural production for export. Topping the list of commodity exports, it is a major cause of recent deforestation. The percentage of forest land to total land area in Thailand has shrunk from 53 per cent in the 1960s to 26 per cent today. Besides the export of logs, cash-crop production of various agricultural commodities, such as corn, sorghum and tapioca, have contributed to deforestation.

To stop this decline of forest land, Thailand imposed a ban on logging in 1989 turning Thailand from a net exporter to a net importer of logs and sawn timber. In 1994, Thailand's exports of logs and sawn timber were insignificant, and only 7.56 per cent of total imports were of these commodities. Today, sawn timber is mainly exported. The increasingly scarce wood is substituted by using parawood, wood obtained from clearing overmatured rubber trees when preparing for new plantations. Chips and sawdust are reused to make products like particle boards. Timber is important for Thailand because it is needed to produce furniture and other value-added wood products for export. These goods account for 31 billion Baht in export revenue or roughly 3 per cent of total exports.

Internal pressure to save forests in Thailand has been strong. Entire watersheds are now the focus of protection in Thailand, as forest resources are viewed as an integral part of a larger eco-system.

The destruction of tropical forests caused not only internal action, but also international pressures on Thailand to better safeguard its forests. A second international issue has emerged; imported wood used in Thailand's furniture production for export. A considerable amount of wood, harvested non-sustainably, is imported from neighbouring states. Due to the commercial involvement of the Thai army in the timber trade, there is little available information on harvesting methods of imported timber.

Thailand needs to ensure that its timber imports come from sustainable sources so as to comply with the demands of importing countries (see Box 12.1). Such pressure may soon come in the form of sanctions against tropical timber imports, voluntary consumer boycotts, and requirements for 'sustainable management' certifications.

12.6.4   Textiles

The textile industry is a major industry in the economic and export development of Thailand but is also the major source of certain kinds of pollutant emissions. It generates air pollution in the form of suspended particulate matter, as well as chemical fumes and vapours from the various production stages. Water pollution comes in the form of chemical and organic wastes. In four out of ten of the most heavily industrialized provinces in Thailand, the textile industry is the worst polluter in terms of biochemical oxygen demand (BOD). The study

Box 12.1   The benefits of sustainable forestry: one example

Smith & Hawken is a mail-order and direct retailing company, selling high-quality gardening equipment, outdoor furniture, and clothing. The company used to distribute teak-based furniture produced by a Thai manufacturer. The manufacturer claimed that the teak, coming from Thailand and Myanmar, was harvested sustainably. After consumer inquiries in 1988, the company launched a study in 1989 to find out how the teak was harvested. The report concluded that in Thailand 'there is no widespread commitment outside the Forest Department to manage the forests in an environmentally sustainable manner'. As for Thai timber, sustainability guarantees could not be given for timber originating from Myanmar.

First, Smith & Hawken asked its Thai producer to use timber supplies from Java, Indonesia, where it had found well-managed teak plantations, guaranteeing sustainability. After a while it became obvious that verifying compliance of the Thai producer would be too difficult to achieve. The company was still using timber from Myanmar for other customers. Smith & Hawken then decided to switch to an Indonesian manufacturer, making it easier to keep track of the company's wood sources.

Smith & Hawken supply the demands of an environmentally conscious group of consumers. Because sustainability is not yet an issue in mass production, trade impacts of not respecting sustainability criteria are small. But consciousness among consumers has been growing and restrictions on tropical timber imports to developed countries have proliferated. The consideration of sustainability criteria, both by the Thai government and by Thai producers, may become essential for the future success of the timber sector.

notes that pollution treatment varies widely. Small producers often do not possess treatment facilities at all, while large plants tend to operate up to international standards. The costs of treatment depend on the degree of clean-up. Minimal water treatment is not expensive, costing less than 0.25 per cent of profits, but costs increase rapidly with more sophisticated facilities.

12.6.5   Electronics

The electronics industry is a second important and dynamic export sector in Thailand. Besides using ODSs for solvent cleaning (see Section 12.5), the electronics industry is responsible for the creation of hazardous wastes containing copper and lead. The plating industry contaminates water supplies with copper, nickel and cadmium. The study notes the difficulties in judging the extent and severity of the pollution problems because pollutants are less visible than, for instance, in the textile industry.

The study concludes that the electronics industry, which is dominated by large firms producing for export, should not have problems adapting to higher environmental standards. As in the case for ODS phase-out, waste-water treatment should not pose any substantial problems to these industries. However, smaller firms, often operating as sub-contractors will find adjustment difficult (see Box 12.2).

Box 12.2   The role of environmentally sound technologies (EST)

Adverse effects of export production on the environment can be alleviated by governmental support of EST. Obtaining foreign technologies was difficult when Thailand was undertaking a policy of import substitution. This has changed with Thailand's export promotion strategy. Tariffs for the import of environmentally sound technologies have been lowered.

The study mentions two ways in which the Thai government supports the use of EST. The Ministry of Science, Technology and Environment grants duty exemptions to EST imports. Duty exemptions are 5 per cent instead of the normal 20 per cent, but the process of obtaining exemptions is lengthy and the criteria for qualification are unclear. According to Wigzell, only equipment that is used exclusively for the purposes of environmental protection or research qualifies for duty exemptions. The second source of support is better accepted. The Board of Investment (BOI) grants tax benefits, a procedure which is supposedly uncomplicated and rapid.

12.7   CONCLUSIONS AND RECOMMENDATIONS

12.7.1   Conclusions

The study finds that external eco-regulations only partly affect Thai producers. External environmental measures are applied to shrimp and canned tuna. Exporters avoid export losses by adapting their production methods (tuna) and their sources of primary input (timber). However, a French ban on fish imports for sanitary and phytosanitary reasons has led to losses in the Thai fish industry. Voluntary eco-labelling programmes, such as the one developed by the EU, have not had a major impact so far. Eco-labelling posed no difficulties for the modern and export-oriented footwear sector. In the technologically less sophisticated textile sector, the less advanced producers have found difficulty in complying with certain of the eco-label criteria. The impact of eco-labelling is expected to increase when criteria for obtaining an eco-label are based on life-cycle analysis. The study suggests that some Thai producers may react to such developments by changing their export markets.

Concerning Multilateral Environmental Agreements (MEAs), up until now producers are only marginally affected. Because Thailand qualifies according to Article 5 of the Montreal Protocol for a ten year grace period for phasing out ODSs, producers have begun the phase-out slowly. Consumption of the most utilized ODSs rose by a factor of three between 1986 and 1991. Most currently produced refrigerators still contain ODSs. Because producers are mainly large multinational firms or joint-ventures, final phase-out is not expected to pose difficulties. If phase-out is undertaken at the last minute, costs could increase drastically. Phase-out at the last minute poses the danger that Thailand may exceed its limit, set in Annex A. In addition, there are indications that foreign companies are using Thailand as a 'pollution haven' and shifting ODS production to Thailand, taking advantage of Thailand's Annex A status.

Complying with the CITES Convention has resulted in trade losses. Also, restrictions on the export of wild orchids has led to their replacement by artificially propagated orchids in certain export markets. Regarding both CITES and the Basel Convention, the amount of illegal trade is difficult to evaluate.

Production for export has affected the environment to a certain extent, but the major impact on the Thai environment is domestic production and can be attributed to the staggering economic growth of the last few decades. Until now, domestic environmental regulations were able to mitigate the environmental damage emanating from the growth of the economy only to a limited extent.

Certain effects of export production on the environment can be traced. The early orientation towards agricultural cash-crop production for export, like rice and cassava, and the export of timber were partly responsible for massive deforestation and soil erosion. In recent years, exports have begun to diversify reducing environmental problems due to agriculture, but leading to the emergence of new pollution problems. Textile production is one example of a major export industry which causes significant pollution problems. In four of the ten most industrialized provinces of Thailand, textile production ranked first in BOD discharge into waterways. However, with exports diversified and with a large home market for most of the goods that are exported, it is difficult to isolate the impact of production for export from production for the domestic market.

Exports may also improve the Thai environment. By contributing significantly to the growth of the Thai economy in recent decades, exports have also provided resources for new environmental measures.

12.7.2 Recommendations

In general, concerning foreign environmental regulation affecting Thai producers, a more proactive stance of the Thai government is advisable. Stricter standards are likely to spread over time to new markets. An early reaction of the Thai government to new developments could allow Thai producers more time to adjust to external regulations. For instance, a quick reaction from the government when the Thai fishery industry was accused of using driftnets, may have been an important factor in avoiding a ban of Thai imports in environmentally conscious countries. Since Thailand's comparative advantage has been shifting from low value-added products to higher quality and technology-demanding goods, external environmental regulations seem to be important, as foreign concerns over shrimp or the phase-out of ODSs have suggested. A proactive environmental stance would contribute to Thailand's international competitiveness.

To be able to follow such a proactive stance, the involvement of the corporate sector, particularly the affected industries, should be encouraged. Information dissemination is crucial. The government could facilitate this process by creating awareness of regulations and voluntary labels in important export markets, and by providing information on available eco-friendly technology. Exporter's councils could also be directly involved in the process of information dissemination.

Regarding MEAs, the slow progress in phasing out ODSs could be enhanced by international cooperation. A measure undertaken in this direction is an agreement of the Department of Industrial Works (DIW) with the US Environmental Protection Agency (EPA) and the Japanese Ministry of International Trade and Industry (MITI). The agreement encourages multinational companies to halt their use of CFCs as solvents in their Thai operations on the same schedule as adopted in their home operations. This project responds to the fact that solvent use constitutes 40 per cent of Thailand's CFC uses, and that up to 97 per cent of solvent use is by US and Japanese companies, and by joint ventures. If no serious negotiations take place, Thailand will have great difficulties completing the ODS phase-out by the year 2006.

To improve the handling of hazardous waste imports to conform with the Basel Convention, the study recommends building increased capacity for customs operations at the port to help in the identification and classification of hazardous materials. Communication and coordination among various governmental agencies concerned with the handling of hazardous wastes should be improved.

However, the study mentions that the major problem with hazardous wastes is not the import issue, but the inadequate handling of domestic waste.

Trade restrictions may be necessary for the effective implementation of MEAs, however they can also be used for protectionist purposes. Protectionist intentions have been suspected in the case of the import ban imposed by the United States on various products regulated by CITES. For example, crocodile products, which are traded by Thailand, fall under this ban. Trade restrictions undertaken in the context of MEAs should therefore be carefully scrutinized to prevent their abuse.

Problems with illegal trade suggest that complying with CITES and the Basel Convention requires more monitoring facilities and expertise.

The domestic environmental problems are overwhelming. Exports contribute only a small share to them. More investment in infrastructure and local environmental improvements are needed. Where exports are responsible for adverse effects on the environment, domestic improvements should be used for mitigation instead of restricting trade. The study suggests that, for example, the abuse of pesticides for cash-crop production can be avoided by disseminating information about the adverse effects of the improper use of pesticides to farmers.

As a consequence of trade liberalization, Thailand has become more intertwined with other countries, but also more dependent on them. Certain measures imposed by importing countries, including those for environmental purposes, may limit the market access of Thai producers for specific products. It is the duty of the international community to pay attention to market access issues, in order to prevent protectionist tendencies in the development of certain environmental standards and regulations.

NOTES

1. The following draws on World Trade Organization (1995) *Trade Policy Review Thailand 1995*, Geneva.

2. The following on trade policy draws mainly on World Trade Organization (1995), op. cit.

3. World Bank (1994), op. cit.

4. This single value is from Wigzell, S., *Thailand and Ecolabelling*, Thailand Environmental Institute, Bangkok.

5. World Bank (1994), 'Thailand: Mitigating Pollution and Congestion Impacts in a High-growth Economy', Country Economic Report, Washington DC.

6. World Trade Organization (1995), op. cit.

7. *Ibid.*

8. *Ibid.*

9. The BMR includes the Bangkok Metropolitan Area and five surrounding provinces.

10. World Bank (1994), op. cit.

11. Wigzell, op. cit

12. World Trade Organization (1995), op. cit.

13. These two laws are the Commerce, State and Justice Department Appropriation Act of 1990 (Public Law 101-102, Article 609) and the Fisherman's Protection Act of 1967 (the so called Pelly Amendment).

14. Additionally, Thailand consumed 0.02 kg per capita of Annex B substances (trichloroethane and carbon tetrachloride) where the Protocol limit is 0.2 kg per capita.

15. Since the report for Thailand was completed, more data have become available. This indicates that per capita consumption of Annex A substances fell from 0.16 kg in 1981 to 0.1 kg in 1996, well within the Article 5 limits. For Annex B substances per capita consumption fell to almost zero by 1996. (Data from UNEP.)

16. Part of the subsection on CITES is from a personal communication with Mr Berney, CITES-Secretariat, Geneva.

17. A ban imposed by CITES is only a recommendation to its members. It cannot be legally enforced.

18. The following on investment promotion draws on World Bank (1994), op. cit.

19. *The Economist*, 27 April 1996.

13. Turkey[1]

13.1 STRUCTURE OF INTERNATIONAL TRADE

Turkey's economy has recently been rapidly moving from import substitution to export orientation. The strengthening of relations between the European Union and Turkey has emphasized this development. The most important development in the Turkish economy since the early 1980s has been the constant and significant increase in exports of manufactured goods. While the export value/GNP ratio has been consistently growing, the share of agricultural exports to total exports has decreased. Manufactured goods such as garments, and machinery and equipment have recently become increasingly important.

The vulnerability of Turkey's exports to external environmental requirements is partly determined by the sectoral composition of exports. Table 13.1 shows the development of the composition of Turkey's imports and exports both in value and relative terms over the period 1980–1994.

The destination of exports also affects vulnerability to environmental requirements. Table 13.2 shows Turkey's exports in 1993 by commodity groups and markets in more detail. More than 60 per cent of exports are directed to OECD countries and most of these go to European Union countries, particularly Germany, Italy, France and the Netherlands. The United States at present represents only a small percentage of Turkish exports, but exporters see this market as their next target. Around 20 per cent of exports are destined for the Middle East, and around 10 per cent for Eastern Europe and the former Soviet republics. In particular, exports to the Islamic former Soviet republics of Asia are expected to increase.

To analyse more closely the vulnerability of Turkey's exports to external environmental requirements, it is necessary to look at the extent to which environmentally sensitive products are exported to environmentally sensitive markets. The UNCTAD secretariat has identified some sectors sensitive to environmental regulations (and sanitary and phytosanitary standards), based on environmental regulations applicable in OECD markets to each sector. Table 13.3 shows the destination and value of Turkey's exports in the identified sensitive product categories that are of most significant export interest to Turkey.

Table 13.1   *Turkey: total exports and imports by main commodity groups, 1980–1994 (millions of US dollars)*

Commodity groups	1980	1985	1990	1991	1992	1993	1994
Imports (in value)							
Food and agricultural products	388.5	930.3	2805.5	2081.2	2449.2	3094.5	2370.8
Fuels	3668.7	3785.2	4639.9	3771.1	3780.0	3988.2	3836.5
Ores and metals	252.9	489.1	1220.7	1172.9	1082.7	1394.2	1393.3
Manufactured goods	3261.6	6135.5	13612.7	13907.4	15487.3	20823.2	15582.5
Total	7572.5	11340.5	22300.1	21046.9	22870.9	29429.2	23267.8
(share in percentages) Food and agricultural products	5.1	8.2	12.6	9.9	10.7	10.5	10.2
Fuels	48.4	33.4	20.8	17.9	16.5	13.6	16.5
Ores and metals	3.3	4.3	5.5	5.6	4.7	4.7	6.0
Manufactured goods	43.1	54.1	61.0	66.1	67.7	70.8	67.0
Exports (in value)							
Food and agricultural products	1881.4	2373.0	3297.8	3902.0	3551.8	3747.8	4249.1
Fuels	41.5	372.6	293.8	291.7	234.5	174.5	240.7
Ores and metals	204.7	342.5	563.7	451.4	421.4	389.9	471.0
Manufactured goods	782.0	4854.9	8796.6	8940.2	10497.2	11028.0	13134.9
Total	2909.6	7958.0	12959.3	13593.5	14714.6	15348.8	18105.2
(share in percentages) Food and agricultural products	64.7	29.8	25.4	28.7	24.1	24.4	23.5
Fuels	1.4	4.7	2.3	2.1	1.6	1.1	1.3
Ores and metals	7.0	4.3	4.3	3.3	2.9	2.5	2.6
Manufactured goods	26.9	61.0	67.9	65.8	71.3	71.8	72.5

Note: Food and agricultural products consist of SITC 0+1+2+4 less (27+28); Fuels consist of SITC 3; Ores and metals consist of SITC 27+28+68; Manufactured products consist of SITC 5+6+7+8 less 68.

Source: UNCTAD, based on the COMTRADE database.

Table 13.2   *Turkey: exports by commodity groups and markets, 1994 (millions of US dollars)*

Commodity groups	World	Total	OECD countries[1] United States and Canada	European Union	Japan	Developing countries[2]
Total	18105.2	10920.5	1520.5	8270.8	186.5	6634.9
Food and agricultural products	4249.1	2392.3	333.5	1692.3	59.1	1811.9
Food	3971.4	2208.4	319.1	1544.9	57.1	1721.5
Agricultural raw materials	277.8	183.8	14.4	147.4	2.0	90.4

Table 13.2 continued

Commodity groups	World	Total	OECD countries[1] United States and Canada	European Union	Japan	Developing countries[2]
Fuels	240.7	193.3	10.0	172.6	0.0	43.4
Ores and metals	471.0	324.5	46.5	206.4	18.1	105.9
Manufactured goods	13 134.9	8 002.2	1 130.4	6 192.2	109.3	4 673.1
of which:						
Chemicals	735.3	311.4	27.0	239.9	7.5	404.9
Textiles and clothing	6 775.8	5 370.9	743.1	4 262.9	15.3	1 058.5
Leather	28.1	14.2	3.8	9.5	0.0	13.3
Footwear	158.8	23.6	0.8	21.8	0.2	127.3
Machinery and equipment	1 698.6	937.4	76.3	806.5	1.5	725.7
Other manufactured products	10 700.9	6 753.4	1 027.1	5 145.8	100.3	3 542.5

Notes
[1] Excluding Austria, Iceland, Mexico, Norway and Turkey.
[2] Excluding South Africa.

Source: UNCTAD, based on COMTRADE database.

Table 13.3   Turkey: exports of selected goods sensitive to environmental regulations by destination, 1994 (millions of US dollars)

Products	World	Total	OECD countries United States	European Union (12)	Japan	Developing countries	Countries with economies in transition
Textiles and textile products	6 252.2	4 957.0	719.1	3 910.2	11.5	483.5	481.9
Fruit	1 453.1	1 078.8	39.7	881.9	4.7	251.7	101.3
Leather and leather products (excluding footwear)	529.7	414.6	26.5	352.5	3.3	8.5	96.7
Cars	322.3	117.8	4.8	98.9	0.1	104.3	91.0
Plastics and plastic products	233.9	63.3	12.7	45.7	0.5	97.1	62.3
Tyres	200.8	114.9	5.0	91.3	10.2	78.6	4.0
Footwear	158.8	23.6	0.8	21.8	0.2	22.4	111.4
Televisions	153.0	126.4	0.0	120.1	0.0	3.5	21.1
Paper and paper products	107.9	34.3	0.1	32.1	0.0	47.4	22.1
Detergents	100.5	9.1	2.2	6.0	0.0	27.1	60.6
Freezers	92.6	65.8	14.2	50.3	0.0	17.2	8.3
Appliances	78.3	44.4	0.1	36.4	0.0	19.6	10.5
Beverages	71.0	37.5	6.8	29.6	0.4	7.4	26.0
Fish	70.1	65.6	0.2	55.7	7.7	3.3	0.4
Wood and wood products	61.9	25.6	0.1	17.2	0.2	24.3	11.8

Table 13.3   continued

Products	World	Total	OECD countries			Developing countries	countries with economies in transition
			United States	European Union (12)	Japan		
Chemicals	56.2	39.3	0.0	39.2	0.0	15.6	1.3
Fertilizers	32.0	21.0	0.0	19.7	0.0	10.9	0.0
Insecticides	30.1	12.7	0.2	3.0	0.3	10.6	8.2

Source: UNCTAD, based on COMTRADE database.

13.2   EFFECTS OF EXTERNAL ENVIRONMENTAL STANDARDS AND REGULATIONS ON TRADE

13.2.1   Structure of the Exporting Sector

The structure through which export trade takes place in Turkey plays a very important role in determining producers' awareness of environmental requirements in export markets, as well as the ability of Turkish exporters to respond to those requirements. The detailed structure of the Turkish system of exporting manufactured goods to OECD markets is rather complicated and has numerous participants. They can be grouped into importers, exporters and manufacturers of export goods.

The most important participants in this structure are the importing European or North American companies who, through their branch offices or buying companies acting as their agents, prescribe the quality, health, safety and environmental standards, and exercise strict control and inspection practices. In the garment and food industries, the importing companies also impose the design and specifications at the manufacturing stage. There is an increasing inclination for European companies to trade through this system.

Buying companies often act as representatives of large developed-country importing companies. Their activities include: sourcing; assistance in legal issues such as preparation of official papers and contracting; assistance during control and inspection practices of the importing company; constant quality control and verification of compliance with international standards, safety rules, packaging requirements, environmental requirements and other conditions demanded by the customer; and delivery of the merchandise with proper packaging, labelling, timing and so on. Buying companies therefore represent the crucial link between the Turkish export sector and the changes and requirements, including environmental ones, in developed-country markets. Together with branches of importing companies, buying companies account for around 40 per cent of private sector manufactured goods exports in Turkey. They are particularly significant in the textiles and garments sector.

Approximately 15 per cent of Turkish manufactured goods exports are realized through manufacturing and exporting companies that produce primarily for the export market and undertake their own exporting activities. Other companies manufacture for both domestic and export markets, and export through exporters. Small and medium-sized enterprises are important in both groups due to their cost-competitiveness and flexibility, especially in garment manufacturing.

Invoicing companies used to be the most important actor in the Turkish export scene in the 1980s due to government policies that forced manufacturers of export goods, as well as individual buying and exporting companies, to sell through these companies. In 1988 invoicing companies accounted for 51 per cent of exports. However, after the abolishment of some of these policies, their importance declined rapidly so that by the early 1990s only about 25 per cent of manufactured goods were exported through these companies. Some manufacturers' associations have established their own invoicing companies to export the products of their member companies. An example is the Export Company of Garments Manufacturers Association (GSD), which mainly exports to European countries and is very knowledgeable about developments in European markets.

13.2.2   Results of a Survey among Exporters

In order to assess the effects of environmental requirements in the European Union and the United States on Turkey's exports to those markets, the research team conducted a field survey. This survey was based principally on interviews with representatives from 61 private sector export companies in three sectors, namely garments and textiles, food, and machinery and equipment. The interviews were conducted, with the assistance of a questionnaire, in the period February to March 1993. In addition, representatives of chambers of commerce, industry associations and government agencies were interviewed.[2]

In interpreting the results, it should be kept in mind that the majority of respondents could not differentiate easily between quality, health, safety, and environmental product standards, generally imposed by the importing companies as a whole. Furthermore, the companies selected for the survey may to an extent represent the most advanced companies in Turkey. This is because only companies that were able to export to developed-country markets were included in the survey. Also, using participation lists in environmental seminars to identify companies for the survey may have brought in companies that are particularly environmentally conscious.

Awareness

The survey revealed that all interviewed companies were well aware of newly emerging environmental policy measures. The study attributed this high level of awareness to the publicity given in Turkey to the German Packaging Ordinance and to the continuously changing quality standards in the European and North American markets, part of which was due to environmental concerns and which had made producers used to finding out about the requirements of their customers. In addition, public interest in environmental matters in Turkey itself was increasing rapidly, as was reflected in the growing attention paid to the environment by the press, environmental groups, and political parties, and in the implementation of new environmental laws and regulations. In general, obtaining the necessary information about environmental requirements was not considered a problem for Turkish exporters, in striking contrast to many other country case studies included in this book.

For most companies (72 per cent), the principal sources of information on environmental requirements in Europe and North America were the importing companies. In addition, national institutions, namely chambers of industry and commerce (in particular those in Istanbul), manufacturer and exporter associations, and some service companies were quoted as significant sources of information. The Turkish Standards Institute (TSE) provides information on international standards to manufacturing and exporting companies. TSE also aims to adjust national standards to international ones in order to reduce compliance problems. Some companies (15 per cent) were themselves active in trying to obtain information on environmental requirements in their export markets.

Impacts on input and technology requirements

A little more than half of the interviewed companies asserted that recent environmental regulations and other requirements emerging from their export markets, in particular packaging requirements, had some impact on their manufacturing and exporting practices. Almost all of these companies stated that environmental requirements in various degrees influenced their use of raw materials and intermediate goods. This is particularly due to the fact that exports are often produced upon purchasing orders from European customers with quality, material, and so on specified by the importing company. However, respondents stated that the necessary production inputs to cope with environmental, health and safety standards were generally obtainable in Turkey, and few companies claimed to have technological difficulties in coping with environmental standards.

As many as 42 per cent of the interviewed companies, in particular in the food, and textile and garments sectors, stated that importing companies had influenced their process and production methods, either by requesting detailed information or through plant visits.[3] Turkish manufacturers appeared to accept some interference with their process technologies as a normal condition of doing business, and did not question the legitimacy of some influence on domestic process and production methods by customers in external markets. This inclination on the part of Turkish industry could also be explained by the fact that, in any case, domestic pressure (by the government, municipalities, and private institutions) was also mounting to improve the environmental aspects of process technologies. Similarly, the wide acceptance in Turkey of the ISO 9000 quality standard had also decreased the willingness to dispute some international influence on domestic process technologies.

Impacts on production costs and competitiveness

While recognizing that it may be difficult to separate the effects of environmental requirements from other factors impinging on costs, it is notable that 72 per cent of surveyed companies believed that external environmental requirements (imposed by importers) increased the costs of production and exporting, and that the majority of these companies expected that these costs would continue to increase in the future. Among the factors resulting in cost increases, the need to acquire new machinery and to switch to different quality raw materials were mentioned.[4]

A little more than half of the interviewed companies (52 per cent) responded that their competitiveness was not adversely affected by the need to comply with external environmental requirements. Five companies (8 per cent), all in the garments sector, stated that they were adversely affected because they could not meet the requirements of certain importing companies, in particular because of their ageing process technologies. Seven companies (11 per cent), mainly from the garments and food sectors, however, maintained that environmental requirements and particularly changing consumer preferences in European countries had actually improved their competitiveness. Two main reasons were given for this. First, that environmental requirements added to pressures to adopt the most advanced production and product technologies which were a prerequisite for effectively competing in international markets. Secondly, that Turkey had certain advantages in supplying environment-friendly products. It has the capability of producing organic raw materials at lower cost than Mediterranean country competitors due to the abundance of land and water resources, the small family farming nature of much fruit and vegetable production, and the availability of cheap agricultural labour. The remaining companies did not have an assessment of the effects on competitiveness of environmental requirements.

Almost all companies which produce both for the domestic and export markets mentioned that complying with developed country environmental, health, safety and quality standards diminished their competitiveness in both domestic and developing country markets. These companies manufacture products that respond to the different requirements between domestic and export markets, between different export markets, and even between individual EU-country markets. As a consequence, they lose economies of scale in production and in the sourcing of inputs. Many respondents expressed a wish for stricter environmental requirements in the domestic market to prevent the production and import of cheap, lower quality merchandise, for example glassware, small household appliances, textiles and garments from ex-Soviet republics, and textiles and clothing from Pakistan and India.

The study found that concerns about the use of environmental measures for protectionist purposes were stronger among government and academic circles than among manufacturers and exporters. This could perhaps be explained by the fact that the companies tended to see the environmental requirements as a reflection of the changing demands of the importing company rather than changing environmental standards in importing countries.

13.2.3 Eco-labelling

At the time of the survey, none of the respondents had applied for any formal eco-label in any export market. They had felt no need to do so, particularly since there were no mandatory eco-labelling programmes affecting them. However, interest in eco-labelling was increasing particularly among the garments and textiles exporters.

In 1993, several institutions jointly started an eco-labelling programme in Turkey. The label, called 'Friend of the Water and the Environment', can be awarded both to companies and products. Compliance with mandatory governmental environmental regulations is not sufficient to receive the Turkish eco-label.

This section examines the possible effects of eco-labelling in the European Union on Turkey's exports. It focuses on textiles and garments, in particular on the case of European Union eco-labels for T-shirts and bed linen. The corresponding research was carried out under the UNCTAD project on 'Eco-labelling and International Trade',[5] in the form of interviews with representatives of various institutions and companies.

Table 13.4 shows that many of the categories for which criteria are being set under the eco-labelling programme of the European Union are of export interest to Turkey. Further, the European Union is the most important export market for Turkey for many of these products, including cotton, T-shirts and bed linen.

Eco-labelled garments, called 'eco-garments' in the study, have been brought to the market by European textile and garment manufacturers as a response to increasing public interest in the environment. However, Turkish exporters felt that the market for eco-garments is still relatively small, and that, at least for the time being, only a limited number of import companies, in countries such as Sweden, Denmark, and Germany, demand and purchase eco-garments. They pointed out that these companies, which also purchase 'regular' merchandise, assign two different sets of criteria for regular products and eco-products.

Table 13.4   Turkey: exports of products earmarked for eco-labelling in the European Union, 1994 (millions of US dollars)

Product category	Exports to		EU share of Turkish exports (%)
	World	European Union (EU)	
Final products			
Tissue paper	21.3	1.6	7.6
Copying and writing paper	8.1	0.1	1.0
T-shirts	909.5	650.1	71.5
Bed linen	86.3	67.3	78.0
Leather products (excluding footwear)	503.8	344.9	68.5
Footwear	158.8	21.8	13.7
Ceramics[1]	91.9	68.5	74.5
Refrigerators[1]	87.2	49.5	56.8
Furniture[1]	18.8	2.0	10.5
Raw materials (themselves not directly subjected to eco-labelling)			
Leather	25.9	7.6	29.3
Cotton	56.6	41.4	73.2

Note: [1] Included in national eco-labelling programmes.

Source: UNCTAD, based on COMTRADE database, and 'A statistical overview of selected eco-labelling schemes', TD/B/WG.6/Misc.5, 2 June 1995.

Turkish exporters also saw that the potential to supply eco-garments is limited for a number of reasons. First, given existing production technologies and especially the limited supply of prescribed inputs (for example, organic cotton, natural soap and environmentally friendly dyes) it is technically difficult to produce eco-garments in large quantities. Secondly, the need for new investment and the costs of prescribed inputs make production of eco-garments expensive.

The study notes that Turkish textile and garment manufacturers generally perceive eco-labels as non-tariff barriers to trade, which may result in discrimination between European and foreign companies on the one hand, and between different suppliers on the other. On the latter issue, Turkish exporters are worried about the rise of Chinese textile exports to European countries. Most Turkish manufacturers and exporters also feel that eco-labelling programmes may not significantly contribute to the adoption of environmentally sounder practices such as the promotion of less hazardous pesticides, wider and more efficient application of waste-water treatment, and the development and production of environmentally friendly and economically affordable dyes and chemicals.

One segment of the Turkish textile and garment manufacturing industry, however, believes that it is in a good position to supply eco-garments and various Turkish companies are interested in or are taking steps in this direction. First, Turkish companies are investing to encourage the production of organically grown and naturally coloured cotton in various parts of the country, and importing this cotton, as well as yarns and fabrics produced from these raw materials (e.g. from the United States and India). Secondly, firms are investing in machinery and equipment in order to establish an approved eco-factory.[6] Thirdly, firms are actively using advertising and other promotion methods to market their eco-garment products in European countries; and applying to obtain private eco-labels, including the 'Öko-Tex 100 standard label' which is considered by Turkish manufacturers and exporters as the most important and influential eco-labelling programme.

As for the criteria designed by the EU eco-labelling programme for T-shirts and bed linen, the representatives of the Turkish textiles and garments sector argued that the exporting segment of the industry would not confront technical difficulties in meeting most of them, except, perhaps, in cases of pesticides used in cotton growing, and dyes and certain chemicals that are solely provided by European chemical companies. For a number of criteria, such as energy use,[7] AOX in waste-water discharges, and volatile organic compounds (VOC), however, it was not possible to make an assessment as no data could be obtained. Similarly, the situation was not clear with regard to occupational criteria, for example, related to cotton dust and noise.

However, according to the manufacturers interviewed, the costs of complying with the criteria would be very high, especially in the case of textile manufacturing companies, and any increase in textile production costs would be passed on to garment manufacturers. Some of the immediately observable sources of additional costs in the EU criteria list, even for modern and relatively environmentally friendly companies, are the use of approved dyes and chemicals, the prohibition of formaldehyde, and testing and certification (especially if the exporters have to rely on the expensive services of foreign testing and certification bodies). At the same time, criteria such as prohibition of detergent and softener use, and the discontinuation of bleaching fabrics before dyeing tend to reduce rather than increase costs.

With regard to waste-water parameters, environmental norms and standards in Turkey, specified in various legal documents including the *Regulation for Control of Water Pollution*, are in general consistent with the norms in the European Union. Some manufacturers even feel that the levels stipulated for certain parameters in the EU eco-label are very lax. On the other hand, there are several other manufacturers who do not have any waste-water treatment plants, and who have had serious problems both with the government and with various European import companies.

With regard to dyes, pigments and carriers, the Turkish textile industry principally uses dyes imported from various European and Asian countries, especially Taiwan and India. European dyes in general are 40 to 45 per cent more expensive than Asian dyes. Some of the manufacturers claimed that the marketing efforts of European dye manufacturers have increased with the rise of import restrictions in European and North American markets. These companies maintain that their production processes comply with the environmental regulations in developed countries, and offer to supply environmentally friendly dyes to Turkish manufacturers. Some European dye manufacturing companies also offer information and education services to Turkish textile manufacturers on various environmental matters.

In recent years the textiles and garments export scene in Turkey has seen an increase in efforts to cultivate organic cotton. Certain textile-producing and exporting companies in Istanbul, Izmir and Adana exporting to Northern European markets, especially Sweden and Germany, have been investing in and financing the cultivation of organic cotton in the western and southern cotton growing regions in Turkey. A list of criteria for organic cotton has been prepared by some import companies and textile producers in Turkey, and this has gained widespread recognition.[8] Some companies employ experts from Germany and Sweden accredited by European importing firms to control, label and verify the organic cotton growing procedure.

13.2.4 Packaging

Packaging requirements, particularly the German Packaging Ordinance,[9] were the only clearly environmental measures felt by the surveyed companies. The Ordinance at first created some anxiety among Turkish manufacturers of export goods, exporters and various branches of the packaging industry, basically due to a lack of information and fears of cost increases and reduced exports.

To help compliance with the regulation, the Turkish National Committee on Solid Wastes, Istanbul Chamber of Industry and various exporters' associations translated the regulation into Turkish and distributed it among exporters, manufacturers and relevant associations, and organized seminars and workshops on the topic. The implementation of the Control of Solid Wastes regulation in Turkey in 1991 also contributed to the ease of compliance with packaging regulations in export markets. This domestic regulation requires the take-back of an annually increasing portion of plastic, aluminium, tin and glass packaging by companies.

Overall, the study indicates that the Turkish export sector has not been unfavourably affected by the German Packaging Ordinance, and that the prices of packaging have not markedly changed. Only in the case of palettes were there problems, since only one Turkish company producing palettes had the label required in export markets, which resulted in a shortage of acceptable palettes, a waiting list and higher prices.

According to the study, the general ease of compliance of Turkish exporters with packaging requirements in export markets is probably due to the availability of acceptable packaging and the gradual implementation of the requirements. The only cost increase associated with compliance was usually the fee for participation in the DSD (Duales System Deutschland) system. Often, this cost item as well as the necessary paperwork were shared by importing companies. Furthermore, in a number of cases, compliance with the packaging requirements in export markets resulted in reducing waste at source, which actually diminished the packaging costs of exporting companies.

13.3   EFFECTS OF TRADE LIBERALIZATION AND TRADE EXPANSION ON THE ENVIRONMENT

Most economic sectors in Turkey sell their products in both domestic and export markets. However, some sectors have become more export-oriented than others due to export market demand, comparative advantage and government export promotion policies. For these sectors, export priority seems to determine or at least have a strong impact on siting decisions, production levels and the choice of production technologies, which, in turn, influence the nature and degree of environmental impact created by these sectors.

In particular, the need to ensure favourable conditions for export industries has involved the siting of industrial enterprises in and around large cities, the occupation of most suitable port areas by export-oriented industries, and the location of industries on seashores and adjacent to rivers and lakes to facilitate cheap or even free effluent disposal. According to the study, this approach has been the most important reason for industrial pollution in Turkey.

The study selected two cases for analysing the effects of trade liberalization and trade expansion on the environment: iron and steel in manufacturing, and cotton in agriculture. Both of these have an important position in the Turkish economy and belong to the country's most important export sectors.

13.3.1   Iron and Steel

The iron and steel sector is one of the most important industrial sectors in Turkey, accounting for 4.8 per cent of GNP and 6.2 per cent of industrial production in 1992. It is also a leading and constantly expanding export sector. Over 40 per cent of iron and steel production is exported, which makes iron and steel the third most important export item for Turkey. In 1992, the value of iron and steel exports exceeded 1.4 billion dollars and an 11 per cent increase was estimated for 1993. The main export markets are in the Far East, the Middle East and the US. South Korea and Iran together account for almost 40 per cent of exports.

The Iskenderun Iron and Steel Factory (ISDEMIR), which is the largest integrated industrial complex in Turkey, is situated in the Iskenderun Bay area. This area has become one of the fastest developing industrial regions in Turkey, and government investment and incentive policies are primarily geared towards developing export industries in this region. Significant capacity increases are also planned for the ISDEMIR.

The establishment of the ISDEMIR has also brought with it other industrial and infrastructural investments in the region. A large-scale cement factory has been built to utilize the by-products of ISDEMIR. Investments in railways, new roads and port facilities have been required. Four large-scale private sector iron rolling factories and hundreds of small-scale rolling mills have also been established in the region to ply the produce of ISDEMIR. The public and private iron and steel plants of all sizes are a major source of air pollution in the region.

The very rapid growth of exports to Middle Eastern countries, especially to Iran and Iraq in the late 1970s and early 1980s, was the dominant driving force behind the dramatic industrial development in the Iskenderun Bay area. However, domestic policy also had an impact. The South East Anatolia Development Project was put in place, with the aim of developing the region, including its exporting capacities. Furthermore, the Iskenderun–Yumurtalik Free Industrial Zone designated for export industries was established.

According to the study, the Iskenderun Bay area is an excellent example of change induced by export-oriented rapid industrialization in a developing country, and of the economic, social and environmental impact of this change. The region is crucial for the goal of increasing industrial exports, which has taken precedence over the requirements of sustainable development. Furthermore, there is a lack of awareness of environmental issues and concepts that has hindered the incorporation of sustainability concerns in the development of export industries.

The rapid pace of the development in Iskenderun Bay has sometimes resulted in hasty, unplanned action, and a lack of coordination among the relevant public authorities and private actors. The study considers it inevitable that this will result in environmental problems and unplanned urbanization, similar to past developments in other comparable regions like Izmit Bay, Istanbul and Izmir.

13.3.2   Cotton

Agriculture in general accounts for approximately 16 per cent of GNP and over 40 per cent of employment in Turkey. According to the study, the most important feature of Turkish agriculture is its dual character. A modern segment exists side by side with a very large traditional subsistence segment. The modern segment uses modern production techniques, including commercial fertilizers and pesticides, provides almost all of the marketed production and covers over 70 per cent of arable land. However, most of the rural population lives on small family farms. Government policies, such as price supports and input subsidies, have been primarily directed at the modern segment to assure a rapid increase in agricultural production. The agricultural sector has not been fully involved in the general trade liberalization policy of Turkey.

Cotton is one of the key export commodities for Turkey, and present production levels are considered to be well below production capacity. It is grown intensively in the fertile and irrigated plains and valleys of western and southern Turkey almost solely by farmers from the modern agricultural segment. Production has a significant impact on the environment, even when compared to other agricultural products. It is erosive, highly irrigated, consumes high levels of fertilizers and is treated with a variety of chemicals to prevent insect infestations and plant diseases.

Growing cotton for export markets has for a long time caused considerable strain on the soils and water resources of the cotton growing regions. Due to export demand and government policies, traditional rotation practices have been terminated, in particular after the 1960s. Thus, there is continuous pressure from the same crop on the soil, and the environmentally beneficial impact of rotation with other, less erosive crops is lost. Lack of rotation may also lead to an increased need to use fertilizers and pesticides in cotton growing. Thus, market forces combined with government policies prevent the cotton farmers from choosing agronomically sound practices which could preserve and perhaps even improve environmental quality.

Almost all cotton in Turkey is grown on irrigated land. While the ratio of cotton area sown to total agricultural land is approximately 3 per cent, the ratio of cotton area to irrigated land is over 24 per cent. Irrigation water is principally provided by the General Directorate of State Hydraulic Works, and the water is virtually free for nearly all cotton growers. But there has also been a rapid and uncontrolled increase in private irrigation projects that causes pressure on underground water resources. The high consumption of water by cotton growing in turn leads to the leaching of nutrients and agricultural chemicals into the sea, surface waters and groundwater. Although precise figures are not available on chemical concentration levels in the waters and soils of cotton growing regions, according to the study the potential environmental consequences of chemical contamination of waters and soils in Turkey appear to be alarming.

It is maintained that the application of fertilizers in cotton growing farms is well above and sometimes exceeds twice the amount suggested by the Ministry of Agriculture. Fertilizer expenses, although heavily subsidized, account for 18 per cent of total costs in cotton growing. For Turkish agriculture in general, domestic policies have been directed towards encouraging the application of commercial fertilizers. For example, at the end of 1990 the total fertilizer subsidy rate in agriculture was 49.6 per cent.

Use of pesticides in cotton cultivation has a severe environmental impact. Irrigated agriculture provides an appropriate habitat for various damaging insect populations and wild weed growth, resulting in increasing levels of chemical use by the cotton grower. Pesticides are applied through dusting from aeroplanes (approximately 60 per cent of the cotton growing area). This may have serious environmental impacts since, in addition to cotton fields, neighbouring rivers and villages are also affected. Moreover, pesticides that are harmful to human health are widely used and agricultural workers have suffered from their effects. Producing and importing companies have promoted the use of pesticides intensely and farmers have tended to apply overdoses. The Ministry of Agriculture is trying to cooperate with the other ministries to control the supply of pesticides in Turkey. Pesticide prices are not subsidized by the government, and the cost of pesticides accounts for over 17 per cent of the total cost of cotton growing in Turkey.

Cotton growing has become increasingly specialized and requires increasing amounts of water, fertilizers and pesticides as inputs. Part of this has been driven by an increased demand for cotton but government trade and agricultural policies that subsidize cotton production, both directly and indirectly, may have played an even greater role. For example, government subsidies and purchases contribute substantially to raising cotton demand. Furthermore, unions of sales cooperatives award to member cotton growers agricultural credits whose interest rates can be half those of bank loans.

Thus, the study concludes that domestic policies affecting agricultural output and the use of inputs in Turkey can create adverse environmental impacts, particularly in the case of cotton growing. These environmental externalities are regarded as necessary and justifiable in order to meet the production levels set by the Ministry of Agriculture.

13.4   CONCLUSIONS

The studies clearly indicate that the importance of complying with the requirements of export markets is well understood by Turkish exporters and governmental and non-governmental bodies, and efforts to comply are intensifying. A critical facilitator here has been the structure of the exporting sector. Exporters are in direct contact with their customers through importing or buying companies, who may also share some of the formalities and costs of fulfilling the requirements. Based on the studies, lack of timely and adequate information, which has in many other countries proved to be one of the most important bottlenecks for compliance, has not been a problem in Turkey.

However, since all requirements are imposed by the importing companies in an integrated manner, Turkish exporters cannot readily distinguish between environmental and product quality standards. This is also reflected in the general perception among exporters that the answer to any problems of compliance with the requirements of developed-country markets, including environmental ones, lies in ISO 9000.

Although exporters do not feel that their competitiveness in developed-country export markets is harmed by strict environmental requirements, they do see that the harmonization of national and international standards, and strict enforcement of national standards would be very important to maintaining their competitiveness in the domestic market.

NOTES

1. This report provides a synthesis, prepared by the UNCTAD secretariat, of the following study on trade and environment linkages in Turkey:

    Celik Aruoba (1993), 'Research on trade and environment linkages in Turkey. Report I: Environment-trade link. Impact of environmental regulations and standards in European and North American markets on Turkish exports. Report II: Trade-environment link. Impact of trade and production in two important export sectors of Turkey: iron and steel and cotton', Ankara. Study prepared for UNCTAD.

    For eco-labelling, it also draws from the following report:

    Celik Aruoba (1994), 'Analysis of probable impact of European Union eco-labelling programme and Turkish textiles and garments exports to the European Union', Ankara. Published under the title 'Eco-labelling in the EU and the Export of Turkish Textiles and Garments', in Zarrilli *et al.* (eds), *Eco-labelling and International Trade*, London: MacMillan, 1997.

2. Two institutions, the Istanbul Chamber of Industry and the Garments Manufacturers Association, actively supported the research throughout the survey period. The government agencies interviewed were the Ministry of Foreign Affairs, Ministry of the Environment, the Undersecretariat of the Treasury, the Export Development Centre and the Turkish Standards Institute.

3. Interference may involve several stages of the production chain. The survey revealed one example where an importing firm had requested a Turkish manufacturer of clothing to change its domestic supplier of cotton yarn because this supplier did not possess a biological waste water-treatment system.

4. One example in the textile and garments sector is the acquisition of new machinery in order to switch from chemical to mechanical shrinking of fabrics.

5. Zarilla, Simonetta, Veena Jha and René Vossenaar (1997), *Ecolabelling and International Trade*, Geneva: UNCTAD.

6. This term has also been used by the Swedish company, Hennes and Mauritz AB in a leaflet prepared and distributed among Turkish exporters to specify the 'ecocotton textile and garment standards'.

7. None of the firms interviewed calculate the consumption of energy during manufacturing in the manner described in European Union's list of criteria.

8. The main criteria for organic cotton, according to this list, are: (a) soil should be unplanted for at least six months before cultivation, in order for it to be cleansed from past residues; (b) cotton should be hand-planted and hand-picked; (c) chemical fertilizers should not be used (organic fertilizers are allowed); (d) insecticides should not be used (biological control is allowed); (e) harmful weeds should be combated only by hand-hoeing; (f) harvested cotton should be stored separately; (g) organically grown cotton should be ginned separately; (h) lint cotton should be packed in pressed bales and be clearly marked for easy identification; (l) packed lint cotton should immediately be transported to special warehouses to await spinning; and (k) organic cotton lint should be spun separately.

9. The ordinance requires: (a) environmentally friendly material for packaging; (b) recyclable material for packaging; (c) minimizing packaging; (d) reuse of packaging material; (e) avoiding the use of different materials in the manufacture of one kind of packaging.

14. Zimbabwe

14.1 INTRODUCTION

A case study on trade, environment and development linkages was completed in 1995 by a research team consisting of Jabavu Clifford Nkomo, Department of Economics, University of Zimbabwe; Benson Mutongi Zwizwai, Institute of Development Studies, University of Zimbabwe; and Davison Gumbo, Environment and Development Activities, Zimbabwe. Information for the study was collected through interviews in relevant government ministries, industry associations and individual companies. This chapter, prepared by the UNCTAD secretariat, summarizes and updates the findings of the study.

Exports are vital for Zimbabwe, especially with regard to the structural adjustment programme undertaken by the country. Zimbabwe has two major preoccupations that relate to external developments that may affect its ability to earn foreign exchange through exports: falling international commodity prices and the potential emergence of protectionist measures and trade barriers in export markets, which, it is feared, may at times include environmental measures. Bearing in mind the dominant share of food in total exports, emphasis is also put on sanitary and phytosanitary requirements of food products.

14.2 BACKGROUND TO ZIMBABWE'S ECONOMY[1]

Zimbabwe has one of the most diversified economies in Sub-Saharan Africa, and among developing countries it belongs to the middle income group. The country has a comparatively strong physical infrastructure, rich natural resources and a well-educated labour force, that puts it ahead of many other countries in the region in terms of development. Further, the level of industrialization is relatively high and broad-based, and the country, independent since 1980, has long been politically stable. The most important sectors in Zimbabwe's economy are agriculture and mining, and related manufacturing industries. International trade plays an important role in Zimbabwe's economy with exports of goods and services exceeding 30 per cent of GDP.

Agriculture remains the backbone of the economy, providing employment and livelihood for some 70 per cent of the population. The main crops include tobacco, corn, tea, sugar and cotton. Normally agriculture contributes 20 per cent to GDP and 50 per cent to total exports. However, the dependency of agricultural production on weather conditions is a major disadvantage of the sector. For example, in 1992 Zimbabwe was hit by the worst drought in its history, and agricultural output declined drastically, seriously hurting several related sectors of the economy.

Zimbabwe has abundant deposits of coal, chromium, asbestos, gold, and other minerals. Mining contributes 5 per cent to GDP and 15 to 20 per cent to total exports. The largest mineral export item is gold. However, the mining sector is very sensitive to world price fluctuations, and there has been a downward trend in the price of metals.

The manufacturing sector of Zimbabwe is relatively well developed, accounting for 25 per cent of GDP and 30 to 35 per cent of exports. The diversity and large size of the sector, compared to countries of a similar size and income level, reflect the decades-long import substitution policy. Over 90 per cent of all manufactured goods are still consumed domestically.[2] The largest industries in the sector are food and beverages, textiles, and iron and steel. The manufacturing sector has strong linkages with agriculture, since almost 60 per cent of manufacturing output is based on agricultural products.

Despite the natural advantages of the country, the protectionist import substitution strategy did not bring the desired economic results. Real GDP per capita levels stagnated through the 1980s, and in 1992 the external debt exceeded 50 per cent of GDP. Zimbabwean companies were segregated from world markets and protected from import competition, and there was a longstanding isolation from state-of-the-art technologies. Also, the government wanted to reduce the dependency of the economy on agriculture and weather conditions by promoting manufacturing and mining, including manufacturing that does not rely on agricultural inputs. This is an interesting case of environmental conditions necessitating changes in economic policy.

Foreign exchange shortage was probably the most serious problem which confronted Zimbabwe, and it also bred other problems such as unemployment, debt crisis and fiscal deficits. After 1985, the shortage began to have such a negative impact on the whole economy that by the late 1980s, calls for structural change of the economy intensified.[3]

For these reasons, in 1991 the government embarked on a five-year economic reform programme with the aim of moving towards a freer market economy. Liberalization of foreign trade and the elimination of price and exchange controls constitute a major part of these reforms. The goal of the government is to create a competitive and efficient economy that can bring economic growth and development through exports. The competitiveness of Zimbabwe's exports in international markets are a critical element in the success of the economic reform programme.

Against this background, changing environmental and health standards for commodities are a very important issue for Zimbabwe if they threaten to have an adverse effect on the country's trading position. Moreover, since almost all Zimbabwe's major industries are based on natural resources, sustained economic growth and continued trade depend very much on effective natural resources management and environmental conservation. The fact that the environmental policy framework of Zimbabwe has not yet been fully developed to deal with issues of environment and trade as they arise internationally, magnifies the importance of dealing with the subject at this point.

14.3   DOMESTIC ENVIRONMENTAL POLICY-MAKING

14.3.1   Environmental Legislation in Zimbabwe

Analysing the environmental legal regime of Zimbabwe as a whole, it has been noted that the areas that are generally working well are wildlife and nature preservation, and chemical regulation. The weaknesses of the regime lie in hazardous waste disposal, water pollution prevention, lack of environmental impact assessment requirements, and in energy and natural resource utilization where environmental considerations have been secondary. Strict enforcement has been difficult due to a lack of financial and human resources.[4]

There are around thirty Acts of Parliament in Zimbabwe that relate to environmental protection; however, only the Atmospheric Pollution Prevention Act and the Hazardous Substances and Articles Act may have a significant bearing on trade. However, the enforcement of both Acts has been difficult. The effectiveness of the Atmospheric Pollution Prevention Act is reduced by the fact that the Act does not stipulate specific emission levels. There is also a need to strengthen the provisions concerning the disposal of hazardous materials in the Hazardous Substances and Articles Act.

Zimbabwe's wildlife resources constitute perhaps the major environmental management challenge for the country, but the environmental policy framework has been able to deal with the challenge successfully. There are 17 well-maintained national parks in Zimbabwe that also support a strong tourist industry. These national parks are among the last remaining habitats for many endangered species such as the white and black rhinoceros and crocodiles.[5] The most notable aspect of wildlife management in Zimbabwe is the role of rural communities who participate in wildlife management and receive economic benefits from wildlife through the CAMPFIRE programme.

Any efforts by industry to reduce negative environmental impacts are rendered difficult because quantitative information on industrial pollution is lacking and much of the country's technology is outdated. Export-oriented sectors are not adequately addressed by environmental legislation. At the same time, some industries feel that they are not sufficiently consulted when domestic environmental legislation and standard-setting takes place. Despite these problems, industry is slowly becoming aware of the importance of decreasing harmful environmental impacts.

14.3.2 Trade Impacts of Domestic Environmental Policy

Most foodstuffs have to comply with the Zimbabwe Standards Association's stipulations. However, these standards do not deal with storage and packaging. Domestic legislation for the sector is set by the Ministry of Health, but the study reported that the food industry felt that most of the legislation and standard setting is hurried and that too little consultation with industry takes place. The Ministry of Health is knowledgeable of international developments (whereas the industry is not) and perceived to be influenced by the strict Nordic countries.

There is an Environmental Labelling Programme (ELP) in Zimbabwe that awards both product labels and corporate environmental labels. It is hoped that the Zimbabwean eco-label could enhance the competitiveness of labelled products in export markets. However, at the moment even the domestic significance of the ELP programme is questioned. The implementation of the programme is undermined by the low level of environmental awareness in the general public. In particular, the link between consumption patterns and the environment may not be easily perceived. Also, the lack of alternative products places limitations on consumers' choice.

The relatively loose nature of domestic environmental regulations and the difficulties in their enforcement could also harm exports in the longer term. An example is food products that may in developing countries include higher levels of contaminants than in developed countries. This is due to the fact that in many developing countries, persistent pesticides and other relevant chemicals (such as DDT) have not been banned and general pollution regulations contributing to a fall in food contamination (for example, of lead, cadmium and mercury) have not been introduced. Countries in hot or humid regions like Zimbabwe also suffer from high levels of biological contaminants that are difficult to deal with.

14.4 EFFECTS OF EXTERNAL ENVIRONMENTAL REQUIREMENTS ON TRADE

The study points out that environmental, health and sanitary requirements in the importing countries are sometimes perceived in Zimbabwe as new non-tariff barriers to trade. The potential emergence of such barriers to trade would be especially crucial for Zimbabwe given the difficulties it is already having in maintaining existing export markets or penetrating new ones. Accordingly, it is feared that environmental and health requirements in the importing countries might have serious adverse impacts on Zimbabwe's market access and export competitiveness.

Food standards and strict limitations on the use of certain substances are likely to have the most significant effects on market access. Among the problems reported by Zimbabwean exporters are the costs and difficulties of testing and verification procedures; the perceived lack of scientific data for specific thresholds or limit values; and the uncertainty arising from rapidly changing requirements in overseas markets. By increasing the risk involved in export operations, environmental factors may delay investment decisions aimed at adjusting technologies to meet overseas environmental standards. Phytosanitary regulations and food standards may create market access problems on account of differing national standards, lack of transparency and inconsistent application of procedures.

Barriers to trade may emerge in particular if the standards are set so that it is easier for domestic producers in developed countries to meet them than for Zimbabwean exporters. This can be the case, for example, if the fulfilment of the standard requires particular inputs that are available to domestic producers on more favourable terms. The dominant participation of local industry in the standard-setting process may sometimes even lead to deliberate lobbying for creating entry barriers to foreign producers.

Compliance with external environmental requirements may be difficult for Zimbabwean producers with regard to both the procedure and content of such requirements. In addition to incremental production costs, trade effects may also arise if Zimbabwe is increasingly forced to source material, service or technology inputs from developed countries in order to meet the stipulated standards.

Moreover, the study suggests that so far, discussions on trade and environment in the OECD countries have tended to focus on the environmental impacts of production and trade in developing-country commodities such as tropical timber and certain minerals. Although admitting that environmental damage may in many cases be caused by these natural resource based products, the study notes that the trade and environment dialogue should not be limited to developing-country products, nor to only raw materials, but it should also cover other products, including those of developed countries, and the export from developed countries of goods prohibited domestically. Further, it is pointed out that environmentally related trade measures are perceived to be applied only to selected sectors while ignoring others, for example, gold whose market access has not been subjected to environmental requirements despite the negative environmental effects of mining.

14.4.1 Vulnerability to External Environmental Requirements

The vulnerability of Zimbabwe's exports to external environmental requirements is partly determined by the sectoral composition of exports (see Table 14.1). Zimbabwe's exports are diversified compared to those of many other developing countries and include tobacco, sugar, maize, coffee, gold, asbestos, nickel, copper, ferro-alloys, iron and steel, cotton lint, textiles, chemicals and machinery. Table 14.1 shows the development of the composition of Zimbabwe's imports and exports both in value and relative terms over the period 1980–1993.

Table 14.1   Zimbabwe: total exports and imports by main commodity groups, 1980–1993 (millions of US dollars)

Commodity groups	1980	1985	1990	1991	1992	1993
Imports						
(in value)						
Food and agricultural products	15.8	69.2	115.9	101.8	439.3	240.9
Fuels	22.4	213.4	288.3	253.6	261.4	266.8
Ores and metals	1.3	23.5	45.3	54.5	33.0	58.3
Manufactured goods	141.4	565.1	1347.3	1555.3	1416.9	1217.2
Total	192.9	896.6	1851.4	2026.8	2206.5	1813.3
(share in percentages)						
Food and agricultural products	8.2	7.7	6.3	5.0	19.9	13.3
Fuels	11.6	23.8	15.6	12.5	11.8	14.7
Ores and metals	0.7	2.6	2.4	2.7	1.5	3.2
Manufactured goods	73.3	63.0	72.8	76.7	64.2	67.1
Exports						
(in value)						
Food and agricultural products	188.0	493.0	753.7	703.4	592.5	642.1
Fuels	12.9	9.8	10.9	6.1	4.7	7.6
Ores and metals	74.2	155.2	234.0	184.3	189.8	164.3
Manufactured goods	155.1	279.4	453.3	382.5	441.8	500.7
Total	433.3	954.5	1467.6	1286.5	1238.8	1320.5
(share in percentages)						
Food and agricultural products	43.4	51.7	51.4	54.7	47.8	48.6
Fuels	3.0	1.0	0.7	0.5	0.4	0.6
Ores and metals	17.1	16.3	15.9	14.3	15.3	12.4
Manufactured goods	35.8	29.3	30.9	29.7	35.7	37.9

Note: Food and agricultural products consist of SITC 0+1+2+4 less (27+28); Fuels consist of SITC 3; Ores and metals consist of SITC 27+28+68; Manufactured products consist of SITC 5+6+7+8 less 68.

Source: UNCTAD, based on the COMTRADE database.

The destination of exports also affects vulnerability to environmental requirements. Around 50 per cent of Zimbabwe's total exports are destined for the OECD markets, where environmental requirements are strictest. Of these exports, the majority goes to the European Union market (where Zimbabwe benefits from preferential access under the Lomé Convention), the United Kingdom and Germany being its main trading partners within the European Union. The United States and Japan also constitute significant export markets; their share of Zimbabwe's exports has typically been 5–7 per cent each. However, the single most important trading partner is South Africa with its share of 15 per cent, while other African countries account for another 15 per cent of exports. All in all, a relatively large share of Zimbabwe's export trade is conducted with low-income countries. Table 14.2 shows Zimbabwe's exports in 1993 by commodity groups and markets in more detail.

Table 14.2   Zimbabwe: exports by commodity groups and markets, 1993 (millions of US dollars)

Commodity groups	World	OECD countries[1]			South Africa	Developing countries[2]
		Total	United States and Canada	European Union		
Total	1 320.5	674.4	97.8	417.3	268.2	346.6
Food and agricultural products	642.1	353.8	40.9	235.7	87.3	184.0
Food	559.8	295.5	39.9	182.0	69.8	178.1
Agricultural raw materials	82.3	58.3	1.0	53.7	17.5	5.9
Fuels	7.6	0.0	0.0	0.0	1.5	6.1
Ores and metals	164.3	97.2	6.9	53.3	19.5	35.2
Manufactured goods of which:	500.7	219.8	49.7	125.2	158.3	121.0
Chemicals	38.4	1.5	0.1	0.8	7.0	29.9
Textiles and clothing	111.6	71.1	11.6	59.0	27.2	12.7
Leather	7.6	4.0	0.0	3.5	3.3	0.3
Footwear	11.3	0.8	0.0	0.8	9.5	0.9
Machinery and equipment	39.6	2.2	0.4	1.5	18.6	18.7
Other manufactured products	292.2	140.2	37.6	59.6	92.7	58.5

Notes
[1] Excluding Austria, Iceland, Mexico, Norway and Turkey.
[2] Excluding South Africa.

Source: UNCTAD, based on COMTRADE database.

To analyse more closely the vulnerability of Zimbabwe's exports to external environmental requirements, it is necessary to look at the extent to which environmentally sensitive products are exported to environmentally sensitive markets. The UNCTAD secretariat has identified some sectors sensitive to environmental regulations (and sanitary and phytosanitary standards) based on environmental regulations applicable in OECD markets to each sector. Table 14.3 shows the destination and value of Zimbabwe's exports in those identified sensitive product categories that are of most significant export interest to Zimbabwe.

Table 14.3   Zimbabwe: exports of selected goods sensitive to environmental regulations by destination, 1993 (millions of US dollars)

| Products | World | OECD countries[1] | | | | |
		Total	United States	European Union	South Africa	Developing countries
Food	152.7	51.9	0.8	48.7	40.6	60.2
Textiles and clothing	117.7	75.5	11.4	62.2	28.8	13.3
Asbestos	56.9	16.8	0.2	4.9	7.7	32.0
Flowers	26.8	26.6	0.2	26.0	0.1	0.1
Wood and wood products	21.5	8.6	0.8	7.7	11.6	1.3
Leather and leather products (excluding footwear)	16.3	9.4	0.1	8.2	5.4	1.5
Footwear	11.3	0.8	0.0	0.8	9.5	0.9
Fertilizers	10.6	0.0	0.0	0.0	0.0	10.6
Plastics and plastic products	7.4	0.6	0.0	0.5	2.0	4.8
Paper and paper products	7.0	0.3	0.0	0.2	1.9	4.9
Detergents	5.7	0.2	0.0	0.2	0.3	5.2
Beverages	5.1	0.9	0.0	0.9	0.3	3.9

Note: See Table 14.2.

Source: UNCTAD, based on COMTRADE database.

US$466 million, or 34 per cent of total exports, were in products identified as sensitive to environmental regulations (and sanitary and phytosanitary standards) in 1993. It is interesting to note that in the EU market, the share of sensitive exports to total exports was 38.5 per cent, while in the US market the share was only 14 per cent (mainly textiles and clothing) and in Japan 13 per cent (mainly asbestos). Of the products identified above, food products, textiles and clothing, asbestos and flowers had most significant markets in the OECD.

The fact that Zimbabwean industry tends to receive information on changing regulations and respond to them rather late augments Zimbabwean exporters' compliance difficulties with external environmental requirements, and thus their susceptibility to resulting negative trade impacts. It is important for exporters to be aware of contemplated changes in environmental regulations before they are adopted so as to have enough time to adapt the products and production processes to meet the required standards.

Information on environmental requirements is already to an extent available from the Standards Association of Zimbabwe. In addition, the national trade development organization ZimTrade has an Export Promotion Support Scheme (EPSS) developed to assist Zimbabwean enterprises in strengthening their exporting capabilities. Assistance from foreign consultants to meet import requirements of specific markets or international standards can be received through a programme also run by ZimTrade. Many industry associations play an important role in educating their members on environmental issues, and the Confederation of Zimbabwe Industries and the Employers' Confederation of Zimbabwe have set up committees geared specifically to disseminating environmental information.

Thus, channels for information dissemination exist, but according to the study they may not be very effective especially concerning export markets and the environment. The extent to which firms are finally able to acquire the necessary information depends on the efforts of individual firms. Since the industry developed in isolation from international markets for a long time until the trade liberalization programme, firms may not be very practised in obtaining information on export markets.

14.4.2   Specific requirements affecting Zimbabwe's exports

Regulatory measures
Food standards   The Zimbabwean export sector most likely to be affected by new environmental standards and regulations is foodstuffs. It is feared that Zimbabwe might lose some of its present and potential markets, in particular if the standards are tightened and extended to cover growing and processing methods, and especially since the required testing and certification procedures are often difficult and sometimes also very costly. And, since it may already be difficult for Zimbabwean small-scale producers to meet food quality standards (as opposed to food safety standards), complying with emerging environmental standards may pose similar difficulties for them. However, high value products such as ostrich meat (see Box 14.1) have sufficiently large margins to absorb some increase in environment and health related costs without losing their international competitiveness.

Environmental requirements are considered troublesome in the sense that they may be unilaterally imposed by importing countries without being subjected to much discussion, and that they may be country specific. Phytosanitary requirements do indeed differ significantly between countries, and the precautionary principle is in extensive use. Since the products of the food

Box 14.1   Ostrich exports

The case of ostrich production is interesting for Zimbabwe. Ostrich meat is in high demand due to its low cholesterol; the main markets for live ostriches are Europe, the USA and Australia, and for ostrich skins Japan and the USA. For ostrich meat producers exporting is profitable: they can expect a net return of US$100 per bird from export sales as compared to US$40 from domestic sales. However, the recent spread of the New Castle disease has complicated ostrich export programmes.

The long-term strategy in the Zimbabwean ostrich industry is to export ostrich meat and skin. This is more attractive to ostrich farmers than the export of live birds due to the higher value added. At present, Zimbabwe cannot export ostrich meat to the European Union. To do that, it should have a European Union approved abattoir. However, there are no clear requirements that the abattoir should satisfy – in fact there is no European Union approved ostrich abattoir anywhere in the world. Nevertheless, an ostrich abattoir facility is being constructed in Zimbabwe at the cost of US$1 million; farmers are contributing 25 per cent of their earnings from exports of ostriches and ostrich eggs towards this fund. If the abattoir is completed and approved, the EU will still check the management of the facility to guarantee that sufficient standards are met.

The rules of the ostrich trade are largely still open. For example, it has not been determined whether ostriches are poultry or wildlife. This makes it difficult for Zimbabwean producers to obtain information about regulations that vary very much from country to country.

Although the strict regulations are based on veterinary concerns, they also protect the poultry industry of developed countries from competition from ostrich imports. Developed countries are also preparing to engage in ostrich production, which means that by the time Zimbabwean producers are allowed to export ostrich meat to developed countries, they will have to meet domestic competition.

The costs of complying with the veterinary requirements imposed by developed countries are high. In spite of these costs, the ostrich industry of Zimbabwe remains viable and competitive due to the high prices obtainable in the international markets. Yet, the future of the sector is not clear in the face of increasing supply and competition from developed countries.

industry are homogeneous, harmonization of the requirements would benefit producers.

The study also notes a perceived lack of scientific basis for certain environmental regulations in the developed countries. For example, in peanut butter processing, Zimbabwe has adopted an aflatoxin limit of 20 parts per billion, but the Nordic countries are proposing to adopt a standard of 4 to 5 parts per billion. The study reports that Zimbabwean industry has raised the question as to whether there is scientific justification for this stricter standard and whether investments should be made in Zimbabwe to adapt to the proposed new Nordic standards. It also questions to what extent technological implications for producers are considered when setting strict requirements in importing countries, especially if there is no domestic production.

Environmental standards typically increase in stringency over time. Because Zimbabwe is at a lower level of technological development than the developed countries, and because it can devote only limited resources to research and development, it is likely that the standards evolving in the developed countries will at any given time exceed the standards evolving in Zimbabwe. Thus, Zimbabwe will be forced to assume the role of reactively adjusting to standards evolving in the developed countries.

In particular, it is feared that horticulture (mainly fresh fruits and vegetables) and beef exports to Europe will be affected unless Zimbabwe can quickly adapt to new requirements. The EU has discussed a wide range of environmental, health and sanitary regulations for possible implementation in the short term and proposed a harmonized system to apply to all member states. Even if Zimbabwean farmers could adapt to the new demands, the proposed phytosanitary checks (requiring that importers inspect all products before they leave the country of origin and that a bill of health be issued) will make it difficult to penetrate the market. As for meat, Zimbabwe has so far not faced problems in meeting its beef quota to Europe, but environmental and health considerations are expected to emerge in the future.

In addition to food standards, standards relating to other commodity exports are also important for Zimbabwe. These may be the national standards of the export markets or emerge in the context of Multilateral Environmental Agreements. However, the decreasing trend in international commodity prices may make it difficult for Zimbabwe to internalize the environmental costs of commodity production.

Bans   The trade measure with most dramatic effects is the banning of a product for environmental or health reasons. This has been the case for asbestos: Zimbabwe's asbestos exports significantly decreased due to a strong anti-asbestos lobby and the banning of products containing asbestos in certain developed countries. Production only picked up after new export markets were found in the former Eastern bloc, and South East Asia is now targeted as a future market.

In clothing and textiles, the concern with external environmental requirements relate to chemical use, since certain chemicals and processes used in Zimbabwe are not allowed in all export markets. Such chemicals include, for example, organophosphorus in dyeing, acrylic in sizing, and banned chemicals such as uria in easy care finishing. It is expected that complying with international regulations will be expensive for the industry. A mechanism for testing imported raw materials and intermediate products also needs to be developed to ensure that Zimbabwean products do not fail to meet required standards because of the properties of imported materials.

Packaging regulations   Exporters to the European Union are increasingly required to use packaging materials that are recyclable and returnable. Most EU member states have implemented or proposed national programmes on packaging which are unique in structure and targets for recovery, reduction, recycling, and permitted means of packaging, as well as the use of instruments to achieve the set targets, such as take-back obligations, taxes, deposit-refund schemes and labelling.[6] As a result of this, Zimbabwe may have to meet a variety of different packaging requirements for its European exports. A number of companies interviewed for the study, for example, Flexible Packaging, reported that packaging which may be acceptable to the target market was not always very expensive to manufacture.

The EU Packaging and Packaging Waste Directive tries to harmonize the national packaging laws within the European Union. However, exporters are faced with the problem of finding out and understanding the regulatory requirements of the many different national or regional packaging schemes, and the acquisition of such information may be a costly exercise. Exporters may also be confronted with technical and resource problems that make it difficult to achieve conformity with a particular country's regulatory requirements. Using packaging materials that are recyclable in the importing country may be difficult for Zimbabwe, and recycled materials may be more expensive than traditional ones. For example, the study reports that the costs of collecting and separating plastic waste result in recycled plastic being 20 per cent more expensive than using virgin resins. Finally, there may also be difficulties in submitting packaging for evaluation and obtaining the necessary certification, especially if on-the-spot inspection of production and packaging facilities is required.

These factors may result in packaging costs becoming high in relation to sales. Further, the packaging specifications of importing countries may force Zimbabwe to source export packaging from the target market. This not only increases the costs of exporters, but also harms the domestic and export market potential of the Zimbabwean packaging industry. For example, Zimbabwe complained that its exports of flowers to Germany were refused on account of environmentally unfriendly packaging, and initially Zimbabwe may have had to import packaging to be able to export to the target market. Eventually the problem was resolved through information dissemination on the specific requirements and consequent adaptation.

Voluntary developments

Eco-labelling   Eco-labelling schemes are in principle designed to enhance the competitiveness of labelled products by pointing out their environmental qualities. They also indirectly convey the impression that unlabelled products in the same product category are relatively less environmentally friendly. Thus, although participation in an eco-labelling scheme is voluntary, it may in practice become necessary to apply for an eco-label in certain markets and for certain products.

The study holds that most of Zimbabwe's paper products and paper industry processes are environmentally friendly and should qualify easily for eco-labels. External environmental requirements are therefore not perceived as a threat to the industry, and it is felt that eco-labelling would affect the industry positively. The use of mechanical pulping processes and recycled materials, as well as replanting of trees, and the use of cotton as raw material for fine paper are among the environmentally friendly features of the industry.

Voluntary international standards   Compliance with the requirements of international standards that include process-related aspects is not easy for Zimbabwean producers. Despite serious efforts by several companies, only two Zimbabwean companies had fulfilled the requirements of the quality standard ISO 9000. There may be similar difficulties in complying with the environment-related ISO 14000 standard series.

Consumer preferences   In the furniture sector, due to pressure from environmentalists in developed countries, demand for hardwood (and hardwood-based furniture) has decreased and correspondingly that of softwood, especially pine, has increased. Thus, timber-producing firms of Zimbabwe are now increasingly exporting pine logs due to the high prices obtainable in the international markets. This has resulted in raw material shortages for the local furniture industry, in particular since the better quality timber tends to be exported. This reduces the quality of Zimbabwean furniture and prevents the expansion of an otherwise internationally competitive export branch with high value added (on average, by making furniture, the value of timber is increased by three and a half times). Hence, as a result of these developments, the sector may be moving down on the value chain.

It is feared that increasing consumer demand for insecticide-free or chemical-free cut flowers in the European Union will lead to a fall in Zimbabwe's exports of flowers to this market, unless methods to produce flowers without the use of harmful chemicals can be developed. Considering the recent growth of the flower industry and its export potential, it would be in Zimbabwe's interests to be able to keep the flower export markets.

14.5 EFFECTS OF MULTILATERAL ENVIRONMENTAL AGREEMENTS ON TRADE

Regarding Multilateral Environmental Agreements (MEAs), globally binding conventions may need to be adapted, for example, through admission of one-by-one exceptions, to better serve the environmental and other interests of individual developing countries. So far, regional developments in environmental regulations relevant to Zimbabwe have been sparse and have tended to focus on specific environmental threats. However, there are now indications that the region may be moving towards adopting regional environmental standards, for example, in the contexts of the Africa Economic Community and the Common Market for Eastern and Southern Africa (COMESA).

Nevertheless, there are advantages in being a signatory to multilateral environmental agreements. As a signatory Zimbabwe is in a better position to voice its concerns regarding the agreements. For example, the recent ratification by Zimbabwe of the Biodiversity Convention might be partly attributed to a desire to be able to participate in the debate (for example, concerning the right of indigenous people to participate in the exploitation of genetic resources by biotechnology) as an 'insider'. Finally, even if Zimbabwe did not sign an MEA, it might still be affected by the decisions taken in the framework of that agreement.

14.5.1 CITES

Zimbabwe has been party to the Convention on International Trade in Endangered Species in Wild Fauna and Flora (CITES) since 1981. However, there is a conflict between the regulations of the Convention and Zimbabwe's interests with regard to the ivory trade. The Conference of the Parties to CITES agreed to include the African elephant in Appendix I of the convention as from January 1990.[7] Zimbabwe, however, considers its population of the African elephant to be well managed and able to withstand exploitation on a sustainable basis. In fact, the elephant populations in Zimbabwe may exceed sustainable levels.

Zimbabwe and a number of other Southern African elephant range states entered reservations against the Appendix I listing of the African elephant. This means that these states could continue to trade in ivory and other African elephant products if they could find buyers. However, parties other than those that had entered reservations against the listing may not authorize the import of ivory and other elephant products for commercial purposes. As a consequence, three years after the introduction of the ivory trade ban, Zimbabwe had from culling operations an estimated stock pile of US$12 million worth of ivory that it could not legally sell.

Thus in Zimbabwe's view, CITES is clearly restrictive. It is thought that international agreements overshadow local initiatives, and can have serious implications for national environmental management and prohibit rural communities from economically benefiting from wildlife. Therefore, case-by-case exceptions should be allowed in global environmental agreements when necessary.

A possibility for such exceptions has been built into CITES whereby the convention provides for the inclusion, deletion and the transfer between appendices of species on the basis of well-documented scientific evidence on the trade and on the status in the wild of the species concerned. At the June 1997 meeting of the CITES Conference of Parties, it was decided to downlist Botswanan, Namibian and Zimbabwean elephant populations to Annex II. The decision contains specific conditions under which the three countries may resume ivory trade with Japan as the only trading partner.

14.5.2 Basel Convention and Bamako Convention

Zimbabwe did not originally ratify the Basel Convention on the Control of Transboundary Movements of Hazardous Wastes and their Disposal, because it believed that the Convention did not sufficiently address problems related to Africa, especially as a potential recipient of wastes. However, Zimbabwe is now planning to ratify the Basel Convention due to increasing incidences of dumping of hazardous wastes by the developed world, against which non-ratification did not provide appropriate protection, especially in the search for compensation or re-export of the hazardous waste.[8]

Zimbabwe is party to the Bamako Convention on the Ban of Import of Hazardous Wastes into Africa and the Control of Transboundary Movement and Management of Hazardous Wastes within Africa, which it considers to be more defensive than the Basel Convention due to its wider scope. The Bamako Convention has entered into force and, as a result, Zimbabwe expects to benefit environmentally. Thus, in the field of hazardous waste management, it is possible for stronger or more specific regional agreements to coexist with a global convention.

14.5.3   Montreal Protocol

Signatory countries to the Montreal Protocol on Substances that Deplete the Ozone Layer have agreed to gradually reduce and eliminate by the year 2000 the production and consumption of chlorofluorocarbons and other ozone-depleting substances (ODSs). Zimbabwe ratified the Montreal Protocol in 1992, and the London and Copenhagen amendments to the Protocol in 1994. The amendments introduced a faster schedule for phasing out CFCs and halons.

The Government of Zimbabwe has developed an ODS phase-out strategy consistent with the economic reform and industrial development programme. The strategy will be adopted uniformly throughout all affected sectors and the government encourages the adoption of alternative technologies for the effective reduction of controlled substances. A registration system for all qualified ODS users will be developed to promote greater discipline in their practices, and targeting the extensive informal and small scale sectors is a priority.

As Zimbabwe's consumption of ozone-depleting substances is only 0.07 kg per capita, the country is allowed an extra ten-year period to fulfil the Protocol requirements with regard to ODSs used to meet basic domestic needs. Almost all ODSs used in Zimbabwe are imported, and the impacts of the Protocol are already felt in increased prices and restricted availability of the affected substances.

There is a high degree of awareness of the Montreal Protocol in Zimbabwe, and a UNEP-supported programme for phasing out ODSs has been set up. Alternative technologies and recycling possibilities are being sought, and in some cases transitional chemicals are being used. For example, air-conditioning manufacturers have replaced CFC12 by alternative chemicals.

According to the government programme, halons 1301 and 1211 will be completely phased out by 2005, and CFC11, CFC12 and CFC113 by 2010. The main uses of ODSs in Zimbabwe are in refrigeration, air-conditioning, fire-fighting, aerosols and agriculture. Accordingly, the sectors expected to be affected by the phase-out programme include domestic refrigeration, air-conditioning, polymethane foams and aerosols. Sectors that depend on refrigeration facilities such as the food industry are also likely to be indirectly affected, and this may have important consequences bearing in mind the export significance of food products.

Methyl bromide is a major substance used in agriculture. It is also used in horticulture and bulk grain storage. There are so far no controls on methyl bromide in developing countries and the Montreal Protocol provides for complete exemption for quarantine and pre-shipment applications. However, the importing country may have standards for the use of methyl bromide. For example, the State of California and the Government of the Netherlands are considering banning the use of methyl bromide. In such cases, Zimbabwe's exports could be affected, in particular given the fact that almost half of total exports are food products.

14.5.4   Climate Change Convention

Zimbabwe's economy is characterized by a heavy dependence on favourable climatic conditions. Economic growth is largely based on reliable agricultural performance and climatic variations such as recurrent droughts are a common concern. Consequently, the issue of climate change is very important for Zimbabwe's economy, and Zimbabwe was one of the first countries to ratify the Climate Change Convention.

Most of Zimbabwe's greenhouse gas emissions come from energy production, in particular the burning of coal. Coal, a domestic energy source for Zimbabwe, is used as a major industrial fuel. National development plans also rely on the use of coal. The study questions whether it is in Zimbabwe's best interests to reduce carbon dioxide emissions considering that 40 per cent of all energy for both domestic and industrial purposes comes from coal-based thermal power stations and wood fuel for rural folk, and that Zimbabwe's greenhouse gas emissions are an insignificant proportion of global emissions. In other words, the cost of adaptation would be high, but the fairness of imposing such a high cost on Zimbabwe is questionable.

It is also feared that the convention might have serious implications if it leads to, for example, trade restrictions on tobacco cured using coal, steel from conventional blast furnaces, and other products which may be assumed environmentally unfriendly by the developed world.

The study states that the objectives of the Climate Change Convention can only be fully implemented if new and additional funds are identified and effectively transferred, environmentally sound technologies are made available at non-commercial terms, and existing GEF funds are made more accessible.

14.6   EFFECTS OF TRADE POLICIES ON THE ENVIRONMENT

Trade policy reform is an essential element of the general economic reform programme being undertaken in Zimbabwe. Therefore, the effects of trade liberalization and export expansion on the environment is a key issue in the overall analysis of trade and environment linkages in Zimbabwe. Such effects may be positive or negative, and may largely depend on accompanying policies.

On the one hand, to the extent that trade liberalization leads to increased production, and if relevant domestic environmental regulations are loose, there may be negative environmental effects (scale effects).

On the other hand, trade liberalization may also have positive effects on the environment. Import liberalization may facilitate the introduction of environmentally sound technologies and access to environment-friendly inputs. For example, prior to the trade liberalization programme, only a limited number of chemicals, including pentachlorophenol (PCP), were available to leather tanneries in Zimbabwe. Now, leather tanneries have easier access to environment-friendly chemicals, at prices which are closer to international prices.

Increased openness also leads to intensified commercial and investment linkages with markets where environmental requirements are stringent. Thus, consumer demand for environment-friendly products in the developed-country markets encourages Zimbabwean producers participating in these markets to modify their products accordingly. Therefore liberalized trade could help to spread environmental standards. This would have a positive effect on the environment in Zimbabwe, to the extent that such standards are also relevant in the context of local environmental conditions and priorities. However, to the extent that environmental requirements in the importing country are inappropriate or irrelevant for the country of production, compliance with such standards, while securing access to developed country markets, would be of limited environmental benefit for the producer country in the short run.

With regard to the environmental effects of export production, in Zimbabwe, the domestic environmental priorities seem to have been oriented towards wildlife management and correcting environmentally harmful land use patterns. Trade-related environmental issues, and the potential environmental damage caused by the production activities of the manufacturing and industrial sectors, which are major exporters and earners of foreign exchange, have not been focused on. However, production in export-oriented sectors may contribute to increased pollution unless improved measures are introduced to monitor and regulate, for example, the storage, handling and disposal of hazardous materials; agricultural chemical runoff into surface waters and aquifers; and surface water polluting by the mining industry.

The scale effects of intensive mineral extraction can be quite damaging to the environment. In Zimbabwe, continuing pollution from mining is largely due to institutional factors. For instance, the Mines and Minerals Act is so powerful that it supersedes all other Acts, including those that are meant to protect the environment. Very few restrictions are attached to mining rights once a mining permit has been issued, and thus incidents like timber felling without reforestation, poaching by mine workers and siltation from eroding dumps can take place. The study attributes this to the need to secure foreign exchange earnings from mining. The extraction and processing of mineral ores has several negative impacts on the environment of Zimbabwe, and including environmental provisions in the Mines and Minerals Act would therefore be beneficial.

Mining interests in Zimbabwe are largely foreign-controlled by a few major transnational companies and a number of smaller foreign companies. The foreign companies are mainly active in the medium-sized to large end of the sector. State participation in the sector is also significant, and in addition, there is a considerable domestic private small-scale mining industry. The larger companies tend to have more resources to address environmental issues than the small-scale miners.

Metal works are also major polluters, and metals are major export items for Zimbabwe. Emissions could be reduced at these facilities by fitting scrubbers to recover sulphur. The problem of industrial waste has also reached significant proportions as a result of a lack of effective waste management systems by most companies. All in all, there is a general lack of awareness of environmental standards, the monitoring of pollutants is poor and waste management measures frequently are inadequate.

14.7   CONCLUSIONS AND RECOMMENDATIONS

According to the study, the central issues in trade and environment for Zimbabwe are (a) to take measures to avoid or mitigate the adverse trade effects of environmental policies, standards and regulations so that the products of weaker trading countries are not discriminated against and so that the environment is not misused as a protectionist weapon by the strong against the weak; and (b) how to identify and minimize the potential negative impacts of trade on the environment.

Inter alia, the need to service debt, especially hard-currency debt, dictates a need for Zimbabwe to export to OECD markets. In addition to international commodity prices, a major concern for Zimbabwe is how possible protectionist tendencies in industrialized countries may affect the country's exports. Consequently, in relation to (a) above, the study questions the scientific justification for certain environmental measures in the developed countries. A protectionist intent of specific measures related to phytosanitary food standards is also perceived, for example, in the case of ostriches.

The study states that exporters from Zimbabwe will have to comply with the new environmental requirements arising in their export markets, be they regulatory or voluntary instruments, or risk losing exports. Meeting the requirements may involve extra costs and the need for technological improvements, but high interest rates on local private sector borrowing are a major constraint for investments in environmental improvements. In addition, the study indicates that in some cases there may be a trade-off between environmental standards and quality standards, as in the case of food production, or environmental standards and productivity, as in the case of cotton growing.

However, since stricter standards are likely to spread with time to new markets, Zimbabwean industry might be better off taking steps to meet the new standards right away rather than giving up market share and attempting to avoid compliance with the standards by diverting exports to other markets. Nevertheless, in cases where the environmental requirements in the importing countries are not environmentally significant for Zimbabwe, the country might at times be environmentally better off by giving priority to environmental improvements in areas which may not be immediately trade-related.

Positive measures can be envisaged to mitigate the potential trade effects of both domestic and external environmental policies and to facilitate industry compliance. Capacity building in Zimbabwe can help the country to participate meaningfully in the international dialogue on trade and environment, and to respond quickly to the challenges arising from the linkages between trade and environment without sacrificing development and growth. The importance of information collection and dissemination on environmental requirements in export markets must also be emphasized. Some channels for this purpose exist, but their effectiveness could be strengthened. Capacity building and improved access to environmental information are important at the company level, especially since Zimbabwean industry tends to receive information on both domestic and international environmental requirements rather late.

Strengthened cooperation between the government and firms would be useful since the government is often much more knowledgeable about international requirements than industry, and industry feels that there is not enough consultation when domestic standards are set. The study also proposes government compensation for the added costs of environmental protection for companies through a system of market-based incentives.

In the light of the prevailing high interest rates that inhibit investments in environmental improvements, improved access to technology and capital could further expedite the compliance of Zimbabwean industry with environmental requirements.

In relation to (b) above, potential negative impacts of trade on the environment, the study points out that the environmental impacts of trade liberalization depend on the environmental policies that accompany the trade policies. In the case of Zimbabwe, the relative looseness of domestic environmental legislation both in design and enforcement could have led to some harmful environmental impacts of production, including export production. It is necessary to strengthen the legislation in certain areas, especially hazardous waste management, and to ensure that the environmental impacts of all sectors of economic activity are properly addressed, taking into account the environmental, economic and social conditions and priorities of the country. On the other hand, the country has in place a good policy for wildlife preservation that is based on sustainable use and involves local communities.

The study argues that instances could arise in which compliance with Multilateral Environmental Agreements has negative consequences both for the trade and environment of a country, unless the specific circumstances of countries or regions are sufficiently taken into account in the design of such agreements. Regional agreements may be particularly relevant for African countries that have very specific problems. Also, due to the structure of its exports, Zimbabwe may be especially vulnerable to the effects of certain MEAs such as the Montreal Protocol. However, in some cases adjustment to the requirements of MEAs can be made quite easily.

The environmental effects of distortions in international trade, such as those caused by agricultural subsidies in the developed countries, and other factors that limit the development of Zimbabwe, should also be addressed when analysing the impacts of exports, or trade policies in general, on the environment. Declining international commodity prices have forced Zimbabwe to increase natural resources extraction in order to maintain its foreign exchange earnings.

NOTES

1. This section also draws on the following sources: *Handbook of International Trade and Development Statistics*, UNCTAD, Geneva, 1993; Wright, Rupert (1994), 'Zimbabwe', *Project & Trade Finance*, **137**, September 1994; *Trade Policy Review, Zimbabwe*, GATT, Geneva, February 1995.

2. Nickerson, Brian J. (1994), 'The environmental laws of Zimbabwe: a unique approach to management of the environment', *Boston College Third World Law Journal*, **14** (2), Summer, 189–230.

3. Kadenge, P.G., H. Ndoro and B.M. Zwizwai (1992), 'Zimbabwe's Structural Adjustment Programme: The First Year Experience', in A.M. Mwanza (ed.), *Structural Adjustment Programmes in SADC: Experiences and Lessons from Malawi, Tanzania, Zambia and Zimbabwe*, Harare.

4. Nickerson, op.cit.

5. *Ibid.*

6. Perrone, M.A. (1995), 'Fitting the environmental piece into the Maastricht puzzle', *The Environmental Law Reporter*, **XXV** (4), April.

7. Appendix I species are those 'threatened with extinction and are or may be affected by trade'. Import of Appendix I species is prohibited for 'primarily commercial purposes'. Appendix II contains species that 'although not necessarily now threatened with extinction, may become so unless trade in specimens of such species is subject to strict regulation in order to avoid utilization incompatible with their survival'. Trade in Appendix II species is allowed if authorities in the country of export determine that the export will not be detrimental to the survival of the species.

8. Any transboundary hazardous waste transaction taking place in contravention of the provisions of the Basel Convention is considered 'illegal traffic'. According to Article 9 (illegal traffic), the state responsible for movement of hazardous wastes has the obligation to ensure its environmentally sound management, if necessary by reimportation into the state of origin. In conformity with Article 8, if disposal is not carried out in accordance with the terms of the contract, the state of export has a duty to reimport. In addition, if a transaction takes place in accordance with relevant provisions, but disposal cannot be carried out as foreseen, the state exporting has an obligation to ensure reimportation of the wastes if alternative arrangements cannot be made for their environmentally sound disposal.

15. Conclusions and guidelines for further work

Veena Jha and René Vossenaar

15.1 CONCLUSIONS

Trade and environment debates have often been stymied by polarized positions, dominated either by an all out effort to promote free trade or an equally strident effort at protecting the environment. Studies such as those summarized in this volume are a valiant attempt at breaking this deadlock, by pointing to cost-effective mechanisms for implementing environmental objectives which prevent trade displacements and promote the dual goals of economic development and environmental protection. These studies by themselves have been an exercise in capacity building, facilitating and even necessitating better coordination and cooperation between different ministries and other stakeholders in the national context.

While these studies suggest that polarizing trade and environment interests of developing countries may be counterproductive to their development strategies, further work is needed to better define the options for developing countries. In this context more work is required in developing an agenda for promoting sustainable development in developing countries.

The country case studies presented in the previous chapters have been one of the first attempts to analyse trade and environment linkages in developing countries. Subsequently, other studies have been undertaken under an UNCTAD/UNEP project, as well as by other organizations. In the Asian region, for example, the secretariats of the Association of South East Asian Nations (ASEAN) as well as the Economic and Social Commission for Asia and the Pacific (ESCAP) have sponsored country case studies on trade and environment linkages, building on the experience of the UNDP/UNCTAD studies.

The studies included in this volume have largely focused on two sets of issues: (a) what are the effects of domestic and external environmental requirements on market access and export competitiveness for developing countries? and (b) what are the environmental effects of changes in production patterns in developing countries resulting from trade liberalization?

With regard to the first set of issues, the studies seem to indicate that, while not yet widespread, such requirements are becoming more frequent in certain sectors, including those of export interest to developing countries. The effects on trade and export competitiveness of developing-country companies tend to vary largely in accordance with a number of factors. Such factors include destination of exports, cost structures, basis for export competitiveness, relationship with foreign firms, as well as the availability of raw materials and other inputs, technology, and information. Firm size was found to be particularly relevant. Indeed, while large companies in developing countries tend to find it relatively easy to comply with most existing environmental requirements in developed-country markets, small and medium-sized enterprises (SMEs) reported finding more difficulties in compliance.

With regard to the second set of issues, (the environmental effects of changes in production patterns as a result of trade liberalization and globalization), the studies show that such effects are unlikely to be either universally positive or negative. These effects differ by country, by sector and by commodity. Both positive and negative effects have been found. Where environmental pressures may increase, it is important to introduce appropriate environmental and macroeconomic policies to mitigate the negative pressures of freer trade. In many cases, and particularly in countries with adequate policies in place, environmental benefits can actually result from trade liberalization. Trade liberalization could drive some countries to have a more efficient allocation of resources, including environmental resources. Economic growth and development resulting from freer trade can generate additional income and increasing demand for environmental protection that, in turn, can be channelled to make environmental improvements. Additional incomes could also contribute to the reduction of environmental damages associated with poverty.

One important lesson from these studies is that trade and environmental policies can be reconciled and made mutually supportive in achieving sustainable development by appropriate policies and measures at both the national and international levels. The studies have been useful in identifying priority areas. Some of these are listed in the next section.

When this project started, very little work had been undertaken on trade and environment linkages in developing countries. Therefore, the project very much focused on awareness-raising and support to building analytical capacity. Emphasis was more on identifying issues than on resolving problems. The studies have certainly assisted in creating awareness and in improving understanding of key issues, particularly at the national level. In some cases, governments have made some institutional arrangements to discuss trade and environment, for example through the creation of national committees on trade and environment. The project, together with other work carried out in recent years, has also had some positive effects on the international trade and environment debate. As more conceptual and empirical analyses have become available, the participants in the debate have become more knowledgeable about what is at stake. The debate has also become more open, more democratic and more participatory. Finally, the developmental dimension has taken a more prominent place in the discussion.

Perhaps one of the major contributions of these studies and associated activities, such as workshops and seminars, is therefore that it has helped to move away from largely defensive attitudes to a more proactive approach to trade and environment in many developing countries. A clear reflection of this is the fact that the governments of several developing countries have decided to initiate, with the help of UNCTAD and UNDP, national projects on trade and environment aimed at promoting dialogue and strengthening policy coordination at the national level.

15.2   GUIDELINES FOR FUTURE WORK ON TRADE AND ENVIRONMENT: TOWARDS THE DEVELOPMENT OF A POSITIVE AGENDA

Trade and environment has become an important theme for many developing countries. There are several reasons for this. First, a key policy objective of developing countries is their further integration into the world economy. In the process of globalization and trade liberalization, the ability of their producers and exporters to respond to environmental requirements and to enhance environmental quality is important to compete in international markets as well as in their home markets. Second, developing countries have become increasingly aware that they cannot embark on a long-term development process without adequate concern for the environment. Third, developing countries have a key interest in the implications of developments in the trade and environment debate for their WTO rights and obligations. Fourth, developing countries are parties to Multilateral Environmental Agreements (MEAs), implying both the need to implement commitments as well as to make appropriate use of facilitating measures under such agreements, for example in the areas of finance, access to environmentally sound technologies, capacity-building and market-based instruments. Finally, many observers expect that 'trade and environment' will be an important issue in a possible new round of multilateral trade negotiations at the start of the next millennium. At the same time, the further development and implementation of the international environmental agenda, for example in the area of climate change, has increasingly strong linkages with economic development and international trade.

A recurrent theme in the implementation of this project has been the recognition of the need for capacity-building, both human resource development and institutional capacity-building, to enhance the capacities of developing countries to effectively address trade and environment issues and to participate effectively in international deliberations. Apart from building analytical capacity, future work should go beyond studies alone and aim at the design and practical implementation of pilot projects seeking to resolve problems that have been identified.

There is also a need to promote the use of market-based as well as other innovative instruments as well as to encourage the involvement of different stakeholders. For example, access to environmentally sound technologies and their successful dissemination and adaptation requires the cooperation of many stakeholders including governments, private enterprises, research and financial institutions.

In designing innovative approaches, emphasis should be placed on measures which do not require extensive infrastructures for implementation, nor overstretch limited and shrinking overseas development aid budgets. At the same time the need to generate additional resources continues to remain an important challenge. Measures should be used to leverage foreign direct investment and complement both internally generated resources as well as the activities of international industry associations, NGOs and other such bodies. To the extent possible, facilitating measures should also have a built-in dynamic notion of equity which is vital to the success of any MEA.

This volume has identified a range of areas on which future work is required, some of which are listed below.

Information

Most studies referred to the need for information, for example concerning newly-emerging environmental requirements and market opportunities for environmentally preferable products. It was noted that industry and exporters' associations could play a key role. In addition, there is a need to establish mechanisms to channel the relevant information to the interested parties, including through electronic means.

Technology

Several studies stressed the need for access to and transfer of environmentally sound technologies (ESTs). This should allow companies to reduce the environmental impacts of their activities, to comply with market requirements and to maintain international competitiveness. Access to technology is also important to assist developing countries in complying with obligations under Multilateral Environmental Agreements (MEAs). Future work is required to promote the effective use of corresponding provisions in MEAs, as well as ways and means to promote technology transfer through joint ventures, foreign direct investments and innovative mechanisms.

Infrastructure
Improvements in environmental infrastructure play an important role in reducing the costs of compliance, particularly for small firms. Similarly, the establishment or upgrading of certification bodies can be of key importance. Government policies to support private sector research and development also facilitate the ability of firms to respond to trade and environment challenges and, in the process, contribute to the goals of sustainable development.

Building partnerships
An important lesson from the studies is that enterprises, particularly SMEs from developing countries could derive benefits from cooperation among themselves as well as from setting up joint ventures and other forms of cooperation with manufacturers in the more advanced export markets. Future studies could focus on identifying ways and means to reconcile trade and environment through the promotion of partnerships between developing and developed-country companies. Future studies on possibilities to promote the production of and trade in 'environment-friendly' products should be followed up by round-table discussions involving producers/exporters in the source country and importers/retailers in the target country.

Participation in international deliberations
Some studies reveal a need for developing countries to participate more effectively in international deliberations and negotiations on trade and environment, in particular in the WTO Committee on Trade and Environment (CTE), the International Organization for Standardization (ISO) and the Conferences of Parties of Multilateral Environmental Agreements. This requires more than finance for travel; it also requires studies and consultations at the national level.

Coordination at the national level
Throughout the implementation of this project it has been felt that there is a lack of policy coordination at the national level. Better policy coordination at the national level requires coordination between different ministries as well as between the government and the private sector. NGOs and citizen groups have a key role to play here. As mentioned above, several developing countries have decided to implement national projects to promote these objectives, based *inter alia* on an in-depth examination of a range of priority issues.

Regional cooperation between developing countries

Several studies have made suggestions to strengthen regional cooperation between developing countries. For example, developing countries could explore possibilities for greater convergence of environmental standards at the regional level. In addition, they could cooperate in enhancing their capacities to provide services, for example in the area of product testing, certification and accreditation. Regional cooperation should also focus on awareness-raising and training, through the preparation of training materials and the preparation of regional studies.

Keeping these broad objectives in mind, future studies could develop some concrete packages of policies which could be implemented on a pilot basis in a few developing countries. The following areas could be explored for further study.

- Developing integrated multi-stakeholder policy packages for specific sectors under specific MEAs such as the Montreal Protocol, the Basel Convention, the Framework Convention on Climate Change, Biodiversity, and so on. Emphasis should be placed on the development spinoffs from such packages, for example, upgrading of refrigeration technology through the replacement of CFCs under the Montreal Protocol.
- Specific sectoral packages for integrating trade and environment concerns, for example, eco-tourism and textiles.
- Case studies for integrating environment and investment concerns particularly with a view to promoting access and dissemination of environmentally sound technologies and practices.
- Packages for promoting awareness and understanding of as well as adaptation of environmental standards, including in the context of ISO 14000.
- Examining the green market potential through the use of umbrella trademarks, green market preferences, potential for replacing environmentally harmful trade with environmentally beneficial trade, and exploring other trade-related positive measures.

In designing such packages three distinct audiences could be addressed. First, what should national governments do in order to better implement the above-mentioned packages and in this context what adaptations should be made to their design at the national level? Second, at the international and multilateral level, what should be the essential elements of a positive agenda and how should MEAs and aid agencies incorporate such an agenda in a dynamic process? Third, what is the contribution that UNDP, UNCTAD and other relevant international organizations can make in developing such a positive agenda?

Index